GENERATION MULTIPLEX

The Image of Youth in Contemporary American Cinema

BY

Timothy Shary

FOREWORD BY

David Considine

University of Texas Press, Austin

Printed in the United States of America
First edition, 2002

∞ The paper used in this book meets the minimum requirements of ANSI/NISO Z39.48-1992 (R1997) (Permanence of Paper).

LIBRARY OF CONGRESS CATALOGING-IN-PUBLICATION DATA

Shary, Timothy, 1967–
Generation multiplex : the image of youth in contemporary American cinema / by Timothy Shary ; foreword by David Considine.
p. cm.
Includes bibliographical references and index.
ISBN 0-292-77752-3 (alk. paper) — ISBN 0-292-77771-X (pbk. : alk. paper)
1. Youth in motion pictures. 2. Motion pictures—United States. I. Title.
PN1995.9.Y6 S53 2002
791.43'652054—dc21 2001008470

TO CAROLYN ANDERSON
without whom this book and much of my career
would not have been possible

AND TO THE FOND MEMORY OF ANDY ANDERSON
beloved professor, colleague, husband, and father

two great teachers who have inspired countless
young people like myself

CONTENTS

FOREWORD BY DAVID CONSIDINE **ix**

PREFACE **xiii**

ACKNOWLEDGMENTS **xv**

Chapter 1. INTRODUCTION:
THE CINEMATIC IMAGE OF YOUTH **1**

Social Representation and Genre Analysis 11

The Study of Youth, In and Out of Movies 19

Chapter 2. YOUTH IN SCHOOL: ACADEMICS AND ATTITUDE **26**

Trends in the Subgenre 27

Schoolkids 30

Transforming the Nerd 32

Delinquents and Their Avenues of Anger 41

Resisting Rebels 50

The Labor of Being Popular 61

The Sensitive Athlete 69

Conclusion 78

Chapter 3. DELINQUENT YOUTH:
HAVING FUN, ON THE LOOSE, IN TROUBLE **80**

Trends in the Subgenre 81

Delinquent Styles 83

Deviant Dancing 86

Natural Encounters 94

Patriotic Purpose 103

Tough Girls 110

The African American Crime Drama 122

Conclusion 135

Chapter 4. THE YOUTH HORROR FILM: SLASHERS AND THE SUPERNATURAL **137**
Historical Context of the Youth Horror Subgenre 138
Trends in the Subgenre 140
Research on the Youth Horror Film 143
Styles of the Youth Horror Film 147
The Slasher/Stalker Film 147
Supernatural Movies 168
Conclusion 178

Chapter 5. YOUTH AND SCIENCE: TECHNOLOGY, COMPUTERS, GAMES **180**
The Three Dimensions 181
Simple Science 183
Games and Computers 196
Conclusion 208

Chapter 6. YOUTH IN LOVE AND HAVING SEX **209**
Trends in the Subgenre 210
Patterns and Images 212
Youth in Love 214
Youth Having Sex 226
Conclusion 254

Chapter 7. CONCLUSION: YOUTH CINEMA AT THE MILLENNIUM **255**

Appendix A. FILMOGRAPHY OF YOUTH FILMS, 1980–2001 **265**

Appendix B. SUBJECTIVE SUPERLATIVE LISTS **279**

NOTES **283**

BIBLIOGRAPHY **301**

INDEX **309**

GENERATION MULTIPLEX

FOREWORD

David Considine

"I'm sorry I didn't tell you about the world."
—MONICA TO DAVID IN *A.I.*

Released in the summer of 2001, Steven Spielberg and Stanley Kubrick's *A.I.* introduced movie audiences to David Swinton, a robot boy, desperately seeking his mother's love. Brilliantly played by 13-year-old Haley Joel Osment, David searches for self, reality, and security through bizarre environments like Rouge City and Flesh Fair. Though the film is set in the distant future, Monica Swinton's portrayal of a mother, unable to meet the needs of the son she desired and "imprinted" with, rings sadly true in the real world of early-twenty-first-century America.

Published earlier in 2001, Ron Taffel's *The Second Family* argued that in modern America "most parents don't understand their teenagers" and "aren't able to pay the right kind of attention to them." Taffel, a child and family therapist, says the most common comment he hears from kids as they discuss their parents is the phrase "They don't have a clue." On "planet youth," as Taffel calls it, parents have little "gravitational pull" and the dominant ideology is "live and let live." It is a world of moral relativism and rubbery rules, where the primary impetus is comfort, and the primary teacher is pop culture.

What our children and adolescents learn from television, movies, music, and other media has become increasingly controversial in recent years. Media messages and marketing were the target of Republican presidential candidate Bob Dole in 1996 and Democratic vice-presidential candidate Joe Lieberman in 2000.

The way the movies and other media talk to and about adolescents has also attracted increasing academic attention. In August 2000, the *Journal of*

Adolescent Health devoted an entire issue to the complex relationship between media content, the nature and needs of adolescent audiences, and the context in which media messages are consumed.

While much of this interest is dominated by a protectionist approach, there is some indication that a more balanced and constructive approach is also being considered. In June 2001, representatives of the White House Office of National Drug Control Policy released a draft document on media literacy and substance abuse at the National Media Education Conference in Austin. Among other "best practices" noted in the position paper were the need to recognize the pleasure young people derive from the media, and the need to avoid media bashing.

This view is consistent with *Great Transitions,* a 1995 report from the Carnegie Council on Adolescent Development. "The world of the adolescent," the report said, "cannot be understood without understanding the profound influence of the mass media . . . in shaping young people's attitudes and values." *Pay It Forward, Welcome to the Dollhouse, This Boy's Life, Kids,* and numerous other examples of the teen screen provide ample evidence of this.

It is in this context that Timothy Shary's *Generation Multiplex* must be considered. It represents an important contribution to our understanding of the relationship between youth and the mass media, in this case movies. From both a personal and a professional perspective, I welcome this work, which builds on themes and issues I addressed in *The Cinema of Adolescence* in 1985. At the end of that book I said it was not intended as the definitive study of youth and the movies. Rather, I hoped that it would be seen as an attempt to "map out a cinematic terrain, the geography of which must now be thrown open for further exploration." *Generation Multiplex* represents the ongoing need to respect and research both youth and youth culture.

While the movies and other media talk constantly to young people about drugs, alcohol, sexuality, and other controversial topics, political pressures and the remnants of the nation's Puritan origins continue to complicate frank and open discussion on these same subjects. In June 2001, for example, Surgeon General David Satcher called for a national dialogue on sexuality and sex education that did more than simply advocate the teaching of abstinence. Conservative groups like Focus on the Family immediately called for his removal from office. At the same time, conservative film critic Michael Medved's column complained that teen movies like *crazy/beautiful* and *The Fast and the Furious* were guilty of "sending utterly irresponsible messages directly to a youthful audience."

Ironically, at the same time young movie patrons were gaining easy access to these films, and Surgeon General Satcher was being criticized for advocating open communication with our young people, the Supreme Court overturned a Massachusetts law that aimed to protect young people from tobacco advertising near parks or schools. We appear to have created a society where parents do not feel comfortable talking to their children about sexuality or other controversial issues; where conservative political pressures and curriculum constraints limit what teachers can say to their students; where the mass media, protected by the First Amendment, are free to say and show almost anything.

Clearly we cannot continue to create an environment in which on the one hand we lament the negative impact movies and other media have on our young, while on the other hand we refuse to take the matter seriously by providing young people with the skills of critical inquiry that enable them to both *appreciate* and *critique* the role of mass media in their lives and in society as a whole.

In the United Kingdom, Australia, Canada, and other Western nations, media literacy has long been an established and legitimate part of the curriculum. Television, advertising, and the movies are considered legitimate subjects of study. This movement remains in its infancy in the United States, surely the most mass-mediated nation on earth. But groups like the Alliance for a Media Literate America, the National Telemedia Council, and a small but growing number of campuses, including my own, are trying to nurture the movement.

Properly understood and utilized, youth media can serve as a bridge between the past and the present. In the process, it may well lay the foundations for our future. Those who fear and lament the influence media have on our young would do well to learn from that media.

In *A.I.,* David's mother and father do not possess the strength of character nor the moral fortitude to assume responsibility for the child they wanted. Instead, they abandon him to the woods and the wild where he struggles to be true, and real and unique, and most important of all, loved. Like so many modern parents, Monica found herself unable to tell her child about the world. In the end, he learned about it from other sources. So it is with so many of our young people and their families today. If the movies talk to them and we do not, dare we blame the children or the movies for what they learn?

If, as adults, we are to have relevance and purpose in the lives of our children on their odyssey to adulthood, we must share David's dream. To put it simply, it is time for all of us to "get real."

DAVID CONSIDINE BOONE, NORTH CAROLINA SUMMER 2001

Carnegie Council on Adolescent Development. *Great Transitions: Preparing Adolescents for a New Century*. New York: Carnegie Corporation, 1995.

Considine, David M. *The Cinema of Adolescence*. Jefferson, N.C.: McFarland, 1985.

Medved, Michael. "New Films Show PG-13 Is Hollywood's Trojan Horse." *USA Today*, July 2, 2001, 11.

Office of National Drug Control Policy. *Preliminary Guidelines for Educating Youth on Media Literacy Specific to Illicit Drugs*, draft. Washington, D.C.: White House Conference Center, 2001.

Taffel, Ron. *The Second Family: How Adolescent Power Is Challenging the American Family*. New York: St. Martin's Press, 2001.

PREFACE

In any study of contemporary popular culture, the field of subjects changes so quickly, and often so comprehensively, that authors are stymied in making claims about "current" trends and themes. I have certainly found this to be the case with studying teen cinema for the past decade, as each revision of this project involved substantial changes not only to the films cited, but to the claims made about patterns in the movie industry, youth styles, and the films' overall significance.

As this book goes to press at the end of 2001, another wave of fascinating films about youth is bringing further changes—and complexity—to the representation of teenagers in American media. *Save the Last Dance* and *The Princess Diaries* have had a surprisingly wide appeal, and freshly provocative features like *Ghost World, Donnie Darko, L.I.E., Our Song,* and *George Washington* are still gaining notoriety in more limited release. Perhaps the surest sign of a revived teen cinema is the appearance of nostalgic homages, such as *Wet Hot American Summer* and *Not Another Teen Movie.*

Alas, just as I have been unable to give thorough analytic attention to some of the great teen films mentioned herein, I can only bring glancing coverage to many of the new youth genre products that are currently changing the cultural landscape. While I have incorporated the newest relevant films whenever possible, this study is primarily focused on the period from 1980 to 1999. The teen films of the early twenty-first century will undoubtedly continue to be quite intriguing, and will certainly be worthy of further coverage in other studies, if not also a future edition of this book. I invite correspondence from readers who may wish to participate in such endeavors, and who have ideas on how the current volume may be improved.

TIMOTHY SHARY   WORCESTER, MASSACHUSETTS   OCTOBER 2001

ACKNOWLEDGMENTS

This book grew out of my doctoral dissertation at the University of Massachusetts at Amherst, so first and foremost, I express my deep gratitude to my committee—Carolyn Anderson (chair), Martin Norden, and Catherine Portuges—who were encouraging, informative, and supportive during the early production of this work. I owe Carolyn a special debt of appreciation, for her lessons have been indescribably valuable in shaping me as a film scholar, and her teaching has been inspirational: she is wise, witty, dedicated, ambitious, and endlessly energetic.

At the University of Texas Press, my sincere thanks go to Jim Burr for having faith in this book from the start and keeping the faith throughout the revision process, and to Leslie Doyle Tingle for seeing it through its final stages.

My family—Cecilia, Robert, and Kevin—have been incredibly supportive in this endeavor as well, and I am as proud of them for enduring my struggle as they may be of me for surviving it. My sweet wife Rebecca Maloney has also provided me with the love, reason, and sheer fun that kept me going through the many years I worked on this project.

So many friends came forth to help me with this book that I am sure I cannot name them all, but in one way or another all of the following people offered me advice, ideas, data, hope, sympathy, and/or willing participation in watching some of the most exciting and unusual films of the past generation of American cinema: Richard Brown, Anne Ciecko, Darci and Rich Cramer-Benjamin, Susan Ericsson, Chris Goodwin, Devin and Rachel Griffiths, Perrin Harkins, Sara Hunicke, Katie LeBesco, Nancy Inouye, Jon Kitzen, Chris LeBel, Gary Marcus, Mark Mierswa, Carolyn Moore, Kelly Mullaly, Nicola Paterson, Jesse Rossa, Tom Scully, John Shields, Mike Wolpe, Zach Woods, and Zsofia Zvolensky. I would also like to highlight the contributions made to this book by two of my former students, Jon Lupo (who helped me work out the title) and Louisa Shein, both of whom provided significant advice, even under crunch conditions.

Major revisions of this book resulted from the thoughtful and careful critiques of David Considine at Appalachian State University and Kathy Merlock Jackson at Virginia Wesleyan College; their suggestions helped shape my lengthy dissertation into an accessible book. For help with specific research aspects, I thank Brian Taves of the Library of Congress and Alexandra Siebel of New York University. Thanks to Christine Holmlund at the University of Tennessee for sharing valuable ideas on issues of youth sexuality.

Further, I must thank my great students at Clark University, where I was first invited to teach a course on youth cinema in 1997 (thanks also to my colleagues in the Screen Studies program, Marcia Butzel and Marvin D'Lugo). I have since taught newer versions of that course at UMass in 1999, and again at Clark in 2000. The students in these courses and others at Clark and UMass have helped me to develop and shape many of the ideas that are contained herein.

The Higgins School of Humanities at Clark University provided a faculty research grant to support the final revisions of the manuscript in 2000–2001; my thanks to Higgins School director Janette Greenwood and assistant Lisa Coakley.

At least one video supplier deserves special thanks: Video to Go in Amherst, Massachusetts. Stills were provided by Jerry Ohlinger's Movie Material Store, except figure 6.3 from Miramax Films and figure 7.1 from Paramount Pictures.

Two teachers in my precollege years had perhaps the most profound effect on my early education: Ty Walker, who taught me into my teenage years, and Lee March, who taught me out of them. Mr. Walker was the first teacher who demonstrated to me the legitimacy of studying movies as well as enjoying them (he had seen *Star Wars* 17 times when I first met him), and Ms. March sparked my early academic film interests, pushing me to write my first essay on a movie, which prophetically turned out to be *The Breakfast Club*. These two teachers not only helped propel me in my educational pursuits, they provided the models that I still follow, showing me and their other students the personal and passionate nature of being a great teacher. I can only hope that this work will similarly inspire other students, regardless of age, to study cinema and to make the most of their youth.

GENERATION MULTIPLEX

1 INTRODUCTION
The Cinematic Image of Youth

American cinema in the late twentieth century revealed a curious and often inconsistent cultural fascination with stories about and images of young people. Various film trends catering to young audiences had emerged over past generations, but movies in the last 20 years of the century appeared almost fixated on capturing certain youth styles and promoting certain perspectives on the celebration (or really, survival) of adolescence. Many arguments persist as to why teenagers have been targeted by Hollywood: youth have disposable incomes that they enjoy spending on entertainment; today's children become the consumptive parents of tomorrow; filmmakers engage in the vicarious experiences of their own lost youth. All of these points are valid, yet this book argues not as much for the reasons behind youth representation as for the issues and trends that representation engenders. As evidenced by the latest massive outpouring of American youth films in the late 1990s, and the parallel production of teen-oriented television shows, magazines, and multimedia outlets, as well as the attention paid to youth attitudes and behaviors in the wake of various scandals, crimes, and accomplishments, the imaging of contemporary youth has become indicative of our deepest social and personal concerns.

Consider, for instance, Todd Solondz's 1996 film *Welcome to the Dollhouse*. As we approach the bittersweet climax, the awkward adolescent heroine, Dawn Weiner (Heather Mattarazzo), is preparing to declare her unrequited romantic longings to an older boy at a party. Dressed in a colorful but garish outfit, Dawn gazes at her crush until she decides that this is her moment: she stands holding her breath, fists clenched, mustering up all her strength to take this plunge, looking as if she could explode. In this one image, Solondz evokes the very intensity that is the nature of growing up, for Dawn is not only confronting her tormented affection for an older boy, she is facing the inevitable conflict of becoming an adult.

All dramas thrive on conflict, and the process of maturing is a natural conflict familiar to everyone by their teenage years. While many filmgoers freely participate in screen fantasies about the possibilities of life as a secret agent or of saving a loved one from the clutches of death, most of our lives are filled with less spectacular phenomena, such as how we come to be accepted by society, discover romance, have sex, gain employment, make moral decisions, and learn about the world and who we are in it. These are the phenomena that most of us first encounter in our adolescence, and how we handle them largely determines how we live the rest of our lives. The gravity of adolescence thus makes for compelling drama, even if many of us would rather forget those trying years. Understanding how we learn and grow in our youth is integral to understanding who we become as adults.

Since the 1950s the American cinema, with varying interests, has been relying on people under 30 to pay for movies about their daily dramas and fantasies.[1] However, there has not always been a prolific output of coming-of-age stories by Hollywood, and the themes of youth films have changed considerably since the days of young Mary Pickford and Lillian Gish in the early 1900s. One of the telling dilemmas of youth films since cinema began is that while they address young people they are not produced by young people, for children and teens are effectively restricted from the commercial filmmaking process. Thus, screen images of youth have always been traditionally filtered through adult perspectives. Virtually all feature films ever made about youth have been produced by filmmakers over 20, even though many are now produced by filmmakers under 30, and most recent youth films have become as complex and sophisticated as adult dramas, no longer content to showcase the trite frivolity of beach parties or the overwrought warfare of urban gangs and schools. Since the early 1980s a number of distinct subgenres and character types within the genre of "youth/teen/young adult" films have emerged and have offered richly provocative images that question the changing concepts of youth in America. The specific number of these categories is arguable, and surely too large to detail in one volume, so I offer here an analysis of five subgenres—containing 18 of the most significant youth film styles and movie roles—to demonstrate the changing nature of teen representation in American media during the past generation.[2]

Young people have always been a concern in American film history, both in terms of their images on screen and their reception of films as an audience.

In the earliest days of cinema there did not exist a distinct youth genre, nor for that matter much of an agreed social sense of what constituted youth. Children in the early twentieth century often left school by the age of 14 to begin jobs (only 6.4 percent of young Americans completed high school in 1900) and many were married and having children by 18, a condition that kept the state of "youth" limited to just a few years between childhood and adulthood.[3] The reception of movies at that time was also affected by social fears about their corruptive potential, especially regarding their influence on children. Many early-1900s moral guardians preached about the dangers of exposing children to typically adult-oriented dramas, and rather than make films that specifically catered to a young audience, the fledgling movie industry tended to side with concerns over propriety.[4] By the 1920s, Hollywood formed the Hays Office and began formal evaluations and restrictions on the moral content of American films, and despite a choice few popular films that featured young characters of the time—Lillian Gish in *Broken Blossoms* (1919), Mary Pickford in *Pollyanna* (1920), Jackie Coogan in *The Kid* (1921), Baby Peggy in *Captain January* (1924)—the industry took a clear position on youth films by the 1930s: children were either preadolescent (such as Shirley Temple or the kids in *Our Gang*) or were developed into early adulthood (such as in the Andy Hardy series starring Mickey Rooney or the old-before-their-time *Dead End Kids*). In either case, young people certainly did not have on-screen discussions about otherwise typical developmental issues like sexuality, drug or alcohol use, or family dysfunction.

The notable youth films that followed in the years after the Great Depression tended to be optimistic and endearing fables starring the likes of Deanna Durbin, Judy Garland, and Rooney, but these films were still directed at and most often seen by an adult audience, or by a family audience consisting of both parents and children. Hollywood studios promoted these small troupes of young stars (also including Frankie Darro, Bonita Granville, Freddie Bartholomew, Dickie Moore, and Joyce Reynolds) who came to represent the contemporary ideals, if not the realistic conditions, of youth. Then with the resolution of World War II, a distinct population in America began to emerge: teenagers. Gradually the age between childhood and adulthood came to be codified, debated, celebrated, and perhaps most significantly, elongated.[5] More young people stayed in school, and with the arrival of postwar prosperity, more began attending college. Other factors contributed to the burgeoning presence of the teenager in the 1950s: the greater availability of automobiles, which allowed youth to travel and thus achieve a certain independence; the recovering economy, which gave many teens extra money for entertainment outside the home; the popular reception of rock and roll music, which clearly flew in the face of previous standards; and the influence of television, which, while giving all Americans a new common entertainment medium, also kept more adults at home. In terms of the U.S. film industry, two landmark legal cases set the stage for the eventual proliferation of young adult fare. The "Paramount Case" was handed down by the Supreme Court in 1948; soon thereafter began the process by which major movie studios divested their holdings in theaters, giving rise to more small independent studios that would take advantage of their increased theatrical access by catering to niche audiences like teenagers.[6] Then the important so-called "Miracle Decision" by the Court in 1952 brought certain First Amendment protections to films, thereby opening the door for depictions of a wider range of moral issues on-screen; this development attracted young people to theaters where they could view more "adult" dramas than were available on television.[7]

However, Hollywood studios did not suddenly bank on hedonistic teen roles in the 1950s: their process of introducing the postwar teenager was careful if not apprehensive, as they gradually exploited the ephebiphobia—fear of teenagers—that was seeping into popular culture and politics. After a few notable "clean teen" performances in the 1940s by Jeanne Crain (*Margie,* 1946), Jane Powell (*A Date with Judy,* 1948), and Elizabeth Taylor (*Little Women,* 1949), the archetypal '50s teen performer was embodied in James Dean, whose performance in *Rebel Without a Cause* (1955) is probably the most influential demonstration of pure teen angst in American cinema. Marlon Brando had already showcased the young rebel image in *The Wild One* (1953), but Dean's affected demeanor was more enduring. Hollywood then continued to mold other performers into troubled youth, as in the milder but still afflicted roles of Natalie Wood (in *Rebel Without a Cause, Marjorie Morningstar* [1958], and *West Side Story* [1961]), John Saxon (in *Rock, Pretty Baby* [1956], *The Unguarded Moment* [1956], and *The Restless Years* [1958]), and Brandon De Wilde (in *Blue Denim* [1959], *All Fall Down* [1962], and *Hud* [1963]).

Perhaps a more notable trend than the emergence of these new young performers was the film industry's fresh confrontation with the conditions of youth. *Rebel* showcased the high school outcast who couldn't fit in (while also considering alcoholism, family dynamics, basic crime, and in more concealed terms, homosexuality); *Blackboard Jungle* (1955) dramatized the potentially violent conditions of urban high schools and tangentially introduced rock music to American cinema, giving rise to the teen "rock movie" that would

Jim (James Dean) struggles to express his archetypal angst to his overbearing mother (Ann Doran) in *Rebel Without a Cause* (1955).

become a subgenre thereafter; and *Peyton Place* (1957) and *Splendor in the Grass* (1961) demonstrated the supposed dangers of teenage sexuality. Each of these films dealt with issues important to young adults, but now that Hollywood was finally making films about the difficulty of being young, a reactionary movement began, as usual in the film industry, in binary form: films were made that avoided or toned down the dilemmas of youth for the sake of celebrating its carefree aspects, or films were made to further exploit and enflame the dangers of teen delinquency and decadence. In other words, good kids were divided from bad kids. Thus appeared a wave of inane beach films in the '60s (many featuring Frankie Avalon and Annette Funicello after their well-attended *Beach Party* in 1963) as well as the popular *Gidget* series (starting in 1959), alongside a lesser-seen but nonetheless visible output of youth exploitation films, a genre that emerged as early as 1936 with *Reefer Madness* and was carried on by *City Across the River* in 1949 and sustained in such productions as *Teenage Devil Dolls* (1952), *Teenage Crime Wave* (1955), *High School Confidential!* (1958), *This Rebel Breed* (1960), *Teenage Strangler* (1964), and *The Wild Angels* (1966).[8] As my study shows, this reactive and divisive pattern of the movie industry is a trend that persists to this day.

By the early 1970s, after the implementation of the Motion Picture Association of America's ratings system (in 1968) and the national suffrage of 18-year-olds (in 1971), not to mention the young ages at which boys were being drafted to fight in Vietnam, American youth began to have a different sense of their identity than that which had been provided for them in so many of the happier, hipper '60s films. The dark and more rebellious aspects of youth that had emerged in the '50s teen films continued in counterculture productions like *Wild in the Streets* (1968), *Easy Rider* (1969), *R.P.M.*, and *The Strawberry Statement* (1970). As was the case with films of the previous generation, most of these movies were not about adolescents but rather young adults, just leaving high school or in college. In fact, Hollywood virtually abandoned its practice of promoting teenage performers in the '60s and certainly had very few to account for in the '70s (the three prominent exceptions being Jodie Foster, Tatum O'Neal, and Robby Benson).

After the dearth of teen stars and films in the 1970s, Hollywood could have maintained its lower output of youth films in the 1980s, but instead the industry concentrated more on young adult dramas than ever before. The most likely factor contributing to this was the emergence of another icon of youth independence, the shopping mall. The mall became a scene of teen congregation where arcades and food courts replaced the pool halls and soda fountains of the past. Furthermore, since the '70s, following the dramatic decline of American movie theaters, Hollywood had come to rely on the centralization of multiple theaters in large retail centers to increase the number of screen venues and to offer moviegoers greater variety and convenience. Thus the multiplex was born. With the relocation of most movie theaters into or near shopping malls in the 1980s, the need to cater to the young audiences who frequented those malls became apparent to Hollywood, and those audiences formed the first generation of multiplex moviegoers.

The clearest result of the multiplex movement was a voluminous outpouring of films directed to and featuring teens, but in order to avoid a stagnating homogenization of the teen genre, Hollywood revised its '50s formula by intensifying the narrative range of youth films through placing teenage characters in previously established genres with more dramatic impact (gory horror, dance musicals, sex comedies), and as a result, a new variety of character types grew out of this generic expansion. Given the categorical choices offered by the multiplex theater, teens in the '80s were then able to go to the mall and select the particular youth movie experience that most appealed to them, and Hollywood tried to keep up with changing teen interests and styles to ensure ongoing profits. This led to constantly evolving efforts by the film industry to maintain the youth market through further generic expansions and revisions; more significantly for the audience, teens were then exposed to a wider range of characters and situations that directly addressed their current social conditions, even if many of the films that did so clearly had puerile provocation as their motive. Unlike the '50s when screen teens were steered down relatively rigid, righteous paths, the '80s teens encountered a complexity of moral choices and personal options on which the multiplex movies thrived. This gave teenage movie audiences at the end of the twentieth century a greater sense of presence in popular media, a deeper potential to be influenced by the films they saw, and a wider range of options from which they could construct and compare their sense of self.

The late '70s suggested the teen trends to come, as the popularity of such films as *Saturday Night Fever* (1977) and *Grease* (1978) with John Travolta—both of which combined music, sex (or the repression thereof), and style—created a segue to the more dynamic stories that young audiences would soon demand. A handful of other films truly inaugurated new cycles: two 1978 American films, the low-budget sensation *Halloween* and the college farce *Animal House,* as well as two unassuming Canadian films, *Meatballs* (1979) and *Porky's* (1981). These were the starting guns of the new youth subgenres of the '80s. *Animal House, Meatballs,* and *Porky's* were raucous comedies featuring goofy and/or hormonal youth pursuing pleasure at college, summer camp, and a '50s-era high school, respectively, and their successes spawned numerous imitations over the next few years that featured desperate variations on this storyline (with such suggestive titles as *Goin' All the Way* [1981], *The Last American Virgin* [1982], *Losin' It, Getting It On,* and *The First Turn-On* [all 1983], *Screwballs, Joy of Sex,* and *The Wild Life* [all 1984]). The new abundance of teen sexuality on screen also coincided with an increasing awareness that the age of first intercourse was dropping for American youth, and the few earlier films that solemnly featured teens losing their virginity—for example, *Rich Kids* (1979), *The Blue Lagoon* (1980), *Endlesslove* (1981)—faded into the new appeal of carnal comedies about the plight of sexual pursuits.[9] At the same time, *Halloween* and similar films like *Friday the 13th* (1980) and *Slumber Party Massacre* (1982) were capitalizing on the reactionary aspect of teen sexuality, slaughtering wholesale those youth who deigned to cross the threshold of sexual awareness, even though these films usually hinged on a major suspension of realism. The early '80s then marked the beginning of a new era in American youth movie production with the release of numerous popular teen horror films in 1981 and the release of *Fast Times at Ridgemont High* in 1982, the first commercially successful hybrid of the contemporary sex, school, and delinquency elements.

Between 1980 and 1985, there were six major approaches to youth cinema offered by Hollywood, most revised from past trends in the genre: the horror film, the science film, the sex comedy, the romantic melodrama, the juvenile delinquent drama, and the school picture that often borrowed generic elements from the rest. Of these approaches, the horror film tended to offer the highest grosses (literally and figuratively) and often showed the least knowledge of true youth conditions. These films were a runaway success in the early '80s and may in many ways be responsible for bringing a new image of youth to American cinema, however incomplete that image was. Within the youth horror subgenre, graphic depictions of sex and violence had come to be expected, and such previous taboos as the depiction of "underage" nudity were broached. The '80s youth horror subgenre depicted teens not only as sexually active but as morally culpable for their explorations of sexuality, paying with their lives for their indiscretions. The youth horror film—especially in its "slasher" and "supernatural" varieties that I explore in Chapter 4—has brought attention to teen sexuality and morality, and other issues, by the most dramatic means possible.

The science film represents the smallest subgenre but I will argue that its inclusion is nonetheless crucial to understanding the industrial treatment of adult and youth difference. The youth science film had early stirrings in *E.T.* (1982) but came into its own in 1983 with *WarGames* and then continued with further nuclear-era projects like *Real Genius* (1985) and *The Manhattan Project* (1986). Youth science films then went into a clear decline as the Cold War came to a close, and even films featuring youth using computers and video games (*Arcade* in 1993, *Evolver* in 1995) were primarily relegated to smaller studios after the '80s, suggesting that Hollywood was aware of changing cultural conditions for youth using technologies of power but chose not to celebrate this liberatory potential. Considering the very vocal debates around children's increasing access to technology, the continuing lack of films about the topic may signal a certain repression.

The sex comedy and romantic melodrama are companions, for despite the often gratuitous content of many of these films, they all consider the trial by fire that is the discovery of young lust and love. All youth love films can be categorized by identifying the obstacle to the protagonists' romance (class, race, age, distance), but in this study I focus on the obstacle most commonly portrayed since Shakespeare's *Romeo and Juliet:* familial conflict. Throughout the early '80s, the depiction of teens' sexual pursuits was primarily ribald and explicit, as in *Private School* and *Risky Business* (1983), but by the mid-'80s a distinct shift took place toward more serious and sensitive representations of teen relationships, particularly in the films of John Hughes, such as *Pretty in Pink* (1986). The stakes of young romantic and sexual practice grew higher in the era of AIDS, and by the mid-'90s, films about youth having sex portrayed a greater diversity of issues that sometimes accompany these practices, as with the three topics I address here: virginity, pregnancy, and homosexuality.

The output of juvenile delinquent dramas has been the most voluminous of youth films, although their attention to contemporary realism is much debated, since they offer a rich appreciation for the aggressive expressions that teens most crave and parents most fear. A clear range of immorality can be studied across this subgenre, from the harmless mischief that youth enact in daily life—such examples as *Ferris Beuller's Day Off* (1986), *Don't Tell Mom the Babysitter's Dead* (1991) and *Snow Day* (2000)—to the life-threatening criminality of teen thugs in films like *Class of 1984* (1982), *China Girl* (1987), *Kids* (1995), and *American History X* (1998). I look at five specific delinquent styles that represent this spectrum, starting with movies about "deviant dancing" and concluding with the African American crime drama of the early '90s, a successful and influential trend that brought a distinct sense of harsh tension to youth films but nonetheless faded in the mid-'90s.

School films are probably the most foundational subgenre of youth films, yet they often consider teenage identities quite separately from other subgenres. In most school films, the educational setting becomes an index for youth issues, featuring a variety of youth culture styles and types, as best represented by *The Breakfast Club* in 1985. Five character roles played out in that film—the nerd, the jock, the rebel, the popular girl, and the delinquent—are the roles most commonly seen in all school films, and my study examines the impulse of smart students to transform, the impact of delinquents on school order, the threat of conformity to rebels, the sensitive depiction of athletes, and the effects of popularity on teen girls. The cycles in school films are thus best revealed through tracing the characters that embody those cycles, from the nerdly outcast of *Lucas* (1986) to the tormented clique queens of *Heathers* (1989) and the jock heroes of *Varsity Blues* (1999).

These subgenres remained in place throughout the end of twentieth century American cinema, and with the ironic exception of the now-dormant science film, they still form the frame in which youth films are made and marketed in the early twenty-first century, even as a number of the particular styles within the subgenres fade or change. Looking back, after a boom in the early '80s, the output of successful American youth films began to decline by the late '80s, as the "Brat Pack" of popular teen stars in the mid-'80s began taking adult roles and Hollywood moved away from the limited market of teen stories. Many little-seen youth films did continue to be made at this time, and while many were quite good, most were by small studios and thus had restricted releases. With the exception of a few notable films focusing on African American teens in criminal settings, this marginalizing effect continued until the mid-'90s, when Hollywood began to cultivate a refreshed interest in youth films, partially due to the recycling pattern of most film genres, but also in an effort to lure youth back to theaters and away from the proliferation of cable-TV channels and new teen-oriented Internet sites.

By the mid-'90s, the latest expansion of youth movie production emerged, especially in the wake of highly successful and/or provocative youth films such as *Clueless, Kids, Dangerous Minds* (all 1995), *William Shakespeare's Romeo + Juliet, Scream,* and *Girls Town* (all 1996). The new Hollywood strategy worked: by 1997, the national teenager-demographic tracking organization Teen Research Unlimited announced that teens labeled "going to the movies" the most popular "in" activity, ahead of (in descending order) using the Internet, dating, partying, sports, and shopping.[10] In fact, just as they saved Hollywood profits in the early '80s, youth movies of the late '90s offered a much-needed boost to a previously sluggish film industry, with relatively low-budget productions such as *Can't Hardly Wait, The Faculty* (both 1998), *Never Been Kissed, She's All That,* and *Varsity Blues* (all 1999) all yielding tidy revenues—not to mention the hugely budgeted and overwhelmingly successful *Titanic* (1997), a film that owed much of its profit to a youth audience captivated by the film's teen romance. Various media outlets began covering the escalating interest in teen culture, which was apparent not only at the multiplex but in television shows such as *Party of Five, Buffy the Vampire Slayer, 7th Heaven, Moesha,* and the relatively huge hit *Dawson's Creek* (developed by *Scream* screenwriter Kevin Williamson), and which thus had a synergistic effect in increasing the output of teen roles in the cinema.[11] The youth population at the end of the century was clearly witness to a new wave of films that catered to their interests and explored their images, and these films were and will continue to be undoubtedly influenced by and built upon the evolution of cinematic youth representations in previous generations.

The rich and compelling history of films about youth informs us of more than the changing social conditions and perceptions of young people; it gives us a special appreciation for how successive generations have endured the conflicts of claiming identity and seeking recognition for their actions. This endurance was seen most visibly in the post–World War II teen films as young people restively entered the Cold War era their parents created, and then again in the '60s counterculture films, and most recently at the turn of the millennium as youth face a future that will be far more fast-paced and removed from the traditions and mores of their parents' generation. This study examines American youth films in the last two decades of the twentieth century to determine how recent generations of young people have been represented in American cinema and what that representation tells us about the various phenomena that constitute the contemporary coming-of-age process. Through this examination I demonstrate not only that youth films comprise a legitimate genre worthy of study on their own terms, but that they are imbued with a unique cultural significance: they question our evolving identities from youth to adulthood while simultaneously shaping and maintaining those identities.

SOCIAL REPRESENTATION AND GENRE ANALYSIS

This is a work of film criticism. I have viewed and analyzed hundreds of films that compose my primary texts of analysis, and my main analytical method uses genre analysis to study social representation. Social approaches to film studies seek an understanding of cinema based on group and individual representations in (and/or reactions to) films—for example, how films portray a given population or their conditions—under the tacit assumption that films are both aesthetic and cultural documents produced by an industry whose aim is to appeal to (often larger) populations who will find the films worth seeing. Genre analysis considers patterns, motifs, and trends across a spectrum of films that share a commonality, usually subject matter and theme (such as science fiction, melodrama, Westerns), and further explores how the elements of a genre are manifested and change over time. My study considers how American films about teenagers have utilized different techniques and stories to represent young people within a codified system that delineates certain subgenres and character types within the "youth film" genre. Unlike other genres that are based on subject matter, the youth genre is based on the ages of the films' characters, and thus the thematic concerns of its subgenres can be seen as more directly connected to specific notions of different youth behaviors and styles.

Pioneering cinematic image studies include Molly Haskell's examination of women in film, *From Reverence to Rape* (1974), Thomas Cripps's examination of African Americans in film, *Slow Fade to Black* (1977), and Siegfried Kracauer's seminal investigation of German film and society, *From Caligari to Hitler* (1957).[12] To this list we could also add many other studies, including those of Native Americans (*The Only Good Indian,* Ralph Friar and Natasha Friar, 1972), Jews (*The Jewish Image in American Film,* Lester Friedman, 1987), and the disabled (*Cinema of Isolation,* Martin Norden, 1994).[13] The authors of these studies employ various approaches to their investigations, all of which are built upon the belief that films are cultural artifacts revealing much about not only the people who are depicted in them but also those who make and view them. These approaches can be primarily interpretive, utilizing a subjective understanding of the films and the population in question, or more quantitative, attempting an objective "content analysis" to reveal various features of the films.

I study the images of youth in American cinema by combining both of these approaches. I feel that in any social study of cinema one cannot and should not rely solely upon quantitative and statistical information, and an "objective" study of a medium as personal and social as film would not be effective in such matters as attitude, nuance, and style. However, I also feel that relying solely upon inferential readings of films is equally problematic, for such a study can become so subjective as to be indifferent to other perspectives. I therefore aim to understand the subtleties and possible interpretations of youth films while also exploring the social and industrial contexts of the films' productions; I try to identify and analyze the "image" of youth with as much information as possible about what inspired and manifested that image and how that image developed over time. I do not study the reception of youth images, and I leave such a study to those who can pursue thorough audience research. Rather, my study expands upon the work done by scholars whose analyses of the images of youth have provided a helpful foundation.

Genre analysis has been developed more recently than social analysis methods. While many critics observed the social influence of movies on viewers from the earliest days of cinema, serious genre examinations did not proceed until after World War II. Paul Willemen (1983) describes the two functions that genre theory was then designed to fulfill: (1) "to challenge and displace the dominant notions of cinema installed and defended on the basis of the assumed excellence of the 'taste' of a few journalists and reviewers, appealing to the 'age-old canons and principles' of Art in general," and (2) "in the wake of the realisation that any form of artistic production is a rule-bound activity firmly embedded in social history, [genre theory] set about discovering the structures which underpinned groups of films and gave them their social grounding."[14] Thus, as genre theories were staked out, many scholars argued alternately for political, aesthetic, social, and industrial methods for studying genres.

Theoretical studies of genre appeared, such as Robin Wood's "Ideology, Genre, Auteur" (1977), in which Wood claimed that genre films are "different strategies for dealing with the same ideological tensions."[15] Rick Altman's ambitious "A Semantic/Syntactic Approach to Film Genre" (1984) proposed studying genre by combining the semantic view of genre study ("definitions that depend on a list of common traits, attitudes, characters, shots, locations, sets, and the like") with the syntactic (". . . definitions that play up instead certain constitutive relationships between undesignated and variable placeholders"), an approach that he has since revised and expanded in his recent *Film/Genre* (1999).[16] Practical methods of studying genre were offered in Thomas Schatz's *Hollywood Genres* (1981) and Stuart Kaminsky's *American Film Genres* (1985), while specific generic approaches were also hotly debated (e.g., Paul Schrader's take on film noir, Jim Kitses's study of the Western, Jane Feuer's and Rick Altman's books on Hollywood musicals).[17]

Some writers insisted upon parameters for describing "genre films," such as how one could claim that certain movies were indeed gangster films, or Westerns, or melodramas (Kaminsky called for a limited scope and definition to genre, in films with clearly defined constants).[18] However, an early critic of this concern, Andrew Tudor, in 1973 pointed to the "empiricist dilemma" of arbitrary definitions and post hoc descriptors that are often used to describe a genre, by which a genre is defined "on the basis of analyzing a body of films that cannot possibly be said to be [a certain genre] until after the analysis."[19] Tudor sees two solutions to this dilemma: first, to "classify films according to a priori criteria depending on the critical purpose," or second, more commonly and more preferably, to "lean on a common cultural consensus as to what constitutes [a certain genre] and then go on to analyze it in detail."[20] Still other writers remained grounded in the broader theories of genre, such as Steve Neale's contention in "Questions of Genre" (1990) that genres represent social and industrial conditions indicative of alternating dominant forces, although using such a model demands an exhaustive and impractical study of a myriad of discourses in order to be sound and is ultimately as interpretive as other text-based approaches.[21]

Genre criticism shares an important role with social criticism in revealing to scholars the complex tastes and trends of filmmakers and audiences. Schatz argues in *Hollywood Genres* that audiences "write" genres within limited contexts, describing to the film industry what films should be made based on what films they go to see. Schatz thus claimed that "a genre represents a range of expression for filmmakers and a range of experience for viewers."[22] I believe this is a helpful way of considering genre, although the ranges of which Schatz speaks can be wide and difficult to define. In the case of the present study, I consider the image of the American youth population within certain ranges of experience that youth are afforded, such as school, relationships, and delinquency. These experiences are essentially what define the more precise "subgenres" within the social genre of youth films.

In terms of defining and analyzing the youth genre, both of Tudor's solutions to the empiricist dilemma can be employed: first, temporarily set aside cultural context in the definition of the genre by simply maintaining a defined and consistent limit on the genre (see "youth picture" described below). Then, in addressing the cultural context, be explicitly aware of the fallibility of generalizing that remains an inherent danger in observing the characteristics of a genre and then extrapolating from those characteristics to make comparisons to social conditions. Since my study argues primarily from the point at which images of youth are produced—the texts of the films—and not their reception within a historical reality of youth, nor their stylistic components (e.g., lighting techniques, editing patterns, use of sound), I can only offer interpretive arguments about the social milieu as well as about the industrial and narrative range of films themselves. While any study that deals with representation must necessarily consider the context of said representation, my study only applies recent historical and statistical information about youth as it is relevant to certain arguments. Conditions of education, employment, and lifestyle among young people are too complex to analyze within the scope of this study, although the representation of certain youth trends or practices in films against the historical or statistical "reality" of youth conditions is considered.

One of the most conspicuous problems of genre analysis over the past generation has been the assumption by most scholars that a genre's characteristics and development can be discerned by studying only the most popular and "successful" examples of a genre or else a random sample of its offerings. Obviously this approach presents a number of dilemmas: how the determination of "importance" is made for the sample selected, what is lost in the films not studied, and how claims about the genre may not apply to every film that can be argued to fit the genre's code. In the dissertation that was the source of this book, I insisted upon a generic methodology in which all of the available films within a genre, and its respective subgenres, are addressed, since this is the only way to ensure complete knowledge of a genre. Nonetheless, a few problems with my approach arose as I wrote the dissertation and revised it into the current volume: many films that may fit within the youth genre are not available for viewing; the restrictions of space do not allow for lengthy commentary on the many films in question; some films that are only partially germane to issues of youth representation may not contribute to an examination of youth subgenres as a whole.

The first problem cannot be avoided—there are simply many films that are so obscure as to be inaccessible, and a scholar is left with the faulty option of making comments on a few films based on plot descriptions; thus, I only offer analyses of the relevant films I have been able to carefully view. The second problem is unfortunate, since it demands that some valuation be placed on films and styles that do warrant more extensive commentary, while others are given shorter coverage or omitted altogether. This and the third problem are indicative of the inevitably judgmental nature of generic definition: I must determine which films are most representative and which address youth issues "significantly," as well as how they operate within the various youth subgenres. I argue that most youth films fall into one of five subgenres, but not all portray youth in such a way that lends deeper insight to the patterns and operations of the subgenres. In selecting the films that are the most germane to my argument and in focusing on the subgeneric categories that are most revealing of youth film trends, I have had to eliminate a number of wonderful films and important issues for the sheer sake of concentration and demonstration. I thus apologize at the start for the absence of numerous teen classics that you may otherwise find endearing, and which I can almost certainly promise have found or will find thorough coverage in other sources.

The difficulty of this type of genre approach has been examined by Janet Staiger (1997) in her analysis of the "purity hypothesis" in genre study, for she claims that "Hollywood films have never been 'pure'—that is, easily arranged into categories. All that has been pure has been sincere attempts to find order among variety."[23] She does, however, go on to say that these sincere attempts are in the service of understanding larger structural and representational patterns in film history, while questioning why scholars such as Tudor can point out the inconsistencies of genre study and then essentially pass over them in excessively precise efforts to study genre films. Thus, to this day an agreement within the field on how to conduct genre studies has yet to be reached, as is evident by the number of current texts that continue to debate the issue, although I proceed through a comprehensive analysis that expands upon the most complex and visible examples of the youth genre's output.[24]

That films about youth actually constitute a genre has only recently been identified in film studies. After the pioneering work of David Considine and a few other authors in the 1980s, two genre catalogs offered codifications for the youth genre. In his massive compendium *Films by Genre: 775 Categories, Styles, Trends, and Movements Defined, with a Filmography for Each* (1993), Daniel Lopez identifies the "Teen Movie," which has also been called the "'Juve' Movie," "Teenage Movie," "Teenpic," and "Youth Picture," although he places undue emphasis on the exploitative nature of many films since the 1950s that have featured teenagers.[25] He then divides the Teen Movie into subgenres, while cross-listing other relevant genres such as the "Exploitation Film," the "Juvenile Delinquency Film," the "Motorcycle Movie," the "Rock Film," and the "Youth Film." Of Teen Movie subgenres, Lopez offers the division of "Beach Films," "High School Films," "Teen-Violence Films," and "Teen Comedies"—which he distinguishes from "Teen Sex Comedies."[26]

His further distinction of the "Youth Film" appears to be a matter of historically specific semantics, since he only cites examples from 1967 to 1972 and claims that these films "highlighted the concerns of young people querying the Establishment, society and its values," as if films before or since this time frame had failed to do so as well.[27] Such a dubious category exposes the difficulty of finding accurate descriptors for generic styles and movements, since Lopez would have done better to label the Vietnam-era films to which he was referring by their thematic concerns, calling them perhaps "Anti-Establishment Films," or placing them in a temporal subgenre such as the "Vietnam-Era Youth Film." Lopez's attempt to define and divide films about youth is still significant, for he locates Teen Movies as a genre unto itself, and sees the necessity of making subgeneric distinctions.

In 1995 the Library of Congress commissioned its Motion Picture/Broadcasting/Recorded Sound Division to study the cataloging of films by types, and by 1997 the group produced *The Moving Image Genre-Form Guide,* which relies on the work of archival sources (such as the *Film Literature Index* and *The American Film Institute Catalog of Feature Films*) to construct a descriptive structure for the various genres and forms of film.[28] This guide locates one comprehensive genre it labels "Youth," which comprises "fictional work portraying aspects of the trajectory through adolescence, including high school years, peer pressure, first love, beach parties, and initial attempts at adulthood, along with strains in the relationship with family."[29] The emphasis in these films is on teenage characters, and the guide thus subsumes the distinction of "Teen" films within this category, moving films about characters aged 12 and younger to "Children," and films set in a collegiate environment to "College." These are essentially the same distinctions that I make (although I do include 12-year-old characters) in delimiting the genre that is the youth film.

As Janet Staiger and other authors have continued to argue, many films do not easily conform to manufactured categories: some films may simply not fit into a clear (sub)generic classification, or may cross over so many themes and styles as to defy any single (sub)generic location. This is a dilemma of which I am keenly aware, and I attempt to address it by always foregrounding the existence of youth cinema as a genre itself, which has a relatively reliable denotative frame—that is, films in which youth appear. Then within that frame, I allow for much categorical interplay and cross-generic influence. Yet because not even all "films in which youth appear" can properly be identified as youth cinema (usually because the young characters are secondary to adult leads), the larger generic frame under which I work is still sensitively constructed. This is a dilemma that I do not feel disrupts the process of examining how youth have been represented in cinema because so many youth images are still being studied; yet from a methodological standpoint, it does bear reminding, if only to argue that describing a truly reliable, consistent, internally and externally integrated model of genre study by social types may be an impossible goal. I believe that this book employs the paradigm that is best suited to the study of cinematic social representation through generic analysis, however incomplete and arguable it may remain.

What delimits youth in this context? For the purposes of my study, I consider the youth population to be between the ages of 12 and 20. This represents a range of years that includes the actual teen years as well as the traditionally recognized entrance into adolescence (or at least in the United States, the beginning of middle school, or junior high school), as well as late adolescence and entry into the post–high school world. (This is the same age range that David Considine analyzed in his work on adolescents in film, beginning with his dissertation and culminating in his book *The Cinema of Adolescence*. It is also the same age range used by Mark Thomas McGee and R. J. Robertson in their study of juvenile delinquency in movies, *The J.D. Films*.) However, I do not analyze films that are about characters in college (who tend to be between 18 and 24 years old) except for the rare cases where clearly defined adolescents attend college in the story. This is not to say that college-age characters are not youthful, but since the college genre has itself already been extensively covered in other studies, and further, because the ages of college characters are often vague and are usually implied as the "early 20s," and most of all, because the majority of college films do not concern the same issues about youth as do teen and high school films, analyzing these films would detract from the primary focus of my study on teen representation.[30] Therefore, the chapters on horror, science, delinquency, and love and sex consider films about characters aged 12 to 20, while the chapter on school covers characters in junior high or high school (generally 12 to 18 years old). Using this subgeneric format allows for a clear demonstration of the diverse and yet confined images of youth that Hollywood produces.

I further delimit my study by concentrating on feature-length films, although I do consider many straight-to-video movies that achieved recognition outside of theatrical release. I do not examine films that, despite the presence of young performers or their appeal to young audiences, are not about the youth experience. As Thomas Doherty and other critics have argued, Hollywood "juvenilized" its films after World War II to such an extent that virtually all movies can be said to appeal to youth.[31] Thus, given the comprehensive reach of what can be labeled "youth" films, I am not only concentrating on those films that are relevant to the dominant subgenres of youth cinema since 1980, but I am omitting films that only tangentially or incidentally depict youth. A filmography of all youth films from 1980 to 2001 (many of which are excluded from the present study) is included as Appendix A; this list is provided in the hope that a complete analysis of all youth films may someday be conducted.

Assembling the filmography for this study proved to be an arduous task. Many of the so-called indexes of genres are incomplete or, as is the case with many generic categories, based on ambiguous or subjective judgments of what constitutes relevant films in the "youth" genre. I conducted numerous cross-referenced searches, generating an initial list of roughly 1,500 films, which I then began to narrow by consulting plot descriptions. This was by far the most reliable and complete method for compiling the filmography, which rounded out at just over 1,000 films, of which I was able to view and analyze about 420 examples. I believe this is the most complete filmography of youth films from 1980 to 2001 that can be assembled.

I have read what I believe to be all of the relevant literature on youth films since 1980, as well as numerous published reviews on each film in the study. While I integrate these writings into my analyses, I do not believe that it is necessary or appropriate to focus on any specific authors' theoretical arguments about youth films, youth culture, or film reception in general. My approach is meant to be pluralistic and inclusive, considering as many pertinent perspectives about these films as possible. For instance, many commercial developments at the end of the twentieth century—multiplex theaters, the availability of films on video, trends in youth fashion—not only have affected the output of youth films but also have changed the representations of youth within films. I thus also consider how certain financial conditions of the filmmaking practice have factored into the social and generic aspects of youth images in cinema.

A note on terminology: I use the label "youth films" to refer to the entire universe of films made about young people. While I often label this population as "young adults," I will occasionally divide "teens" from "20-somethings" when such a distinction is demanded. "Adolescence" is an ambiguous term that can be applied to youth before the age of 12 and after 20, so I reserve use of the term for when I specifically discuss the social or biological process of entering adulthood and leaving childhood.

THE STUDY OF YOUTH, IN AND OUT OF MOVIES

A study of cinema and youth offers an interesting historical parallel: motion pictures were invented in the 1890s and "youth" as an area of academic research emerged less than 20 years later in 1904, when social psychologist G. Stanley Hall wrote his pathbreaking two-volume tome *Adolescence: Its Psychology, and Its Relations to Physiology, Anthropology, Sociology, Sex, Crime, Religion, and Education,* which may be credited as the beginning of youth studies.[32] That the proliferation of cinema and the founding of youth studies coincide within the same historical generation may not be indicative of a cause-and-effect relationship; however, the relationship between cinema and youth is significant. The twentieth century produced a series of "moral panics" around young people and social behavior, and the cinema—both as a gathering place and as a site of influence—has been a perennial source of those panics.[33]

Of course children and teenagers existed before the twentieth century began, but the social perception of the preadult population was considerably different before the early 1900s, and certainly before the Industrial Revolution. Many girls and boys left school at preteen ages in the nineteenth century and started families soon thereafter, often entering the labor force in their early teen years or younger. As the modern era took hold, certain researchers like Hall (and later Havighurst, Piaget, Winnicott, Erikson, and Anna Freud) began recognizing a distinct age of specialized development between childhood and adulthood that had been initially described through characteristics of sexual development and was then later examined as a more complex sociopsychological manifestation of cultural and internal conflict.[34] This age of development was adolescence, and its study by researchers (including Keniston, who even divided adolescence from youth) and its acceptance by society during the progressing twentieth century resulted in a new notion of youth, if only to distinguish a crucial transitional period during the teen years between childhood and adulthood.[35]

Until the 1960s the study of youth remained largely a discipline within the behavioral sciences as researchers studied the changing attitudes and "pathologies" of youth during the various cycles of twentieth-century life. Then in the '60s, certain global political events brought about a visible change in the activities of young people, not the least of which were the escalating war in Southeast Asia and the student revolts in France in 1968. During this same decade Philippe Aries wrote the next paradigmatic study of youth, shifting attention away from behavior and toward history in *Centuries of Childhood: A Social History of Family Life* (1962).[36]

Throughout the 1960s and the 1970s, the new research on youth history was taken up by the growing field of cultural studies, which eagerly considered how the youth uprisings of that era could be representative of previously repressed or diffused class, gender, and race conflicts. First appeared the work of James Coleman in his 1961 book, *The Adolescent Society: The Social Life of the Teenager and Its Impact on Education,* after which British scholars in the 1970s, among them Stuart Hall, Angela McRobbie, and Dick Hebdige, studied patterns of resistance and revolt within what was now called "youth culture."[37] By the 1980s, as the Reagan/Thatcher era brought about a series of new moral panics based on the vision of the New Right, the trend in youth research shifted back toward studies of youth "pathologies" (e.g., teen pregnancy, unemployment, crime) within a cultural studies method.[38] One of the first such studies was *Hooligan: A History of Respectable Fears* (1983), in which Geoffrey Pearson claimed that essentially the same moral accusations about youth had been recycled for the past 150 years. One of the more notable later studies in this vein was *The Road to Romance and Ruin: Teen Films and Youth Culture* (1992), in which Jon Lewis relied much upon the observations and opinions of Hebdige and Hall as he studied various teen "vices" in recent cinema.[39] The influence of British cultural studies remains evident in more recent youth studies, such as *Teenagers: An American History* (1996), by Grace Palladino, which studies the emergence of the American teenage population in terms of its institutional identification through the rise of high schools in the early twentieth century, and its economic identification through the greater consumptive capacities that teenagers developed in the years after World War II.[40] Regardless of how youth studies have focused on deviance and development (psychology) and/or resistance and economics (politics), one aspect of youth studies has been undoubtedly clear since the 1980s: youth culture is not homogeneous.

The 1980s became a time of distinct change in youth studies as the trajectories of sociology, history, and cultural studies merged over concerns about refreshed conservative attitudes that were largely vilifying youth.[41] These concerns were legitimate given conditions of the time; however, these conditions were not necessarily being visibly addressed in the American cinema at this time. Most Hollywood films about youth in the 1980s relied upon formulas that exploited youth issues, especially sexual development, while gradually revealing an increasing tension and confusion about the role of contemporary youth. By the early '90s, in the wake of the Reagan and Thatcher years and the patriotic swell of the Persian Gulf War, teens in American films had been entirely reconfigured, if not often extinguished, as increasing emphasis fell on portraits of the post-teen "20-something" generation in movies after *Slacker* in 1991 (examples include *Singles* in 1992 and *Reality Bites* in 1994). Popular studies of youth thus shifted their attention: in July 1990, *Time* magazine published an extensive and influential article entitled "Proceeding with Caution," which debuted the skeptical "20-something generation"; over the next few years more magazines followed suit (including dueling cover stories in *Atlantic Monthly* and *The New Republic* at the end of 1992) with studies of young adults now labeled "Generation X" after Douglas Coupland's eponymous 1991 novel.[42] "Youth" by the mid-'90s thus covered a wider age range than ever before, spanning the first year of postelementary education (the age of 12) to the first few years after college (or, considering that the majority of young people do not complete college, at least the mid-20s).[43]

This perception had already been supported in Susan Littwin's *The Postponed Generation: Why America's Grown-Up Kids Are Growing Up Later* (1986), in which she argued that American adolescents now require over 10 years after the onset of puberty (usually the early teens) to become adults.[44] Further evidence of the widening age range and the concentration on recent information about youth came from more demographic studies like *Marketing to Generation X* by Karen Ritchie (1995) and *Welcome to the Jungle: The Why Behind "Generation X"* by Geoffrey T. Holtz (1995).[45] These studies argue that "youth" has been reconfigured as a specialized and crucial age group for American commercial marketing, and they show how certain youth attitudes—notably cynicism and narcissism—have been amplified and exploited by advertisers, businesses, and even politicians. (Janet Weeks has suggested that part of the reason for the decline in youth films from the late '80s to mid-'90s was that Generation X youth were "less enamored of cinema" than previous and current youth, although considering that many Gen Xers were teens in the early to mid-'80s when American youth films were thriving, such a generalized audience claim is likely specious.[46]) Most recently, a psychosociological interest in studying youth conditions has emerged following Mary Pipher's very successful *Reviving Ophelia: Saving the Selves of Adolescent Girls* (1994), which chronicles the tales of a wide range of troubled teenage girls facing negative body images, difficult familial conditions, and confusing romantic and social experiences.[47]

The shift in youth studies and the general perception of youth over the past generation thus makes for intriguing research; but studying how the image of youth has changed, and further how it has diversified into a heterogeneity of styles, attitudes, and ages, offers insight into the significant and often contradictory notions of who young people are. The cinema, with its limited range of products with unlimited ranges of meaning, is a system of representation that provides a useful index of issues about various conditions; and in the case of this book, the conditions studied are those of youth.

In terms of general studies about youth in cinema, the most important and complete work to date is Considine's *The Cinema of Adolescence*.[48] Considine employs a method that most other studies omit or minimize: he provides narrative descriptions of virtually all the films he discusses within the context of a thematic examination of the history of a population he calls "screenagers." His overall argument is that American youth films over the course of the century have lacked verisimilitude since "the American film industry has been spectacularly unsuccessful in realistically depicting adolescence," and thus the image of youth in films has been distorted.[49] Considine proceeds chronologically (up to the early 1980s) through chapters divided into sections on family, school, delinquency, and sexuality, and thereby lays out a structure that other critics and I have followed. (I do not locate "family" as an individual subgenre of the youth film after 1980: few recent youth films actually concentrate on family issues—indeed, much of Considine's examination of family is from pre-1970 films—or the family issues are contained within dramatizations more relevant to other subgeneric qualities.)

Considine strikes the best balance between historical and social analysis of any study I have found (with emphasis on the sociological), and his study demonstrates quite well the ways in which Hollywood had portrayed youth until the early '80s, predominantly in negative images. I build from Considine's thematic model and narrative approach in *The Cinema of Adolescence,* updating his study with a deeper consideration of how youth themes have become subgenres and how individual movies themselves became the paradigms for those subgenres.

A less sympathetic study is *The Road to Romance and Ruin* by Jon Lewis.[50] As I have argued in "The Teen Film and Its Methods of Study," Lewis preserves a thematic approach similar to Considine's (yet he never cites him), with a perspective that is often pessimistic and occasionally condescending.[51] He proceeds through six chapters, each of which addresses a different teen vice: anomie, delinquency, sex, consumption, rebellion, and regression. Lewis uses these issues to support his ultimate thesis that "despite stylistic, tonal, industrial, and by now even generational differences within the genre, teen films all seem to focus on a single social concern: the breakdown of traditional forms of authority."[52] Lewis works within a conspicuously limited range of films to demonstrate this argument, and ultimately the light he sheds on teen films and youth culture is as negative and misinformed as the selective films he examines.

I agree with Lewis that genre "begins with the text, not with industry intent or with target audiences," but Lewis often gives the teen texts he discusses scant coverage.[53] He ultimately does appear more concerned with teen films' audiences, moving away from film analyses to incorporate ideas on youth movements (mods, rockers, punks), music, and to a lesser extent, sociopsychological commentary. This could have resulted in a comprehensive study that would have cast new light on the conditions of contemporary youth culture, yet so much of what Lewis says about young people is recycled from notions that are two or three generations past. When he concludes, "For this [current] generation of teenagers, the present is dominated by images and narratives of their parents' youth," his overall argument is revealed as exaggerated and lacking in serious study of recent teen films, which are occupied much more by a nostalgia for the present—the instant recycling of, and ironic longing for, contemporary phenomena—than by scenes of an extinct parental history.[54]

More focused overviews of youth films worth noting include Armond White's article "Kidpix" from 1985; Kathy Merlock Jackson's study of preteens in *Images of Children in American Film: A Sociocultural Analysis* (1986); Thomas Leitch's "The World According to Teenpix" (1992); "Teenage Films," a chapter in Randall Clark's *At a Theater or Drive-in Near You: The History, Culture, and Politics of the American Exploitation Film* (1995); Wheeler Winston Dixon's essay "'Fighting and Violence and Everything, That's Always Cool': Teen Films in the 1990s" (2000); and Steve Neale's coverage of "Teenpics" in *Genre and Hollywood* (2001).[55] Murray Pomerance has coedited a collection of recent articles on youth in film and television, *Pictures of a Generation on Hold: Selected Papers* (1996), from a conference on the same topic; Pomerance is also the coeditor with Frances Gateward of a study of girls in popular media, *Sugar, Spice, and Everything Nice* (2002).[56]

As of this writing, the newest comprehensive analysis of teens in films can be found in Jonathan Bernstein's popular book *Pretty in Pink: The Golden Age of Teenage Movies* (1997), which is an often refreshing although generally uninsightful examination of '80s teen films, since Bernstein only briefly mentions the many significant social, political, and economic conditions of the time, a shortcoming that is more glaring when he then attempts to study the representations of youth in films.[57] What becomes quickly evident, as Bernstein admits, is that he has no intention of examining an "exhaustive collection" of these films, and even though he does address about 120 teen films (more than any book other than Considine's and the present study), his review process is rather skewed to easily fit his generalizing remarks about the hedonism and angst portrayed in the films he describes. This yields sentimental reflections that can be amusing, while Bernstein's arguments remain self-fulfilling and lacking in depth.

In their 1980 reference catalog *The Screen Image of Youth: Movies about Children and Adolescents,* Ruth Goldstein and Edith Zornow describe a 1972 article by *New York Times* film critic Vincent Canby entitled "Stop Kidding Around," in which he portrayed a 10-year-old boy who was so angry about the "lies" that films told about children that he was going to write a corrective book, "The Image of the Child in Film."[58] Neither Canby nor the mythical boy ever produced such a book, although the critic did indeed recognize a significant need for research, revision, and appreciation for the ways in which young people are represented in cinema. Most of the authors above, knowingly or not, have participated in fulfilling that need articulated by Canby 30 years ago, and I attempt to augment that tradition by examining young adult films in this book.

2 YOUTH IN SCHOOL
Academics and Attitude

You see us as you want to see us, in the simplest terms and the most convenient definitions. But what we found out is that each one of us is a brain, an athlete, a basket case, a princess, and a criminal.
—BRIAN TO HIS PRINCIPAL IN *The Breakfast Club*

I use my great IQ to decide what color lip gloss to wear and how to hit three keggers before curfew.
—VERONICA IN *Heathers*

I'm fucking tired of being wrong before I open my mouth.
—LESTER TO A COP IN *Light It Up*

The school film is perhaps the most easily definable subgenre of youth films since its main plot actions focus on the setting of high school or junior high school campuses. The vast majority of school films present the educational building as a symbolic site of social evolution, with young people learning from and rebelling against their elders (and each other) in the ongoing cycle of generational adjustment and conflict. In certain instances, school films have actually considered how the design and structure of the educational facilities of a school impact upon the students and teachers, but most often the school itself is an indifferent location wherein various gender, race, class, and above all, popularity issues are contested among students.

School is also a site of individual growth through not only educational achievements but also the earning of social acceptance. Young people learn very early that certain traits—good looks, money (in the form of nice clothes or cool toys), intelligence, athletic skills, toughness—yield special attention from their elders and their peers. The struggle for gaining attention in any school system is a complex contest for recognition of genetic privilege and negotiation of social status, for young people without naturally attractive traits must learn to cultivate whatever characteristics will most successfully earn them acceptance, unless they can deny the process of acceptance and adopt an alternate means of gaining self-identity and esteem. Yet by the teen years, with the onset of puberty and adolescent angst over conforming to the adult world, all young people are faced with even larger confrontations about acceptance, and their physical placement in the school environment becomes a visible reminder of their plight. School may be a land of opportunity to demonstrate one's worth or a locus of oppression where one's attempts to gain worth are met with resistance or ridicule.

The majority of American teens' socialization takes place at or around school. (Most school districts offer junior high school, or middle school, to students between the ages of 12 and 14, and high school to students age 15 through 18.) Since the school is thus a prime location for a wide range of youth development, movie studios have capitalized on the variety of applications to which the school setting can be utilized generically; all of the other subgenres in this study contain some films in which schools are used as various narrative devices. What makes the school film a specific subgenre is its focus on the actual socialization process at the school, as opposed to other youth issues which are less integral to the school setting, such as crime, sex, terror, or family (although these issues are often developed in films around school settings). This chapter examines the American school film as a subgenre dependent upon the social recognition of junior high and high school as contained milieux for the educational development and cultural disciplining of youth, where youth are most often clearly divided into distinct types with certain levels of achievement and acceptance according to that development and disciplining. In environments of such change and containment, conflicts are inevitable; since such containment is rendered upon a population teeming with physical energy, sexual curiosity, and psychological tension, the dramatic potential of those conflicts, and their resolutions, seems limitless.

TRENDS IN THE SUBGENRE

The school film as a subgenre has moved through discernible waves of popularity. From the debut of postwar high school discontent in such teen trouble films as *City Across the River* (1949) to the more popular image of tense school conditions in the two 1955 classics, *Rebel Without a Cause* and *Blackboard*

Jungle, both major studios and smaller independents tapped into (or exploited) the burgeoning cultural anxiety about reckless youth. With the rapid proliferation of multiple teen subgenres, the school film became only one avenue for representing teens, and as tensions of the 1960s shifted to college campuses, fewer high school films were made. While the youth film market boomed in the 1980s after the tamer 1970s, the school film did not maintain any consistent popularity of its own.

The film that perhaps presaged the '80s high school cycle (while openly borrowing from the '50s crime dramas) was *Over the Edge* in 1979. The film features a young Matt Dillon as a James Dean–style rebel who galvanizes a small group of suburban tough kids to fight for a certain liberation from their alcoholic parents and misguided school system. In one of the most extreme teen fantasies ever filmed (although the film's premise was based on a true story), the students ultimately lock their parents and teachers in their high school and set it on fire. The film may now be viewed as an examination of social anxieties about delinquency and discipline in the late '70s, although, according to Jonathan Bernstein, the film was in fact kept from public release for a few years because the studio feared copycat violence.[1]

The next major school film of the era took a decidedly different approach. *Fast Times at Ridgemont High* (1982) arrived just as the new trend in teen sex films was developing (notable examples include *Foxes* and *Little Darlings* in 1980 and *Porky's* and *Endlesslove* in 1981), and while the film was at once a lighthearted portrait of suburban youth making their way through the curricular and extracurricular maze of high school life, it also gave viewers a full array of sexual melodramas, complete with titillating nudity and sex talk. Many other school films of the early '80s also incorporated the same attitudes and themes about young sex, although the novelty quickly wore off as popular films such as *Teachers* (1984) and *The Breakfast Club* (1985) offered more focused interrogations of schools and their effects on students.

The later '80s marked a decline in the overall number of successful school films (although, as is the case with some other youth film subgenres, the number of school films in total increased, even if many of these were barely seen by audiences). After the previous movement from sexual themes to character dramas based on school and family problems, the school films of the late '80s covered a range from such tasteful coming-of-age comedies as *Lucas* (1986) to more tasteless attempts to agitate teen tensions, as in *The Principal* (1987) and *Johnny Be Good* (1988). With the exception of *Stand and Deliver* in 1988, which concentrated on the role of an inspirational math teacher, there were no school films between the seminal *Breakfast Club* in 1985 and *Heathers* in 1989 that matched their popularity.[2] Such a cycle would soon repeat itself, for after the release of a few more successful school films in 1989 and 1990 (*Bill and Ted's Excellent Adventure, Dead Poets Society, Lean on Me, Pump Up the Volume*), the school film again declined in recognition through the early '90s. As if the genre were on a prescribed cycle, it returned in 1995 with *Angus, Clueless, Dangerous Minds,* and *Powder,* and then again in the late '90s with *Can't Hardly Wait, The Faculty,* and *Rushmore* (1998), *Election, She's All That, 10 Things I Hate About You,* and *Varsity Blues* (1999).

The reasons for the alternating wavelength of popularity in the contemporary school drama may be deceptively easy to explain. As with all genres, new styles and approaches to the same subject matter appeal to audiences for only a short time. The sexual and narcotic hijinks of the early-'80s films may have been an initial reaction to the Reagan era's puritan ethic for youth (movies at least were a site where teens didn't have to "Just Say No"), but declining box-office returns for the ongoing imitations of *Fast Times* (e.g., *Private School* and *Losin' It* in 1983, and *The Wild Life* and *Joy of Sex* in 1984) indicated that interest in rowdy teen sex stories was waning.

Another certain factor was the emergence of Hollywood's first coherent teen screen machine in decades, the so-called Brat Pack. From 1984 to 1986, photogenic young performers such as Molly Ringwald, Anthony Michael Hall, Andrew McCarthy, Judd Nelson, Rob Lowe, Ally Sheedy, and Emilio Estevez found themselves in a series of successful teen dramas. Their appearance in the teen market was built upon wistful, tormented, and ultimately clean images of mid-'80s youth who proffered occasionally sincere questions about sex and drugs as they engaged less in these practices (on-screen, at least) than their previous counterparts. The success of this troupe was nonetheless short lived, and by the late '80s the performers had either gravitated toward adult roles or faded into obscurity. As has been the case with child and teen performers throughout the century, the aging process swiftly carries young actors out of their original personae, and few are welcomed into more assertive adult roles.

Trends in American schooling and social fads are further factors in the oscillating popularity of school films. Each high school "generation" itself lasts for only three or four years, and these short successive generations do not want to be associated with the outmoded styles and fashions of the groups that preceded them, lest they be perceived as unoriginal and conformist. Thus, the appeals of certain types of music, styles of dress, manners of speech, and even social attitudes are bound to be limited to relatively short lifespans among youth, especially those in school who are constantly monitoring the changing cultural landscape. The same phenomenon applies to films about school: with the exception of the rarely successful period film (e.g., *Dead Poets Society* in 1989), young viewers pay to see their current conditions celebrated and exaggerated on the screen, but the conditions of 1999 cannot look like those of 1995 (or perhaps even 1998).

This brings up a final point that may explain the dips in school movie production and/or success. Given the critical acuity of youth audiences, studios must understand the hit-or-miss dilemma of marketing films about youth to a young audience. Whereas adult films that appeal to youth may at least draw a wide audience, contemporary teen dramas have a more limited appeal, and a financial investment in a school picture (unless it has the adult crossover potential of *Stand and Deliver, Lean on Me,* or *Dead Poets Society,* each of which featured a major adult star) is a considerable gamble for a studio. Even the late-'90s resurgence in school films was brought on by relatively low-budget hits like *Clueless, She's All That, Election,* and *Varsity Blues.* During the boom in African American youth films in the early '90s, major studios avoided traditional high school movies while television took up the school setting in popular shows like *Beverly Hills 90210, Saved by the Bell, Blossom,* and the nostalgic *Wonder Years.* Hollywood has more recently developed a synergy between film and television in school depictions, using popular shows and their stars to promote films, such as *Buffy the Vampire Slayer*'s high school demon chaser Sarah Michelle Gellar starring in *I Know What You Did Last Summer* and *Cruel Intentions.*

SCHOOLKIDS

There has been little effort by filmmakers to experiment with or change the types of characters featured in school films, even as the conditions of the school environments and the context of youth images have inevitably continued to evolve. Most school films before the 1980s focused on one type of school character and his or her relation to others, such as the misunderstood rebel played by James Dean in *Rebel Without a Cause,* the sexually curious but nonetheless repressed virgins played by popular schoolgirl Natalie Wood and jock Warren Beatty in *Splendor in the Grass* (1961), or the outcast nerd played by Sissy Spacek in *Carrie* (1976). But by the 1980s, many school films began showcasing an ensemble of school characters, as was shown in *Fast Times at*

Ridgemont High, based on Cameron Crowe's "exposé" investigation of real school life, and reaching an apex with the "experiment" of (stereo)typecasting in *The Breakfast Club.*

Both *Fast Times* and *Breakfast Club* feature the five basic characters of school films that permeate the subgenre: clean-cut and essentially repressed (and thus occasionally aggressive) nerds; delinquent boys and girls "from the wrong side of the tracks" who either pay for their crimes or learn to reform; psychologically distraught rebels who may dabble in crime but are usually looking for a more acceptable outlet for their malaise; "popular" types whom every-

The Breakfast Club (1985) presents the five types of characters who populate schools in American youth films, and this publicity still demonstrates some of their traits. Delinquent John (Judd Nelson) lurks behind shades and working-class garb, rebel Alison (Ally Sheedy) is coiled up and nonconforming in the shadows, athlete Andy (Emilio Estevez) is tensely wrapped in his wrestling jacket, popular Claire (Molly Ringwald) exudes an elite nonchalance, and nerd Brian (Anthony Michael Hall) is drably trying to blend in on the edge.

one at school knows and who support their status through fashion, appearance, and attitude; and jocks, usually shown as physically focused and prouder than their counterparts, dedicated to a given sport yet surprisingly emotional as well. These stereotypes can embody different ages, races, classes, and genders, but as my study shows, there are indeed not only codifications for the behaviors of each type but also certain patterns that reveal narrative modes of acceptance within each type. The ways in which school characters are portrayed may offer an index of identifiers and signifiers for the young viewers who are presumably meant to relate to one or more of these types, and thus the films can be seen to "teach" the proper mannerisms of each school persona.

This chapter analyzes the five basic character types in school films through an evaluation of their primary conflicts: the ways nerds seek to transform, the means delinquents use to express anger, the actions rebels take to resist conformity, the efforts popular girls make for notoriety, and the signals athletes use to show their sensitivity.

TRANSFORMING THE NERD

The roles of intellectually ambitious school characters in youth films since 1980—who are portrayed as socially inept and uncouth—indicate that nerds lack the respect of their teen counterparts, but most films featuring nerds (a.k.a. dweebs, geeks, dorks, brains, and whizzes) reveal that they, like most school characters, are simply struggling to be understood and accepted in the face of social oppression. The irony of nerds' oppression is that they excel at the very practice that school is designed to promote—learning—but such a blatant conformity to institutional expectations gives nerd characters a reputation for being unoriginal and excessively vulnerable. Further, their capacity to excel is viewed with jealousy by other students, who occasionally exploit nerds' skills (many nerds in school films are used to help struggling students overcome academic obstacles). Nerds most often attain their liberation through some abandonment of academics—joining a sports team, falling in love, committing a crime—but they always reaffirm the value of learning as a way of life. In many ways, nerds face the greatest struggle of all school characters because they must make the most forceful denials of their true nature, but this often gives them a distinct sense of accomplishment and respect. In his 1986 review of *Lucas,* Joseph Gelmis noted, "The nerd is to the high school movies of the '80s what the rebel without a cause was to the high school flicks of 30 years ago: an unlikely hero."[3]

Nerds in school films from 1980 to 1999 were almost always males (who did occasionally find nerdlike girlfriends; and *My Science Project* [1985], *Lucas* [1986], *Heathers* [1989], and *American Pie* [1999] contained small roles by female nerds). In 1996 *Welcome to the Dollhouse* offered the first extended portrayal of a female nerd in junior high school, and *She's All That* (1999) presented the female high school nerd as yet another compromising conformist. Some nonschool youth films, such as *A Nightmare on Elm Street 4: The Dream Master* (1988) and *She's Out of Control* (1989), portray female nerds, but in the case of the 1988 horror film the character is killed, and in the 1989 romantic comedy she is transformed into an attractive socialite. This seems to be the option for all nerds: change or perish.

Save such exceptions, which nonetheless employ many of the same stereotypes that are used for male nerds, the reasoning behind this gendered portrayal of nerds may arise from the more compelling tensions generated by bookish boys compared to girls: smart boys are generally portrayed as tormented by their lack of physical presence in relation to their jock peers, and are further ridiculed for their assumed lack of social skills, whereas girls are shown to use their intellect to their advantage. Nerds are also either virgins or sexually inactive, a condition that most nerd films attempt to eradicate through the transformation of nerds into other school types (but nerds who remain nerds almost never have sex). Given the sexualized imaging of female characters in Hollywood history, the neutered role of the nerd does not comply with the traditional vision of screen "girls." In fact, in other films that depict particularly smart female teens—such as *Pretty in Pink* (1986), *Say Anything . . .* (1989), *The Unbelievable Truth* (1990), *Hackers* (1995), and *10 Things I Hate About You* (1999)—much effort is made to make the characters appear attractive and stylish and thus avoid stereotypically nerdish codings, although the intimidation of female intelligence to male characters is alleviated though other means, such as depicting the girls as poor, shy, neurotic, or even feminist.

Nerds tend to come from poorer class backgrounds than their other school counterparts (the most dramatic exception is in *Class Act*). The reasoning behind this characteristic is not clear, although some explanation may lie in nerds' assumed lack of fashion sense, which can be result from impoverished familial conditions. Most nerd characters also have career goals that exceed the ambitions of their classmates, indicating that their sense of professional drive is inspired by a desire to rise above the class conditions into which they were born. Perhaps the clearest connotation of class for these characters is derived from their exaggerated lack of acceptance for other reasons: poverty itself is not popular, and nerds' working-class status further motivates their need to change.

The Endearing '80s Nerd

Even though its characters are in college, the film that has offered perhaps the most dominant image of nerds is *Revenge of the Nerds* (1984), about a group of outcast freshmen who are ridiculed by popular campus characters such as jocks and party girls until they form their own fraternity and ultimately exact a very clever series of pranks to retaliate against their tormentors. In the process, the nerds show not only their ingenuity but also, somewhat ironically, their common interests with their college cohorts in having a good time. The nerd transformation that is common to virtually all other such depictions is thus somewhat challenged by *Revenge,* since its characters achieve pleasure, power, and popularity without shedding their nerdy images, which may seem more legitimate in a college setting as opposed to high school.[4]

Like *Revenge,* many school films feature nerd characters as part of an ensemble depiction of various school stereotypes. In these films, nerds tend to fill background roles, clustering together in tribes, awkwardly bumping into each other, and speaking with big words. Most ensemble films tend to focus on another type of school character, leaving nerds to be less developed and therefore more easily viewed with pity and occasional contempt. For instance, the main nerd character in *Fast Times,* Mark Ratner (Brian Backer), is chastised by his best friend, the lubricious Mike Damone (Robert Romanus), for his lack of sexual prowess. Mark is thus seen as timid and immature; however, his patience in waiting for sex does afford him the film's one lasting romantic relationship. The nerds in *Heathers* are more extreme caricatures, assembled at a table in the opening cafeteria sequence, with their hallmark pocket protectors, eyeglasses, and braces. They shudder at the fleeting attention of the popular Heathers, but they are oddly absent from much of the rest of the film.

A more complete picture of the nerd type in an ensemble film is Brian (Anthony Michael Hall) in *The Breakfast Club,* who is portrayed with a tentative pathos that points to the alienation of nerds in school films. Brian wears khaki slacks and a bland sweatshirt, signifying his lack of fashion sense, plus he has "pale skin, pale-blue eyes, and almost milky blond hair; he's bodiless, almost translucent," as David Denby observed.[5] This lack of corporeality causes Brian to be constantly shut down in conversations with his fellow students, and they don't even learn his name until many scenes into the film. The story's premise is quite simple: five students, three boys and two girls, spend an entire Saturday in detention and systematically open up to each other about their personal problems. By the end of the film, after Brian has confided the dark secret that he is failing a shop class (his recognition that he's not so smart after all, as well as his badge of communal tribulation), the other students take advantage of his usually boastful attitude toward his academic skills by asking him to write their assigned "punishment" essay on their behalf. As Brian is writing the essay, the two remaining couples pair off, leaving him as the lone character without a partner, except of course for his studies: in virtually parallel sequences, the other couples exchange first kisses while Brian, alone in the library, kisses the essay he has so proudly rendered on their behalf.

While the role of Brian in *The Breakfast Club* may be more complete than many other nerd characterizations, it supports as well as challenges some of the usual nerd typings. Brian is indeed ostracized, ridiculed, physically and socially inept, and desexualized, but his yearning for a transformation from his nerd status to a more acceptable or dramatic personality is minimal. Unlike most nerd characters in school films, Brian ultimately appears to accept his nerd labeling, and his peers eventually show some sincere appreciation for the difference he represents (Brian is especially funny when he smokes pot with the others, and he's the only one who admits to contemplating the classic teen temptation of suicide). When the students leave school at the end of the day, Brian may be alone unlike the others, but he has thus ironically maintained a certain independence that is not afforded to them. His resistance to romance and to changing himself to look like or act like the others—something the rest do—indicates that he is the least conformist of the bunch. As other school films show, nerds must either aspire to a homogeneity with their peers to gain acceptance or endure a compromised acceptance that consequently preserves their individuality.

Many nerd stories in the '80s took a somewhat endearing perspective on their subjects—such as *Class* (1983), *Lucas* (1986), *Can't Buy Me Love* (1987), *Three O'Clock High* (1987), and *The Beat* (1988)—but such sweetened portrayals became rare by the '90s, as the torment of teen intellect began to take more serious turns in the late-'80s films. The goofy protagonist in *Three O'Clock High* eventually turns to violence to prove his worth, *The Beat*'s enigmatic nerd kills himself, and even a comedy like *How I Got into College* (1989) shows that its hero's attempt to appear smart to attract a pretty, popular girl is tantamount to social suicide. *Class, Lucas,* and *Can't Buy Me Love* had enacted more positive nerd fantasies of achieving love and popularity through "self-improvement," which in all cases comes with a price: broken friendships, family crises, social disappointment, or literal money in the case of the last film, wherein a nerd pays his pretty neighbor to date him and fails to see what a jerk his resulting fake status makes him.

The most sincere nerd depiction of the '80s is *Lucas,* whose plot sounds familiar even though its story is actually unique among nerd films; as David Edelstein observed, the film is different from other teen romances because it "strolls up to each of the genre's clichés, sniffs it, and makes a gallant show of casting it off."[6] The title character, played by Corey Haim, is a bespectacled and undersized freshman overachiever who gains the attention and sometimes affection of everyone at his high school—one shy classmate who longs for him is Rina (Winona Ryder)—when what he really wants is the love of a junior named Maggie (Kerri Green), who enjoys Lucas's friendship but is more attracted to football star Cappie (Charlie Sheen).

What makes *Lucas* shine is its sincere (almost saccharine) handling of Lucas's coming of age, and its earnest refusal to elevate Lucas from his otherwise lowly nerd position. David Denby called *Lucas* the first high school film "told from the point of view of the nerd," a strategy that "might have been disastrous, but Lucas's being a bit of a pain, as well as a bright boy, absolves the movie of self-pity."[7] For all of his quirks and embarrassing demonstrations, Lucas remains proud of his intellect and still wins favor among many at school (even Cappie befriends and defends him, since Lucas helped him study once when he was injured). However, since Lucas's romantic pursuit of Maggie is still the film's central plot, and since even the most tame sexualizing of his innocent desire would disrupt his secure status as a nerd, the film uses Lucas's failed and ultimately dangerous attempt to play on the football team as a device to display both his lack of virility and his abundance of heart. In the end, Lucas still doesn't win Maggie (a rare romantic comedy in which the lead character is left alone), but he's still desired by Rina, who is implicitly a better match since she is closer to his age, size, and intellect. When the guys on the football team give him a varsity jacket in the last scene, he proudly dons it to signify his triumphant ascent to a potentially new level of masculinity in which he may gain both physical and sexual confidence. This notion that a better life is waiting for the nerd is common to most of these films, a suspended promise of success in a world where intelligence and sensitivity are valued, a world unlike school.

Nerds in the '90s

The major nerd films of the '90s—*Class Act, Angus, Powder, Welcome to the Dollhouse, She's All That*—eschew easy categorization, although each typically advocates a transformation from the shyness associated with intellect and difference to characteristics that offer greater social acceptance, even if that acceptance isn't achieved. *Class Act* (1991) is the only one in which real acceptance for the nerd is gained, using an interesting variation on the switched-identity theme by crossing a street hood with a nerd. *Angus* (1995) endeavors to show how an overweight ninth-grade pariah achieves pride through standing up against the popular jocks in his class, placing its emphasis less on his social integration than on his gaining self-respect. *Powder* (1995) presents its superintelligent albino outcast as more cosmically mysterious than simply shy, a portrait of the nerd as alien life-form, with his cosmic qualities never explained and never appreciated either, a condition that many prodigies must feel.[8] *Welcome to the Dollhouse* (1996) is a discomforting examination of a seventh grader's confrontation with adolescence through the mania of junior high grief. *She's All That* (1999) revises *My Fair Lady* by proposing that a girl nerd is really an intelligent beauty, yet weakens her integrity through her ambiguous longing for a popular boyfriend. And while it isn't a school film per se, *Can't Hardly Wait* (1998) does feature a prominent nerd fantasy, with William (Charlie Korsmo) becoming a party animal and a sex machine for the evening thanks to a low dose of alcohol; in the end, after his temporary acceptance, he is again rejected by the popular school jocks, yet a closing credit tells us that he went on to become rich through the computer industry, signaling his eventual true revenge.

Class Act teams up African American rappers Kid and Play (real names Christopher Reid and Christopher Martin) as Duncan and Blade: these names already foretell that Duncan is a smart and dull nerd who, as signified by his high-top haircut and glasses, is dramatically different from Blade, a bad boy with attitude who is fresh out of prison and ordered by the court to return to high school. By chance their school files are switched at the beginning of the year, and since Blade wants to avoid the derision of being placed in the "delinquents" class and Duncan is susceptible to his pressure, the two decide to let the school continue believing that they are each the other, resulting in Duncan being feared by his classmates as a criminal and Blade being placed in a special class for gifted students. The different treatment that the two receive, and the way each changes in relation to that treatment, demonstrates the film's central message, which David Denby describes well: "[T]eenagers, particularly black teenagers, get typed early on in life and then act in ways that fulfill the expectations placed on them. Change the circumstances and expectations and—presto!—you get a different teenager."[9] The racial and class commentaries of the film further call attention to the differences that *Class Act* attempts to highlight in its portrayal of nerd and criminal youth: very few smart teens in films before the '90s were nonwhite, and Duncan is the only nerd in 20 years of teen movies who comes from a financially prosperous background.

Nonetheless, the film preserves much of the explicit moralizing that African American youth films typically contain: crime does not pay, staying in school is better than being on the streets, true success is measured in respect and not dollars. Or as Jami Bernard saw it, "The movie manages to keep to today's requisite anti-drug, pro–safe sex agendas without getting too bogged down in do-goodism, and gently mocks the stereotypes of uncool intellectuals and idiot homeboys."[10] Duncan is able to make an initially slow but ultimately complete transformation from unhip nerd to stylish dude thanks to Blade's training and the school's attitude toward him, but he thus achieves a certain balance with Blade, who softens some of his toughness and negativity to enjoy the admiration that comes from being (perceived as) cool but smart. By the end of the film, the two opposing types meet at the center of a fulcrum of teen acceptability: Duncan will always be smart but can now be appreciated by his peers as also being cool, and Blade will always be cool but can now be appreciated by his superiors as also being smart.

As with *Class Act*'s treatment of race, *Welcome to the Dollhouse* is notable for implicitly examining gender, being the first full portrayal of a female nerd in American school films since smaller roles in the '80s. Dawn Weiner (Heather Matarazzo) is a seventh-grade target of ridicule, which is assured by her dressing in tacky clothes and wearing the trademark thick glasses.[11] What makes Dawn a nerd to be reckoned with is her intense anxiety about her awkward image, something she recognizes but can't seem to change. The other girls at school clearly dress differently and aggressively intimidate Dawn, as when one even forces Dawn to defecate while she watches, a complex psychological degradation that other films have never risked depicting. Her peers make clear that it's not her intelligence they envy (for Dawn is the rare nerd who's not also book smart), but her sheer appearance that they so easily abhor. Dawn asks the girl who taunts her in the bathroom, "Why do you hate me?" Her flat response: "Because you're ugly."

Rather than cower into shyness, Dawn has learned to fight back or, more often, to vent her anger in other ways (such as her active disgust for her younger sister). Dawn doesn't crave acceptance by the social order at large, and initially doesn't seem to crave acceptance at all, until she develops a crush on her older brother's friend Steve (Eric Mabius). This crush makes Dawn consider her image more seriously, as does the violent interest a class delinquent, Brandon (Brendan Sexton Jr.), shows toward her. Brandon threatens to rape Dawn, but in an unexpected revelation, he shows Dawn that he's more innocently attracted to her, even if he doesn't want anyone else to know. Brandon's sensitivity thus becomes an interesting foil to Dawn's: both students want the affection of someone who can't provide it (Dawn tells Brandon she's in love with Steve, but she still wants to be friends), and both face the embarrassing discovery that the images they've cultivated deny them both acceptance and security. Brandon ultimately runs away from home and Dawn tries a similar tactic, albeit with the purpose of finding her younger sister, who is temporarily kidnapped, and thereby steals more attention away from the long-suffering Dawn.

Dawn realizes in the end that, rather than finding a way out, she must endure five more years of school, and one can only hope "that Dawn Weiner—and Heather Matarazzo—will one day soon bloom into talented and beautiful young women," as Lisa Schwarzbaum wrote in her review.[12] Indeed, the film proposes that Dawn can only wait and hope for nature to bring better options, and perhaps this powerlessness is integrally linked to her gender positioning: unable to capitalize on either smarts or savvy, the nerd girl must hope for change from without to gain a respectable place in society, since the changes she has made or will make from within are clearly not recognized by those around her. After Dawn's crush rejects her and Brandon runs away, she is really left alone, more so than the many male nerd characters in earlier films, who had at least won their crush's attention if not some friends.

She's All That (1999) offers a more insidious depiction of a teenage female nerd, in a plot that originates in Pygmalion: brainy Laney (Rachel Leigh Cook) is cast aside by the popular and wealthier schoolkids for her artistic aspirations and social insecurity, until elite jock Zack (Freddie Prinze Jr.) takes on a bet that he can change even this "loser" into a desirable girl. He does this not out of any affection but to save face after his girlfriend dumps him, for his task becomes not only romancing the wallflower but turning her into a prom queen. Thus is set in motion an explicit transformation narrative, in which once again an already-pretty performer simply needs to doff her glasses to start looking attractive.

At first Laney shows an informed suspicion of Zack's intentions, which makes her seem confidently independent, yet she gradually gives in to the lure of being accepted, despite the fact that the popular crowd still resists her. In this way, the film is harsher than many of the previous nerd tales, for Laney so openly compromises her sense of identity in spite of herself (setting aside her dedication to political causes as well as her expressive artistry) that her embarrassing efforts at gaining acceptance become more self-deprecating than socially integrating. Further, Zack's unusual intelligence does not appear to impede his unethical manipulation of Laney, as he boosts his inflated ego by being not only the motivation for her change but the organizer of it as well. This is somewhat alleviated by an ending in which Zack finally realizes that he has really fallen in love with her, yet Laney still retains the artificial appearance that he has desired all along, and while she may have gained some pride in winning the prize boy, she's still unaccepted, unknown, and essentially deindividualized. Jane Ganahl expressed a common sentiment among critics: "Just once, I'd love to see a teen flick that doesn't send out a message to young girls that to be acceptable, you have to conform."[13] The true deception of *She's All That* is that it suggests its heroine is indeed all that—smart, comely, talented, caring, resilient—and concludes that such great qualities do not guarantee happiness without social and, more strikingly, masculine endorsement.

The main emphasis in most nerd films of the '80s was on transformation, on changing from someone who is smart and physically awkward to someone who is merely clever but popular and sophisticated, and this emphasis became more complicated in the '90s. Nerds are always "told" to transform, that their present image holds them back from being socially accepted and that social acceptance is indeed more valuable than idiosyncratic individuality, but nerds are usually portrayed as being smart enough to realize the fallacy of this expectation. If *Can't Hardly Wait* is any indication, nerds will continue to be ostracized as teenagers, but will have the last laugh as they become successful (and popular) adults. Some films may continue to acknowledge this, even if other films in the *She's All That* mold are likely to also continue the stereotypical depiction of smart youth as inherently conflicted by their intellect—a conflict that, after all, grants nerd characters a greater dramatic interest.

DELINQUENTS AND THEIR AVENUES OF ANGER

The delinquent character has long been a staple of school films, and is certainly the most common screen image of students since 1980. (I analyze the larger topic of teen delinquency in the next chapter.) Like their roles in films since the '50s, delinquents are used to demonstrate that crime is not a proper means of acceptance, and unless the delinquent reforms, he or she is destined for a life of misery (or else the delinquent dies before the end of the film). Delinquency in school films is portrayed through characters who not only violate the moral code of the school, but who also usually carry their troubling behavior outside of school, and thus often use the school as a refuge from even greater repercussions for their acts. Delinquents sometimes act aggressively toward other students, but often teachers are the targets of their anger, and in the case of a certain type of delinquent film, the teachers' reformation of delinquents is the focus of the plot. Acts of delinquents' aggression range from simple teasing and taunting to fistfights and gun battles, and because delinquents have what they perceive to be valuable territory and/or a reputation to uphold, they often launch their attacks against defenseless victims, inadvertently demonstrating their false sense of power.

Some school films, particularly of the "reforming teacher" variety, portray some or most of a school as being troubled from the start, either due to the presence of a few especially bad students or, in more politicized dramas, due to inept management on the part of the school administration. A few school films in the early to mid-'80s concentrated on one or a small group of troublemakers—such as *Up the Academy* (1980), *Class of 1984* (1982), *Teachers* (1984), and *Tuff Turf* (1985)—but since the late '80s, films have dealt with delinquent school characters either as a large group, as in *The Principal* (1987), *Lean on Me* (1989), and *The Substitute* (1996), or in smaller roles beside other school types, as in *Three O'Clock High* (1987) and *Class Act* (1991). Since the late '90s, school films have depicted fewer and less-violent delinquents altogether (the "bad boys" of *The Faculty, Can't Hardly Wait* [both 1998], and *Light It Up* [1999] all show softer sides, revealing that they aren't inherently dangerous).

As with nerd characterizations, the great majority of delinquent characters are male and from lower-class backgrounds. The Hollywood rationale for this pattern may be clearer than it is for nerd roles, since males are responsible for the vast majority of crimes in the country and poverty is a major contributing factor to violent crime. Delinquent characters over the past generation of school films have nonetheless evolved from the reckless abandon they displayed in early-'80s films like *Class of 1984* and *Tuff Turf* to more sensitive portraits of misunderstood underachievers who really want to succeed, from *Stand and Deliver* in 1988 to *Dangerous Minds* in 1995. (There are a few minor exceptions to the trend, such as *Class of 1999* [1990] and *187* [1997].) This sensitivity is intriguing given the long-standing social concerns about crime on high school campuses, for in this instance Hollywood filmmakers appear to be more carefully examining the causes of teen delinquency. On the other hand, as I demonstrate in the next chapter, there is still a sensational aspect to portrayals of teen crime such as there has been since the '50s, even if most of those portrayals do not involve a school setting.

Like other school types in youth films, the delinquent character is often featured within a school environment filled with a variety of characters or simply provides tension in films that otherwise center on issues not necessarily integral to delinquency. Such tension is provided by delinquents in *My Bodyguard* (1980), *Three O'Clock High, Summer School* (both 1987), *Pump Up the Volume* (1990), *Sister Act 2: Back in the Habit* (1993), *Powder* (1995), and *High School High* (1996). (Most of these films do feature or focus on an influential teacher, but one who is not presented as an agent for the disciplining of delinquents.) The clearest trend in Hollywood's recent depiction of delinquents has been not only the shift from less-forgiving images in the early '80s to more-sincere depictions in the later '80s and early '90s, but also an effective neutralizing (if not erasure) of the delinquent school character altogether. Following the numerous real-life acts of terror at high schools throughout the country in the late '90s, movie studios are understandably nervous about depicting delinquency, and may be considered negligent if they continued showing delinquents in the increasingly sensitive style of previous films. The threats of school violence suggested by pre-Columbine films seem almost tame after recent tragedies, and youth need no greater messages about the dangers of violence than current news events.

I divide delinquent school roles into two styles of conflicts, which essentially correspond to the division of early-'80s films and late-'80s/early-'90s films: conflicts with other students and conflicts with the school and teachers. While there is some overlap in this division, the films that feature conflicts with the school tend to focus equally or more on the teachers and administrators involved, and the fewer films that feature delinquents fighting other students thus tend to appear more fanciful by comparison, as if students could carry out criminal activities in school without encountering the wrath of their elders. Perhaps, with the exception of *Class Act* (which was a comedy), that is why these types of delinquent dramas vanished after the mid-'80s: the depiction of delinquents who were not in conflict with school officials strained credibility.

Students versus Students

Two films from 1985 that considered how students handle each other's delinquency (with minimal input by teachers) also feature delinquent characters confronting their peer reputations. In *The Breakfast Club,* John Bender (Judd Nelson) gains the most attention of his detention hall colleagues through his endless rants and rowdy actions, even though he seems to be clearly disconnected from them socially. Bender initiates the dialogue on personal terms, and takes an early stand for his authority in a brief showdown with the principal. This begins to galvanize the group, as David Edelstein observed: "When they realize they're united against a common enemy—the teacher, their parents, adults in general—they begin to open up, confessing sins and fears and telling stories. And all, in their way, feel trapped by their images."[14] Despite the students' initial disdain for Bender, they recognize that his lack of concern for social acceptance is not genuine but is indeed demanded by his image—after all, he works incredibly hard to gain their attention—and as he reveals more of his sensitivity to being understood if not accepted, they come to appreciate and envy his capacity to express his feelings. During the film's climactic set piece, Bender has the least to reveal because he has already exposed so much of himself earlier. Bender is the classic delinquent, disgusted with his place in the world but unsure of what place would be better, taking on a demonstrative toughness to shield his vulnerable desolation.

Bender's toughness can also be displayed without his resorting to violence. This is not the case in *Tuff Turf,* where Morgan Hiller (James Spader) has come to a new suburban high school after being expelled from prep school. However, Morgan isn't guilty of the usual delinquent crimes: he simply finds himself dealing with the violent thugs at his school (a gang plainly called the Tuffs), and struggles to escape his middle-class family values to achieve his own identity. Morgan's own rebellion takes the form of taunting the Tuffs and openly romancing their leader's girlfriend, Frankie (Kim Richards). The premise is clearly lifted from *Rebel Without a Cause,* complete with an overbearing mother who wears down Morgan's financially struggling father, and with Morgan's fawning friend Jimmy (Robert Downey Jr.).[15] This updating includes far more fighting, swearing, and some sex, and it raises the stakes for its reluctant rebel—Morgan's father is shot by the leader of the Tuffs—before resorting to a happy ending in which Morgan beats the Tuffs' leader to death, sees his father recover, and wins Frankie's affection.

What makes *Tuff Turf* more a study in delinquency than rebellion is the fact that Morgan's rebellion is so underdetermined (he lives in the shadow of a successful older brother and the threat of losing class status, but that doesn't explain why he actively aggravates the dangerous Tuffs), and the film ultimately supports the message that might makes right. Or, as Michael Wilmington remarked flatly, "The basic problem with *Tuff Turf* is a question of values. *Rebel Without a Cause* had them, dealt with them. This movie doesn't."[16] While Morgan has every opportunity to ignore the Tuffs or to at least call the police when he witnesses their crimes (which include street robberies, car stealing, vandalism, and attempted murder), his deliverance comes not from a stand of individuality but from using a dart gun and two-by-fours to beat up the Tuffs. *Tuff Turf* shows its delinquents in a world practically devoid of authority and identity because they have only each other to fight, and as other school films in the '80s and '90s would show, a clear force of authority is exactly what supplies delinquents with their identity.

Dangerously Close (1986) and *The Beat* (1988) also feature delinquents in conflicts with other students, although the plots of these films contain the weakest examples of delinquent psychology and contemporary school conditions, and they can largely be dismissed as attempts to capitalize on teen tensions portrayed in earlier films. *Dangerously Close* does have an interesting premise: the students at an otherwise happy high school are "protected" by a group of upper-class student "guardians" who call themselves the Sentinels, who also gather at night to terrorize disadvantaged students. The film thus shows the corruptive element of youth empowerment, since the Sentinels become the most dangerous type of delinquents, effectively destroying the school with their misguided attempts to preserve its vaguely selective integrity. The class critique inherent here—that wealth breeds contemptible elitism—is unfortunately too obvious and easy, and the fact that the harassing students attain so much power without being checked makes the film play like a juvenile fable. Such insincere and incomplete depictions of delinquents as those in *Dangerously Close* and *The Beat* gradually vanished in the subgenre of school films, but the emphasis on sensationalism, especially in confrontations between teachers and delinquents, is still evident in films made before and since.[17]

Students versus Teachers

Most films focusing on youth with disciplinary problems take themselves quite seriously, as in the heavy-handed *Class of 1984:* the prologue states that the events depicted in the film are "partially" based on actual scholastic incidents, a tactic that highlights the film's occasionally prophetic realism but also makes its excessive depictions somewhat dubious.[18] The story revolves around a gang of punks led by talented but violent Peter Stegman (Timothy Van Patten), who clashes with the school's new music teacher, Mr. Norris (Perry King). The school itself is under the grip of Stegman and his cronies: graffiti is everywhere, the extensive school security is nonetheless rendered inadequate, and one teacher even resorts to pulling a gun on his class to keep them in line. Norris attempts to turn the drug-running Stegman over to the police, but he is told that prosecuting juveniles is next to impossible. With the law thus rendered impotent, and the school administration looking the other way, Norris abandons his originally altruistic efforts at reform. After the delinquents attack and rape his wife. he lowers himself to their level, killing three of them and letting Stegman fall to his death.

Class of 1984 is the first film of the 1980s to depict an American school as overrun by delinquents, a drama that has been nonetheless extant since the late 1940s. Many of the earlier dramas, such as *Blackboard Jungle,* also featured a tough and idealistic teacher who was attacked by his students outside the classroom as well as at school. However, this film does draw attention to two opposite shifts in the depiction of "bad" students and "good" teachers: Stegman is clearly shown to have a potential for success that he denies for a criminal lifestyle, and thus he is portrayed as more culpable for his acts than many of his predecessors who were "victims" of society who lacked opportunities; and Norris does not prevail with his educational ideals but instead resorts to killing off the delinquents. The film's blurring of responsibility for delinquency—everyone is at fault, especially when teachers become delinquents themselves—is a theme that saw further manifestation in *Teachers* in 1984 and was maintained in virtually all of the "reforming teacher" films of the '80s and '90s.

The next three "reforming teacher" films in the late '80s showed students under further difficult conditions. In *The Principal* (1987) and *Lean on Me* (1989), urban schools have become cesspools of corruption, with helpless teachers unable to control their wayward students until a new administrator arrives to shake things up. The primary significance of *The Principal* is the way the film delicately handles the issue of race. The featured delinquents are African Americans, but the white principal's allies tend to be Latino students, who obviously maintain an uneasy distance from the black gang. While these two groups never actually fight or even talk much to each other, and the film has little to say about the implicit tensions between them, the fact that earlier delinquent films in the '80s didn't even point to racial issues gives *The Principal* some relevance, especially since race is a prominent topic in most depictions of delinquents that followed. This was certainly the case in *Stand and Deliver* (1988), where the school conditions aren't quite as bad, and the inspirational Latino teacher takes on a smaller portion of the population to enforce his reform, turning his math class from potential street hoodlums into calculus geniuses, and later defending them against racist charges of cheating on tests. Delinquent students abound in all three films, but each film goes out of its way to demonstrate that at least some (if not all) young people really do want to learn and be successful, and given the success of students in the latter two films, this message represents some sense of hope compared to the fate of previous delinquents.

Stand and Deliver and *Lean on Me* derive similar bold messages from their true stories: students need leaders who exemplify the discipline and dedication they preach, and hard work must be done to reach tangible goals as well as more philosophical ideals. *Stand and Deliver* is a rare depiction of delinquents who not only learn to "behave" but also work toward lasting educational results. The delinquents in *Lean on Me* aren't given quite such a chance. The film chronicles the reforming efforts of Joe Clark (Morgan Freeman), who is appointed principal at a run-down urban high school. Clark's first executive act is to gather up all of the "miscreant" students and summarily expel them all, and he thereafter makes vocal and stern demands of his faculty and staff, in whom he tolerates no questioning of his authority, as he oversees the transformation of the school from its drug-infested and decaying, dank state into a bright and cheerful environment. Only one of the expelled delinquents appeals to be readmitted, and Clark agrees to give him one more chance—but not until he has stood the student on the school roof and challenged him to jump off if he doesn't want to learn.

There is a glaring problem with the reform that Clark brings to the school, which Charles Epstein has well identified:

> His "unconventional" tactics, brutal in any other context, are made acceptable, even heroic, by the nightmarish universe he attempts to subdue, affording

us ample opportunity to let loose with a few cathartic cheers—and to suspend judgment. But questions persist. Clark's methods did produce short-term results, but the ends, as they say, don't invariably justify the means, especially if those means border on the fascistic.[19]

The film does offer a running criticism of Clark's actions by his staff and the students' parents, but despite this and the emotional appeal that Epstein points out, the film has a distinct lack of sympathy or understanding for the students. While simply casting the "bad apples" out to society and away from the students who use school for an education more than a drug operation is a way to promote a serious attitude for the school, it also begs the question of how secondary education, especially in urban areas, can afford to ignore the very serious problems that produce delinquency in the first place. A film like *Lean on Me* is deceptive in a way that *Stand and Deliver* is not: the kids obviously need help and get it, but their achievements are less the result of their dedication than of their dodging delinquent influences that are supposedly chased away by their dictatorial principal. The film thus ends appropriately with students receiving their diplomas at graduation, a proud accomplishment indeed, yet also a symbol of passage to even more difficult adulthood, a treacherous state that this film, and all films about school delinquents, safely avoid confronting.

The school films of the '90s featuring the delinquents-versus-teachers plot are wildly different from each other, from the cute humor of the tame *Sister Act 2: Back in the Habit* and the dark comedy of *Teaching Mrs. Tingle* (1999) to the curiously apocalyptic *Class of 1999* (1990), a "sequel" to *Class of 1984* in which the real villains are cyborg teachers who carry out their violent discipline against unruly youth gangs until a proletarian student uprising brings down the greater adult evil.[20] Each of these depictions points to interesting adult dilemmas in handling contemporary school delinquents, yet only one, *Dangerous Minds* (1995), can be viewed as a realistic story.[21] Here Hollywood banked on another urban student transformation tale, although this time based on the true story of high school teacher LouAnne Johnson (Michelle Pfeiffer). Johnson is a former marine (at least three of the teachers in delinquent school films of the '90s have some military background, as if that is required to teach school today), and after initially failing to reach her unruly English class with poetry, she shows her street "cred" by teaching them karate skills. The film proceeds to develop a few student characters in Johnson's class, which is composed of "especially challenging" delinquents, most of whom are

African Americans or Latinos in stark comparison to Johnson's suburban lily-whiteness; she takes on a saintly concern for all of them, trying to turn them away from the criminal lifestyles that they all seem to lead. Johnson shows an amazing acuity for understanding their concerns—death, survival, fighting, and pride are more important to them than grammar and punctuation—and she works these issues into her lesson plans.

The racial tension between Johnson and her charges still pervades the film, despite her efforts to mollify it. Jeannette Sloniowski points out that Johnson "implies to minority teens that they, too, can fit into the 'normal' world of white society—a world that both the teacher and the film tend to portray as more legitimate than the world that the teenagers inhabit."[22] This sense of white legitimacy is embodied by Johnson bribing her students to learn by passing out candy bars, taking them to an amusement park, and even treating one student to a fancy dinner. Perhaps these "bribes" are effective inducements, for many of her students do come to appreciate poetry—the film oddly uses Bob Dylan and Dylan Thomas in place of the rap songs that Johnson used in real life—but *Dangerous Minds,* like virtually all delinquent dramas, does not offer a clear vision of a better future through education, and Johnson's tactics seem like placebos designed to promote high graduation numbers rather than dedicated learning skills.

The film shows that the delinquents in Johnson's class can indeed be calmer citizens if they are faced with friendly leadership and clearly gratifying rewards, and perhaps in that way it is offering a suggestion to American educators. Yet unlike *Lean on Me, Dangerous Minds* must struggle to depict learning and reform as good for their own sake, and similar to *Lean on Me,* the film only implies the long-term results of education, opting to end—like *Teachers* and *Stand and Deliver*—with the teacher's decision to stay and teach future classes of delinquents, if only so she can "make a difference." *Dangerous Minds* thus lays bare a myth more applicable to adults than to youth: by winning over delinquents, the reforming teacher finds her purpose, despite the fact that her students may still lack direction.

The few following school delinquency films of the mid-'90s did little to advance the issues of previous films, although they did escalate the amount of violence before vanishing in the late '90s. *The Substitute* (1996), like *The Class of 1999,* is another school-as-battle-zone film, with a mercenary posing as a teacher to systematically expose a school's drug-running students as pawns of the principal, yielding another vision of youth delinquency turned back upon more corrupt adult forces.[23] A more deliberately ridiculous delinquent student film that appeared in 1996, *High School High,* parodies many that had come before; it features a naive new teacher at an urban high school filled with outrageously dangerous students who casually check their automatic weapons at the door. The fact that *High School High* can make jokes about drug abuse, violence, and undereducated youth—the valedictorian graduates with a 2.35 average—indicates that images of school delinquents have become so common, if not excessive, that they are difficult to take seriously anymore.

187 (1997) testifies to this in its slick style and animalistic imaging of delinquents, but it ventures into further excess with its reforming teacher who secretly begins to maim and kill his most trouble-making students. The criminal youth are themselves so thinly drawn that they become caricatures of adolescent menace wallowing in an environment of urban violence that makes the deviant teacher's actions appear almost justified, and the film actually seems to propose murder and suicide as the existential solutions to the cycle of school crime, especially after the teacher and his last student nemesis each end up killing themselves in an absurdly macho game of Russian roulette, an ending that loses its pathos by leaving no viable alternative to the crisis. Hollywood by this point seemed to have no reasonable way of dealing with the very complex topic of school violence—*187* appeared at the start of the late-'90s wave of student mass murders, and given the standard of irresponsibility it represents, the film industry was smart to steer clear of further school violence parables, which is a much better option than further promoting such inflammatory, unsympathetic images of troubled teens. Even the farcical *Teaching Mrs. Tingle* had its title changed from *Killing Mrs. Tingle* in an attempt to ease concerns about its story of three students (hardly the deviants of past films) executing an ultimately effective kidnapping of a mean teacher. The film proved to be the Waterloo of late-'90s teen movie revivalist Kevin Williamson, who was faced with small audiences and harsh criticism after his previous successes; the mere threat of student-teacher violence is no longer a welcome topic in youth films.

Just as there are two conflicts school delinquents engage in—against other students and/or against teachers—there were two images of delinquents that school films of the '80s offered: they were either irresponsible and unreformable troublemakers who were the cause of the social decay of high schools or they were misunderstood and simply defensive adolescents seeking identity in the face of serious struggle. By the '90s, after the supposedly successful reforms brought about by teachers and administrators in late-'80s films, depictions of delinquent schoolkids retained this division yet more thoroughly implicated teachers and administrators in students' behavioral problems, and the adults' utilization of their disciplining power—and capacity to educate—became more suspect.

RESISTING REBELS

The distinction between delinquents and rebels may seem superficial, especially given that every school delinquent is rebelling against something or someone. The difference for the rebel type in school films of the past generation is in the sophistication of the rebellion. Whereas fighting and crime are dramatic and dangerous forms of rebellion, there are rebellions waged by schoolkids that are not so visible or even consequential. Thus, the rebel type is more heterogeneous, ranging from undisciplined revelers who have more interest in socializing than learning to neurotic youths who aggressively confront their own complex psychologies. Most youth rebellion in school films is founded on an angst generated by the social and/or physical tensions of being in school, but not all rebellions point in the same direction: some rebels become heroes, some become enigmas, and some remain troubled young adults. Rebels are best defined by what they do not want to do—conform—but if they are to make it in school (or society) they must find some means of surviving with their adamant individuality intact, which necessitates the sophistication of their techniques.

Rebels are most often male, but there have been a number of female rebels, in strikingly different roles (e.g., *The Breakfast Club* [1985], *Heathers* [1989], *Just Another Girl on the I.R.T.* [1993], and *The Faculty* [1998]). Rebels also come from a rather wide class range, incorporating the toughness associated with working-class conditions—as in *Scent of a Woman* (1992) and *Light It Up* (1999)—or the demonstrative anger that seems to come from the ignorance of wealthy parents, as in *Heathers* and *Pump Up the Volume* (1990). Rebels do tend to be white (at least until *Light It Up*), which is interesting in comparison to the number of black and Latino delinquents who populate the school and delinquency subgenres after 1987. Certainly nonwhite students have plenty to rebel about, but Hollywood shows little interest in accommodating those voices of rebellion unless they are heard through crime on the streets and not in school classrooms.

Offering an ordered chronology of rebel students in films of the past generation is especially difficult given the variety of roles. Even within ensemble films—such as *Fame* (1980), *Fast Times at Ridgemont High,* and *The Breakfast Club*—the rebel students are dramatically different; in *Fame* the students' attitudes are fueled by their intense drive to succeed in the performing arts; the rebel of *Fast Times* is a generally harmless pothead surfer; *The Breakfast Club* offers a reclusive "basket case" who seems to be on the verge of suicide—thus demonstrating that stereotyping rebels may be fruitless, a dilemma that would make most rebels proud. As this analysis shows, not only are rebels diverse and diffuse (they don't travel in gangs like most delinquents), but they face the losing proposition of either accepting a rebel identity that no one challenges or denying the rebel attitude that has ostracized them. In only a few instances, such as *The Chocolate War* (1988) and *Pump Up the Volume,* does a rebel character maintain his distinctive identity and become accepted for it.

One pre-1980 school rebel worth mentioning is Riff Randell (P. J. Soles) from *Rock 'n' Roll High School* (1979). The film is a fusion of past rock music rebellion movies and the classic fantasy of students taking over their school: Riff plays rock on her school's small radio station against the orders of the stuffy principal, and eventually the administration orders all of the school's rock music to be burned, resulting in Riff's friends—and her favorite band, the Ramones—blowing up the entire school. Unlike the shocking ending of *Over the Edge* from that same year, the climax of *Rock 'n' Roll High School* is set within a hyperbolic comedy, and the film is meant as a parody of the exploitative school films of the '50s and '60s (e.g., *High School Confidential, The Cool and the Crazy* [both 1958], and *Platinum High School* [1960]). Riff's ability to rally her peers around the power of rock music to declare that they'd rather have no school than a dull school was a refreshing (if still not serious) image of youth taking control of the educational environment, and that attitude would permeate many school films of the '80s, up to and particularly including *Pump Up the Volume* in 1990. Oddly enough, that spirit was completely truncated in the film's eventual sequel, *Rock 'n' Roll High School Forever* (1991), which is evidence of the awkward shift that took place in school films from the late '70s to the early '90s, as screen students not only became less visible but largely lost their sense of purpose.

Two other rebels became archetypes of their generation, from dramatically different positions yet for equally intriguing reasons. Jeff Spicoli (Sean Penn) in *Fast Times* is an unlikely rebel because his rebellion is very casual and even pleasurable. Spicoli spends far more time catching waves and smoking pot than he does studying homework, with his only visible resistance coming from his history teacher. Otherwise, Spicoli is known by his schoolmates as a mellow stoner dude, radical for his disinterest in social acceptance and school achievement, yet no upholder of ideals (or even ideas). As the end credits tell us, Spicoli goes on to continue his wayward ways of surfing after graduation, so while he may indeed reject social conformity, the rejection is founded more on hedonism than anxiety.

Anxiety has become a lifestyle for Alison (Ally Sheedy) in *The Breakfast Club,* as she embodies the neurotic girl rebel of the late twentieth century. Alison wears black makeup and clothes (casting a "goth" look that would become more popular in the '90s) and doesn't speak to her detention hall peers until the day is half over. Unlike rebels who wear their woe on their sleeve, Alison's problems demand to be unearthed, which she invites the others to do late in the film by dumping the contents of her very full bag on a couch and lying that she's a nymphomaniac. However, the students around her are too busy with themselves to be shocked much, and Alison's only solid quality is her cynicism: when another student wonders if they'll grow up to be like their parents, Alison delivers the memorable mantra, "When you grow up, your heart dies." Her supposed psychological problems are revealed to be a tactic directed at her parents' ignorance of her—and all the students in the film indicate that their parents are the root of their problems. Alison's role, however, is compromised the most of any character when Claire (Molly Ringwald), the popular prom queen, convinces Alison to let her change her into a more common-looking girl. This wins Alison the attention of Andy (Emilio Estevez), the attractive jock, but it also superficially makes her a more acceptable member of the group, thereby diminishing her previous rebel status and providing simply another false facade behind which she can hide her anxieties. As in virtually all films featuring psychologically disturbed young women—going back to *David and Lisa* (1962), *The Sterile Cuckoo* (1969), and *I Never Promised You a Rose Garden* (1977)—*The Breakfast Club* doesn't offer the means for its subject to overcome her troubles, and thus perhaps Alison is ironically the ideal rebel, destined to remain excluded even when she looks included.

Prep School Rebels

The prep school environment would seem particularly fertile ground for producing rebels, since its orderly traditions and high expectations readily invite challenges. A number of youth films since 1980 have presented the rebel character in prep school, although many of them have shifted their focus away from actual school activities. In most cases, the prep school drama is set in the past to emphasize the rebellion of earlier youth resisting traditions that have become even more archaic from a contemporary perspective. This is the case in at least five examples: *Heaven Help Us* (1985) is about a group of Catholic schoolboys in the 1960s who continually find themselves in trouble with the morally rigid priests running their school. More famously, *Dead Poets Society* (1989) portrayed the classic "inspiring teacher" role within a 1950s prep school where a group of boys are forever changed by the lessons of their English teacher. The first film is about modern notions of adolescent mischief running into old traditions of Catholic discipline, and the latter film focuses more on the ideals of discovering individuality and unlocking creative potential. The main student character in *Dead Poets* rebels by pursuing his interest in acting, and faces such stifling opposition from his strict father that he eventually kills himself, the ultimate act of passive-aggressive rebellion. *School Ties* (1992) is another prep school period film, about a Jewish football quarterback in the McCarthy-influenced '50s who stands up to the anti-Semitism he encounters at school after trying, unsuccessfully, to hide his ethnicity. More recently, *Outside Providence* (1999) tells the story of a free-spirited teen in the '70s whose father sends him to prep school in an effort to keep him out of trouble. *All I Wanna Do* (2000), which was originally called *Strike* during its limited theatrical release in 1998, is about a group of prep school girls in 1963 resisting their school's conversion to co-ed status. This unfocused but enjoyable film failed to achieve the notoriety of similar films about boys, perhaps because the image of young female rebellion is not as compelling or appealing to young audiences, which has often been the case with the more prolific 'tough girl' films, as described in the next chapter.[24]

Taps (1981) presents the most literal youth rebellion depicted in any film of the '80s: the cadets at a boys' military academy stage a takeover rather than allow the school to be closed. The narrative is a morality tale on themes of honor and duty, with the students defending their notion that the traditions of the school—training young men to become disciplined soldiers—are worth preserving over the changing times that have rendered their institution an anachronism. Brian (Timothy Hutton) is the highest-ranking cadet, and thus he organizes the students, coordinating their entrenchment and maneuvers with the high-strung David (Tom Cruise). Brian's roommate Alex (Sean Penn) has doubts about their success from the start, and even Brian is unsure of what they will achieve. Their initial demand is to communicate with their former headmaster, who unexpectedly dies, resulting in a growing number of students defecting to their parents, who are waiting outside the school's gates.

The story further changes course with the accidental shooting of a cadet by one of the adult soldiers who have been stationed outside the school walls, a symbolic gesture of the warlike conditions that the students have brought upon themselves. Brian, under the influence of Alex, resigns to declare their standoff a victory and to surrender, a decision that David cannot live with. David opens fire on the outside troops, drawing their fire in return, and as Brian tries to stop him, both are killed. *Taps* ultimately confirms what its characters so valiantly attempt to deny: that despite the aspirations to masculine pride upheld by the military, the manufacturing of soldiers has become a suspicious, if not altogether unnecessary practice. Brian and the other cadets actually fail in their rebellion; in the process the school is destroyed, and they become the victims of the impractical ideals they sought to preserve.

The Chocolate War (1988) indicts the preparatory educational system's contradictions in a similar way to other prep school films, only suggesting that the rebels are lonely and sad. The story is set at a Catholic boys' school where Jerry (Ilan Mitchell-Smith) seems to want nothing more than to earn a place on the football team and get over the death of his mother. All of the students are coerced to join the school's annual chocolate sale, but after Jerry is given an "order" by the school's secret gang, the Vigils, to not sell the chocolates for a few days, he decides to continue his resistance after the assignment is over. Jerry's introspective sense of rebellion is what begins to influence other students, who secretly join him in a passive strike against the chocolate sale, although the reasons for his fight are rather ambiguous compared to the motivations of school rebels in other films. Jerry initially shows no clear resentment toward the Vigils, but as they continue to pressure him to sell the chocolates, he realizes that he has gained a level of attention and obstinance that earn him a veiled respect among many of the students. The film concludes with a dramatic boxing match in which Jerry is set up to be beaten by a Vigil leader, only Jerry surprises them all by winning; after this, the defeated former leader is shown taking orders from a younger Vigil, with the continuation of prep school tyranny now complete. While the rebellion launched by Jerry in *The Chocolate War* appears unfulfilling, the film offers a sensitive parable about the defense of individuality without resorting to condescending sermonizing: Jerry, like most school rebels, remains the same confused kid at the end of the film, but the inadvertent testing of his identity by the school affords him a powerful pride that many rebels do not achieve. This is the one instance in which a school itself is shown to actually *create* a rebel.

In *Rushmore* (1998), the suave 15-year-old Max (Jason Schwartzman) juggles an absurd amount of student activities at his private academy while becoming embroiled in a more pressing crush he develops on Ms. Cross (Olivia Williams), a first-grade teacher twice his age. Max is too hyperconfident and cocky to let his nerdish qualities get in his way, although his attraction to Ms. Cross throws him so badly that he is expelled from school for plotting to build an aquarium in an attempt to impress her. Max nonetheless reconstructs his overachieving identity at his new public school, showing that his drive and not his environment is his primary identifier, as the film proposes (through Max's fierce romantic competition with an older man who also desires Ms. Cross) that his creativity and ingratiating manner are rooted in his desperate longing to be treated like an adult. Yet where previous prep school rebels were motivated by sincere interests and admirable ambitions, Max is caddish and ultimately puerile, or as Kevin Courrier described him, "monotone and morose," adding, "We don't believe that this kid is dynamic enough to be writing numerous hit plays for the school, playing chess, and learning French and German on the side."[25] Indeed, Max is so focused on making a name and image for himself that his supposedly selfless efforts for his schools are exposed as egotistical, and his endless extracurricular activities betray his disinterest in developing his academic abilities, and shield him from finding truly effective ways to channel his energies. He is a rebel with too many causes, none of which are consequential.

The film does introduce an interesting class issue, since Max attempts to hide his humble background through his private school facade, but once he is expelled (and later drops out of school altogether) he comes to understand that his hard work ethic is more respectable than his previously pompous efforts to appear rich. Curiously, like *The Chocolate War, Rushmore* avoids markers that label its contemporary setting, relying more on '60s motifs and styles that hint at its spirit of assiduous determination, and reminding us that Max—who manages to win back favor from everyone by staging and playing the hero in a Vietnam War play—could only pull off his sham revolt in an era less cynical and disaffected than the '90s. Similarly, the academic traditions and ideals of prep schools themselves seem better suited to period nostalgia than current cinematic depictions of postmodern youth.

Lone Rebels

The disparity in representation among other school rebels is striking, demonstrating the diverse backgrounds and tactics of contemporary rebel types. For instance, the rebellion of Bill and Ted (Keanu Reeves and Alex Winter) in their postmodern odysseys, *Bill and Ted's Excellent Adventure* (1989) and *Bill and Ted's Bogus Journey* (1991), is not founded on any typical resistance to conformity; what characterizes these two heavy-metal flunkies the most is their sheer lack of ambition, their utter revelry in middle-class suburban stupidity. The goofy plots of both films have the duo traveling through time, in the first film meeting important historical figures to gain their help with a school project, and in the second film going into the future to inadvertently save the world. The intended irony is that even hedonistic dolts like Bill and Ted become heroic (and wise) by maintaining their integrity, however frivolous it may be. In that way, the two Bill and Ted movies offer a sustained fantasy for spoiled and laconic young men seeking identity through the least rebellious and laborious means possible.

Permanent Record, Heathers, and *Pump Up the Volume* appear to be more homogenous depictions of high school rebellion, if only because their plots focus on otherwise well-to-do students who simply ask the usual adolescent questions and demand to be accepted on their own terms. Each of these films feature teens committing suicide, and each depict a rebel character trying to deal with his or her troubled surroundings; but each film approaches youth rebellion—and high school—from distinctly different perspectives. *Permanent Record* (1988) follows the confused friend of a suicide victim who becomes the conscience of his peer group, telling everyone that there's no sure way to find happiness as a teenager. The film is daring in that it leaves open the question that haunts these teens—*why* their friend committed suicide—but in lieu of providing answers it offers an artificial and temporary panacea for teen suicide: life is worth living when you have good friends and a good school. Because no one knows why their friend failed to recognize this, he cannot be the martyr or rebel he might have been, and only students who actively fight their frustrations survive. High school itself must be survived, rebel characters tell us, not enjoyed.

Such is the message driven home by *Heathers* (1989) and *Pump Up the Volume* (1990), both of which star Christian Slater as a deviant out to expose various problems in his high school's social and academic systems. In the satirical *Heathers,* Slater plays Jason Dean, a.k.a. "JD" (his name is not far from its 1950s James Dean inspiration, and his initials remind us that he is indeed a juvenile delinquent), who becomes the boyfriend of Veronica (Winona Ryder) just as she is staging a revolt against "the most powerful clique in the school," of which she is a member along with a trio of her fellow rich friends who are all named Heather. In many ways, Veronica is the true rebel character of *Heath-*

ers: she uses the popularity and attention she has gained from hanging out with the Heathers to forge her own confident identity, recognizing from the start that her friends are really conformist and superficial. Veronica actually talks to the school's outcast population, including JD, whom she initially believes is a kindred spirit sharing her disdain for the school's social order, and whom she soon takes as her lover without question.[26] What Veronica does not anticipate in JD is the extreme to which he takes his disdain. Veronica and JD inadvertently poison and kill one of the Heathers, and later, in a prank that supposedly goes wrong, they end up fatally shooting two football players. (Veronica writes a line in her diary that would prove to be prophetically eerie by the late '90s, "My teen angst bullshit has a body count.") While Veronica is disturbed by this series of events, she agrees to cover up the crimes with JD, disguising both as suicides and thereby marking suicide as a chic practice for the popular.

Heathers takes youth rebellion to its greatest extreme, climaxing in JD's attempted bombing of the school, and Veronica's restoration of order by defusing the bomb and cornering JD into killing himself (although no typical popularity awaits him). Along the way, *Heathers* points accusations at all elements of the secondary educational system for why such strife exists among adolescents, placing responsibility on teachers and administrators who are sorely out of touch with their students, parents who are self-absorbed and as immature as their children, and the students themselves, who succumb too easily to the pressures of peer acceptance. JD is a failed rebel, one whose efforts to find identity lead to a psychotic inability to accept others, whereas Veronica finds a way to manifest her rebellion more successfully, disrupting the school's oppressive caste system and exposing, however briefly and unintentionally, the inability of high school to provide social acceptance at all.

Slater's performance in the more serious *Pump Up the Volume* reveals a sincere appreciation for the desolation and confusion of teen rebellion. He plays Mark, a shy new kid at school who has trouble making friends but no problem communicating to his fellow students who listen to his clandestine low-band radio show every evening. During his shows, in which he calls himself Happy Harry Hard-on, Mark unleashes all manner of frustrations, be they sexual, parental, political, or simply musical. The world according to Mark has come to suck—"All the great themes have been turned into theme parks," he rants—and high school is only an enforced concentration of the commodification and sterilization that has disenfranchised young people. Mark does not realize the impact he has on the students at school until a fellow shy stu-

As pirate radio host Happy Harry Hard-on in *Pump Up the Volume* (1990), Mark (Christian Slater) uses his basement studio to instigate an unexpected revolution among the mistreated students at his corrupt high school, telling them to "Talk hard!"

dent calls in to ask if he should kill himself, and Mark, by not talking him out of it, becomes complicit in the suicide.

What began as Mark's attempt to alleviate his loneliness escalates into a call to arms among students: despite the suicide, other students take his advice to rebel, to "steal the air" and express themselves. Teachers and parents immediately try to quell the uprising. Mark is eventually apprehended by authorities, but not before he publicly exposes the villainous actions of the school administration and inspires dozens of other students to form their own radio stations. This character undoubtedly represents the most culturally powerful teen rebel in school films of the past generation. Mark's rebellion is not contained within his personal and familial environs, but rather it reaches out through its technologically sophisticated means and psychological simplicity: by describing to his listeners his deepest suppressed emotions—fears, anxieties, perversities, fantasies, curiosities—Mark becomes a model for their liberation from the roles that they endure on a daily basis. And the fact that he reaches so many of the students at school, from expelled delinquents to nerds to the popular types, is ironic in light of his continual anonymity. *Pump*

Up the Volume supports a vision of teen independence and identity that is rare among all school films: it not only says that students should surrender their accepted images in order to end repression and oppression, but it demonstrates a practical method of achieving this supposed empowerment.

Pump Up the Volume also marks an interesting moment in the history of school films. After its premiere in August 1990, the only other notable school films in the next five years to even feature the contemporary white suburban population, which had been the staple of teen films through the '80s, were the farcical comedies *Buffy the Vampire Slayer* and *Encino Man* (both released in 1992, and discussed in the next section). Perhaps the movie market had simply lost its demand for school films, but I propose that the level of political confrontation brought up by *Pump Up the Volume* essentially warned studios away from tackling further issues about the serious dilemmas facing contemporary students. Not only does *Pump Up the Volume* take a certain jab at the previously rebellious ideals of students in the '60s (who became the parents of the '80s), thereby further discomforting any adult audience, but the film features such potentially "controversial" youth issues—a pregnant student is expelled from school, a gay student comes out on the air, less intelligent students are exploited by the administration, wealthy students come to hate their parents' privilege—that any subsequent films would necessarily have to up the ante and confront even more sensitive and serious issues. Films about African American youth in the early '90s did do this, but outside the school setting and within the context (and generic traditions) of criminal action, offering compelling images of troubling youth conditions that were nonetheless centered on a small portion of the young population. Even the proud black protagonist of *Just Another Girl on the I.R.T.* was only shown as a student in a few scenes, and thus the film is discussed (in Chapter 6) as a movie more about pregnancy than school rebellion.

Then in 1999 *Light It Up* finally did raise the ante with its confrontation of contemporary conditions among a mixed-race group of school rebels, led by the pensive Lester (Usher Raymond), a black student who unexpectedly rallies a small group of his classmates in taking over their decrepit school to demand improvements. Lincoln High is a prison vision of a school: dark, dank, and cold, and recently under the watch of an edgy cop who, in trying to detain the protesting Ziggy (Robert Ri'chard), is accidentally but not seriously shot. This is the match that lights Lester's latent fire of anger at the school administration, and he and Ziggy take the wounded cop hostage in the school library with a group of variously dedicated peers, including Stephanie (Rosario

Dawson), a smart Latina, and three school outcasts. Two of the students are white, yet racial tensions do not divide the group.[27] Rather, the broader conflict of racism is spoken by Lester's burning rage at the police who recently killed his unarmed father, a generational oppression that he screams at his cop hostage: "I'm sick and tired of being treated like a fucking criminal, of never being listened to." This frustration is exactly what fuels the efforts of the students to be heard, and perhaps not coincidentally, the students of color are the most vocal (the two whites may be token, but they may also be intended to diversify the students' cause, and to lighten the tone of black militancy).

The film's image of armed students in a library is eerily reminiscent of the confused cowards who killed their classmates at Columbine, only these teens are not hatemongers; they're simply trying to draw attention to their plight. That is exactly what they achieve by the end of the day, when media crews and the local community converge to watch Lincoln's fight for emancipation, as scores of police surround the barricaded building. The students realize they have a spotlight and, to their surprise, are asked by the authorities for a list of demands, giving them a false sense of confidence. They think that these adults might listen to them, and thus they begin making very reasonable requests for the school—better facilities, more books, the reinstatement of a fired teacher—which they convey most effectively by going online to news outlets. These rebels thus quickly find their causes, although they soon realize that none of the adults outside are actually interested in fulfilling these requests; they simply want to return the school to their own control. Mick LaSalle aptly points out a symptom of the film that explains essentially all youth rebellion: "The adults in power don't want to listen and don't want to know anything. They want to make assumptions and impose their authority."[28]

Despite the heavy media exposure, the students are unable to convince the authorities to meet their demands, and the group finds itself cornered in an attic where Ziggy has quite symbolically painted an urban homage to the Sistine Chapel. In this place of contemplation and artistry, the students realize they can't escape, leading Lester to threaten killing the cop, a gesture that backfires, resulting in Ziggy being gunned down by police. The film's epilogue is quite telling, since all of the students serve brief prison terms and get on with supposedly better lives, but only Lester and Stephanie go to college and retain their passionate ways. In a solemn voiceover, Ziggy suggests that the protest was indeed successful (the school got its improvements), and that even two members of the "Lincoln Six" are enough to preserve their purpose. The rebels have thus achieved their respect, although again the film is careful to indicate that this respect comes from within, for no adult figures acknowledge their accomplishment. The very fact that students had to expose the terrible conditions of their own school, unlike the "reforming teachers" of earlier films who took matters into their own hands, indicates that rebellion has become even more solitary for youth. Given the lack of such rebels in school films over the past decade, their rare actions thus appear even more courageous.

Rebels in school films since 1980 always think they have objectives, even if they can't articulate them, and this faith in individual purpose can make their self-dedication endearing to their elders, whose condescension and expectations are exactly what rebels require to know how *not* to be. The idea that teen discontent arises from predictable patterns in psychological and social development is endorsed in these films, as is the tradition of young people not going gently into adulthood. Among school characters, rebels fight the most emphatically for their understanding of self, even if sometimes their fights are directed more at themselves than at others, and they face the same inevitable realization that all teens must face: high school is just a proving ground for the greater challenges of adulthood. As long as young people continue to recognize these foreboding challenges, they will continue to resist them, and that dramatic conflict will permeate virtually all characterizations of high school students, even if relatively few of these roles offer the conflict *as* their character's identity.

THE LABOR OF BEING POPULAR

As with the struggle for identity, the struggle for high school popularity—in other words, maximum acceptance—is an enduring process. Perhaps ironically, popularity among high school students is often determined by a fine combination of conformity *and* rebellion, as popular students must appear and act acceptable to a wide range of people while also staking out an individual identity that makes them special and desirable. Of course, physical attractiveness is a sine qua non for popular students, as is fashion sense, agreeable attitude, and usually wealth. Most popular students find their acceptability bestowed upon them at an early age—they are the most pretty or handsome, the most coordinated, the most endowed—and thus high school becomes an opportunity to demonstrate their privilege. In rare instances, popularity can be systematically learned and earned, usually through association with already popular students. Popularity and its concomitant acceptance are only achieved by a minority of fortunate students, who can hope that with popularity will come a lessening of the strife they would otherwise face in the social challenges of high school.

However, in many contemporary youth films, students who have embodied the popular image have been troubled by the tacit acceptability bestowed upon them, and those who have fought to become popular often find that the rewards of acceptance do not outweigh the costs of compromising one's individuality. Despite how effortless the lives of popular students seem, most school films focusing on popularity portray the great effort involved in maintaining it. Since high school is already a site of struggle, perhaps well-adjusted and widely liked students simply enjoying their educational experience would strike audiences as unrealistic, and thus school films depict the popular as having their own special problems, primarily related to the stress of supporting their fragile image. Few high school films have been made about boys seeking popularity for its own sake (at best, sports provide them with a different sense of popularity, as I discuss in the next section); boys must earn popularity systematically. This leaves girls in high school films in an odd position of always already being popular or denying their desire for popularity. This provides a more sensitive conflict for girls than it does for boys, and the vast majority of popular characters are indeed girls.

The development of youth films focusing on popularity has been inconsistent over the past generation. Popularity is either studied within the context of other character types (after all, how do popular students know they are popular except by comparison?), as in *The Breakfast Club, Can't Buy Me Love,* and *Clueless,* or is used as a mere plot device to advance other aspects of the narrative, as in *Just One of the Guys* (1985), *Buffy the Vampire Slayer,* and *Sugar and Spice* (2001). The only consistency over time has been in the gendered determination of popular characters, with only a handful of films considering boys' aspirations to popularity outside of sports, such as *Ferris Bueller's Day Off* (although most of the action takes place outside of school), *Encino Man* (in which two losers try to "create" a popular friend), and *The Brady Bunch Movie* (which flatly ridicules the elder brother's delusions of grandeur). Girls have a far more dominant relationship with popularity, and as the following review demonstrates, they have been shown cultivating similar notions of popularity over time despite the changing environments and appearances that signify that popularity.

Popular Girls

Where popularity for boys in school films is a matter of "faking" it, the attainment of popularity for girls is far more complex. Despite the fact that maintaining a popular image takes considerable work—and as these films show, it induces considerable stress—it must nonetheless *appear* natural and effortless. Popular girls in school films are always pretty and well dressed and come from wealthy backgrounds; their parents' genetics and class status seem to ensure them a large measure of automatically acceptable features.

Once again in *The Breakfast Club,* John Hughes provided an archetype for the popular American movie girl: Claire (Molly Ringwald). While the film actually limits the demonstration of Claire's popularity by confining her exposure, the four students who surround her are clearly aware of her highly visible image at the school, which they simultaneously acknowledge and detest. The wealthy Claire exhibits a snobbish attitude toward John and Brian, the working-class members of the group, and is initially only friendly with Andy, a jock made popular by his wrestling skills. However, as the students move through their therapeutic afternoon, Claire reveals two unexpected aspects of her personality: she is attracted to John's delinquency because she longs to be deviant herself, and despite her privilege, Claire is just as unhappy at home as the other students. Claire openly protests the special treatment she receives for being popular, which keeps her restricted to the very expectations and standards of acceptance that have ensured her popularity. Claire clearly uses her attraction to John—at one point she even smokes pot with him, all the while reminding everyone of how wild she can be—as her demonstration of deviance *and* acceptability. Claire ultimately retains the privilege of her popularity despite her complaints against it, and when she hands John one of her diamond earrings at the end of the film, the gesture is as much an example of her pity on him as it is her appreciation for his reciprocal affection. She, like the rest of these students, may also return to ignorant parents, but back at school on Monday she will still be the prom queen who does not need the rest of the school to understand her like these few students do, since the majority will still honor her superficial status. *The Breakfast Club* reminds us that while acceptability comes from privilege, there is no greater venue for popularity than the rarified milieu of high school.

Further ironic commentary on high school popularity lies at the heart of *Heathers*. The three Heathers who rule over Westerberg High are pretty, porcelain, and prosperous, with a bitter sense of confidence: one of them looks down upon the other students and proclaims, "They all want me as a friend or a fuck." The Heathers' invitation to Veronica to join their clique is contingent upon her not only having the same traits but also rejecting her past affiliations with the "losers" of the school, something that she refuses to do. Veronica sees beneath the artificial acceptance that the Heathers have carved out for themselves, even though she initially wants to be a part of it: she tells JD early on that the Heathers are "like these people I work with and our job is being popular and shit." As Veronica gets involved with JD and loses interest in being inducted by the clique, the Heathers begin to realize that their popularity is threatened the moment that any guy doesn't want them and any girl doesn't want to be like them. At one point, after overweight outcast Martha "Dumptruck" (Carrie Lynn) attempts suicide, one Heather tells Veronica that the losers at school are only trying to imitate the deaths of the popular students.

Heathers thus uses its dark comedy to exploit the ignorance and conceit of these popular students, who achieve their greatest popularity through death; unlike Claire in *The Breakfast Club*, the Heathers never come to a pro-

The cafeteria scene in *Heathers* (1989) demonstrates the hierarchy of popularity in high school. Haughty Heather Chandler (Kim Walker, standing) lords it over the outcast nerds (signified by their glasses and books) while Veronica (Winona Ryder, second from right) sits among them, implicitly negotiating her power and acceptance.

found realization of their tenuous position. In the end, Veronica offers the most critical commentary on school popularity through demonstrating the reincarnating nature of acceptance: even though she supposedly comes to reappreciate the losers of the school, when she tells a dejected Heather that she's the "new sheriff in town," Veronica is simply staking out her final achievement of the authority she desired in the first place. Of course, the popularity that she now proposes—which would include the previous undesirables of the school, as evidenced by Veronica's invitation to skip the prom with Martha—is a popularity that could not hold up under the conditions of contemporary teen acceptance, and the *possibility* of such popularity, while promising, is only a facade itself.

Heathers turns the otherwise serious high school business of popularity into a farce, and that is exactly what films of the '90s continued to do with the roles of popular female school characters. *Buffy the Vampire Slayer* (1992), *Clueless* (1995), *Jawbreaker*, and *Election* (both 1999) all feature popular school girls who are at once dedicated to maintaining their accepted image but who struggle (or fail) to recognize the contradictions and ironies of their position. The films thereby become parodies of popularity, although only *Clueless* and *Election* offer the same wide social scope as *Heathers*.

Clueless is a more complex and more humorous examination of the same Southern California high school scene that is staked out in *Buffy*. The film is a loose adaptation of Jane Austen's *Emma*, in which Cher (Alicia Silverstone) attempts to use her good fortune to discover the supposed joys of selflessness. Cher and her friend Dionne (Stacey Dash, playing a rare popular African American character in a mixed-race school film) share more than their pop-singer names: both come from conspicuous wealth and maintain a high-profile elite image at school. "What matters to the kids in *Clueless*," Owen Gliberman astutely claims, "is looking good and hanging out with other kids who are looking good."[29] Therefore, when they spot the less attractive but friendly Tai (Brittany Murphy), they decide that they can transform her frumpy image and make her an acceptable member of their small clique. This process reveals the classic standards of school acceptability: first Cher and Dionne work on Tai's appearance, giving her a makeover and changing her wardrobe, and then they inculcate her to their ways of speaking and dealing with boys. While Tai's changes are noticed by many at school, she nonetheless fails to gain the affection of her snobbish crush (he tells Cher that Tai is simply beneath his class status), which would have signified her attainment of equal popularity. Ulti-

Clueless (1995) celebrates the highs and lows of being popular for Cher (Alicia Silverstone, fourth from left), who juggles a crush on a gay classmate (Justin Walker, far left), maintaining her fashion sense with her best friend (Stacey Dash, third from left), transforming a misfit (Brittany Murphy, fourth from right), and falling in love with her stepbrother (Paul Rudd, far right).

mately, Tai directs her attention to a more appreciating, if less popular, rebel skateboarder, thereby confirming the same statement on popularity that is preserved in virtually all school movies: acceptance is given, not earned.

Cher, on the other hand, does not question or concern herself with her own acceptability except when she doubts her ability to win favor with it. After receiving lower grades than she expected on her report card, she makes variously smarmy appeals to her teachers, all of whom agree to raise her grades except for her debate teacher. Upset but not undaunted by this, Cher softens him up by matching him with a spinster teacher, and Cher eventually persuades him to raise all of his students' grades, thereby gaining further popularity for herself. Cher later encounters another lack of acceptance when she pursues a good-looking guy whom she quite slowly realizes is gay; more telling is Cher's eventual coupling with her college-age stepbrother—which makes for a rather strange statement on the "safe" acceptability afforded by finding romance close to home. These relational conditions are all in contrast to Cher's confident social status, symbolized by her stylish clothes, high moral standards (she only smokes pot at parties and is waiting for the "right guy" to lose her virginity), and buoyant but refined personality. Popularity comes easily for Cher, but she must ultimately struggle to help others, finding her calling through raising money for a "beach relief"; her fulfillment in self-sacrifice rather than enjoying her usual constant consumption is an ironic discovery, which her narcissistic ways had previously concealed.

Three 1999 films also examined school popularity in farcical and often dark tones: the *Taming of the Shrew* adaptation *10 Things I Hate About You, Jawbreaker,* and *Election*. The first film is more of a romantic conflict based on family tensions, although it does examine numerous contemporary school issues: a popular girl's father won't let her date until her uptight firebrand sister also dates, setting in motion a morality play about contemporary teen acceptability in the age of desperate consumerism (the popular girl) and tough-girl chic (her feminist sister). *Jawbreaker* is no less critical in its examinations, reaching for a *Heathers*-level satire in its portraits of popularity. After three girls accidentally kill one of their friends, they decide to cover up the death rather than face the possibility that their image at school could be tainted. This film also sets up an intriguing duality, showing that a popular girl who is focused on maintaining her status rather than being a responsible friend is ultimately cast out of social acceptance altogether, while the girl who endures shows that she can properly manage being attractive, smart, and caring, the qualities that mark *lasting* popularity.

In many ways, *Election* presents an even more menacing portrait of popularity, further showing the increasingly sophisticated characterizations of '90s school films. The story begins with Tracy Flick (Reese Witherspoon), an over-ambitious student who doesn't want popularity in the traditional sense—through acquiring elite friends—but through the more formal process of being elected student council president. As Cindy Fuchs wittily observed, Tracy is "the girl everyone admires and despises, the model student and scary Heather (without a posse, because who could hang with her? she's far too self-involved), the delectable Lolita and the don't-fuck-with-me chick."[30] Such qualities earn Tracy the scorn of her adviser Mr. McAllister (Matthew Broderick), who fears not only that her winning the election would rack him (his love/hate feelings for her stem from a disastrous affair she had with his colleague), but that Tracy's implicit lust for power would only grow more monstrous if she won. As McAllister tries to thwart her efforts, providing a jock and a lesbian rebel competitor as a demonstration of his social savvy, Tracy engages in her own unethical conduct, raising the stakes of the generally inconsequential election to a validation of all her dreams and desires.

Unlike most other screen girls, Tracy wages her war of acceptance in rather solitary terms, losing sight of the very people whose approval she needs to secure; for she has taken popularity to an altogether new level, where it is not simply granted by informal recognition but enforced through political structure, a critique of the '90s mania for litigious revisions of reality. Most of the film focuses on McAllister's blithe torment, since not only does Tracy win the election but he loses his job after rigging the ballots, thereby showing how his own irrational immorality (wrought most poetically by his failed affair with his fired colleague's wife) arose in response to Tracy's dominating influence. The mildly gynophobic ending suggests that girls like Tracy, who is shown rising in the ranks of the federal government, do indeed carry their drive for acceptance to potentially destructive levels, and given the film's plausibility, this is a harrowing scenario compared to the popularity parodies that came before.

The state of popularity for female high school students, as films from the '90s tell us, has become increasingly suspect, despite the ongoing value placed on being popular. Characters like Buffy and Cher are popular in the face of their visibly materialistic goals, and even *The Brady Bunch Movie* (1995) ridicules the older-sister popularity bestowed upon Marcia (Christine Taylor), showing the effortless enjoyment of her scholastic and familial acceptance. Popular characters in '90s school films are enterprising at earning social value, but most are also intellectually or morally deficient; their acceptability usually comes without question, unlike the more troubled depictions of characters in *Just One of the Guys, The Breakfast Club,* and *Can't Buy Me Love.* Stephen Holden questioned this backlash to popular girls in late-'90s films by pointing out that "the beautiful are the bad":

> The underlying message seems to be that teen-age girls, having finally been given license to swear like truck drivers and sleep with whomever they want, deserve to be punished. Being born beautiful means being born bad. Only ugly ducklings who have turned themselves into swans have a right to be happy.[31]

The recent harsh depiction of popular teenage girls may thus be a symptom of reactionary Hollywood sexism—it crosses over to films such as *The Faculty* and *Disturbing Behavior* (1998), *She's All That, Never Been Kissed,* and *Varsity Blues* (1999)—while more sympathetic popular girls have been less visible (*Can't Hardly Wait* [1998] offering the only prominent late-'90s example). Yet perhaps Hollywood filmmakers in the '90s simply found a way to balance the appeal of popular characters with the evolving cynicism of teen audiences, resulting in the many bold critiques of these characters that have been produced since *Heathers*. Because being popular is so coveted and yet so rare, conflicted and/or parodic depictions of the popular would understandably appeal to the majority audience who simultaneously desire and detest the privilege of popularity. These roles thus demonstrate that even the most attractive and accepted images of school characters are filtered through suspicion or downright contempt.

THE SENSITIVE ATHLETE

For many boys (and an increasing number of girls) in American schools, athletic ability is a more important asset than intellect, looks, or wealth. Athletes are thus often stereotyped as being stupid and preoccupied with their sport, since their abilities in that sport may be their main means to success at school, or even later in life. Nonetheless, school movies featuring jocks in leading roles have, for the most part, offered rather sensitive portraits of athletes who are often very ambitious and determined, and sometimes smart. Of course, any film can be difficult to sell with an unsympathetic lead character, which may explain the added depth that these films provide their jock leads, and the films that feature jocks in supporting roles often do resort to the common notion of jocks as dumb or mean.

The jock movie has been surprisingly unprosperous among school films since 1980, despite the overwhelming popularity of school sports in American communities.[32] Of the many movies since 1980 that focused on a jock and his or her role in school, few were popular successes, although a handful featured jocks in notable ensemble roles (*Fast Times at Ridgemont High, The Breakfast Club, Lucas, Heathers, The Faculty, Can't Hardly Wait*). In the '80s, jocks were generally featured in common high school sports—football, basketball, wrestling—while in the '90s, otherwise unsung schoolkids began to find pride in their more daring mastery of martial arts, and more traditional sports remained the subject of only a few films. The trend of the '90s was incredibly interesting given the nation's unwavering interest in traditional sports and the number of sports films that focused on college students in the mid-'90s: for example, *The Program* (1993), *Rudy* (1993), *Blue Chips* (1994), and *Last Time Out* (1994). Martial arts became increasingly popular, both as a form of self-defense for youth and as a new holistic form of fitness in the healthy '90s, but I still cannot explain the lack of otherwise traditional teen jock movies through the decade.[33]

The Invisible Female Jock

More remarkably, there have been extremely few films focusing on female athletes, in school or out, despite the fact that in real life girls participate in sports almost as much as boys. Even a film like *Ladybugs* (1992) compromises its story about a girls' soccer team by casting a boy as the (disguised) best player. The only prominent example of an athletically proficient girl in youth films before 2000 is the protagonist of *The Next Karate Kid* (1994), the fourth in the *Karate Kid* series. (The first three [1984, 1986, 1989] starred Ralph Macchio as a growing boy finding pride—and plenty of fights—outside the confines of his oppressive high school.) The female role in *The Next Karate Kid* is essentially a raison d'être for expanding the series, and the "jock" in this case does not participate in a school sport, nor for that matter does she ever formally compete against her peers—something the male martial artists in the previous *Karate Kid* movies, as well as *Sidekicks* and *Only the Strong* (both 1993), are afforded. The absence of female athlete roles may be easily blamed on the Hollywood tradition of casting young women as delicate and sexy coquettes, or alternatively tough rebels and delinquents, based on a chauvinistic attitude about women's physical capabilities compared to men's.

Some clues to the state of young female representation in terms of athletics are indeed available in *The Next Karate Kid*. The film stars Hillary Swank as Julie, a distraught senior whose parents have died and who finds purpose and self-esteem through Mr. Miyagi (Noriyuki "Pat" Morita), a martial arts instructor who volunteers to babysit her for a few weeks. Julie initially wants nothing more than to get through her bizarre school, where teachers are all but absent and a paramilitary gang of students called the Alpha Elite roam the halls and enact "discipline" under the excessively aggressive orders of Dugan (Michael Ironside), their drill sergeant instructor. Julie is stalked by Ned (Michael Cavalieri), the leader of the group, who implicitly threatens to rape her, until she develops her martial arts skills and prepares to defend herself against him.

While the plot then becomes a classic tale of finding inner strength through athletic development, Julie's transformation from dolor-ridden brat to proud young lady is indicative of Hollywood's awkward handling of female physical power. Julie is despondent at school and home until Mr. Miyagi shows up and takes her away for her training; then, upon her return to school, Julie agrees to go to the prom with Eric (Chris Conrad), the one nice guy at school who's ever spoken to her, who's also an Alpha Elite defector. Mr. Miyagi buys Julie a sexy prom dress and approves of her date, but she and Eric are harassed at the prom by Ned and his gang, who lure the two into a climactic showdown. After Eric is beaten down by the gang, Julie takes on Ned and soundly beats him, until Dugan orders the rest of the gang to fight her, which they refuse to do. Mr. Miyagi then fights Dugan into submission, and Julie walks away with him and Eric. The film clearly demarcates traditional masculine roles while questioning Julie's capacity to maintain her tomboy image, even after she has become a better fighter than the guys. The fact that Julie comes to the rescue of her boyfriend may seem to be a progressive twist, but Miyagi is the ultimate victor in the film, as his fighting skills have defeated the most evil character and his parenting skills have directed Julie out of her asexuality and toward a "healthy" heterosexuality. Even Julie's victorious fight with Ned is diminished by its location—on a dark pier—thereby excluding the school from witnessing her defeat of its fascist oppressors. The jock role in films about boys is considerably different, as the male jock achieves victory and increased masculinity, usually with hundreds of people watching. *The Next Karate Kid* shows that since increased athletic ability cannot be equated to increased masculinity for girls, the obvious solution is to win the fight and a more pronounced "feminine" appearance, at least as determined by males.

However, recent films portend a potentially positive change in this situation. *Love and Basketball* (2000), about two African American athletes who become romantically involved into adulthood, at least features a section showing how the boyfriend and girlfriend develop their basketball skills in high school. More prominently, the independent film *Girlfight* (2000) tells the story of a teenage female boxer who not only gains impressive pugilistic power as she redirects her frustrating home life into the ring, but who defeats her boyfriend in a title bout. And in terms of girls' team athletics at school, *Bring It On* (2000) could actually be a turning point: the plot revolves around competing cheerleaders who are the main attraction at school games (since the football team is so weak), and makes a clear statement that the girls' (and boys') routines are indeed athletic contests. Alas, Hollywood is still waiting to make the step of showcasing teenage girl athletes in established sports, which may finally happen now after the success of the U.S. women's soccer team and the rise of female athletes in other team sports such as basketball, softball, and football.

Male Jocks in the '80s

Issues around masculinity abound in all other films about jocks, especially jocks in leading roles. The jocks in ensemble roles are obviously less developed, save Andy in *The Breakfast Club:* the football hero in *Fast Times at Ridgemont High* vocalizes more grunts than words; the leading football stars of *Heathers* are nothing more than abusive and stupid (although their pronounced homophobia connects them with a jock conflict that was somewhat developed in earlier films); Cappie in *Lucas* is a rare football player of some integrity, yet he's also not very intelligent and he bluntly lures Lucas's crush away from him; even the basketball players of the nostalgic hit *Hoosiers* (1986) were secondary to the film's focus on its adult characters. Recent school ensemble films maintained the tradition of depicting jocks as dim-witted, albeit with a touch more heart, as in *Can't Hardly Wait* and *Election*.

Evidence of a crisis in masculinity within jock roles of the '80s is provided by films addressing the very physical sport of wrestling, which was disproportionately prominent in youth films relative to its popularity in real life vis-à-vis football or basketball. Three teen wrestling characters were portrayed in the mid-1980s, the first in *Hadley's Rebellion* (1984), about a churlish boy who goes to an uppity boarding school to pursue his wrestling ambitions. A more notable wrestling role that was also a dramatic exception to the usual jock ensemble typecastings is Andy (Emilio Estevez) in *The Breakfast Club*. A wrestler with classic jock traits—he has an enormous appetite and wears a muscle shirt—Andy is also at odds with his demanding father. He immediately comes to blows with John, who has disarmed Andy's usual sense of control, and thus they vie for the role of most masculine (Brian is eliminated due to his nerd status). Andy later reveals that he earned his detention by beating and wrapping tape around the butt of a smaller student, an act that he claims was inspired by his father's attitude to be a "fighter." Like the other students, Andy wears his identity (literally on his sleeve, in the form of a wrestling patch), and he desperately wants to break free of its confines. While his wrestling abilities secure him an equal physical position against the larger John, he realizes that his instilled antagonism comes from his father, and he expresses a vulnerability that would otherwise seem rare for his toughness. His most sensitive side is brought out by the distraught Alison, for whom he shows concern and to whom, after her transformation by Claire, he becomes attracted. Andy is the jock as conflicted masculinity, determined to maintain his physical power but desiring to explore his more emotional—if not intellectual—dimensions.

The third teen film of this brief period to feature a wrestler was *Vision Quest* (1985), in which Louden (Matthew Modine) is more concerned with his sport, and more concerned with one particular competition, than his larger life goals. For Louden, defeating his wrestling rival—Shute (Frank Jasper), the best wrestler in the state—will secure his manhood, and in the course of training for the big match, Louden is able to confront his other obstacles: he cannot achieve success until he loses his virginity, which will chase away his tacit confusions about his sexuality, and he needs to secure a college athletic scholarship to rise above his working-class background. However, he needs to lose 23 pounds to qualify for Shute's weight class, and his brutal training regimen brings on nosebleeds and fainting spells that threaten to thwart his chances. Most of the film is then taken up by Louden simply fighting his own body, an appropriate metaphor for a young man who has no secure career or life ambitions, as he has to become as strong and lean as he possibly can to even compete against the best. (The homoerotic overtones of the film are rich, beginning with a gay man's pass at Louden, his own excessive attention to his thinning body, and his passionate desire to physically dominate a better-looking young man. The film both alleviates and enhances these tensions through Louden's daydreams of becoming a gynecologist so that he can "look inside women to discover the power they have over me," and through his eventual loss of virginity to a slightly older woman who's boarding at his house, while his greatest fulfillment still comes through his conquest of the slyly named Shute.)

The idea behind Louden's "vision quest" is to find some Emersonian self-reliance that will emerge from his dedication to perfection (he knows this through an English teacher), a lofty ideal to which David Edelstein responded, "This is the stuff of adolescent epics, and *Vision Quest* brims with portents and seizures and mystical tussles."[34] However, the film offers a notion of masculine fulfillment that is narrowly focused on sexual and physical achievement, a jock fantasy sustained through getting the girl and beating the guy. As in all school jock roles, the protagonist seems to have some greater potential lurking beneath his temporary goal of victory—and since Louden *is* victorious in the big fight his goal is fulfilled—but he is ultimately neither smart nor sensitive enough to understand the necessity of achieving larger goals, a supposedly noble quality of athletes that is just as limiting as the image of manhood to which Louden aspires.

The tough-but-vulnerable jock is also featured in two early-'80s football stories: *Choices* (1981), about a teenage football player denied a role on his team because of a hearing impairment, and the more popular *All the Right Moves* (1983). Like *Vision Quest, All the Right Moves* examines the search for manhood identity that is an inherent obligation of boys' varsity sports, and shows the serious meaning that sports represents to its protagonists, working-class students who are just looking for a way out, if not a way up. *All the Right Moves* offers one of the most gritty realist images of high school life in the past generation: Stef (Tom Cruise) is a senior cornerback on his high school football team in Ampipe, Pennsylvania, a fictional steel town based on the many such real towns spread across Appalachia. Like so many other jocks, Stef just wants his sport to carry him away from the depressing conditions of his hometown, but unlike other jocks, Stef does not exploit his popularity at school, and he sees football not as a ticket to fame and fortune but as a way of securing a college scholarship so that he can be an engineer. Stef has a pretty girlfriend and a rather supportive family (his father and brother both work in the town's steel mill), and he's a good enough player to be recruited by colleges, but his coach turns on him after Stef criticizes his play calling, kicking him off the team, and for the second half of the film Stef has to confront the loss of his life goal. Rather than resort to the jock mythology that would have Stef coming back to the team to save the season, *All the Right Moves* chronicles the lost dreams of Stef's fellow athletes: one is arrested for robbery, another loses his scholarship after getting his girlfriend pregnant, and most are destined to work in the steel mills. The same fate seems to befall Stef, who gives up on football to work at the mill, until his former coach miraculously invites him to his new job at Cal Polytech U., with its football scholarship and excellent engineering program.

While the film thus recuperates a happy ending, *All the Right Moves* is the first notable film of the '80s to portray the teen jock as troubled and frustrated. The dour conditions in Ampipe and the heavy criticism that Stef receives from locals—high school football is very big in this town—do not compose the glorious and rewarding environment of athletic success that so many jocks long for. Stef struggles with his girlfriend, who resents his ambitions because she can't get very far with her musical talents, and who reminds him that while his best friend is becoming a father, Stef is still a virgin. Even though Stef is an otherwise effective and valuable player to his team, once his coach cans him

Stef is left with nothing but his family's heritage, of which he is not proud. The ascent to manhood that Stef was following is thus threatened to collapse into a manhood that everyone else succumbs to. High school sports in this instance are shown to be a humbling rite of passage for young men who may not excel at much beyond their practical skills, but *All the Right Moves* also reminds us that what is gained from the jock image—strength, pride, determination—may indeed be more valuable than excelling at any particular sport.

The jock image offered in three '80s school comedies is only superficially different. *Teen Wolf* (1985) replaces a macho attitude about athletic achievement with its supernatural conflict of pubescent development: the hero, who occasionally turns into a werewolf and saves his high school basketball team, learns to give up his popularity and power as a wolf, because he just wants people to accept him for who he really is. *Wildcats* (1986) is more a study of a female coach, who tests the masculine mettle of a ragtag football team. As a portrait of school jocks, the film is skewed toward the most stereotypical extreme, that of inconsiderate chauvinist beasts needing to be tamed, even if the taming does reveal that the beasts are not so uncivilized or untalented after all. *Johnny Be Good* (1988) begins to consider the corruptive potential of school athletics before becoming yet another message movie about male pride. The title character is a high school football star who is such an outstanding quarterback—he can pass, run, *and kick*—that college recruiters throw themselves at him, at least until he gives up his inevitable fame to live a more humble life. The film is not very remarkable except for its excesses (it was desperately reedited to an R rating for video release, adding nude scenes in an attempt to lure a wider male audience) and the fact that it was the last notable film about a white teen athlete in a traditional school sport until 1999. There is no clear correlation between this hiatus and the release of *Johnny Be Good,* although the film does show the straining of believability required to watch a film in which a contemporary teenager rejects his chance to have a life of glory for the sake of the athletic pride and social morality connected to the noble jock image.

Male Jocks in the '90s

Team sports became rarer in student athlete depictions in the '90s, and a definite martial arts trend emerged. Three of the more obscure sports films featured solo athletes: *Diving In* (1990) is the story of a high school diver who becomes derailed by a fear of heights, *Windrunner* (1994) portrays a student who enlists the help of Native American Jim Thorpe from beyond the grave so that he can come to terms with his inadequacies on the football field, and *The Break* (1995) is about a failing teen tennis player who won't give up his dreams of being a professional.

As for the martial arts films, since the majority of American high schools do not have an organized program or competition in martial arts, these narratives portray their jock characters outside of the school mainstream. (In fact, martial arts as a theme in youth films proliferated in the '90s, as in *The Power Within* [1995], *Tiger Heart* [1996], and the *3 Ninjas* franchise [1992–98].) In the case of Julie in *The Next Karate Kid,* a lonely girl takes on and defeats the closest thing her school has to a team, its gang of oppressive thugs. *Only the Strong* (1993) uses the same premise, except here the evil gang is composed of older drug lords who intimidate the students. Once again, an ex-soldier has become a teacher, training his previously "trouble" students in *capoeira,* a Brazilian martial art that looks like acrobatic break dancing, and through honing their skills, the students not only become better fighters but begin to take pride in the craft of their fighting and come to respect each other as well as their school, banding together to clean up their campus. The film's deemphasizing of the usual violence in '90s teen gang films—few guns are drawn, no bullets are fired, and little blood is shed—shows a perhaps unrealistic but still optimistic perspective on effectively channeling the energy of angry youth into an athletic context. *Sidekicks* (1993) is a more conventional daydream in which an underdog student uses the inspiration of his hero, Chuck Norris, to overcome his intimidation by the school bully and win a karate competition. In all three cases, school is only the backdrop for an external contest of martial arts waged off campus, and unlike previous jock roles, these characters have to literally fight to earn their sense of pride and achievement.

Like *Wildcats,* another portrait of a determined woman coach at the helm of a boys' high school sports team is *Sunset Park* (1996), which, unlike most '90s depictions of African American jocks, is not entirely aligned with the delinquency subgenre, even though the teens' behavior is an issue. The novice white coach stands out within a virtually all-black urban high school setting, where the basketball team has become undisciplined and unruly, if only due to their greater problems off the court. The film has the opportunity to play like *Dangerous Minds,* with its white woman leader ultimately showing her charges that their game is only a metaphor for their progress through life—she persuades them to take their closing championship loss as a step in a larger struggle—and within the context of darker depictions of youth in films by the mid-'90s, *Sunset Park* suggests that life will indeed be more difficult for these student athletes than the game they play.

Varsity Blues (1999) harked back to the more mythical image of high school sports, and became the first successful film in this category in many years.[35] The story itself is not very unusual: a dominant football team led by an overbearing coach begins to break down under his abusive pressure, and when the smart second-string quarterback takes over for the injured starter, dissension brews among the ranks. The film definitely owed some of its profits to heavy MTV marketing and the casting of *Dawson's Creek* star James Van Der Beek as Mox, the new quarterback who initially cares more about getting into college and getting out of his small Texas town than he does about the team. Mox's early indifference to his role is what gives the narrative a twist: he's a casual hero, ambivalent about the town's attention to the game and everyone's artificial acceptance of him, even if it has advantages. As Owen Gliberman pointed out, "The emotional hook of *Varsity Blues* is the way it presents Mox caught between his own sane vision of athletic elation and the revved-up dreams of victory his new status as a hero forces him to confront."[36] As he gains popularity and authority, Mox encounters a deeper connection to his teammates—who all have their personal fears and frustrations—and a deeper suspicion of the coach, whose zeal for winning blinds him to the torture he inflicts on his players' young bodies.

The story proceeds through various episodes in which the team parties and plays ever-bigger games, even losing one as a result of a drinking binge the night before; and meanwhile the sensitive, loyal Mox consoles colleagues ranging from an obese lineman to a passed-over African American receiver. When the Big Game arrives, Mox confronts his coach's practice of injecting injured players with painkillers, leading to a dual showdown, first of the team's solidarity against their failed father figure, and then of their insecurities out on the gridiron. Of course they win the championship, but Mox's closing voiceover places an unexpectedly sober tone on the moment, reminding viewers that this was only one great night in these young men's lives before they faced their less exciting adulthoods, yet keeping intact the symbolism of athletic victory signifying the ultimate masculine achievement.

What perhaps makes the '90s jock images most different from those of the '80s is their emphasis on athletic *development,* in that the accomplishment of athleticism comes as much from work (easy as it sometimes appears) as it does from natural bodily qualities and talents. While all of the serious portrayals of athletic characters in school films hinge on a discovery of self beyond physical skills, and the resolution of a dilemma in which the characters must rely on their integrity and pride as much as their bodies, the trend in portraying jock characters has largely shifted away from organized team sports and toward even more intensively personal conflicts. The 1998 drama *He Got Game* further illustrates this, with its depiction of a renowned basketball star facing the choice of which college he will attend, who is then thrown by an unexpected visit from his convict father. The film contains virtually no scenes of the teen in school and only a few of him with the team (even the climax is a one-on-one contest with his father), for the emphasis here is on his sense of familial and moral obligation, showing how the strong work ethic his father instilled in him and the solid values his mother gave him have made him not just a great athlete but a righteous man.

Perhaps the minimizing of team play as a unifying force for athletes in school films betrays a certain cynicism in Hollywood's imaging of all high school youth: students have more serious conflicts to deal with (in school and out) than athletic competitions, and the resolution of these personal confrontations makes for more exciting drama than the organized and controlled arena of sports. The few recent sports team films even exemplify this (as in *Remember the Titans* [2000]), and in the broader sphere of schools in reality, jocks no longer get so much attention for their abilities—as delinquents do for their crimes.

CONCLUSION

The school subgenre is a helpful starting point for the analysis of youth images in cinema: it provides the character codes with which most youth films portray their protagonists, and it demonstrates the classic conflicts that adolescents face in their ascent to adulthood. Because school is signified as a formal environment, unlike more variable teen settings such as home, hangouts, and places of employment, it offers to filmmakers a consolidated location against which to dramatize youth, and more so, it provides for youth a certain index of accomplishments (popularity, good grades, sports, dating) and thus of identity.

The school subgenre, unlike the subgenres that follow in thus study, is virtually dependent on the sustained characterization of certain youth types to ensure the recognition of its styles and narrative interests. Other subgenres, while also employing these types, are more dependent on narrative devices themselves—curiosities of science, obstacles to romance, varieties of horror, means of rebellion—to provide their senses of style and motivation. Youth in school films tend to declare and/or resist their identification through character stereotypes, yet remain identified accordingly. Youth in other subgenres either are less concerned with identity issues or, most often, find themselves struggling for identity more mightily within the context of such arbitrary and inconsistent experiences as love, fear, and delinquency.

3 DELINQUENT YOUTH

Having Fun, On the Loose, In Trouble

Nobody puts Baby in a corner.
—JOHNNY, REFERRING TO HIS DANCE PARTNER IN *Dirty Dancing*

I'm not a baby. You don't have to hold my hand.
—AMY TO HER FATHER IN *Fly Away Home*

Any fool with a dick can make a baby, but only a real man can raise his children.
—FURIOUS TO HIS SON TRE IN *Boyz N the Hood*

Young people would seem to be natural candidates for trouble, from mischievous misadventures brought on by playful curiosities to criminal acts induced by more violent and angry drives. Indeed, the range of plots in films dealing with youth in trouble is quite wide. Sometimes teens wander into their delinquency with little effort or intent, turning a day off from school or a night of babysitting into a series of unexpected (and usually humorous) exploits; more often, however, teens approach their delinquency quite deliberately, rebelling against uncaring or uninformed parents, against a misdirected society, or as demonstrated in the previous chapter, against the educational system. Rebellion is thus the usual inspiration for teens in these films, whether on a large or small scale, and regardless of intent. Some teens are clearly out to just have fun while others envision themselves as crusaders bent on upheaval.

Teens in real life inevitably find themselves acting in deviant ways because they are only beginning to learn the social codes of proper behavior and are learning how to test those codes. This is why delinquency covers such a broad spectrum of behaviors: what in one cultural setting or period is considered transgressive (say, staying out late) may be more acceptable in other settings, in which teens would have to commit rather dramatic offenses (such as violent crimes) in order to demonstrate their deviance from the norm. Not all teens become deviant simply as a means of testing their social acceptability—the etiology of delinquency runs to class and race issues, family dynamics, genetics and psychology, and political conditions. Yet all teens find themselves accounting for their delinquent behaviors through the very systems that determine exactly what is delinquent: the family, school, society, and law. Teens' struggle to gain a sense of self and independence is most often wrought through their challenging of these systems and institutions, and thus delinquency becomes the means through which many teens achieve not only an identity (or at least a reputation) but also a sense of who they are in relation to the structured world around them and the adult life ahead of them.

Films about delinquent teens thus make for great drama, and the subgenre of delinquent youth films is the most voluminous in this study. Further, due to the diversity of deviant styles and themes in these films, the subgenre is perhaps the most broadly defined. Here the generic trends that are visible in each of the other youth subgenres (e.g., the cyclical prominence of school films, the rise and fall of the slasher cycle) are more difficult to discern. The commonalities among films about runaway teens, for instance, testify to the certain sorrows of their protagonists, but from such different perspectives and within such different settings as to put asunder any coherent argument about their chronological development, or even their influence on each other. More than any other chapter, this chapter is founded on an examination of youth representation through the characters' actions in the films, relying less on generic trends and thematic motifs. In that way, this chapter demonstrates the range of youth delinquency, but more significantly, the general inability (or disinterest) of the film industry to codify any particular delinquent style for any length of time. Perhaps this is indicative of the ambidexterity and revolutionary nature of youth delinquency itself.

TRENDS IN THE SUBGENRE

Despite their diversity of delinquency styles, teen delinquency films from 1980 to 1999 followed certain production patterns. Like most other American youth subgenres, teen delinquency films were at their most prolific in the mid-'80s, with more than 15 in 1986, and then slowly declined until 1991. However, the uprising of African American crime films that year, such as *Boyz N the Hood* and *Straight Out of Brooklyn,* seemed to revive interest in youth delinquency dramas, even though other youth subgenres were still in decline at the time. Hollywood produced at least a dozen teen delinquency films each year from 1991 to 1996, raising their levels of violence and social consciousness. Then, in the late '90s, the youth delinquency film again declined in production, despite the increasing media attention paid to high-profile youth crimes (when in fact the overall crime rate among teens was declining).[1]

Within the range of youth delinquency, some acts of rebellion became more prominent while others became less so. For instance, films in which dancing was portrayed as deviant and energizing essentially vanished in the '90s, after '80s dance films had so often attempted to connect themselves with perceived musical trends of the time: rap and hip-hop in *Beat Street* (1984) and *Fast Forward* (1985), or Latin influences in *Rooftops* (1989), *Lambada*, and *The Forbidden Dance* (both 1990). Actually, the weeklong phenomenon of "lambada" movies in early 1990 signaled the end of dance as a form of delinquency in teen films. Likewise, films about teens frolicking at the beach—which in the '60s became a conspicuous alternative to the relatively troubling delinquent dramas about the suburban youth population—also lost their popularity after the '80s.

Meanwhile, other images of rebellious youth became more prominent in the '90s. Stories about wayward youth learning valuable lessons about themselves through their relationships with animals and/or nature became rather popular in the '90s, after being little-seen in the '80s. Another interesting trend was the increase in films depicting hardened teenage girls who rebel against their schools, parents, and/or society in general: most such depictions in the '80s featured a lone troubled girl, whereas in the '90s these girls were usually operating in pairs if not small groups. Perhaps the clearest trend in delinquent depictions arrived with the African American crime films of the early '90s, which were not only quite profitable, but addressed previously under-discussed issues about the effects of race, class, and cultural conditions on youth.

Overall, teen delinquency depictions have become increasingly confrontational about the source of their protagonists' rebellion, whether it is the typically unsatisfying home life brought on by inadequate parents or the more complex operations of social institutions. The earliest youth delinquency films—such as those featuring the "Dead End Kids" of the late 1930s and the "East Side Kids" of the early 1940s, and then the teen rebellion films of the 1950s such as *The Wild One, Rebel Without a Cause,* and *Blackboard Jungle*—examined these sources as well, albeit under the guise of traditional moral values, which these films were just beginning to question on larger social and historical terms. The questioning of teen rebellion in films of the past generation has been comparatively explicit and informed, and often sides with the youth who ultimately want to achieve success and independence but have simply chosen impractical—not necessarily "wrong"—ways to proceed.

Yet in the case of youth films in which the rebellion is more subtle or less deliberate, the narratives do not explore the reasons behind the protagonists' activities as much as they *celebrate* rebellion, and this is a charge that can be leveled against many of the "serious" films as well. As in the larger action/adventure genre, many youth delinquency films find their appeal in the raw exhilaration of danger and daring, and any excessive examination of the characters' motives within the film could distract from that essentially simplified sense of thrill chasing and pleasure seeking. Youth quite often think of themselves as fearless, if not invincible, and that notion of confidence and irresponsibility finds an audience in youth who long for creative means to express their courage and unleash their frustration, and in adults who fondly remember (and may still relate to) those impulses. This dual attraction of delinquency to young and old was demonstrated most dramatically in five adult-child age-switching fantasies released from 1987 to 1989 (*Big* being the most popular), and was sustained as a theme in films of the '90s that featured problem parents (as in *House Arrest* in 1996), where the rebellious teens of the last generation have become the reluctantly responsible parents of the current generation.

DELINQUENT STYLES

As is common among youth film subgenres, a certain amount of categorical overlap exists between the youth delinquency film and other subgenres. Chapter 2 looked at the image of the delinquent within the school setting, although most delinquency in youth films occurs outside of school. Where the strange teen behaviors in the horror subgenre could be labeled delinquent, not to mention the errant experiments of "science teens" and the unleashed carnality of sexually curious teens, the delinquency film is generally concerned with the act of delinquency as defiance and empowerment within a relatively typical cultural context, a concern that these other subgenres generally eschew. Some delinquency films do offer the fanciful wish fulfillment of these other subgenres, but most are deliberate confrontations with troubling (and hence provocative) youth issues.

There is a huge range of delinquent styles that I cannot possibly cover within the scope of this book, although I will summarize them before focusing on particular delinquency themes. On the least deviant end of the spectrum are "harmless mischief" films, in which youth rebellion is represented by wild parties, escaping parental control, and skipping school. Such films deal humorously with the more serious social and moral issues that are addressed in most other youth delinquency films—here the emphasis is on fun derived from ultimately safe transgressions, as in *The Wild Life* (1984), *Ferris Bueller's Day Off* (1986), *Adventures in Babysitting* (1987), *House Party* (1990), *Dazed and Confused* (1993), *Good Burger* (1997), and *Detroit Rock City* (1999).

While I do explore the "deviant dancing" film, there is another category of youth delinquency that hinges on the representative rebellion of speed, achieved through fast cars, biking, or skating; respective examples include *License to Drive* (1988), *Rad* (1986), and *Airborne* (1993). These films celebrate the common independence of teens mastering their "hot wheels," although the delinquency committed by youth with such vehicles is generally less problematic than that represented by drugs or guns, and the emphasis in these films is on the sense of accomplishment and adventure resulting from proficient use of the wheels featured.

I also examine films that highlight the encounters of delinquents with animals and nature, but have here jettisoned the rather extinct "fun in the sun" movie, which also has a companion in the "snow and ski" movie. Beach movies were a veritable staple of youth cinema in the '60s, gathering frolicking teens for sexual sublimation in the surf, but the few '80s films that took up the tradition—such as *Beach House* (1982) and *Private Resort* (1984)—were not very distinct from other teen sex comedies of the time, nor were their snowbound counterparts—such as *Hot Dog . . . The Movie* (1984) and *Snowballing* (1985). Less lascivious and little-seen examples such as *Aloha Summer* (1988), *An American Summer* (1991), and *Phat Beach* (1996) further confirmed the erosion of teen beach movies. The animal and nature films, by contrast, deal with more compelling and revealing "primal" issues.

At the moral midpoint of the youth delinquency subgenre is a range of rather disconnected films that deal with teens' social struggle, in which the setting and style of the movies appear generically arbitrary and the narratives' depiction of youth confronting social oppression becomes the focus of the films. This category would include such popular titles as *Suburbia* (1984), *Amazing Grace and Chuck* (1987), *War Party* (1989), *American Heart* (1993),

American History X (1998), and *Black and White* (2000). These films raise particular and clear issues about the nature of youth rebellion through a wide range of plots, each of which is thematically dissimilar from other styles of youth delinquency. Such a categorical designation points to the methodological difficulty in defining coherent and consistent classifications within a subgenre, for these films clearly have common interests yet few distinctive generic traits.

More films locate the roots of youth delinquency in specific causes, and construct their narratives accordingly. Thus we also have a host of movies about problem parents (*Ordinary People* [1980], *At Close Range* [1986], *The Day My Parents Ran Away* [1993], *House Arrest* [1996], *American Beauty* [1999]); runaways (*I Am the Cheese* [1983], *Fire with Fire* [1986], *Where the Day Takes You* [1992], *Niagara, Niagara* [1998]); fighting and gangs (*Rumble Fish* [1983], *China Girl* [1987], *Gladiator* [1992], *Tiger Heart* [1996], *Six Ways to Sunday* [1999]); criminality (*Bad Boys* [1983], *River's Edge* [1987], *The Liar's Club* [1993], *Hurricane Streets* [1997], *Pups* [1999]); and drug abuse (*Foxes* [1980], *Less than Zero* [1987], *Terminal Bliss* [1992], *The Doom Generation* [1996], *Traffic* [2000]). As with the "social struggle" film, these depictions are quite revealing but unfortunately rather incoherent as a study group. For instance, in films addressing actual youth crimes, there are not only a wide range of crimes committed, but the juvenile offender is alternately vindictive, repentant, gullible, and/or dangerous. All youth crime films show the practice to be generally unappealing, of course, but as I will demonstrate in my focus on the African American crime film, some of these films provide a latent stimulation with their moral lessons. Even certain films about problem parents, running away from home, and drugs had taken on a lighter, inconsistent tone by the end of the '90s, as evident in *Go* (1999) and *Almost Famous* (2000).

Thus, I focus on three other categories of youth delinquency films that have more clearly developed patterns and cycles. The first is the "patriotic purpose" film of the mid-'80s, which celebrated Reagan-era nationalism through the efforts of teens resisting foreign aggressors. I then examine the still-evolving "tough girl" roles that have emerged over the past generation: images of young women taking authority and demanding respect through often angry acts. The last category I explore is the African American crime film of the early '90s, which offered perhaps the most conspicuous style of youth delinquency dramas in the past two decades and which addressed a complex range of issues including race, class, gender, politics, violence, and morals. All films featuring delinquent youth deal with at least one of these issues, and in the '90s films that showcased African American youth facing criminal lifestyles, these issues found their most comprehensive and persuasive form.

DEVIANT DANCING

There has long been a connection between youthful expressions of energetic passion and dance, especially dance inspired by certain musical trends. With the emergence of rock and roll music in the 1950s, American youth began dancing more forcefully and, to the chagrin of moral custodians of the time, with more sexualized movements. (The term "rock and roll" itself was a euphemism for intercourse.) Various dance trends appeared, such as the Twist and the Shag, and a variety of musical styles—calypso, tango, cha-cha—were borrowed to encourage new dances. Youth used dance not only as a release, but to distinguish their culture from that of their parents; with its increasingly controversial nature (rock music not only celebrated sexuality but implicitly challenged the status quo by promoting kinetic outbursts by teens, crossing race, class, and gender lines), youth saw that their styles of dance represented forms of rebellion.

The intersections of youthful sexuality and rebellion in dance made the medium appealing to young movie audiences, as witnessed by the dozens of dance-and-music-inspired films after World War II—for example, *Rock Around the Clock* (1956), most Elvis Presley movies in the '50s and '60s, the rise of the rock concert documentary, and the advent of disco in *Saturday Night Fever* (1977), which was still detectable in *Fame* (1980). Similar dance films remained popular in the '80s, through rap and hip-hop music and break dancing, Latin-influenced couples dancing, and more conventional rock and roll. Yet after the last deliberate attempt by the film industry to introduce to youth a "new" form of Latin dance, the lambada, virtually no other youth dance films appeared. *Lambada* and *The Forbidden Dance* (both 1990) were box-office bombs, and the dance itself did not take off. Hollywood thereafter dodged the potentially lingering appeal of dance in youth films, despite the continued popularity of various musical styles within youth cultures. Perhaps the emphasis on particular *dance* styles has waned, yet given the relative safeness of dancing as a form of sexual and creative expression, one can only wonder why the movie industry has not found more ways to capitalize on recent dance-and-music trends.

Break dancing became popular in the mid-'80s, although its origins date back to the beginning of the century, if not earlier. A number of break dancing films appeared with the trend, most of which featured performers in their early 20s, even though the form was reaching widespread practice among teens and preteens, especially urban African Americans. Movies such as *Breakin'* (1984), *Breakin' 2: Electric Boogaloo* (1985), *Body Rock* (1984), *Breakin' Through* (1984), and *Krush Groove* (1985) appeared alongside films featuring teenagers break dancing like *Wild Style* (1983), *Beat Street* (1984), *Delivery Boys* (1984), and *Fast Forward* (1985), although by 1986 no further teen break dancing films appeared, and the trend, at least in movies, was over. All of these films used break dancing in what were otherwise rather traditional musical narratives—dancers need to put on a show to raise community funds and spirits, and young people hope to achieve fame through their dance skills. Anne Billson rather cynically called these films "bopsicals," about "hip-hoppers [who] bopped their way out of the ghetto on their heads and elbows, pausing in mid-bop to wrestle with their consciences and pick up a chick or two," although clearly the films were meant to highlight the distinctive qualities of breaking as a dance form and rap and hip-hop as musical forms.[2]

Beat Street proved to be a popular archetype with its story of Kenny (Guy Davis), a black Bronx teenager who is an aspiring mix disc jockey. Along with his friends Chollie (Leon Grant) and Ramon (Jon Chardiet), a Latino graffiti artist, the three go to parties and discos where they watch music/dance exhibitions, including those of Kenny's inventive younger brother Lee (Robert Taylor). The film makes clear that these contests have become safer alternatives to the street violence that marked youth competitions years before, which led to the murder of Kenny and Lee's older brother. Yet the dancing does not prevent other teen problems, such as Ramon's resistance to getting a job and to marrying his girlfriend after he fathers her child. Ramon's story becomes the most compelling in the film, as he eventually decides to take a grocery store job and move into a meager apartment with his girlfriend and child, which his buddies help him set up. Yet soon thereafter he encounters a rival graffitist destroying his latest work and chases him down a subway tunnel, where both are accidentally killed. Kenny, who has at last been hired as a DJ at a club, dedicates his debut to Ramon, turning the closing number into a multimedia celebration of youthful creativity.

Beat Street, in addition to featuring youth who fulfill their modest dreams of musical and dance excellence, also features one of the more thoroughly positive young women of color in '80s youth cinema, Kenny's girlfriend Tracy (Rae Dawn Chong). She does serve as a love interest to the protagonist, but she also attends college and encourages Kenny's and Lee's artistic development. Kenny is himself a rather undeveloped character, which may be due to the film's attention to its many production numbers. What the film achieves in using these numbers to showcase the talents of its energetic youth is a vision of racial integration and a channeling of their ideas and impulses into slightly radical but nonthreatening expressions such as break dancing, rap, and graffiti painting. J. Hoberman observed that the film presents hip-hop culture as "a utopian community, an explicit black-Latin synthesis that, as the film progresses, reveals the capacity to encompass all races, sexes, and classes."[3] Ramon's untimely death is thus made all the more striking, with its harsh senselessness poignantly disrupting the film's otherwise cool harmony. Unlike white youth in other films who use dance to simply rebel against their parents and gain notoriety, nonwhite youth are connected to dance as a means of survival, not only in *Beat Street* but also in *Rooftops, Lambada,* and *The Forbidden Dance*.

The destined demise of break dancing movies may be detectable in the 1984 comedy *Making the Grade*. When the white urban protagonist attempts to show off his break moves to his preppy cohorts, the scene becomes an unwitting demonstration of how little the dance style was catching on with white youth: despite his finesse (carried out by a body double), the other characters consider his dancing strange, or perhaps more accurately, too difficult to emulate. Given the dominance of white teen images in American cinema of the '80s, the primarily black culture of break dancing and rap was restricted in its exposure.

Footloose (1984), one of the two most successful youth dance films of the '80s, provides an easy demonstration of the dance-rebel motif and the whitewashing of the youth dance musical. Ren (Kevin Bacon) is new to his religiously rigid midwestern town, fresh from Chicago where he loved to dance and compete in gymnastics, but now stifled by the town's ordinance against dancing. He's filled with frustration over his father deserting him and his mother, and his pent-up emotions come pouring out in solitary clandestine dance fits. The local preacher's daughter, Ariel (Lori Singer), witnesses one of these outbursts, and becomes attracted to Ren's handsome vitality, especially after he beats her boyfriend in a game of chicken using farm tractors. Ren shows Ariel the joy of dancing (although she is already so involved in defying her father by more dangerous means that she needs little encouragement), and he further teaches his clumsy friend Willard (Christopher Penn) how to dance. Ren gradually aligns his high school senior class in proposing a prom to the town coun-

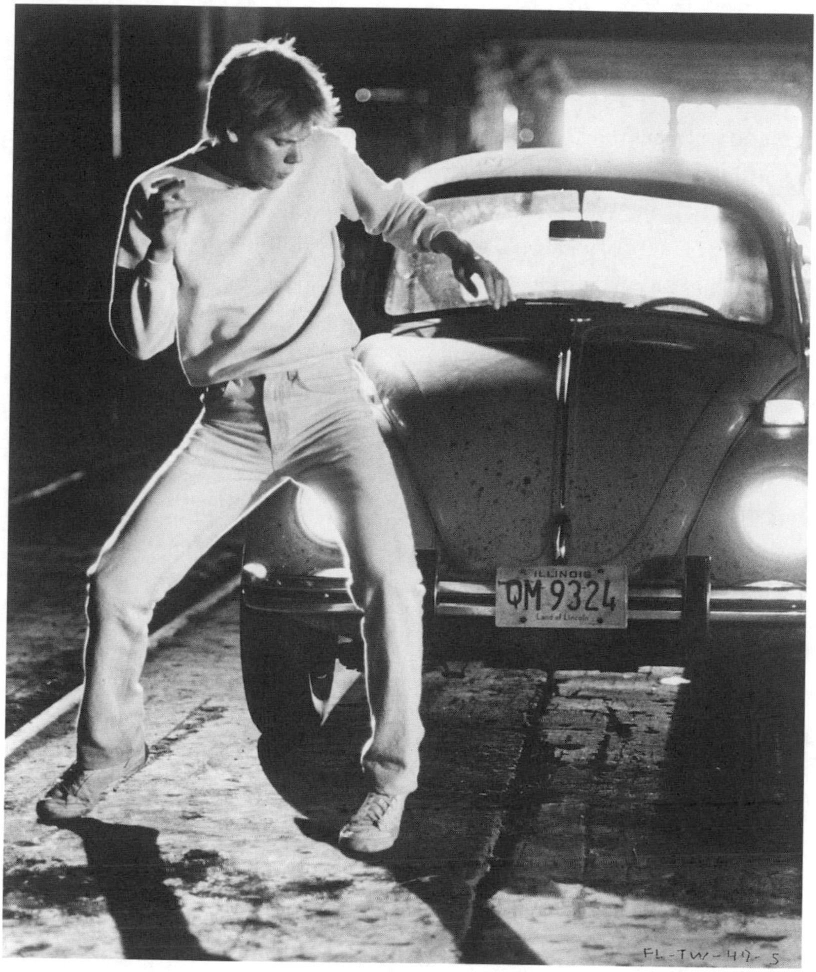

In *Footloose* (1984), Ren (Kevin Bacon) steals away to remote locations where he can satisfy his choreographic desires.

cil, but they remain resistant. Finally, after moving the prom to a granary just outside of town, Ren pulls off the event, much to the delight of the senior class, and even wins glancing approval from Ariel's parents.

Here dance is most explicitly labeled as problematic by the town's parents, who are admittedly drawn as such puritans that they burn schoolbooks, and who all seem to be of one voice, despite how many of them have children teeming over with rebellious impulses. Ren brings dance to the town like a religion itself, a message that the town's hungry youth have never heard. In a challenging gesture, Ariel gives Ren a list of biblical citations to read to the town council, mentioning the many references to dancing as a form of religious celebration. Ren does not present the prom as a specifically religious event, although that is his implication: dance will make these young people free, and will focus their rebelliousness on a much safer activity than the drinking and dope smoking they do behind their parents' backs. On the night of the prom, Ren and Willard are brought to use their fighting *and* dance skills in fending off a set of local bullies, and after they do, the parentless prom provides further proof of just how liberating dancing can be.

From a generic angle, as Donald Greig points out, "*Footloose* is a combination of two proven formulas so obviously made for each other that their marriage seems to have been unaccountably delayed: the recent musical tradition of *Fame, Flashdance,* and *Saturday Night Fever* and the '50s melodrama of rebellious youth and families in crisis (principally *Rebel Without a Cause*)."[4] Yet despite the box-office profits of this "marriage," relatively few youth films followed its lead. Two would soon try the formula from a female perspective; the first was ignored (*Girls Just Want to Have Fun* in 1985), but the second created a sensation.

That second film was *Dirty Dancing* (1987), the most popular youth dance film of the '80s.[5] The film makes no concessions to disguise the relationship between dancing and sexual expression, and becomes another teen polemic on dance as a method of ultimately acceptable deviance.[6] The story takes place in 1963, which is not insignificant, since this time marked an era of change in American social dancing, away from the controlled formality of prewar dances that kept partners rigid or separated and toward dance styles with unrestrained, suggestive gyrations, which is what many of the youth dance films in the late '50s and early '60s promoted. Such cultural changes parallel the protagonist's development. Baby (Jennifer Grey) goes on a summer vacation to a resort hotel in the Catskills with her staid upper-middle-class family just after she graduates from high school. There she finds herself fascinated by the "underground" culture of workers at the hotel, who let loose in vibrant, sensual dances during the evenings, out of the view of the guests who regard them as little more than nameless servants. Baby soon falls in love with a worker named Johnny (Patrick Swayze), who's also a dashing dance instructor, and his supposedly bad reputation not only fuels her desire but raises further her conservative father's ire, especially after she volunteers to replace a dancer in the resort's big show.

Unlike the religious conflicts of *Footloose,* here the resistance is about class and social image, as Baby seeks a sense of self away from the privilege of her family, and seeks a sense of abandon in the apparently primal nature of real working people who not only earn their free time but turn it into such dynamically carnal celebrations. However, Roger Ebert (and other critics) have pointed out a more subtle conflict, since Baby's family is Jewish and obviously has "opposition to a Gentile boyfriend of low social status," even though this is never explicitly expressed in the film.[7] Such an ethnic tension, which many dance trends and dance films seek to transcend, introduces another level on which Baby is trying to find individuality through dancing. Thus her eventual mastery of dance techniques through Johnny's training becomes her ascension to sexualized womanhood, literally and figuratively: after learning both dance and lovemaking from Johnny, and standing against her father's wishes, Baby makes her debut at the hotel's show, where she proves to her family that her own hard work has paid off and, as Johnny dances while looking up at her on stage, she achieves the visible heights of adoration and confidence that her previous lifestyle could never have allowed. As in *Footloose* yet more formally so, the transformed dancer and her transforming male leader are given temporary approval for their efforts, and convince a community that dance—even the more mildly erotic choreography she and Johnny perform at the show—unites people across class lines, backgrounds, and ethnicities.

In the wake of *Dirty Dancing* followed no less than seven youth dance films over the next three years. *Rooftops* (1989) found director Robert Wise trying to cash in on the lingering fame of his *West Side Story* from some 28 years earlier, but his new approach went largely unnoticed in this dark story of urban teens using dance as a form of fighting and expression (the *capoeira* style later featured in *Only the Strong* in 1993). *Rooftops* failed by overemphasizing the violence of dance rather than the romance, a mistake not made by subsequent dance films, although *Sing* (1989) also tried to connect young urban street styles with modern dance and was also passed over by audiences. Three dance-themed films that found better reviews, if only slightly larger audiences, were each celebratory period stories, and two of them were directed in loving spoof style by John Waters: *Hairspray* (1988) points to race and gender tensions around dance in its story of teens competing on a '60s TV dance show, and *Cry-Baby* (1990) parodies '50s rock movies with its story of a young rebel who stirs up local tensions through his melodramatic relationship with a "good girl." *Shag* (1989) is also a nostalgia piece, about four girlfriends spending a wild weekend together at the peak of the Shag dance craze in that significant dance year of 1963.

Yet despite these efforts to keep the youth dance film on its toes, the two lambada films that appeared in the spring of 1990—*The Forbidden Dance* and *Lambada*—would effectively be the last steps of the decade. The fact that two different studios were willing to take such a calculated gamble on an unknown dance signaled the confidence that the industry still had in youth dance films, but after their unmistakable failure to win audiences and start an expected revival, studios retreated. Curiously, both lambada films were unusually political, exposing North American audiences not only to the South American dance but to issues of Latino struggles against Anglo oppression. *The Forbidden Dance* addresses the deforestation of the Amazonian rain forest and the exploitation of Latin peoples by American capitalists, and features one of the few interracial *and* class-crossing romances in teen cinema. A displaced tribal princess comes to the United States to save her culture, which is most represented by the lambada—a dance so arousing in its bump-and-grind moves that it was banned in Brazil, but which she has no trouble teaching to a wealthy white boy whom she is thus able to convert to her cause. The problem with the film's handling of the protagonists' relationship and their plea to save the rain forests is that both are built around the recurring gratuitous display of the lambada, which forces emphasis upon the exotic foreign sensuality of the dance and away from the film's two dominant conflicts (environmentalism and racism), exposing these plot points as mere contrivances. In many ways, the film's biggest flaw is its idealism, suggesting that dance in itself could induce spoiled rich kids to become passionate about addressing the developing world's needs.

Lambada took a more believable consciousness-raising approach, one more directly related to domestic race issues. New high school teacher Kevin (J. Eddie Peck) teaches math to his suburban Beverly Hills class by day and breaks out as a lambada dancer at a local club by night. But the married teacher is not sneaking around on his wife—his lambada act is simply a cover to his more passionate practice of teaching barrio kids at the club how to study for their general equivalency diplomas, who call their ersatz school "Galaxy High." Sandy (Melora Hardin) is one of Kevin's wanton wealthy white students back at school who happens upon his dance moves at the club and comes on to him; Kevin resists her seductive moves throughout the story, taking advantage of her affection by asking her to keep his double life a secret. Ramone (Shabba-Doo, who also choreographed the dance scenes), the self-styled leader of the barrio group, resents Kevin taking over his popularity at the club yet is won over by Kevin's dedication to teaching him, as well as Kevin's pride in his Mexican heritage. The difference between the well-off and aimless schoolkids and the ambitious barrio students provides a contrast in educational priorities that Kevin ultimately exposes to the disapproving school principal: after a fight breaks out between the two groups one night at school and Kevin loses his job, Sandy petitions to bring him back and the principal agrees to do so if Kevin can demonstrate that the barrio students know math better than the school students.

With this mental showdown thus staged, the narrative pits Kevin's school teaching skills against his club teaching as much as it pits the urban whites against the ghetto Latinos, and the climax thus hinges on a nervous racial tension. Ramone wins the contest for the Galaxy team by recalling a billiard lesson Kevin taught him about rectangular coordinate systems, and Kevin immediately rushes to the stage to give an inspirational speech about his own barrio past and the value of education, regardless of race. He asks the opposing teams to make amends, and the film closes with the entire student population doing the lambada outside, as dance once again unifies diverse cultures. Then, over the closing credits, we see that each of the barrio students ends up with a successful job. While *Lambada* can be characterized just as much (if not more) as a school movie, the film is sold on its use of the title dance and the ongoing erotic tension between Sandy and Kevin (although there is less dancing here, and less discussion of the cultural background of the dance, than in *The Forbidden Dance*). *Lambada,* very much like *Stand and Deliver* before it, preaches a message about the capacity of underprivileged youth, even if its gimmick of exotic dancing and sexual-cultural intrigue somewhat dilutes that nonetheless clear lesson.

The lambada films of 1990 alas suffered the same fate as other post-*Dirty* dance films, and with these last gasps, the youth dance film, deviant or not, exhausted itself for the next ten years.[8] A few odd entries did continue to appear, such as the anachronistic orphan musical *Newsies* (1992), which wasn't really about dancing per se, and the pre–World War II story *Swing Kids* (1993), in which a group of German teens find themselves electrified by big band music and dance, a force that gives them the energy and inspiration to resist the rising tide of Nazism. With such heavily dramatic historical plots, these films seemed doomed from the start, at least in trying to appeal to young audiences, who may have been more receptive to *Swing Kids* during the late-'90s revival of swing. Despite that revival, and the emergence of rave culture in urban centers, not to mention the continuing popularity of dancing for teenagers as a social activity, movie studios have still tended to avoid youth dance movies, and have struggled with most efforts to reintroduce them. *Center Stage*

(2000) represents a cautious attempt, choosing ballet as its dance style and mixing late-teen characters with early 20-somethings, but this strategy of trying to gain a wider audience and exploiting a realm of dance not based on current trends was unsuccessful at the box office. *Mad About Mambo* (2000) was even less popular, despite starring television's *Felicity* protagonist, Keri Russell.

Even the prolific dance films of the '80s, with the exception of *Footloose* and *Dirty Dancing* and the specialized appeal of the break dancing films, did not provide teens with images of dancing that made them want to join in, a liability that has been a cause of the continuing dearth of popular dance films. Youth may simply want to see exciting dances that they can duplicate, and as the most profitable '80s dance films revealed, the dancing must be done within a challenging romantic context. This could explain the unexpected success of *Save the Last Dance* (2001), directed by Thomas Carter of *Swing Kids,* who revised his previous narrative formula and made the first youth dance film to gain serious attention in over a decade. Instead of primitive Nazi oppression, the film features as its conflict a timely interracial romance between two dancing teens that yet again lends itself to certain frictions among the characters (even though interracial dating remains more common among real teens than Hollywood has acknowledged). In place of big band swing are contemporary music and dance styles that are relatively familiar to current young audiences, who responded to the film with enthusiasm. *Save the Last Dance* may thus indicate a revival of the youth dance movie repackaged for a new generation, with fresh dancing maintaining its connection to traditional deviance for teens, who continue to break down racial and cultural divisions with their shared moves.

NATURAL ENCOUNTERS

Films about youth engaging with nature have been relatively popular for generations, growing out of a long literary tradition and offering images of often misguided teens who discover direction, peace, and/or maturity through their encounters. Such films fall into two categories: those depicting children's interaction with animals, and those that place their young characters in a more adventurous narrative built around surviving the challenge of the wilderness, desert, or ocean.

Animal movies tend to focus on preteens, but animals obviously have an inherent appeal to youth of all ages: their playfulness and cuteness are endearing, their usual smallness gives young people a sense of dominance over another creature such as they perceive adults have over them, and in terms of wild animals, their struggle for survival and the mysteries of their lifestyles—especially how they may communicate or express emotion—are intriguing. What all animal youth films portray is a sense of personal connection between the animals and their protagonists, a connection that most adults in the films fail to understand, and that the youth usually use in defense of the animals' worth since a humane relationship between them has been achieved. The effect of this becomes youth's defiance against unsympathetic, and apparently unperceptive, adults, in which the animals are aligned with fighting for senses of purpose and freedom that the youth are just beginning to discover for themselves.

Animal films appeared quite prominently in the '90s compared to the '80s, despite the presence of many popular movies of the past, such as the numerous *Lassie* and *Benji* films. Two little-seen examples from the '80s are the equine tales *Wild Pony* (1983) and *Sylvester* (1985), which are about troubled teens gaining wisdom through their care for, respectively, a pony and a show horse. Both of these common plots borrowed from the many previous child-loves-horse films, such as *My Friend Flicka* (1943), *National Velvet* (1944), its sequel *International Velvet* (1978), *The Red Stallion* (1947), *The Red Pony* (1949), *Misty* (1961), *The Black Stallion* (1979), and its sequel, *The Black Stallion Returns* (1983). This same plot was used again in the '90s, first in *Dark Horse* (1992), in which a tormented girl, rapidly becoming a delinquent after the death of her mother, stumbles upon a new direction in life after being ordered to care for a horse. Less youth-oriented takes on the horse story include *Black Beauty* (1994), the classic tale of a proud stallion that has been adapted to the screen at least five times, and *The Horse Whisperer* (1998), in which a teenage girl's mother hires the title character to "heal" her daughter and horse after a traumatic accident. And, in a less horse-oriented approach, *Wild Hearts Can't Be Broken* (1991) tells the true story of a runaway girl who becomes a carnival attraction by riding a diving horse into a tank of water, until she is blinded in an accident and finds the courage to rebuild her life.

Other '90s animal films employed a wide variety of animals, many from the wild. *White Fang* (1991) and its sequel, *White Fang 2: Myth of the White Wolf* (1994), are adapted from one of Jack London's novels of the same name, about a youth and his supercanine who in both films help themselves and others through the Alaskan gold rush. *Far from Home: The Adventures of Yellow Dog* (1995) is another common tale of a teenage boy who is aided by his loyal dog after they are stranded on an island. An inevitable aquatic animal movie was *Flipper* (1996), which in many ways replays the popular *Free Willy* plot on a smaller scale, with an irritable teenager befriending the titular dolphin, who aids in battling a toxic waste crisis.[9] A more unusual animal is the gorilla in *Born to Be Wild* (1995), where again the politically correct aspect of animal rights is combined with the story of a boy who learns to stand up to adult misunderstanding. *Wild America* (1997) featured the widest range of animals yet, in its true story of teenage animal documentarians who discover their talents for capturing the fascinating and thrilling behaviors of wildlife on film. And still another version of the perennial canine favorite *Lassie* was produced in 1994, about the caring collie who in this incarnation teaches a teenage boy the importance of family values, with the dog "trying to tell us something" through her special animal perception. Youth learning to appreciate animals' special perspectives, and learning to appreciate who they are themselves—especially in the wake of familial strife—are the main features of all these animal movies. This would be borne out again in the *Air Bud* trilogy (1997–2000), in which an athletic golden retriever helps an adolescent boy overcome the death of his father by "training" him in basketball, football, and soccer.

By far the most successful animal film of the '90s was *Free Willy* (1993), the whale saga that had become a trilogy by 1997.[10] (A quite similar but much less popular film was made before in 1976, *A Whale of a Tale,* about a boy training a killer whale for a marine show.) *Free Willy* is the story of Jesse (Jason James Richter), a 12-year-old who has become hardened by a life spent partially on the street in the years after his mother left him. Jesse has been in and out of foster homes, and his latest new parents look as if they won't be able to tame him either. Yet after a night of vandalizing a local amusement park, Jesse is assigned to work there, where he quickly becomes fascinated by Willy, the park's disappointing animal attraction. The narrative makes a bold parallel between Jesse and Willy: both are rebellious adolescents and both long for their real family, and over the course of the story both give each other affection and teach each other how to behave. In Jesse's case, that means being responsible to a job, and for Willy, that means performing tricks that he's been reluctant to do. The stronger theme of the film remains its statement on building and sustaining family relations, as demonstrated by Willy and Jesse, leading Hal Hinson to claim, "[W]hat's great about this uncommon movie relationship is the emphasis it places on the fact that families are made and not born, that they are the products of hard work and compromise and trust that has to be earned."[11] And through each other, the adolescent boy and whale find the trust that leads them back to their respective species families.

As in other animal films, protagonist and animal openly communicate with each other in a way that no one else understands. After Jesse trains Willy for a big show, Willy rebels by not performing for the audience, and Jesse can tell that he's scared, and even implies that he feels exploited. The park owners' decision to have the whale killed for an insurance settlement leads Jesse to try to save him by enlisting the help of sympathetic adults, including his foster parents, who have grown to respect Jesse's devotion to his new pet. The film concludes with a spectacular race to the ocean so that Willy can be returned to his family in their natural habitat, after which Jesse returns to his new home with his foster parents, with whom he has earned a mutual love. The film suggests that Jesse merely needed to find a nonthreatening channel for his emotional longings, and that by setting Willy free, he has ascended to a more mature level of experiencing love on a selfless, familial level.

Free Willy 2: The Adventure Home (1995) is less interesting as an animal movie but revealing of certain differences in Hollywood conventions between portraying preteens and early teens. Like the first film, the sequel concentrates on a quest for familial belonging, but also introduces a shift toward romantic fulfillment for Jesse, who is now entering puberty and encountering the hormonal changes that come with it, as he develops a crush on a teenage whale-watcher who eventually helps him to again save Willy from a disaster. This plot point proclaims a normalizing heterosexuality for its main character, whose love for his whale may have otherwise begun to appear abnormal now that he's a teenager, even though the film's raison d'être is the connection between the boy and the whale. (A similar character device is used in *Born to Be Wild,* where a girl serves to displace the pubescent protagonist's potentially perverted affection for a female gorilla.) The third film in the trilogy, *Free Willy 3: The Rescue,* was released in 1997, and here Jesse befriends a 10-year-old boy whose father is secretly hunting whales, leading to another family confrontation that is resolved through saving Willy.

Setting a new standard of both aesthetic style and scale of animal involvement is the 1996 film *Fly Away Home,* one of the few '90s animal films with a girl protagonist. Amy (Anna Paquin) is devastated when her mother dies in a car accident that she herself survives, and must then move to Canada with her formerly estranged father Tom (Jeff Daniels). The 13-year-old spends her days alone and distraught, until she discovers some goose eggs among the wreckage of a nearby construction site and incubates them in her father's barn. The geese hatch and become more than pets, since they "imprint" Amy as their new mother goose, but local animal authorities remind Amy that domesticated birds cause problems if they are allowed to fly. The narrative thus sets up a familiar environmental conflict (also established through the destruction of local woodlands), and as Amy discovers a sense of purpose and belonging with the birds, her strained relationship with her father becomes more caring. Tom, who is an inventor, convinces Amy that they need to teach the birds to fly south for the winter, and suggests that they build small planes to do so. Through the help of other friends, they train each other and train the birds, culminating in a dramatic flight from southern Ontario to North Carolina. Along the way, national media get news of their flight, and another environmental fight ensues since Amy plans to land the geese at a wetlands preserve that is being razed for a housing project. The developers eventually relent, and Amy lands triumphantly with the whole world watching, showing the geese their winter home. The next spring, a closing caption tells us, all of the geese flew back to Amy's house.

What makes *Fly Away Home* particularly special is the sense of liberating flight that the extensive aerial shots induce, as well as the image of a teenage girl leading her surrogate children to safety via her commanding mastery of a small airplane. Where other animal films concentrate more on a communicative relationship between youth and animals, *Fly Away Home* leaves the connection between Amy and her goslings on a symbolic, if still emotional, level. This actually renders Amy a somewhat less developed character than the pent-up protagonists of other animal films, since her drive to raise, train, and preserve the birds is meant as a tacit statement on her own survival without a mother, as well as the harmony she has long desired with her father. When Tom's plane crashes just before they reach their final destination, he tells Amy that she can go on without him, because she has the determination and spirit of her mother, a gesture that verifies her independence and the maternal inspiration that she has been unable to come to terms with. By completing the mission (and later reuniting with her dad), Amy becomes the rare teen girl heroine who fulfills a motherly fantasy in a typically masculine mechanical endeavor, and a closing shot of the jubilant geese indicates that she has indeed been successful on both counts.

All of these films establish a compassionate relationship between children and animals, employing not only youth's abilities to understand animals in a way that adults do not, but also the very closeness in innocence and wonder that animals are personified to share with youth. These films portray potentially delinquent youth in their early teens, before they have grown hopelessly cynical, who discover a sense of discipline, concern, and humanity through their devotion to animals. Within the context of other '90s youth films about the demise of family unity, which all of the animal youth films address, the story of youth learning to love and become caring through humanizing animals points to a certain crisis in contemporary childhood development. These films reveal that their characters' abilities to align with animals turn them back to their natural familial impulses, a notion that is problematized by the relationships of youth with nature depicted in adventure films.

The youth adventure film is in many ways similar to the animal film but refers to larger social and political conditions (if less so to environmental concerns). These films are not about the potential joys of "getting back to nature" but about the inner natural qualities of youth when they are forced to fend for themselves outside of their usual familial and cultural structure. In that way, the adventure film offers a clear parallel to the challenge of surviving the rigors of school and society for youth, who must confront their inner fears and ambitions against the arduous demands of the outdoors, and in some cases, must confront the primal nature of their friends.

The inspiration for many of these films is an examination of the human condition, although the '90s films take a certain departure from the themes of the '80s films. Up to 1990, youth adventure films generally suggested that humans are more barbaric and ignoble than we, through our refined social relationships, would admit to being. The adventure films after 1990, however, depict youth as determined and driven, casting a generally reassuring light on their capacity to adapt, and to do so in "civilized" ways. While notions of civility are particularly arguable, the change in these films' perspectives reveals an increasingly optimistic image of current teens. By using youth to tell such stories, the films attempt to demonstrate that supposedly basic human traits are instinctual and fundamental, and the films can further capitalize on the preadult state of youth as being particularly volatile and impressionable. Ultimately, these films suggest that codes of socialization are necessary, and that youth have a choice between barbarism and humanity, and if they are to choose humanity, a healthy respect for nature is required to survive.

There have been a number of these films since the '80s, yet most gained little attention, despite studios' efforts to mix adventure tales with other subgenres, as in the sexual dramas of *Out of Control* (1985), the horror elements of *Zero Boys* (1986), and the political messages of *Survival Quest* (1989). Even casting popular stars such as Kevin Bacon and Sean Astin brought few audiences to *White Water Summer* (1987), and the *Cry in the Wild/White Wolves* franchise—which produced four films from 1990 to 1998—was prolific and well regarded but only marginally successful on video. Many adventure films are in fact met with positive reviews, and studios continue to experiment with the style, as in the promising high-seas journey *White Squall* (1996), which also failed to attract much box office despite star casting and a dynamic true story. Youth may actually resist seeing these films because of the plots' blatant celebrations of the liberatory potential of nature, which is difficult for teens to appreciate within the confines of a movie theater, not to mention from the perspective of a comfortable suburban milieu. A case in point is the highly successful *Stand by Me* (1986), the story of four 12-year-old friends who set off into the woods in search of a missing boy's body. The film has the hallmarks of an adventure movie, but it likely owes its appeal to a minimizing of the boys' actual wilderness encounters, focusing instead on their interpersonal issues.

The apparent paradigm for many of these films is William Golding's 1954 novel, *Lord of the Flies,* in which British schoolboys find themselves marooned on an island and, despite their efforts at structuring themselves into certain roles, resort to animalistic brute impulses. The book was originally made into a film in Britain in 1963, and was again adapted by Hollywood in 1990. Its clear examination of human social psychology and its youth-versus-youth plot factor in many of the adventure films.

The 1990 version is relatively faithful to the novel, with its group of military schoolboys whose plane crashes into the ocean. They are forced to swim to a tropical island, where they systematically resort to savagery. Initially, Ralph (Balthazar Getty) is casually elected leader of the group since he has the highest rank, but another boy who is slightly older, Jack (Chris Furrh), develops a group of followers as well. The boys first concern themselves with gathering water and food, until Ralph pushes them to spend more time trying to be rescued. Jack begins to resent Ralph's orders, as well as his friendship with an overweight boy nicknamed Piggy (Daniel Pipoly), and he takes his band of "hunters" away to the woods. The narrative sets up two distinct rival communities: Ralph and Piggy, who live on the shore and whom everyone turns against, and Jack and the hunters, who carry spears, wear face paint, and kill animals for food. The hunters become afraid that a monster is living in a cave on the island, which another boy later learns is only the dying crazed pilot from the plane; when the boy runs to tell the group, who are dancing around a fire with spears, they fear he is the monster and kill him. Ralph tries to appeal to their sense of reason, but to no avail: his patience and tolerance are of no interest to the hunters, who next kill Piggy as he is trying to tell them that they must stop acting like children. The hunters then turn to Ralph as a target, setting the woods on fire and chasing him to the shore, where they are unexpectedly met by marines who have come to save them.

The story is a rich political allegory: as more boys shift alliances from the rational Ralph to the aggressive Jack, a statement is made about the perception of strength through violence, a statement that is broadly applicable. Gary Giddins argued that "the biggest disappointment is the film's refusal to acknowledge the implications raised by the theme applied to 1990 America."[12] Save a passing reference to Rambo and Piggy's expressed fear that Russians could find them, the film's updating of the story does not bring with it much commentary on current political issues, which would have been relevant in its late–Cold War context. Another flaw in the film is its failure to illuminate Ralph's insight, since Jack's powers of persuasion are so strong. After all, he holds out the possibility of gathering more and better food, which is a higher immediate priority to the boys' survival than Ralph's suggestion that they maintain a fire so that adult authorities can find them. What becomes clear is that Jack and many of the boys do not want to be found, that they actually enjoy the freedom from adults and social structure. What rises in the place of those oppressions is the youth's impulse to conform and follow other hierarchical structures. Military rank, for instance, is quickly revealed as irrelevant within their setting. Jack is the meanest and toughest of the group—as signified by his increasing swearing, shoving, and use of weapons—and his rank as the most militant savage demotes Ralph's assumed leadership role. The boys who then follow Jack are, as Ralph later tells them, analogous to the willing slaves of dictators.

Within their jungle surroundings, this message is particularly political, yielding a critique of colonization that was perhaps more apropos of the novel's British schoolboys. These colonizers are not "taming" the land but branding it with their own style of primitive brutality, plundering its resources and losing their respect for human life and humane principles. This makes the film's final scene all the more ironic, since the boys are saved from themselves by the American military's fiercest division, who have presumably achieved such controlled survival skills that they would not resort to the boys' savagery under the same circumstances (a symbolism that may challenge the above claim about the film's lack of current commentary). Thus the film can also be viewed as a parable of puberty, with Jack representing the most unruly element who, through his anarchy and rebellion against established civility, only creates a more oppressive order, and with Ralph representing the individual resisting conformity and upholding mature ethics.

Gold Diggers: The Secret of Bear Mountain (1995), like the tough girl films of the mid-'90s described below, represents a new image of hearty female adolescents. The story takes place in 1980 for no apparent reason (thus becoming one of the first "period" teen films about the '80s), and begins with young teen Beth (Christina Ricci) moving to a small town in Washington with her mother after being raised in Los Angeles. Beth is restless for something to do, and the only local excitement appears to be a rough-and-tumble tomboy named Jody (Anna Chlumsky), who takes Beth on trips through the woods. Other girls tell Beth that Jody is trouble: she lies and steals and her mother is an alcoholic. But Beth befriends Jody all the same, finding in her an appreciating ally, since Jody relates to the recent death of Beth's father and Beth feels that she understands Jody's deviant behavior.

The adventure begins when Jody convinces Beth to go exploring a legendary mountain cave that is reportedly filled with gold. Jody tells Beth the story of a pioneer woman named Molly Morgan, who posed as a man to escape a life of female servitude and become a miner. After a mine collapse, Molly was never found, and neither was the stash of gold rumored to still be on the mountain. Such a legend illuminates the film's promotion of young female independence and intrigue, and Jody is clearly determined to follow Molly's lead. Beth is reluctant to join her, but when Jody tells her that she killed her mother's abusive boyfriend Ray (David Keith) the night before and is running away, Beth promises her loyalty. Unfortunately, Beth cannot control the boat that they've used to get to the mountain, and she becomes trapped under rocks, prompting Jody to brave treacherous terrain on foot as she goes for help. Jody saves Beth's life, yet no one other than Beth believes Jody's stories of abuse. As it turns out, Jody didn't kill Ray after all, but Beth finds Jody's mother beaten by Ray, and realizes that he's kidnapped Jody to go find the gold. Beth sets off with her own mother and the local sheriff to find Jody, revealing that she has inherited Jody's strength and determination. She leads the sheriff to the cave and later finds Jody herself, with a strange woman saving them both from Ray. At the end of the film, the anonymous woman—who both girls know is the long-lost Molly Morgan—gives them each a bag of gold, the symbolic reward for their preservation of her rugged spirit.

Gold Diggers is notable for a number of reasons. It is one of the few (but presumably growing number of) adventure movies about girls; the girls are inspired by a legend, built from a feminist mythology, that is revealed to be true; the main characters' ability to survive in the wilderness is based not on their little specialized knowledge of outdoors skills but on their sheer will. The scene of Beth valiantly braving the rising waters of the cave while waiting for Jody to bring help is evidence of this last point, as is Beth's sisterly devotion to Jody, which compels her to return to the cave to find her friend. The girls are portrayed as insightful—they know each other's true feelings, and take them seriously—as well as resourceful—each saves the other under particularly arduous circumstances. Their closeness is thus largely conveyed through their actions, since there are relatively few scenes of dialogue between them. This is in keeping with buddy action film conventions, but it also demonstrates that teenage girls can be developed as screen characters in terms of their sense of adventure, a narrative trait that has been granted to boys in films since the start of cinema, and long before in literature, as in the Tom Sawyer and Huck Finn stories that *Gold Diggers* has revised.

Other '90s adventure films continued to be produced on both ends of the studio scale, such as the relatively high-budget *A Far Off Place* (1993) and the more modest *Alaska* (1996). Such films maintained an emphasis on becoming balanced with nature and learning to adapt under scary circumstances, and like the animal films, their narratives were founded on fears of family disintegration. Almost all natural encounter films operate on a threat to the disruption of typically safe familial surroundings. The protagonists' families tend to be dead or disrupted, and the youth must reestablish a sense of familial belonging through an animal or must learn to survive on their own, at least temporarily, in an otherwise dangerous environment that is analogous to the adolescents' ascent to adulthood. By finding community with animals and security in the wilderness, the youth in these films verify that they can be responsible to a family and endure adulthood, and they provide an image of the literally wayward youth who navigates unsafe terrain and ultimately thrives through channeling delinquent impulses into primal "survival" skills.

PATRIOTIC PURPOSE

One of the most distinct trends in the youth delinquency subgenre was the output of nationalistic teen films in the '80s, during the height of the Reagan presidency and the last days of the Cold War between the United States and the Soviet Union. Science films like *WarGames* (1983) and *Defense Play* (1988) entertained the notion of youth becoming directly involved in Cold War conflicts from a technological angle, although these films were not nearly as propagandistic in their trumpeting of American values as the patriotic rebellion films of the same era. Here the pride and sustenance of American youth were brought to the task of preserving the country from foreign aggression and/or preserving traditional American beliefs from being trampled by opposing foreign influences. The defiance in these films was thus not against mere parents and adults, but against the potential corruption threatened by any alien force; and the conservation of *American* identity, not just youth identity, became the priority. These films were in many ways simply shifting the age focus of the numerous post-Vietnam films of U.S. military dominance, most notably *Uncommon Valor* (1983) and *Rambo: First Blood Part II* (1985), wherein real American losses and shame from the war were recuperated by narratives in which one or a few men earned honor and valor through combat. An interesting contrast was provided by *Platoon* in 1986, which is set in Vietnam during the war: the teenage protagonist experiences a classic loss of innocence as he encounters the horrors and absurdity of the war, within a context that is far more dour and graphic than the contemporarily set patriotic purpose films.

The duration of these films was brief, from 1984 to 1988. Three sequels have been made to the 1986 film *Iron Eagle,* the most recent in 1995, although all of them were made in other countries, and were far less successful than the first; more tellingly, after the first sequel in 1988, the enemy in *Aces: Iron Eagle 3* (1992) was no longer a foreign military force but a Peruvian drug lord, and in the 1995 installment, the U.S. Air Force itself had become the enemy. Such a shift is indicative of the changing geopolitical atmosphere, which was probably responsible for the earlier demise of this style. Further, the image of youth with various guns and weapons, regardless of their intended target, would have likely become more suspect even had the Cold War continued, given the increased attention to gang violence and teen murder in recent years.

Red Dawn (1984) was the first and perhaps most prominent of the patriotic youth delinquency films. The story opens with the invasion of a small Colorado town by Cubans and Nicaraguans who have come in advance of a larger force of Russians. Twenty-something Jed (Patrick Swayze) and his teenage brother Matt (Charlie Sheen) escape to the mountains and bring a few male friends, planning to survive off the land until the apparent global war is over. Jed becomes the brave leader of the boys, teaching them hunting rituals and reassuring them in times of doubt. The boys are soon joined by two local girls

Stalwart boys Jed (Patrick Swayze), Robert (C. Thomas Howell), and Matt (Charlie Sheen) have their guns drawn to defend themselves, and American values, against the invading Russians of the Reagan-era nightmare *Red Dawn* (1984).

and thus form a tentative family unit, although the girls are hardened and somewhat suspicious of the boys. The boys are more troubled by what occurs with their parents back in the besieged town: one boy's mayoral father is collaborating with the brutal Russians, and Jed and Matt's dad is shot for their role in a skirmish with Russians in the hills. A new father figure arrives in the form of a downed U.S. pilot, who tells the kids of certain military strategies before he too is killed by the Russians.

Feeling a lack of identity, the group adopts the name of their high school mascots, the Wolverines, and like local sports heroes, they inspire the community with their spirit, going on a guerrilla run of sabotaging Russian positions, although as Lenny Rubenstein points out, "Revenge, not victory, seems their sole interest," and the film "even ignores the most interesting features of underground warfare: the attempt to grow in size and power and to play a role in future events"—features that would have presumably appealed to a young audience.[13] The Wolverines do show resolve in their game of war, yet bring the foreign military forces down on them, resulting in all of them being killed except Jed and Matt. The foreboding ending of this xenophobic tale shows the wounded boys being allowed to escape by a sympathetic Cuban commander, portending that the Russian invasion may fail on its own terms, and that the future of the United States lies in the hands of the few strong men who can continue to fight the foreign invaders.

The film may have aged in its politics, but at the time it was obviously designed to play to American—especially young American—fears of not only invasion and death, but also loss of cultural identity. (Although the argument can be made that the threat of nuclear holocaust was a more pressing concern of the '80s, as depicted in films such as *Testament* and the TV movie *The Day After,* both in 1983.[14]) The surviving townspeople who resist the caricatured Russians and Cubans—donning Red Stars and killing innocent civilians—are imprisoned in a "reeducation" camp built in a movie drive-in, an ironic symbol of this entertainment site being turned into a propaganda device by a people who have no appreciation for the "sacrilege" they are committing. The Wolverines remain loyal to the nationalist pride they have developed at home and in school, especially in relation to the Russians, and they hold firm to the two social systems that they feel ensure their citizenship: traditional gender roles and familial loyalty. As a leader and the emergent father of the group, Jed becomes the savior of conservative American values in avenging and replacing his own father: the oldest man has the most control, and protects the group from their own weaknesses. Yet *Red Dawn* is founded on an inherent racism, toward Russians as well as Hispanics; David Denby said the film "stretches right-wing paranoia into masochistic wish fulfillment," and it remains rather reactionary with its ending, suggesting that cultural integrity via masculine authority must prevail if national identity—any national identity—is to be sustained.[15] These are rather sophisticated issues for teenagers to confront, and the film does clearly simplify them to a choice between "democratic capitalism" and "oppressive communism," although it also questions the confidence of American nationalist power.

Born American (1986) received less attention and was somewhat more ambiguous in its declarations of nationalist pride, despite its ludicrous premise: three teenage boys vacationing in Finland—Savoy (Mike Norris), Mitch (Steve Durham), and K. C. (David Coburn)—daringly cross a remote border into Russia for a thrill and are soon captured by locals who think they have killed a young girl. Another local girl helps save them, but before they can make it back to Finland, they are captured by the Russian military and thrown in prison. There Mitch is subjected to torture, most symbolically with a Pepsi bottle, before he is cast into a special dungeon laid out like a chess board, where prisoners battle each other to the death under the gladiator gaze of other crazed inmates (surely one of the most absurd scenes in any youth film). K. C., who is dying from a gun wound, is euthanized by another prisoner, who then aids Savoy in planning an escape. Savoy rescues Mitch, only to see his friend killed in the attempt, but he manages to break free with the help of a black American secret prisoner known as the "Admiral" and a doting Russian girl, the latter of whom goes with him back to Finland. Before Savoy returns to America, the Admiral, who is out to topple the KGB *and* the CIA, gives Savoy his secret manuscript that details the atrocities of these government agencies, and Savoy optimistically assures him that it will be the Admiral's ticket back to the States.

Born American necessarily operates on the level of nightmare-fantasy, even though it seems to take itself seriously. The casting of Mike Norris as the triumphant hero exemplifies the film's agenda: he is the real-life son of action star Chuck Norris, who was busy in other films at the time, such as *Missing in Action* (1984) and *Delta Force* (1986), upholding the American cause through fighting stereotypically brutal Vietnamese and Arabs. Like *Red Dawn,* the film appeals to a masculinist mentality (especially in its abundance of gun play, explosions, and accommodating Russian girls), although its lack of character and plot development keeps the political implications of the narrative rather shallow. In some ways the film is a wild party plot gone wrong, with the boys' fun-loving ways eradicated by Russians who are merely zealous barbarians, and the film's final nod to dual government corruption speaks to a universal oppression of youthful energies.

The original *Iron Eagle* elevated the military competence of its protagonist to a higher level. Doug (Jason Gedrick), who aspires to be a fighter pilot, is rejected from the Air Force Academy because of his bad high school grades, but this doesn't stop him from organizing his fellow aviator friends—who give themselves the sporting name "Eagles"—to gather secret military information after his father is shot down over an unspecified Arab country. Having demonstrated his concern for his father as well as his tactical skills, Doug convinces retired Colonel "Chappy" Sinclair (Louis Gossett Jr.) to help him rescue his father since the State Department is reluctant to intervene. (Gossett would go on to star in all of the *Iron Eagle* sequels.) After being aided by the efforts of the dedicated Eagles, who include two girls and a boy so proud of the president's potency that he calls him "Ronnie Ray Gun," Chappy and Doug stage a daring air raid on the Arab base where Doug's father is being held, engaging in a dogfight with enemy planes that leads to Chappy being shot down. Doug fortunately has a tape that Chappy left for him, which talks him through the rest of the mission: Doug rescues his wounded father and shoots down more planes, including one improbably piloted by the Arab minister of defense, before being escorted to safety by other Air Force jets. (The aerial assaults are set to a pulsing rock music score, which makes them play like a video game, a technique that would reach perfection in *Top Gun* later that year.) Back under military supervision, Doug discovers that Chappy safely bailed out of his plane, and the two avert a court-martial by swearing secrecy about their mission, which is ensured through Doug's admission to the Air Force Academy.

Iron Eagle is indeed a film about patriotism, but it is more about how that patriotism is vivified through filial duty to paternal loyalty. J. Hoberman even adroitly called the film "a mixture of *Star Wars* and *Uncommon Valor* in which fighting for the absent father is elevated to a divine principle."[16] Doug's chief ambition is to be like his heroic father, and when his father is threatened, he takes his role, despite his youthful liabilities. He also enlists a clear father figure in Chappy, whose race as an African American is made an explicit issue to the white Doug because Chappy tells him his father was one of the few white soldiers who respected his status as an officer. Chappy thereby transfers his fatherly admiration for Doug's dad onto Doug's son, and his racial identification may be seen as a subtle reminder of Doug's—and the military's—confrontation with cultural difference. Of course, that difference is accommodated within Doug and Chappy's mutual contempt for the Arabs, and together their alignment as "men with a mission" unites them in a masculine bond that overcomes age and race.

As in *Red Dawn,* the preservation of masculine authority, and moreover, *American* masculine authority, is truly the subject of the film. Doug's duel with the Arab leader is a direct confrontation with "corrupt" patriarchal authority, and his ability to destroy the enemy—with his own incapacitated father literally behind him—verifies his recognition of proper paternal power. Doug's mastery of the phallic control he gains over his fighter plane then signifies his ascent to manhood as well as his competency to be a member of the elite military. Further, Doug's leadership role within the Eagles verifies his authoritative potential, especially since he convinces these young people to do the military job that the disorganized government cannot, and once again the image of teenagers confidently working to dispatch foreign aggressors in preserving their sense of familial and cultural order is celebrated.

The Rescue (1988) borrows directly from *Iron Eagle* in its tale of teenagers rescuing their captured military fathers from North Korea after the U.S. government fails to take action. The film's major revisions over its predecessor are the increased number of youth (five), their wider age range (from 10 to 18), and a girl character who becomes an active participant rather than a mere member. Beyond these changes, the film plays strikingly like *Iron Eagle:* the youth, who are stationed with their families in South Korea at a U.S. military base, steal the Navy's aborted rescue plans and a private boat, which they use to infiltrate heavily armed North Korea, eluding various attacks en route. They meet up with a South Korean ally, who helps them find the prison where their fathers are being held by the barbaric North Korean Communists. The group then activates their plan to use the North Koreans' fireworks displays in rescuing their fathers and getting them back to safe, democratic, American-influenced South Korea.

Once again paternal obligation is present: the leader of the group, J. J. (Kevin Dillon), has longed for the love and respect his father has always given to the Navy instead of him, and knows that this is his chance to win his father's devotion through proving his military mettle (signified most appallingly when he helps his dad kill a North Korean soldier). Another boy, Max (Marc Price), is finally able to put his electronic skills to good use by gaining intelligence information for their raid. The girl in the group, Adrian (Christina Harnos), convinces the boys through her martial arts skills that she can handle the arduous expedition, and to the film's credit, she is as capable as her male counterparts, yielding a timely women-in-combat message. The film's portrait of tough, courageous, and smart teens is rather puissant, and again their motivation is the preservation of family filtered through a hatred of America's foreign enemies, a hatred that ultimately questions the nobility of their cause, and as in past patriotic purpose movies, exposes how these films use young characters as figureheads for deep-seated adult political prejudices that youth themselves have barely begun to develop.

The Rescue represented the last of this short-lived trend, although at least four other films of the time, it may be argued, fit the category: *Terror Squad* (1987), which depicted students fighting off Libyan terrorists who take over their high school; *Hangmen* (1987), which improbably featured a teenager trying to escape a corrupt CIA faction; *Hell on the Battleground* (1987), which was a quickie revision of *Platoon* with young recruits being unexpectedly pressed into combat in Vietnam; and *Little Nikita* (1988), which carried the patriotic theme into the family drama genre, as an American boy comes to terms with the fact that his parents are Soviet spies, and in the end the family leaves the KGB to pledge their allegiance to America. The film thus sutures *family* with *America,* an equation that all of the patriotic purpose films propagandistically promote.

The demise of this youth film style, as previously stated, was most certainly connected to changing political relations between the United States and its past enemies in the Soviet Union, Iran, Libya, and various Latin American countries. Promilitary American films in general saw a decline in the '90s, despite the Persian Gulf War in 1991, and an example of how little international political tensions were handled in youth films after the '80s is *Toy Soldiers* from that same year. In this story, a boys' boarding school is seized by South American aggressors, and a bold group of students must quickly employ their dormant tactical skills to retaliate, a conflict that is staged under a rather politically indifferent tone. The bad guys are still foreigners, yet the youth in the story pay no attention to any issues of nationality or nationalism (they are themselves from diverse nationalities); they are simply fighting to prove their worth and survive. The presence of Louis Gossett Jr. in *Toy Soldiers* as the boys' father figure, however, is a lingering reference to the politics of the brief wave of teen-combat films in the '80s, when the defeat of foreigners in these films was used as a signifier of masculine achievement and familial preservation for Reagan-era youth.

TOUGH GIRLS

A distinct and interesting category of the youth delinquent subgenre is the tough girl film, in which one or more girls stake out their identity through rebellious acts. Since most youth delinquency films dwell on male delinquency, films about females usually take on a different and specific tone. In some cases, the protagonists are reacting directly to mistreatment by men, but in all cases these characters appear knowingly to question and defy patriarchy, through a wide range of means.

As the tough girl persona slowly evolved in '80s teen films, she was primarily a victimized survivor, and then by the mid-'90s many stronger girls appeared, becoming more enterprising and dynamic. Yet not all films featuring rebellious young women (such as the recent *Election* or *She's All That*) could be fully included within this category: the tough girl is not only conscious of her challenge to gender norms, be they enforced by men and/or women, but she often employs a confident aggression in expressing herself, and on a generic level, films about tough girls focus on the exhilaration of their toughness via delinquency, rather than the sensitive negotiation of power that still troubles most teen girls in other films. To be sure, the roles of many girls in recent American movies have begun to reflect a potent image of young femininity, yet these demonstrably delinquent roles have provided a particularly crucial and often questionable empowerment for girl characters, since this most conspicuous empowerment remains aligned with deviance and criminality.

In spite of their often feminist possibilities, tough girl films can unfortunately be easy devices for exploitation, just as various "women's" genre films have been over the years. While perhaps the most prominent tough girl character of the '80s, Angel from the *Angel* trilogy (1984–88), showed a certain autonomy through being an "honor student by day and street-smart hooker by night," and did reform over the course of the trilogy, the films also capitalized on their lead actresses' sexuality, and were marketed accordingly. When the mid-'90s saw a distinct increase in the number of tough girl films, their themes changed as well; after all, girls were at least establishing their buying power in the marketplace, and the swell of girl-oriented magazines and TV shows were supporting young feminist ambitions. In 1996 Peggy Orenstein wrote in her article "The Movies Discover the Teen-Age Girl" that the recent films about girls featured characters "in charge of their own fates, active rather than reactive" since they are films "about girls' relationships to one another rather than to boys, that tackle the big themes of teen-age life, like anger, sexuality, alienation and displacement."[17] Orenstein's examples are not limited to the delinquency subgenre, but include school comedies such as *Clueless* and romances such as *The Incredibly True Adventure of Two Girls in Love,* although the most noticeable evidence of the shift in young female representation remains within delinquency films.

The common past practice of depicting girls within delinquency films as the spectators to or victims of male rebellion clearly changed in the mid-'90s, and girls not only banded together to seek unity through their own rebellion, but often found themselves in the same predicaments as their male cohorts because of it. The consequences of crimes, drug use, and sexual irresponsibility (which rarely weighs as heavily on boys) became problems for the tough girls, who also juggled confusing aspects of their gendered existence such as choosing careers, being attracted to boys (or girls), wanting to have children, and wanting to get married. Yet Orenstein adds, "The ground for exploration in these films becomes not the stuff of day-to-day life but the wreckage that occurs when the boundaries of feminine behavior are crossed."[18] Tough girl films often become examinations of the tensions around young women declaring their independence from men and traditional gender roles and their seeking of a new cultural identity based on feminine ideals that have not been engendered by patriarchy.

Depictions of tough girls in American films before the 1980s were often diffuse and degrading. As Thomas Doherty points out, a cycle of "dangerous teenager" films began to appear in the 1950s, such as *Teenage Doll* (1957) and *Teenage Bad Girl* (1959), movies in which girls were often shown to be just as corrupted by postwar excesses as boys. In that way, these films addressed the patriarchal fear of teenagers *and* women, since in virtually all cases the transgressors in these movies were either killed or brought back under the authority of (adult male) law. The cottage industry of women's prison films sometimes took on teenage inmates, as in *Reform School Girl* (1957) and *Girl on a Chain Gang* (1965), an exploitative tradition that continued into the '80s in campy productions such as *Bad Girls' Dormitory* and *Delinquent School Girls* (both 1984), films that openly employ ruinous depictions of captive young women subjected to various mistreatments, usually at the hands of misogynist men or angry lesbians. Again, these images could hardly have been seen as progressive. Perhaps the roles of young female survivors of trauma, as in *The Exorcist* (1973) and *I Never Promised You a Rose Garden* (1977), could arguably be called the first signs of a stronger, stoical portrayal of young women, even though the narratives of these films hinged on their protagonists being violently abused.

Yet the best sign that the tough girl was becoming a recognizable teen role arrived in '80s films that featured groups of girls helping each other through good and, more often, bad times. The first and most prominent was *Foxes* in 1980, in which four girlfriends struggle through their teen years with scant adult guidance, partying hard along the way until one of them dies from a drug overdose. A more obscure example is *Ladies and Gentlemen, The Fabulous Stains* (1981), about a rebellious teenage girl who joins her friends in forming a renegade punk rock band. Ten years after *The Exorcist,* Linda Blair starred in *Savage Streets* (1983), leading a gang of high school girls against a much meaner street gang who raped her deaf sister; the rape scene is excessively violent and prolonged, pointing to the film's exploitative aims, even though vengeance is carried out by the end of the film. As these "girl gang" movies began to appear, depictions of lone tough girls were emerging as well, such as *Scarred* (1984), which bears comparison to the relatively popular *Angel* released that same year: the story is of a single teenage mother who becomes a prostitute to support her baby.

Angel may have had similar aspirations to portray the Madonna/whore role in its teenage protagonist. Molly (Donna Wilkes) attends Catholic school as a straight-A student, resisting the advances of nerds and jocks alike, but every night she cruises Hollywood Boulevard as Angel, a child prostitute. The 15-year-old is surrounded and supported by a street family of curious characters—a homeless former Western star called Kit Carson (Rory Calhoun), a benevolent transvestite named Mae (Dick Shawn), and a protective lesbian landlady. Stanley Crouch interprets this cast arrangement as the film's parallel to *The Wizard of Oz,* and adds, "[I]t is perhaps a comment on our era that the tin man, the scarecrow, and the cowardly lion have been replaced for our young heroine by old movie cowboys, transvestites, prostitutes, and a butched-up lady who would herself be a lady killer."[19] On a narrative level, these figures represent Angel's orchestrated attempt to replace her own parents, both of whom left her years before (we are led to believe that they were simply selfish and unloving). Thus she walks the streets to raise money for living expenses, and her hardened job persona fuels the confidence and drive she has at school (of course, when she finds time to do homework is unclear). Angel is the teen female who seems in charge of all aspects of her life, and while she still longs for the return of her parents, she is raising herself relatively well.

The plot revolves around a psychopath who is killing hookers on the strip in brutal ways. After Angel finds one of her own friends murdered in a motel room, she turns to a detective for help, who later discovers her secret life. A group of lecherous jocks from school also discover her secret, but she dispatches them by brandishing a gun she's bought. Now that everyone knows the truth, Angel goes after the killer, who first kills Mae. The scenes of Angel chasing the killer through the streets with a gun bigger than her forearm are charged with a palpable energy, yet alas she doesn't kill the killer—the detective shows up to save Angel, and Kit Carson, who has demonstrated what a good shot he is, fills the killer full of lead. This ending thereby feels like a compromise of the determination and strength Angel has developed through the course of the story, especially when she cowers under the detective, but the film as a whole preserves a very autonomous image for its title character. The irony is that her financial, sexual, familial, and social autonomy all arise from her selling of her pubescent body to despicable men, and given that by the end of the film Angel has *not* vowed to give up hooking, this deplorable condition remains a statement on the power imbalance between young men and women. Even when she's about to be gang-raped by her jock classmates, Angel escapes only by wielding a phallus more dangerous than theirs, reminding us that the very power she has achieved in her life has been through the operations of patriarchy. (On another level, the film is easily readable as a black comedy, given some of its stranger touches, and thus its ironies may be intended as a critique of past child hooker roles in films like *Pretty Baby* and *Taxi Driver*.)

The two sequels to *Angel* follow the character later in life: in *Avenging Angel* (1985) she has become a law student, and now takes to the streets only to avenge the murder of the detective who, we learn, turned her away from prostitution after all. With *Angel 3: The Final Chapter* (1988) the story returned to prostitution, only now Angel is trying to save her long-estranged sister from the life she previously led. Both of these films continue to feature the main character in powerful positions; but by moving her into a more successful and less immoral lifestyle, the films expose their exploitative motive, the contrast between "good girl with a purpose" and "bad girl on a mission."

Another important '80s film spoke to the developing mythology of the tough girl role through its name alone, *The Legend of Billie Jean* (1985). Helen Slater plays the title character and Christian Slater (no relation) plays her younger brother Binx, two poor Texas teenagers. After Binx accidentally shoots a lecherous local who tried to rape his sister, the siblings and two female friends go on the run, drawing media attention and hordes of young followers, especially after they manage to air Billie Jean's plea for justice on television. As their notoriety continues to grow, more youth rise up in solidarity with the outlaws, protesting their abuse by adults, with girls emulating Billie Jean's appearance and helping the "Billie Jean Gang" evade arrest. The heroine eventually arranges a surrender that becomes its own media event, especially when she confronts the man Binx shot and stages a revolt against his exploitation of her body, which was first enacted by his sexual assault, and more prominently by his selling of merchandise emblazoned with her image. Her speech becomes a rally, and the crowd joins in by burning their Billie Jean memorabilia, resulting in a fire that engulfs a large effigy of her as well.

Billie Jean becomes such an automatic authority figure in the film not only through her uprising but thanks to the typical absence of the children's parents; all of these kids have such a commitment to defiance because they have been left to raise themselves. In terms of Billie Jean's use of the media, she shows her deft understanding of visual persuasion through adopting the look

Helen Slater strikes an iconic pose as the tough title character in *The Legend of Billie Jean* (1985), aiming for a contemporary version of Joan of Arc.

of Joan of Arc, self-consciously making herself look like a martyr for the cause by simply cutting off her long blonde hair and tearing off her shirt sleeves—a symbolism driven home when her effigy "burns at the stake." She then uses the media's interest in youth rebellion to generate support for their protest—exploiting the exploiters—squarely placing the responsibility for their oppression on the adults who otherwise run the media. Some question can be raised as to whether the narrative is offering this message as critique or irony, as David Edelstein points out:

> *The Legend of Billie Jean* . . . has nothing to do with civil disobedience or self-reliance or feminism. Like a lot of our myths these days, it's about the thrill of overnight celebrity. . . . And what these girls [in the film] really love is not her deeds but her stardom: they want to look like her and act like her and someday be as famous as her.[20]

Yet the film is indeed promoting at least a *vision* of young fortitude, for if its characters are inspired to *act* like Billie Jean through being manipulated by the media, they are still being encouraged to rebel, a postmodern paradox to be sure. When a small army of girls emerges looking like Billie Jean and promoting her continued flight, the potential of organized youth rebellion is demonstrated, and is made more remarkable for its feminist social aspirations, which would not again be prominent in American teen films for nearly a decade.

Less popular films, however, did continue to introduce various incarnations of the tough girl. *My Little Girl* (1987) embodies the style in a more subtle way, with its story of a headstrong rich girl who turns away from her preoccupied parents and takes a job at a home for delinquent women. A film that utilizes the image of erstwhile delinquent girls within a rock music setting is *Satisfaction* (1988), which presents a rare organized girl "gang" of the '80s, whose loyalty to their band is their means of *avoiding* delinquency, since their only hope for self-improvement appears to be staying together. The film's ending, with two of the girls rejecting romantic options, is an endorsement of female self-determination, yet the film was attacked by critics and failed at the box office. Not until the mid-'90s would another film about teen female unity become praised or popular.

Far from Home (1989) could have provided a boost both for tough girl roles and for its star Drew Barrymore (in her first teen role), but failed to do either. Barrymore plays a self-assured and rebellious teenager on vacation with her father who becomes the unwitting target of a killer, and the film was so poorly received that its faint release has rendered it obscure. *No Secrets* (1991) is slightly less obscure and more bizarre, the strange tale of three high school girls who take in a deceptively handsome male drifter while staying at a cabin in the woods. The girls are really too dissimilar to be friends, and thus the film implicitly argues that all girls long for a liberating sense of adventure through competing against other girls for the attention of an alluring, even dangerous man. Unfortunately, the girls lose interest in each other, like the story loses interest in the girls, for the sake of celebrating masculine mythology.

Another problematic depiction of tough girls appeared in *Brutal Fury,* which presented the first organized girl gang of the '90s (the film was released in 1992, although it was made in 1988); in this well-intentioned morality play, a secret high school sisterhood calling themselves the Furies sets out to eradicate the drug dealers and date rapists that have sullied their school (not unlike the Sentinels in *Dangerously Close* [1986]). The repressed, molested Misty (Lisa-Gabrielle Greene) joins the quasi-occult group as they traipse about in black leotards for their attacks, but she goes beyond the group's intimidating assaults and becomes consumed with homicidal mania. An undercover female cop eventually catches up with Misty, whose rampage leads to her own death, only this expected ending vitiates the film's possible lessons on vigilante justice, and reveals its ultimately insulting image of potent young women whose efforts at gaining power corrupt and destroy them. As the decade continued, more of these vengeful and sometimes violent portraits of girls appeared, although the characters tended to become more purposeful and understanding.

For instance, in 1994, two films about girl delinquents were released that not only staked out new terrain in the depiction of tough young women on screen, but brought up previously unspoken issues about the influences of race, class, and sexual preference on their protagonists. The less visible (although no less powerful) of the two was *Fun,* in which two girls meet one afternoon and, after sharing stories of their childhood abuses and going on a cross-neighborhood prank spree, end up murdering an elderly woman in a cathartic rampage of unleashed aggression. Their lack of motive for the crime and their passionately nonsexual devotion to each other baffle the authorities who question them: for these effectively parentless children, the path from conversation to confession to stealing to games to jokes to murder is a logical progression, and the film leaves open the unsettling possibility that many young women are simply waiting for the right partner with whom to follow a similar epiphanic trajectory. In the end, after being imprisoned, one of the girls kills herself when she learns that the two of them will be separated, which becomes her twisted attempt to immortalize their uniquely understanding relationship. The film wisely concludes that the diffuse yet damaging oppressions of girls may lead to all manner of inexplicable adolescent outbursts and reactions.

Mi Vida Loca (*My Crazy Life*) depicts young barrio women in Los Angeles, all Latinas, who have formed the Echo Park Home Girl gang. Members of the gang, Sad Girl (Angel Aviles) and Mousie (Seidy Lopez), had been friends, but after both having children by the same kind-hearted drug dealer, Ernesto (Jacob Vargas), they meet for a fight. At that same time Ernesto is killed over a broken deal, and Ernesto's gang vows revenge against his killer, who they believe is a rival named El Duran (Jessie Borrego). Sad Girl and Mousie make up, and are concerned for their home girl Whisper (Nelida Lopez), who was shot in the incident; the women decide to sell Ernesto's customized truck to pay Whisper's hospital bills and help support his babies. In a related subplot, Sad Girl's sister Alicia (Magali Alvarado), who has not joined the gang and goes to school, is crushed when her ex-convict pen pal stops writing, only to discover that he is El Duran, when at that moment Ernesto's gang kills him. In retaliation, El Duran's girlfriend tries to kill one of Ernesto's friends, but inadvertently shoots a young girl, leading to a somber closing scene where the home girls gather at her funeral.

Mi Vida Loca testifies to the sad chain that is gang warfare through the struggles of its strong female characters who long to break it. These girls do not enjoy the thrill of violence, yet have become defensive of their home turf and friends due to the treacherous conditions of their surroundings, which are made so primarily by the activities of men. They clearly enjoy the vibrant energy that otherwise runs through their neighborhood—fancy cars, children playing, decorated buildings—only they have tried to bond with each other to create an insularity that can protect them. This protection is not only from other gangs (who make their presence known by specialized hand signals), but from the deterioration of their local identities; their ability to preserve their group is integral to the preservation of their individuality.

Despite the success of the male-focused African American crime films of the early '90s, no similar films about African American girl gangs have been made (with the arguable exception of *Set It Off* in 1996, about a group of four black women in their twenties who take to robbing banks for a variety of personal and political reasons). One way *Mi Vida Loca* distinguishes its Latina gang members from their black male counterparts is by letting us hear their childhood memories through voiceover (Ernesto narrates as well), imbuing them with a sense of innocence that would threaten the virility of most male gangsta characters. White filmmaker Alison Anders was nonetheless criticized for her handling of the characters in *Mi Vida Loca* by critics such as Kevin Thomas, who claimed that regardless of her good intentions, "Anders has ended up confirming a decidedly negative stereotype of young Latinos as aimless, dangerous, and incapable of thinking for themselves, not to mention welfare-dependent.... (none seem to be employed)."[21] Yet Anders also provides points of contrast to the gang girls, such as Giggles (Marlo Marron), a former member herself, now out of prison and looking for a computer job to help support her daughter, and Alicia, whose tender appreciation of El Duran—at least before she knows who he is—speaks to the romantic resolve that sustains many "women reared on cheap romance and the religion of the gun," as Leslie Felperin saw the characters.[22]

What *Mi Vida Loca* may best demonstrate about the image of young tough Latinas is the tension they bear in wanting better lives for themselves despite the fact that they have few concrete ideas about how to achieve them, which is the essence of most delinquent depictions. These young women suffer the indignities of the men around them, all the while hoping—or gambling—that the men they pick as partners will help them survive. The film paints this hope as futile, with single motherhood an inevitability. In that way the film is fatalistic, but it shows that these women's enduring identities are symbiotically dependent on each other, and given that Anders cast many actual Latina gang members in the film, it further offers a tentative verisimilitude based on a feminine constancy and reliability that films about male gang members seem determined to break down.

As previously stated, the mid-'90s saw a boom in the output of tough girl films, which met with varying degrees of success. Lesser-known films such as *Spitfire* (1994), *True Crime* (1995), *Freeway,* and *Ripe* (both 1996) offered increasingly complex interpretations of the hardened teen female—especially the latter two, which were, respectively, a postmodern updating of "Little Red Riding Hood" in which the cast-off heroine escapes from prison to kill a murderous psychopath (read: wolf), and a true-life account of fraternal twin sisters who wind up on a military base where they discover different aspects of their emerging sexuality, leading one to kill the other's lover.

Foxfire (1996) offers a more coherent image of young female "outlaws," four high school seniors who are joined by a runaway girl of the same age and begin a latent feminist movement on campus while trying to cope with their own personal issues. First they retaliate against a sexually harassing teacher, and then begin hanging out in an abandoned house, casually drinking whiskey, smoking dope, and dancing, but unfortunately revealing little more about themselves. The runaway girl is the group's catalyst, only she is a necessary cipher, since the film suggests that these girls have been longing to break free and simply needed a shove to do so. In the end, the runaway continues on her run after helping out the other girls one more time, and a final shot of one of the remaining girls ascending to the top of a bridge tower indicates that she has gained similar independence and strength. Despite the clear messages of the movie, which is based on a Joyce Carol Oates novel, the characters are kept remarkably distant. Like *Ripe* and *Freeway,* the film plays as a parable, and given the realism of its setting, this makes the narrative's force a bit weaker, denying these strong, growing characters more complete identities. The film is not subtle in message—it is loudly telling girls to unite and stand up for themselves—yet it leaves its characters too subtly drawn.

Girls Town (1996) offers more developed characters and presents them in a more informed way. The story begins with four New Jersey high school friends about to graduate: Patti (Lili Taylor), a single Latina mother who has grown into her early 20s as she has had to put school aside; Emma (Anna Grace), a white girl contemplating college; Angela (Bruklin Harris), a middle-class black girl also planning to go to college; and Nikki (Aunjanue Ellis), a black writer who has already been accepted to Princeton. The four meet to exchange the daily frustrations of their lives: Patti and Emma come from impoverished backgrounds, Angela rebels against her working mother—only Nikki is hiding her gnawing self-contempt, which the other three do not realize until she suddenly kills herself. Reading through Nikki's diary, they learn that she was raped by a man at work, leading them to begin confronting each other about the problems that they don't share with each other.

The narrative proceeds with each of the three remaining friends accounting for their anger at both men and women. Emma, who had been raped by a school football star, vandalizes his car with Patti and Angela, writing "rapist" on the hood. After her confused boyfriend hears of the incident, she becomes impatient with his lack of understanding and tells him to go away. Patti enlists the other two in stealing items from her abusive ex-boyfriend to pawn so they can buy food and clothes for her baby. Angela, who has kept a stolid composure, lets loose on a smaller girl when she brings up Nikki's death in a disparaging way. Their acts are all motivated by a realization of their inner anger and a resolve to stop tolerating their teenage plights, especially those imposed by men—a more clearly political agenda than the tough girls of past films. The girls become "feminist in praxis rather than ideology," Emanuel Levy noted.[23] Yet their implicit ideological agenda emerges after they begin a list of sexually abusive students and teachers on a bathroom stall at school, and other girls come forth to add to the list, quietly augmenting their rebellion. Slowly they realize that their sole strength is through each other, and "institutions like church, school, police, and family are uncaring, absent, or ineffective," as Phil Riley observed.[24] The girls' harmonious diversity of race, class, and interests further testifies to the similar problems shared by a wide range of women, as well as the solidarity they must rely on to overcome those problems. (Queen Latifah's closing song "U-N-I-T-Y" makes this message adamant.)

While the film was directed by Jim McKay, the director worked through improvisation with his performers, who developed each of the character's stories and identities collaboratively. This lends the film a certain realistic cohesion of vision, as each of the girls becomes more fully aware of changes she wants to make in her life; in that way, Levy claims, the story "conveys effectively the sheer joy and catharsis in the girls' reluctance to quietly accept their place in society."[25] Their climactic collective step in that direction is when they pay a surprise visit to Nikki's rapist and beat him in the street, not to the point of serious injury, but enough to make their virulent rage known. The film concludes on a bittersweet note, as the girls realize that their summer will pass quickly and they will then be separated, yet they have given to each other a sense of confidence and control they never had before.

After these portraits of girl groups in the mid-'90s, the film industry returned to more solo depictions of tough girls, such as *The Opposite of Sex* (1998), which is perhaps most indicative of late-'90s tough girl roles, even if the heroine is somewhat sinister. Christina Ricci plays Dedee, a disenchanted teen who moves in with her upwardly mobile gay half-brother and proceeds to seduce his boyfriend. She later finds that she's pregnant and goes on the run, although she eventually decides to have the baby so that it can be raised by her more caring brother. Dedee is the tough girl as confident to the point of being self-centered, and thus she doesn't stand up for a cause like previous protagonists, although she does reveal by the end her sense of frustration with the world, and she does come to realize her limitations without succumbing to them. Such a character thereby retains her sense of humanity—these girls may be tough, but they're not brutes—while remaining dedicated to finding her own direction in life.

In many ways the tough girl films are still seeking an identity for their attitude and style, just as the characters are within the films, since this remains relatively new terrain in youth cinema. The handful of tough girl films before the mid-'90s never found a specific identity, let alone a niche in the movie market. By the end of the '90s, as Bernard Weinraub has pointed out, teenage girls had become a more potent force at the box office as well as on screen.[26] Now that many films about tough girls have established themselves within the juvenile delinquency genre, their ethos is more successfully crossing over to other genres such as horror in *The Craft* (1996), *Scream* (1996), *Disturbing Behavior* (1998), and *The Rage: Carrie 2* (1999); dark dramas like *All Over Me* (1996), *Crime and Punishment in Suburbia* (2000), and *The Smokers* (2000); thrillers like *Wild Things* (1997), *The Mod Squad* (1999), and *Go* (1999); and comedies such as *That Darn Cat* (1997), *Can't Hardly Wait* (1998), and *10 Things I Hate About You* (1999), and *Ghost World* (2001). Even period films like *Whatever* (1998), *A Soldier's Daughter Never Cries* (1998), and *Dick* (1999) present revisions of the tough girl image through their protagonists, suggesting that the drive for young female authority began manifesting itself long before the current generation.

As a result, teenage girls in American cinema at the end of the twentieth century emerged as more aware of their past mistreatment and misrepresentation and more in control of their destiny, both in terms of politics and sexuality, and films like *Girlfight* (2000) and Jim McKay's *Our Song* (2001) have offered the hope of continuing this progress in the twenty-first century. The blockbuster success of *Charlie's Angels* (2000) and *Tomb Raider* (2001) can also be attributed to changing attitudes toward young female power, despite some lingering sexist aspects. Most of the recent representations of tough girl roles reveal a cautious effort by the film industry to provide increasingly active images of young women, even if many tough girl characters tend to remain conflicted about their new sense of power. As these films and their characters continue to discover the range of their identities, young women in cinema will continue to achieve greater authority, and they won't have to appear "delinquent" to do so.

THE AFRICAN AMERICAN CRIME DRAMA

One of the most distinct and significant styles of youth delinquency films, and of youth films in general, emerged in the early '90s in the form of the African American crime film. Few youth films before the '90s had chronicled the lives of African American youth, or had integrated them as characters within the generally Caucasian confines of most teen settings. Those that did were usually nostalgic period pieces, like *The Learning Tree* (1969) and *Cooley High* (1975), which addressed issues of racism and social struggle from a reflective perspective, without directly confronting contemporary conditions.[27] By the '90s, especially after the provocative portrait of racial tensions offered by Spike Lee's 1989 film *Do the Right Thing* (which features, but does not concentrate on, many young characters), other African American filmmakers began addressing race issues in their films, and more often than not, the films that were about youth essayed their plight within violent urban conditions. Ed Guerrero went so far as to claim that the racial discourse of *Do the Right Thing* was taken up in these youth films, beginning with *Boyz N the Hood* in 1991.[28] Significant as well were the age and race of the makers of many of these films, since most were under 30 and most were African American themselves, and thus very much in touch with the experiences they were depicting. This marked another departure for youth cinema, since for the first time young adult filmmakers began controlling their own images, a trend that would be carried over immediately in the early-'90s films about (predominantly white) 20-something Generation X characters.

There were exceptions to the association of African American youth with violence, such as the films of Kid and Play (the *House Party* series and *Class Act*), and relatively few of the young characters in the emerging crime films were violent themselves (often only one character within a group of teens is the violent one). Nonetheless, a certain trend developed in which African American youth were shown in films fighting for their lives, under the hegemony of a racist legal and political system, under difficult family and class conditions, and under the influence of the media that were rapidly codifying the image of young black "gangstas" through certain rap music acts. This presented a set of tricky issues to the films that portrayed urban African American youth, for many wanted to reveal the long-suppressed conditions of their characters' real-life equivalents, but many also appealed to a notion of criminality as a way of life, despite all of these films' explicit messages that crime does not pay. Jacquie Jones called these films "homeboy cinema," and voiced a common concern about their alliance with current cinematic and social conventions:

Sadly, the monolith of imagery spawned by the current interest in Black film may threaten the viability of other types of mainstream Black cinematic expression. And it promises to codify a range of behaviors as uncharacteristic of the Black experience as those represented in films made by whites (though they may be executed with a greater degree of truth and sensibility). Films that attempt to delve more deeply into any cultural actuality not directly associated with teenagers or crime have no better chance of being widely distributed today than they did five years ago.[29]

Jones made her comments in 1991 just as the African American youth crime film was developing, and her last point, while perhaps true then, has fortunately been challenged by the wide release of films such as *Waiting to Exhale* (1996), *Soul Food* (1997), *The Best Man* (1999), and *The Brothers* (2001). Nonetheless, her cultural concerns were shared by many critics of the time and bear emphasizing for their importance to racial representations. As Jones goes on to conclude, the film industry's "wholesale investment in films that explore only ghettoes and male youth ignores the existence of a Black community beyond these narrow confines—inclusive of women as valuable participants—as well as films that refuse to cater to these prescriptions."[30]

This argument may help explain the gradual, and now apparently certain, demise of the African American youth crime film. More diverse and less ghettoized representations of African Americans began reaching the screen by the mid-'90s, and the repetitive themes—and problematics—of the youth crime film had become apparent. The youth film market had also become saturated with these films, and further, less violent portraits of African American youth began appearing by the mid-'90s on a variety of television programs, as well as in the popular documentary *Hoop Dreams* (1994), and in spoofs of the "hood" films (*Friday, High School High,* and the well-titled *Don't Be a Menace to South Central While Drinking Your Juice in the Hood*). The African American youth crime film may have ended, appropriately enough, with Spike Lee's film *Clockers* in 1995. Similar to the only other African American crime film of that year, *New Jersey Drive* (for which Spike Lee was executive producer), *Clockers* was well received by critics but not by audiences.[31]

As significant as these films were in exposing audiences to (male) African American youth culture and questioning the current state of race relations in the nation, from a generic perspective these films were instrumental in reviving critical and financial legitimacy for all youth films, which had been declining throughout the late '80s. The African American youth film was the dominant style of American youth film from 1991 until 1995, when a wider range of youth films began to again appear. Further, for as much as these films addressed violence among youth, they not only always condemned it within their narratives, but seemed to have a cross-generic influence in raising critical issues about youth conditions, as in many of the '90s delinquency films detailed in this chapter, and in school and love/sex films as well. Whether or not the African American youth crime drama of the early '90s was a mere industry fad is moot, although I argue that the more unsettling and direct representations of youth conditions presented in these films have had and will continue to have a lasting influence on the cinematic depiction of youth, if only in terms of questioning their cultural context, specifically issues of race, class, and morality.

Most chronicles of the '90s African American youth crime film would begin with John Singleton's massively influential *Boyz N the Hood* in 1991, yet four other relevant films appeared just before *Boyz*. In *Up Against the Wall* (1991) an African American youth from the city transfers to a school in a wealthy white suburb where he unsuspectingly becomes a drug-runner for his older brother. The film was directed by erstwhile blaxploitation star Ron O'Neal and debuted three months before *Boyz N the Hood,* going virtually unseen, even though in many ways it had already set the tone for the Singleton film and others like it that would follow. The teen protagonist vocally questions race and class problems in the Black community, and further criticizes his father, from whom he'd been estranged since birth, for not caring more about him and his mother. All of the African American crime films of the '90s directly or implicitly raised the same issues.

Two other influential films that opened just before *Boyz* but are not entirely appropriate in this context were *New Jack City* (1991) and *Hangin' with the Homeboys* (1991), since most of the characters in these films are in their 20s. However, they are worth mentioning as examples of the emerging style. The first film was made by young African American director Mario Van Peebles and stars rapper Ice T and former teen actor Judd Nelson in a relatively action-packed story about a drug lord and the law enforcers who bring him down; it was an unexpected success at the box office, and perhaps to the chagrin of makers of youth-themed films that followed, it set a high expectation of violence for films about urban problems. The second film, which had its release delayed and overshadowed by *Boyz,* was less violent and, perhaps consequentially, less visible, but it gained some popularity nonetheless. *Hangin'* is about four friends, two African Americans and two Latinos, who spend a rowdy night together, revealing their various insecurities and racial prejudices as they encounter how white prejudice is used against them. These characters do not resort to the violence of other characters in similar films that would follow—their run-in with the police is for jumping turnstiles—yet their rebellion and confrontation with social conditions remain clear.

Straight Out of Brooklyn (1991) opened just weeks before *Boyz,* but did not receive wide distribution until after the success of the later film. Independently shot by 19-year-old filmmaker Matty Rich, the film is a sensitive portrait of three black teenagers from a housing project in Brooklyn, focusing on Dennis (Lawrence Gilliard Jr.) and his troubled family.[32] Dennis is witness to his father's drunken abuse of his mother, which is fueled by his frustration at their impoverished lifestyle. He convinces his friends that they need to take their destiny into their own hands, and they can begin by robbing a local drug-runner, although his girlfriend warns him against turning to a life of crime after he tells her of his plans to make it big by moving to Manhattan. After Dennis and his friends pull off the robbery, he tries to give the cash to his parents, which only leads to a fight in which his mother is accidentally but seriously injured. The jarring conclusion features Dennis and his sister watching their mother die in a hospital as their father is meanwhile gunned down by the robbed drug dealer.

Straight Out of Brooklyn is gritty and unrelenting in not romanticizing the rough lives of its characters. Part of this is owing to the film's low-budget production values and Rich's vérité technique, yet its greater potency lies in its depiction of these genuinely human characters who desire a better life than their social confines can provide. The film is able to convey the poignancy of their situation without being didactic, and the teens in the film come across as young men who are old enough to know that they can change their lives but not wise enough to know how. The politics of the film draw on the economic connection between race and class while still considering the individual's role in that connection: Dennis's consoling parents are a reminder to him that their struggle grows out of their lack of opportunities for better jobs due to racist employment conditions, but also due to their personal failings, such as his father's alcoholism and his mother's tolerance of being beaten (at one point she is denied a job because she looks so battered). Dennis envisions the better life he could have just a few miles away, if only he could move out of the housing projects that seem to ensure an ongoing cycle of poverty, yet he disregards his girlfriend's idea of college for a more immediate, demonstrative means of breaking that cycle. In the end, we see that Dennis is thinking not only of himself; he is trying to save his whole family, a task that is far larger than any teen can handle. Dennis robs a drug dealer because he be-

In *Boyz N the Hood* (1991), Cuba Gooding Jr. plays Tre, a proud African American teen trying to balance typical coming-of-age rituals with the violent confusion of the Los Angeles milieu around him.

lieves that the act is actually not criminal itself; however, by aligning himself with such criminality, he has destroyed the family that he so desperately wanted to preserve and support, and is likely to face a much worse life for it.

When *Boyz N the Hood* opened in the summer of 1991, the film received an unfortunate amount of negative publicity due to fights that broke out at a small number of theaters. (*New Jack City,* which had opened a few months earlier, also became associated with a handful of criminal incidents that erupted at its screenings.[33]) The violence that occurred during and after the film's showing in some venues—and which was exaggerated by the media—seemed to arise from the narrative's tense depiction of harrowing urban conditions, and more specifically, from the fresh frustration with which the film examined those conditions.[34] *Boyz* was not just about life on mean streets, but about the hopes of young African Americans to avoid the tragedies of those mean streets and enjoy life on their own terms.

The story opens with young Tre (Cuba Gooding Jr.), the son of a strong-willed mother, in his rebellious years as a preteen, and then moves on to his teen years spent living with his equally strong-willed father, Furious (Larry Fishburne). Director Singleton, as Jack Mathews claimed,

> deals with a lot of issues here: the permanence of psychological damage on children living with unchecked violence; the degrading attitude of many black males toward women; the economic opportunism of people from outside the neighborhood; and the frustration of many blacks toward black cops in their community. But the point he drives home hardest is the need for more African American men to take responsibility for raising their sons, to give them direction and make them accountable for their lives.[35]

This message of paternal responsibility is made clearest through Furious's straightforward lectures to his son about standing up to oppression and overcoming adversity, and by the time Tre is a teen, he has become one of the most respected kids in his community. He stands out among his group of friends, particularly the heavy drinker and dope dealer Doughboy (Ice Cube), who went to juvenile prison for killing an older youth, and has now returned home, disinterested in finding a job or going back to school. Tre and his pals have the same interests as other guys their age—cars, parties, and girls—and for much of the film these are their sole pursuits. Tre has a girlfriend in Brandi (Nia Long), who has been resisting his requests for sex because she doesn't think it is worth the risks involved, and Tre reluctantly respects her. Brandi wants to go to college after high school and would like Tre to come with her, so Tre must decide between his hanging-out lifestyle in South Central Los Angeles and the prospect of college in Georgia with Brandi.

This decision becomes secondary to a more central conflict in which Tre and his friends find themselves the target of a small black gang, who eventually murder Doughboy's brother, aspiring football player and teen father Ricky (Morris Chestnut). This prompts Tre and Doughboy into retaliatory action, although Tre becomes racked by his conscience and backs out before the climactic gunning down of the rival gang, which is carried out by Doughboy. The film ends with the forlorn Tre realizing that he needs to leave his hardened neighborhood as Doughboy wonders whether his own death will be next; a closing title tells us that Tre did indeed go on to college with Brandi, and Doughboy was murdered just weeks later. Despite this sobering ending, the climax can still be seen as a testament to vengeance, and the film's depiction of Tre as wiser than such behavior is effectively undermined by Doughboy's tough hero status and off-screen demise.

Yet *Boyz* is not about moral retribution as much as it is about the struggle for righteous survival; an opening title alerts us to the statistic that 1 in 21 black men is murdered, setting the tone for the film's examination of the sad and senseless violence that is part of the lives of certain urban African Americans. This is what made the film so provocative and influential at the time of its release, and from a generic perspective, such a story was already well suited to drama. *Boyz* helped establish an altogether new image of youth in American cinema—the young black warrior-survivor—and while none of the films that featured this new role achieved the same success, the image would be pervasive and profound in many other films over the next four years. Paula Massood, in comparing *Boyz* to Allen and Albert Hughes's later film *Menace II Society,* argues that the first film "lays the groundwork and maps the route for the narrative and signifying systems which the Hugheses then use in a shorthand manner."[36] I would expand this point to include essentially all of the African American youth crime films that followed *Boyz*.

Juice (1992) owes much as well to *Straight Out of Brooklyn* in its story of four black youth from Harlem who think they can better their lives by robbing a store. (Despite the fact that only two similar films had appeared before, by the time of *Juice*'s release many critics called it formulaic.) Yet where *Brooklyn* symbolized its robbery as a specious way out of poverty, the robbery in *Juice* becomes the teens' violent passage to manhood, since none of them really need the little bit of cash the robbery nets. The robbery goes wrong when one of them kills the store owner and then a member of the group, leading to a confrontation between two surviving members. When the characters should be more concerned about the effects of their actions on their families, if not their community, they are focused on a macho showdown, for which Ed Guerrero criticized the film, since it "tends to reduce pressing collective issues to the drama of individual weaknesses and victimization."[37]

Menace II Society was the only film in this category to appear in 1993, and it remained much a part of the new style, being set in the Watts neighborhood of L.A. and chronicling the downfall of a young African American criminal.[38] Tyrin Turner plays the not-so-subtly named Caine, who has just graduated from high school when his jumpy friend O-Dog (Larenz Tate) fatally shoots a Korean store owner and his wife after they suspect the teens of shoplifting. O-Dog retrieves the surveillance camera tape of the incident and plays it for friends, boasting of his brute toughness, while Caine is less inclined to celebrate the event and more worried about the fallout from rival gangs in the area. As it turns out, a gang shoots Caine and kills one of his cousins, prompting him and O-Dog to seek vengeance. Their plans are thwarted when Caine's desire for upward mobility as a drug dealer leads to his arrest for car theft, and the police, suspecting him of being involved in the store murders, beat him so badly he lands in the hospital. Caine's girlfriend Ronnie (Jada Pinkett) tries to convince him to move with her to Georgia, and Caine decides to go, at least after another girl sends her cousin to harass him for impregnating and then abandoning her, whereupon Caine beats him. Just before Caine and Ronnie leave, the girl's cousin guns down Caine in front of Ronnie.

Menace has strikingly similar concerns (and plot points) as the previous films, and yet the film's youthful twin directors, Allen and Albert Hughes, imbue the story with a less preachy style than *Boyz* and a more emotional core than *Juice*.[39] In flashback sequences, we see how Caine's violence was instilled in him as a child by his ruthless drug-running father, who casually killed a man in front of his son (and, Caine tells us in voiceover, killed many more). His heroin-addicted mother was of little help, and both parents died from their abuses before Caine reached his teen years. The story presents Caine's background against a certain historical argument, as Peter Rainer points out: "The cyclical nature of Caine's story is just part of a larger story; the movie is saying that miseries move down the generations, just as the Watts riots of '65 (which we see in newsreel footage) are replayed in '92."[40]

After his father's death, Caine finds a mentor in another father-figure criminal, Pernell (Glenn Plummer), who is himself taken away to prison. Now living with his religious but ignorable grandparents, Caine dodges every message sent his way about responsibility and direction. As in *Juice,* there is an association of masculinity with violence in *Menace,* to which Paula Massood speaks: "In a film in which relationships among men are predicated on violence, it is no coincidence that Caine's father and Pernell influence Caine in the most sustaining ways."[41] The lone authority figure Caine will listen to is his former teacher Mr. Butler (Charles S. Dutton), who warns him of the trouble awaiting him if he doesn't change. Butler and his son try to convince Caine to move with them to Kansas, only their offers and lessons evaporate in Caine's misguided impatience to be as tough as—and survive longer than—his father.

And still Caine shows glimmers of wanting to reform, of wanting to break out of the bleak destiny of O-Dog and his friends and turn to Ronnie for his salvation. Pernell, who fathered a child with Ronnie, tells him from jail to take off with his former girlfriend and find a better life for all of them, but Caine's pride and fear of accountability for his crimes and misdemeanors continue to erupt in violent outbursts. The Hughes brothers also show how the largely white legal system maintains the cycle of murder among urban ethnic youth, especially when the brutalizing police drop off the battered Caine on a rival gang's turf, assuming the gang will finish their abuse and kill him. Yet the film is not dourly simplifying the social crisis it presents; David Denby points out:

> [*Menace*] doesn't lay off the problems on somebody else; it doesn't say that whitey is to blame for everything, or that there's no way out. There *are* ways out; the tragedy is that people aren't always ready or able to take them.[42]

Whether Caine is unready or unable to reform, he lacks the remorse and determination to do so, and because one girl's dedication will also not be enough to make him reform, he pays with his life, an equation that the film implies is the inevitable outcome of a complex social machinery. The implications of this equation for youth trying to escape it are starkly daunting.

Above the Rim (1994) combines the style and commentary of the African American youth crime film with a typical sports drama in its story of a promising high school basketball player from Harlem who is lured into a more corrupt world by a young local crime lord. The tension and occasional brutality of previous crime films are softened by the film's sentimental sports clichés, but a clear moral lesson about crime is not absent: the protagonist's ascent to a successful sports career is obviously marred by his temptations to run with the wrong element, which he does out of doubt that his career will ever take off, even though by the end he is playing for championship-bound Georgetown. The only problem with this, from a real-world perspective, is how very few young men, black or white, will ever realize professional athletic success, and how much more accessible is the criminal lifestyle, something that was hinted at in the *Hoop Dreams* documentary later that same year.[43]

Fresh (1994) returns to a rather direct depiction of the criminal lifestyle among African American youth, only this time the main character is a mere 12-year-old who has been hardened by his days on Brooklyn streets running drugs for a local dealer. Again the narrative emphasis is not only on the destructive nature of crime, but on the longing for familial unity that has been lost in the wake of degenerative social conditions. The film avoids the didactic approach of most earlier films, letting its rhetoric come across in the title character's tacit determination to break out of his imminent criminal lifestyle by turning its worst elements in on themselves. *Fresh* calls attention to at least two crucial factors in the representation of troubled urban youth: their strength lies in their insight and compassion and not their displays of ferocious bluster, and youth must come to realize this at strikingly younger ages—before they are even teenagers—or they may not live through their teen years.

With *New Jersey Drive* and *Clockers* in 1995, the African American youth crime drama apparently came to an end. By then the moral lessons of these films had become worn, and the characters familiar, though both these films remain stylish and well developed. *Drive* focuses on a Newark 17-year-old who hangs out with friends, stealing cars, joyriding, and drinking beer. He is ultimately one of the least cognizant protagonists of all these films, since he seems to have little moral comprehension of his acts, and continues to expose himself to trouble for little apparent gain. One by one his friends are killed by police, thereby exposing the most distinctive quality of the narrative, since the teens' deaths are not at the hands of other criminals, but the law. Yet this leaves a large fault in the film: given that the protagonist lacks understanding, and that the enemy is the law, too much of his criminal activity appears fun, if not forgivable. Despite the deaths of his friends, his sullen survival leaves an image of youth delinquency that is indifferent to the problems it creates.

Spike Lee followed up producing *New Jersey Drive* by directing the slightly similar cops-versus-youth film *Clockers*. Rather than cars, here the criminal object is drugs; and rather than corrupt cops, here the "enemy" is more ambiguous. Strike (Mekhi Phifer) is a teenage "clocker," a hustler of crack, who has both the Brooklyn cops and the community against him. His supplier is an unassuming gangster named Rodney (Delroy Lindo) who, as a test of Strike's reliability, asks him to murder a local troublemaker. The twist in this story is that Strike's older brother Victor (Isaiah Washington) turns himself in for the murder, even though he has no criminal connections and is a respectable family man. The cops don't believe Victor and continue to pressure Strike, whose mounting stomach problems are a sign that the stress of his lifestyle is getting to him. Like all of the other drug-running black youth in these films, Strike never ingests what he deals, and he warns his fatherless 12-year-old protégé Tyrone (Pee Wee Love) against ever taking the drugs, even as he's molding him into a pusher. After the police arrest Rodney under suspicion of murder, he orders a hit on Strike—only the hit man is gunned down by Tyrone with Strike's gun. In another twist, Strike and Victor's mother comes forth to confess that Victor is indeed the killer, and one of the nicer cops who has been following Strike takes him to a train so that he can get out of the city and get on with a new life.

Despite Strike's centrality to the story, the plot spends much time on the white investigating detectives (Harvey Keitel and John Turturro), most likely due to the actors' star presence, but also to shift attention away from Strike's culpability in his gangster lifestyle. While Spike Lee is known for exploring issues of racism in his films, here race relations are less suspect. Strike is like all of the other hardened heroes of these films; he owns his decisions and cannot blame them on the system. However, he actually shows evidence that he can't handle the gangster lifestyle, and unlike many other similar protagonists, he gets out of town in the end, despite his past transgressions. This indicates a certain optimism on the part of Lee that may have ironically signaled the further resolution of tensions within African American crime films, which thus made audiences lose interest in them. James Berardinelli commented on this change in the story's resolution compared to other films in the subgenre:

> Productions like *Boyz N the Hood* and *Menace II Society* deliver their final blow through bloodshed. While Lee doesn't shy away from violence, his methods are less straightforward. Like 1994's *Fresh, Clockers* uses unexpected narrative turns to accentuate the themes of lost innocence and uncultivated potential, and affirms that tragic melodrama is not a prerequisite for emotional impact.[44]

The tragic melodrama of the film actually arises from its unusual imaging of family relations. For all of Strike's sense of independence (he lives alone on money from his dealing), he has a nefarious, if generically inevitable, surrogate father in Rodney, and yet he looks toward Tyrone as a surrogate son. This hints at not only Strike's longing for familial unity—which is even further strained after his brother goes to jail—but his capacity to accept parental responsibility. Of course, his moral standards are still very much in question: no sooner does he share his love of toy trains with Tyrone than he's teaching him about running drugs. Then, after Tyrone saves his own surrogate father's life, Strike must face his lack of parental presence as Tyrone is taken away to jail, feeling a sense of failure as a father where previous protagonists felt their failures as sons.

Otherwise, *Clockers* provides even more of the same clear messages as the past films, and continues the trend in alleviating the moral indiscretions of its protagonist by displacing the most violent acts onto another character. The rules to be learned from the African American youth crime films were plainly clear by this point: that broken families cannot be unified by crime; that crime is not lucrative, at least not for long; that crimes perpetrated against other blacks only reinforce the racist social system; and that youth do not have the moral grasp to appreciate the repercussions of their crimes, even though they may gain it if they stay criminal long enough. The eventual outcome of a crime-based life, as Hollywood has told audiences for years, is prison or death, unless the character has the enlightenment to leave town. Those who stay in the hood (as in *Straight Out of Brooklyn, Juice,* and *Fresh*) do so in the face of tragedy, with their own futures in great doubt. This cycle of films encouraged young black men to find alternatives to crime, their action-violence notwithstanding, and did not deny race as a factor in the difficulties their young characters face. Rather, these films all suggested that the greatest menace is the city itself, where crime, racism, and death are pervasive and constant. Those who survive must find a way out of the hood, which is their best way out of trouble.

Since all of these films focus on young men, some mention must be made of how these films handle, or fail to handle, images of young women. As Jacquie Jones previously stated, women in these films are largely disenfranchised and not treated as valuable participants in their stories. While a certain level of respect is still reserved for the protagonists' mothers, their girlfriends and sisters are clearly kept as secondary elements within the story, even when they may be integral to the characters' motivation, as in *Boys N the Hood, Straight Out of Brooklyn, Juice, Menace II Society, Fresh,* and *New Jersey Drive*. Further, many of the secondary male characters treat their female counterparts with contempt and ridicule; the main male characters show more consideration, but do little to address or change the sexist attitudes of their friends.[45]

As discussed in the tough girl section, there is a conspicuous absence of African American girls in youth films that deal with issues of delinquency, or even racism, at least apart from male-centered narratives, despite the fact that in reality these issues are often just as relevant to the lives of many black females. The one notable film that does portray African American girls confronting some of these issues, *Just Another Girl on the I.R.T.,* does not make up for the paucity of female-centered films, or more so, for the inadequate ways they are portrayed in films about boys. One reason for this absence may well be a perceived lack of "action" in female depictions; after all, the selling points of many of the male films are crime and violence, and to promote the image of sympathetic criminal women would be to bring up a host of threats to the patriarchal media (*Thelma and Louise* did this with its quasiviolent characters in 1991). This lack of representation may also occur simply because few filmmakers feel confident enough to portray the young African American female experience, and on a larger scale, it may be due to the continued marginalization of African American women within the film industry.[46] Even *Mi Vida Loca*'s examination of the lives of Latina tough girls was directed by a Caucasian woman, yet there remains no equivalent in African American roles. Given the apparent decline in filmmakers' interest in representing racial and criminal problems among youth, this may remain the case for a while, although given the recently increasing popularity of tough girl films, this situation could change.

CONCLUSION

The complex and varied images of youth presented in these delinquency films evinces the spectrum of character concerns, behaviors, and types that the film industry has employed in examining the way young people express their most tormented anxieties and enjoy their most liberatory outlets. Unlike the school film, more than five character types are visible in the delinquency subgenre—at least one for every style of delinquency—and even within each style the motivations and actions of teen characters often cover a wide range. The increasing articulation of anger by youth in the '90s was revealing, for fewer youth films showed teens engaging in harmless deviance than in the '80s, while the newer films that attempted to connect youth delinquency to larger social conditions appeared to be implicating so many sources of unrest—parents, school, law, race, class, gender, drugs, television, music, capitalism—that the examinations of these potent forces were diluted. The open evaluation of youth rebellion that has been a hallmark of juvenile delinquency films for generations may simply be moving toward more implicit arguments, yet this evaluation also seems to be embodying greater ambivalence, unable to offer either clear critiques or celebratory assurances. These films ultimately seem to understand why youth rebel, but most of them conclude that such rebellion is an inevitable necessity, for both the teens who wreak it as they confront adulthood and the adults who endure it as they try to comprehend constantly changing youth.

4 THE YOUTH HORROR FILM
Slashers and the Supernatural

All of you are very pretty. I love you. Takes a lot of love for a person to do this. You know you want it. You'll love it.

—KILLER TO HIS LAST FEMALE VICTIMS IN *Slumber Party Massacre*

Grown-ups think it's funny to be scared.

—SOON-TO-BE-KILLED TEENAGER TO LITTLE GIRL IN *Friday the 13th Part 6: Jason Lives*

Where do all these movies come from anyway? How do we know Spielberg, Lucas, Sonnenfeld, Emmerich haven't been visited by aliens?

—SUSPICIOUS STUDENT TO FRIEND IN *The Faculty*

Of all the subgenres in this study, youth horror has been—perhaps appropriately—the most enigmatic. It enjoyed massive financial success and public popularity in the late '70s and early '80s: in 1981, *Variety* claimed that "slasher" films (many of which featured teens) accounted for 60 percent of all U.S. releases that year, and 25 of the 50 top-grossing films of that year were "slashers" as well.[1] Given this voluminous and lucrative output of horror films at the time, and considering how many of them were about teenagers, certain popular beliefs and assumptions emerged: the youth horror film was excessively violent and gory; the vast majority of its violence was perpetrated against female characters; characters engaging in sexual activities paid for their indiscretions by being killed. Like all clichés, these perceptions were partially based in fact, since a number of youth horror films seemed to follow predictable formulas and motifs.

Nonetheless, many teen horror films since 1980 have deliberately challenged the structure and consistency of the subgenre, and the subgenre itself has gone through varying cycles of popularity, style, and content. The true consistency in virtually all of the teen horror films of the past generation has been their concentration on youthful fears of being different, becoming sexual, and confronting adult responsibilities—fears that the horror film is ideally suited to examine (at least on a metaphorical level), and which themselves may not have changed much in the past few generations. These fears take on a strikingly wide variety of manifestations—there are more types of horror movie "killers" than varieties of teen characters themselves—and are thus confronted in a number of ways, making the youth horror film far more complex and significant in its representations of young people than popular belief would generally allow.

HISTORICAL CONTEXT OF THE YOUTH HORROR SUBGENRE

Perhaps the most peculiar feature of the 1980s teen horror film was its excess, at least compared to its predecessors, of sex and violence. There had been few horror films about youth before the late '70s, although each had indeed been pushing the boundaries of acceptable excess: the violence of *I Was a Teenage Werewolf* in 1957 and *The Blob* in 1958 may have been shocking then, but was relatively tame compared to *Teenage Strangler* in 1964, which in turn was far less gory than 1976's *Carrie,* a film that became a literal bloodbath and essentially came to represent the starting point of contemporary youth horror films. In the wider horror genre, the gorefests of directors like Herschell Gordon Lewis and George Romero had been gaining mild attention in an era of otherwise declining cinematic attendance in the United States, and the overwhelming popularity of *The Exorcist* in 1973 further demonstrated two phenomena of the genre that would be integral to its greater success in the late 1970s: audience acceptance of and fascination with morbid gore, and the use of a young character as the victim of (and in this case also the perpetrator of) inexplicable terror.

Carrie capitalized on these two phenomena, only now the protagonist was a teenage girl facing adulthood, as evidenced most dramatically by the onset of her first menstrual period. *Carrie* was thus able to explore classic youth fears of adult transformation, although its title character also had the further "dilemmas" of telekinetic powers and a zealously religious mother. In the film's remarkable climax, Carrie uses her powers to unleash years of pent-up aggression at her high school tormentors—who have gone to great extremes in humiliating the shy girl by dumping a bucket of pig's blood on her at the prom—and at her mother, whom she "crucifies" with knives.[2] *Carrie,* based on a Stephen King novel, set a high standard in the teen horror subgenre for character development as well as overall graphic violence. Unfortunately, most of the films that followed in the subgenre minimized the former and amplified the latter.

A notoriously nervy 1974 horror film called *The Texas Chainsaw Massacre* began to have a clear influence on certain filmmakers over the rest of the decade. The film featured a family of psychos whose two sons stalk and murder four young victims, while a fifth barely manages to escape the carnage. As Carol Clover notes in her perceptive study, *Men, Women, and Chainsaws: Gender in the Modern Horror Film* (1992), the film was instrumental in codifying what would become the classical practice of "slasher" films in the late '70s: a seemingly indestructible killer tracks down and brutally murders a number of helpless young victims, sparing the last one, who is (according to Clover) always female, a character type she dubs the "Final Girl."[3] Coupled with the success of *Carrie* and *The Exorcist, The Texas Chainsaw Massacre* heralded a new era in Hollywood, not only for the graphic depiction of youths being brutally murdered by mysterious forces—hence the "slasher" moniker—but for low-budget films that became so successful they provided an industrial antidote to the blockbusters emerging at the time (e.g., *Jaws* [1975], *Star Wars* and *Saturday Night Fever* [both 1977], *Superman* and *Grease* [both 1978]—all of which were largely aimed at a young audience).[4]

The film that confirmed the new era of youth-oriented horror was John Carpenter's *Halloween* in 1978. The film earned at least 60 times its production costs, a massive profit ratio for an independent "exploitation" film.[5] With *Halloween* the teen die was cast: a mysterious figure stalks and kills four teens, all of whom are sexually active, while a fifth escapes with her life, ostensibly since she is a virgin. *Halloween* thus added an explicit sexual dimension to the formula (*Texas Chainsaw Massacre* and plenty of previous horror films offered copious, yet often implicit, sexual issues), and further evacuated the expansive subgenre of the character development seen in *Carrie.* Much time in *Halloween* was spent on lengthy creepy silences and suspenseful pauses in action that did not provide much background on the featured characters other than their ages, their respective senses of hedonism or puritanism (the four who are murdered have or are planning to have sex, and the survivor is dutifully babysitting), and their ignorance to the danger at hand (the babysitter continually tells her charges that they're only imagining the "bogeyman" they see outside). What the film did provide was a rousing time for its audience, as well as a paradigm for the image of most youth in the horror films of the next few years.

Thus ensued the onslaught: *Halloween* was followed in 1980 by two Canadian films that featured the now-typecast Jamie Lee Curtis (the babysitter in *Halloween*), *Prom Night* and *Terror Train,* in which a killer systematically eliminates high school and college students, respectively, and *Friday the 13th,* in which teenagers at a summer camp are stalked and killed by a dead boy's mother. The killers in all three films were avenging previous abuses or neglect inflicted by past teens, a prominent motive that would characterize most future villains; the youth in all of these films also remained rather firmly divided between the sinners and the sinless, with death coming to those of lesser moral stature. In this way, the teen horror subgenre that would thrive in the '80s relied upon classical notions of misfortune falling upon transgressors of purity, only now such "transgressions" as premarital sex and youthful hedonism were resulting not in punishment by social institutions like parents, teachers, or the law, but in death at the hands of a greater evil.

By 1981, as previously mentioned, a cycle of "slasher" films was firmly established in the American cinema, and at least six such films that year concentrated on teenage characters (many more were about older characters). Proof of the "slasher" as an emergent category of the teen horror subgenre also came that year in the form of *Halloween* and *Friday the 13th* beginning their franchises with sequels, and a parody called *Student Bodies* that easily referenced the many slasher films of the previous few years.[6] The image of contemporary youth presented by these 1981 horror films was facile and incomplete at best, but it was undoubtedly a prominent image compared to other subgenres (I locate only 14 other nonhorror youth films that year, most of which are obscure), and it forms a strong starting point for the current study.

TRENDS IN THE SUBGENRE

The slasher film, particularly its teen variety, was already showing signs of lost prominence by 1982, and by 1983 only three youth films featured the slasher/gore formula of past years. Then in 1984 the teen horror subgenre found new momentum with the release of *A Nightmare On Elm Street,* a successful and somewhat refreshing take on the slasher scenario. The number of teen horror films released in 1985 doubled over the previous year, as a new industrial practice was emerging: the release of low-budget horror films straight to the video rental market, whereby youth who were otherwise barred from seeing the R-rated films alone in theaters were now able to watch the frightfests at home. The majority of teen horror films released from 1986 to 1990 all had scant, if any, theatrical releases, but many gained their profits in the growing video trade. In fact, there were more teen horror films released in these five years than in the more discussed 1977–81 span.

The slasher scenario itself remained a dominant style of the subgenre in the late '80s, but a wider variety of youth horror had been appearing: supernatural and occult stories, vampire and zombie movies, and a plot that seemed to hark back to postwar society's reactionary fears of 1950s youth: the rock-and-roll horror parable. Sequels, which were often akin to remakes, became standard practice for any film that gained the slightest attention; the three most enduring franchises became *Halloween, Friday the 13th,* and *Nightmare* with at least seven versions of each, and lesser franchises emerged with *Slumber Party Massacre* (1982; a trilogy by 1990), *Sleepaway Camp* (1983; a trilogy by 1989), *Children of the Corn* (1984; seven versions by 2001), *Return of the Living Dead* (1985; a trilogy by 1993), and the Canadian releases of three *Prom Night* sequels (1987; four versions altogether by 1992).

After the industry's run of youth horror films on the video market in the late '80s, conditions changed: very few teen slasher movies were released after 1990, and even fewer new youth horror films released since 1990 have had more than one sequel. The plots of many films shifted focus notably toward more sophisticated narratives dealing with social issues (e.g., *The People Under the Stairs* [1991], *Society* [1991], *Tales from the Hood* [1995], and *Apt Pupil* [1998]), and the overall output of youth horror films declined precipitously (the combined releases of 1993–96 were fewer than the 24 youth horror films released in 1988 alone). However, the unexpected success of the revisionist *Scream* in 1996, along with *Scream* screenwriter Kevin Williamson's similar film *I Know What You Did Last Summer* and then the sequels to these films, revitalized the subgenre in the late 1990s. By 2000, films like *Scary Movie* and the impressively sardonic *Cherry Falls*—which features the twist of a psycho killer targeting teenage virgins—were both exploiting and satirizing the subgenre's most visible elements.

As in other youth subgenres, the question of generic cycles and evolution is germane to understanding the changing representations of youth within the teen horror subgenre. If the sheer industrial exploitation of the video market in the late '80s can explain the uprising of youth horror films at the time, what explains its popularity in the late '70s before video and its decline in the early '90s when video was still thriving? Perhaps the novelty and extremity of violence in the late '70s films helps explain their success, as special effects artists were making their reputations by developing ever more gruesome gore and the MPAA was allowing more gratuitous graphic violence to pass for an R rating, fulfilling audiences' fascination with excess. The late '70s were also characterized as an era of greater consumption by Americans, and with the expansion of malls and multiplex theaters within them, studios must have seen the advantage of tapping into social tensions of the time, with the literal consumption of people by mysterious forces becoming a metaphor for the excess consumption of goods by the new yuppie generation. For youth, moral lessons about consumption were becoming ever more conspicuous in horror films about them—those who engaged in sex and drugs paid the price—a message that sublimating adults in the disco era must have felt compelled to drive home.

Yet by the early Reagan era, a new notion of American conservatism was sweeping the country, and horror films about wild youth were replaced by less metaphoric narratives about youth actually enjoying the pleasures of rebellion and sensuality; thus the teen sex film flourished in the early '80s (as detailed in the next chapter). Later, with public awareness of AIDS growing by the late '80s and a marked shift in the teen sex film from promiscuity to romance, the youth horror film again seemed to capitalize on otherwise classic youth fears of sexuality and adulthood. Perhaps the relative drought of teen horror films by the early '90s was only indicative of the general decline in all teen film output at the time; perhaps the new realism of youth crime films in the early '90s made the supposed terrors of the supernatural seem less frightening than real social conditions; perhaps the subgenre simply ran out of new ideas and, given the theatrical failure of virtually all youth horror films after 1988 (*A Nightmare on Elm Street 4: The Dream Master* that year was the subgenre's last "hit" until *Scream* eight years later), studios concentrated on more reliable products.[7] In any case, the roles of youth in these films remains intriguing, if only as an indicator of their development within a subgenre that initially afforded them a minimal sense of identity: indeed, the youth horror film may have also declined because it relied on less intelligent, less sophisticated young characters, an image of themselves that recent youth have been rejecting (a case in point being the welcome reception of *Scream*, wherein the hero *and* villains are all smart, tough teens).

While other youth film subgenres have been occasionally taken up by previous scholars, the horror film has generated much literature over the years, and Carol Clover's *Men, Women, and Chainsaws* is the most integral to this study, even though little of the book addresses issues about youth. Clover's thesis is that recent horror films have problematized certain received notions about gender identification in cinema, if only because these films reveal "the possibility that male viewers are quite prepared to identify not just with screen females, but with screen females in the horror-film world, screen females in fear and pain."[8] I argue that the teens in most of these films are presented in images that are superficial and accessible enough for a dual gendered appreciation of their plight, especially since men and women are equally likely to be victims (other research on this follows), and even though more attention has been paid to female survivors, a role that Clover calls "the female victim-hero" in her coining of the phrase "Final Girl."

Clover's articulation of the Final Girl role in recent horror films sheds some light on the use of teens in the horror film system. As previously mentioned, Clover identifies the Final Girl character emerging in the 1974 film *Texas Chainsaw Massacre* and traces her role through horror films of the next 15 years, describing her as such: "She is the one who encounters the mutilated bodies of her friends and perceives the full extent of the preceding horror and of her own peril; who is chased, cornered, wounded; who we see scream, stagger, fall, rise, and scream again. She is abject terror personified."[9] She is thus the sole survivor of the terror wreaked in the film, and usually she is identified as the most morally "pure" of the group in which she travels, most often as a virgin. While Clover is wrong in her claim that since 1974 the survivor figure in slasher films has always been female, a point that calls attention to the skewed direction of her argument, she traces an important change in the image of the Final Girl after *Halloween* in 1978: the Final Girl begins to fight back, often killing the killer on her own. Another interesting characteristic of the Final Girl in the post-*Halloween* films is that she becomes less "feminine":

> Just as the killer is not fully masculine, she is not fully feminine—not, in any case, feminine in the ways of her friends. Her smartness, gravity, competence in mechanical and other practical matters, and sexual reluctance set her apart from the other girls and ally her, ironically, with the very boys she fears or

rejects, not to speak of the killer himself. Lest we miss the point, it is spelled out in her name: Stevie, Marti, Terry, Laurie, Stretch, Will, Joey, Max.[10]

As I describe in the analysis of these films that follows, the identification of the *Final Girl,* as well as the identification of other victims, killers, and parents, is indicative of a struggle with various notions not only of feminine empowerment but of youth empowerment and difference. Clover's observation of this character type is heavily focused to accommodate her central argument on gender identification, yet I use her term and its application throughout my analysis, and further develop the changing image of this role, especially in regards to the changing nature of the teen horror subgenre itself.

Another study of contemporary horror films worth mentioning is Vera Dika's *Games of Terror:* Halloween, Friday the 13th, *and the Films of the Stalker Cycle* (1990), in which she explicates various generic characteristics of nine slasher films from 1978 to 1981. Dika is otherwise so concerned with the theoretical establishment of a generic methodology (particularly in comparison to the Western) that she avoids discussing the role of youth in these films except in terms of their use as plot elements.[11] However, in the short section in which she discusses characters of the stalker cycle, she amplifies Clover's assertions about the Final Girl type.[12] Dika notes that "the heroine of these films is usually presented as a strong, practical character with a variety of well-developed skills," whose "ability to see and to use violence gives her the status of a valuable character."[13] She goes on to say that "in contrast with the killer's deformed and destructive qualities, the heroine and her friends are attractive, healthy, and lively."[14]

The most valuable observation that Dika makes about these young characters is that they form "an easily identifiable series of binary oppositions," which she goes on to label "valued/devalued," "strong/weak," and in terms of the youth community, "in-group/out-group"—labels that have clear applications within the films' narratives.[15] Dika also describes three oppositions that are more conceptual, if not subjective: "normal/abnormal," "life/death," and "controlled/uncontrolled."[16] What these oppositions foreground is both the very dialectical tension of horror film narratives—how will the conflicts set up by these oppositions of right and wrong be resolved (or will they)?—and the subsequently conflicting images of the young people within the films, who, as I will argue, tend to be firmly ensconced on the sides of good (in Dika's terminology, the valued, strong, in, normal, live, and controlled), or else they face terror for their transgressions. These "sides" parallel natural adolescent identity crises, which is another reason why horror films can be such rich, if obvious, texts for studying images of youth.

Robin Wood's work on horror films, while applied primarily to adult roles, is also integral to the imaging of youth. Wood describes a Freudian "return of the repressed" in his "Introduction to the American Horror Film," using rather arguable psychoanalytic theory to advance a nonetheless compelling taxonomy of horror movie repressions.[17] Wood points out four social repressions of sexuality in American culture—sexual energy, bisexuality, female sexuality, and the sexuality of children—the last of which Wood notes is a repression in the form of oppression, "from the denial of the infant's nature as sexual being to the veto on the expression of sexuality before marriage."[18] This is an important insight into the future operation of teen horror films: repressed or displaced sexual energy and anxiety are almost always the central sources of conflict in the films' narratives, and transgressions by premarital youth into the sexual realm are met by the oppressive terror of pathological, supernatural, or simply parental forces.

Wood goes on to describe another important horror concept, that of "the Other" that must either be annihilated by society or assimilated within it, listing such recognized others as women, the proletariat, ethnic groups, and finally children, about whom he says,

> When we have worked our way through all the other liberation movements, we may discover that children are the most oppressed section of the population (unfortunately, we cannot expect to liberate our children until we have successfully liberated ourselves). Most clearly of all, the "otherness" of children (see Freudian theories of infantile sexuality) is that which is repressed within ourselves, its expression therefore hated in others: what the previous generation repressed in us, and what we, in turn, repress in our children, seeking to mold them into replicas of ourselves, perpetuators of a discredited tradition.[19]

This observation about children can be applied to the imaging of youth in films in general, and certainly in the horror genre: the burgeoning preadult population that threatens to express the repressed, in the form of sexuality, crime, hedonism, and basic resistance to social norms, must be contained and controlled. When parents fail to do so and institutions such as schools and the law cannot make up for the parents' shortcomings, "higher" natural and supernatural forces are brought down upon the youthful others. In teen horror films, figures such as monsters and indestructible killers become parental surrogates demanding that youth conform to more repressive ways or else be destroyed, and since those who are already repressed tend to be the only teens who survive, the teen horror film formulation of "natural selection" hinges upon the social elimination of undesirables and the preservation of the obedient.

Another relevant article is "Content Trends in Contemporary Horror Films," in which Barry Sapolsky and Fred Molitor assemble a number of interesting content analyses that clearly indicate that women are more often "seen in fear" than men in slasher films of the 1980s (by an overwhelming margin) but that there is no significant difference between the number of male and female murder victims.[20] Sapolsky and Molitor thus go on to conclude that, contrary to popular perception, "females have not been found to be the primary victims in slasher films," and more arguably, they claim that "sex and violence are not frequently connected in slasher films."[21] The authors suggest that political/psychological reasons and faulty methodologies in other studies are explanations for why perceptions of the slasher film have become so extreme, at least in terms of female victimology and the "sex = death" link, although I will take them to task on this point. While their approach does not single out or examine issues particular to youth, my following analysis further questions the common assumptions made about these films.

One last review of youth in horror films is Jonathan Bernstein's chapter "Dead Teenagers" in *Pretty in Pink: The Golden Age of Teenage Movies* (1997). Bernstein makes a few relevant observations ignored by other studies, such as the idea that teens relate to horror films because they sense a familiarity with the monstrous (every teen is "morbid and miserable, paranoid and tragic, sick and scared").[22] Bernstein goes on to claim that slasher movie franchises of the '80s were more likely supported by young male aficionados of gore than by teens at large; the general decline of the slasher film may have come from teens' realization that "when an enemy cannot be killed, the victory of the last man or woman standing is an empty one."[23] Bernstein does promote the sex-and-death connection typical of most arguments, making the point that the virginal survivors of '80s slasher films represented "the *real* revenge of the nerds," but that "the amount of sadism and cynicism that went into these movies increased apace, swiftly sucking the fun out of them."[24] Bernstein says little else about the roles of teens in horror films and proceeds with lengthy plot synopses, missing many opportunities to explore critical issues about youth representation.[25]

What I borrow from Bernstein and have expanded upon (in the dissertation on which this book is based) is his further division of the horror subgenre into categories relevant to the types of terror involved. As in other youth subgenres, certain generic conventions of the youth horror film are often integrally linked to certain depictions of teens, connecting the actual image of the teen or teens being depicted more to the film's style than to its attempted messages about youth. Thus, I have divided the subgenre of teen horror according to the films' already established notions of larger horror subgenres. Bernstein catalogs the slasher, monster, and "modern" varieties of teen horror (subdividing monsters into vampires, werewolves, ghosts, and zombies, and only mentioning one example of the "modern").[26] I would add to his taxonomy the category of "supernatural" (wherein I incorporate occult and ghost stories), yet the limitations of space do not allow me to include analyses of other categories such as "sociopaths" (e.g., the *Children of the Corn* films [1984–2001], *Society* [1991], *Tales from the Hood* [1995], and *Strangeland* [1998]), nor the connection between zombies, mutants, and other monsters (e.g., the *Return of the Living Dead* films [1985–93], *The Lost Boys* [1987], *Ticks* [1993], and *Idle Hands* [1999]), nor the short-lived phenomenon of "rock and horror" films in the late '80s (e.g., *Trick or Treat* [1986], *The Gate* [1987], and *Black Roses* [1988]). Nonetheless, the slasher and supernatural categories do contain the most examples and have proven to be the most visible of the subgenre, and their examination here speaks to broader issues in the teen horror subgenre at large.

As in other youth subgenres, the image of teens as both social types and historical references is complex and evolutionary in horror films of the past generation. This subgenre offers a surprisingly understanding notion of the most excessive teen tensions through its exploitation of the more realistic displaced fears of all teens: difference, alienation, rejection, sexual and bodily transformations, aging, authority, and the unknown, especially the future in which adulthood may appear more terrifying than any bogeyman.

THE SLASHER/STALKER FILM

The youth horror film featuring a maniacal killer on the loose stalking victims one at a time has been the dominant mode of the genre. While Vera Dika most appropriately referred to these films as being part of a "stalker cycle," the more common moniker for such films has been "slashers," referring to the killer's practice of (usually) killing his/her victims with sharp objects. Such films constitute nearly a third of all teen horror films since 1980, have consistently earned the most box-office profit compared to other varieties of the subgenre, and have thus become the most popular style of teen horror film. Six different "series" of films emerged in this category (in addition to a number of single films), four of which are the most recognizable of all teen horror titles—*Halloween, Friday the 13th, A Nightmare on Elm Street,* and *Scream*—and two of which retained a low-budget look with low-profile releases but which are nonetheless notable, *Slumber Party Massacre* and *Sleepaway Camp*.

Most of the slasher narratives are built upon a revenge scenario, usually realized at the end of the film after the killer has been captured or killed (although typically the killer eventually escapes, even from death); a main character stumbles upon the motive behind the killer's actions, which usually involve avenging the past irresponsibilities of youth (and/or their parents) so that now further youth will be killed to accommodate the killer's anger. Such revelations are almost always brought out only in the last instance, after the ambiguous killer has stalked and murdered a number of victims for what seem like arbitrary reasons. David Edelstein has commented on the generic ironies of the slasher film in relation to this sense of oblique identification:

> Slasher movies *are* teen sex comedies; the only difference is the presence of an outsider, someone who watches the fun—like a moviegoer—and, presumably, becomes enraged by it. I say presumably because, while we frequently observe the action from the killer's point of view, no anger is verbally expressed—most of the psychos in these movies say nothing and wear blank masks. They slash away in anonymity, partly, I think, because they *are* anonymous.[27]

The lack of audience empathy toward characters in these films—victims or killers—is striking, if only because the stories are meant to shock but inevitably allow us to too easily enjoy the "pleasure of terror" against their defenseless characters. The use of teens seems especially effective in this regard, since they embody a wanton exuberance for experimentation with sex and drugs, which is continually met with virtually instant death, although little suffering. Teens in these films are often murdered for their forays into adult morality, providing a skewed justification for punishing them, and more so enforcing a certain safe distance for their teen viewers, in the notion that since sex and drugs do not *really* lead to death in the ways depicted in these fantasies, the reality of sex and drugs must pose less threatening consequences. As Edelstein implies, teens can enjoy their depictions within these films as comical extremes, and the box-office success of these films over more realistically moralizing tales—at least before the African American crime films of the early '90s—can be explained accordingly.

The *Halloween* Series

Halloween established a variety of slasher modes in 1978, foregrounding the killer's motives with an opening sequence in which young Michael Myers witnesses his teen sister's sexual congress with a boy and then hacks her to death with a butcher knife. Michael is sent to an insane asylum and escapes at the age of 21 to go back to his neighborhood on Halloween, where he locates other sexually active teenagers and kills them. Tension in the plot is built upon Michael's slow discovery and murder of these teens as a doctor desperately attempts to find Michael and stop his killing. The film's virginal and dutiful protagonist, Laurie Strode (Jamie Lee Curtis), became the paradigm of the Final Girl.

Four sequels to *Halloween* were made over the '80s, one of which, *Halloween III: Season of the Witch* (1983), had effectively nothing to do with the storyline established by the first two. At the time of *Halloween II* in 1981, the slasher style was enjoying its peak of success, and while the film was indeed a true sequel to the original story (revealing that Laurie and Michael are siblings), it went further afield of the original's psychological tension and relied more upon what had quickly become slasher stocks-in-trade: the killer who won't die, the car that won't start, gratuitous sex met with gratuitous violence. About the only interesting element of this film is how it points to the mounting dispensability of teen and adult characters in slasher films; lest one lose count, a cop at the end of the film lets us know that ten characters have been killed, which does not include a teenage boy who was run over and killed by a cop because he was wearing a Halloween mask that looked like Michael's. Perhaps the "accidental murder" of this teen is the most important contribution of *Halloween II* to the subgenre, in that anonymous death by association is validated even by the criminal justice system, which is already incapable of controlling young killers.

Halloween 4: The Return of Michael Myers (1988) clearly signaled to audiences that the killer was back, and as in *Halloween II,* where he was trying to kill his estranged sister Laurie, here again his motive is to kill a surviving family member. Laurie has since died, leaving a nine-year-old daughter (Michael's niece) whom Michael stalks for the entirety of the film, a drive that is only explained in terms of his familial blood lust, although as the series progresses he will become determined to kill other surviving family members at increasingly younger ages, as if trying to halt his family's reproductive process altogether. Here Michael hacks his way through a group of teenagers until he is again "killed" by police, leaving his niece somehow possessed by his spirit, as she then kills her foster mother with a pair of scissors. This ending suggests that Michael's mission may actually have been to stop the terror that his genetic line represents, to stop the inevitable cycle of horror that his bloodline produces; however, in yielding a virginal Final Girl who is a new menace, the film problematizes the slasher film tradition of good girls prevailing over their evil male killers.

The *Halloween* series, unlike the *Friday the 13th* and *Nightmare on Elm Street* series, continued to consistently kill off one young couple for having sex in each film, although the films' depictions of teenagers otherwise remained relatively flat. In *The Return* and its sequel, *Halloween 5: The Revenge of Michael Myers* (1989), the teen characters are again little more than mere targets for the lunatic killer. *The Revenge* picks up with Michael's niece Jamie (Danielle Harris), now a mute struggling to accept her matricide and the lingering memories of Michael, who inevitably returns and begins to kill more sexually active teens. Michael is eventually caught, leaving Jamie to again become the Final Girl, who sees at the end of the film that a mysterious dark figure has nonetheless freed Michael from jail.

This dark figure returns in the next sequel, which was actually not numbered but obviously constituted the sixth film in the series, *Halloween: The Curse of Michael Myers* (1995). Now Jamie is pregnant and being terrorized by a cult who want to sacrifice her baby boy; the dark figure is later revealed to be a colleague of the previous investigating doctor who believes he can harness the seemingly limitless powers of Michael's evil. As with the later films in the *Friday the 13th* and *Nightmare on Elm Street* series, this installment ages its protagonists to their 20s, supporting my observation that the filmic image of teens expanded to include college-age young adults in the '90s Generation X era. The college students in this story become involved in saving Jamie's boy after she is killed by the resurgent Michael, two of whom apparently kill Michael after he kills all the members of the cult. The film thus preserves a Final Family, with the obviously nonvirginal (but morally upstanding) parents raising their own son as well as Jamie's baby.

In what yet again promised to be the final film in the series, *Halloween H2O* (1998), Jamie Lee Curtis returned to play Laurie Strode, who, like her brother Michael, has cheated death, since she had to fake her demise to escape his reign of terror. Now she's a middle-aged private school headmaster trying to keep the secret of her tormented past, only she realizes that her son is about to turn 18, which she fears will once again invoke Michael's return. This sequel focuses much more on the mother's personal torment than the activities of teens at the school (a few of whom nonetheless become Michael's victims), and it abandons many of the plot details that had built the series over the past 20 years, presumably to draw in a younger audience not familiar with those films. Its most significant revision is Laurie's more authoritative destruction of Michael, whom she ultimately beheads after saving her son. The *Halloween* series has followed a trajectory from saving virgins to saving mothers and their children, an interesting aging of the female victim-hero over the past generation as well as a testament to changing social concerns in America: the potential dissolution of the family is a greater threat than the possible loss of virginity, at least to teenagers. The dissolution of the series, alas, seems to be a perennial threat to the film industry, as witnessed by the making of an unnecessary yet interesting eighth installment, *Halloween: Resurrection* (2002).

The *Friday the 13th* Series

The original *Friday the 13th* in 1980 launched the most prolific, if least creative, of the slasher franchises. The film plodded through the murders of various teens at Camp Crystal Lake, where years earlier a boy named Jason Voorhees drowned while his counselors were off having sex and being killed by an unseen assailant. Years later, the newly murdered teen counselors are revealed to be the victims of Jason's avenging mother, whose head is eventually lopped off by a final surviving teen girl. While the mother, unlike most other slasher killers, actually dies accordingly, her undead son returns at the start of *Friday the 13th Part II* (1981), five years later in diegetic time, for another season of killing counselors. The sequel provides at least twice as many teens to become potential victims, and builds somewhat more complex characters, setting the stage for sexual and suspenseful tension as the counselors are killed by Jason while they are in a variety of sexual situations. The escalating connection of sex and death in the long climactic sequence is obvious, although only "normal" sexuality is practiced: two mildly perverse counselors never so much as touch before being killed, and a disabled teen is not allowed to enjoy his supposedly intact sexual capacity; but the one long-term couple have hot, sweaty sex, resulting in Jason impaling both of them on a long spike after their orgasms but while still engaged, providing a lingering image of phallic terror that excessively violates the otherwise expected pleasure between these characters.

The following sequels proceed with relatively little improvement on the plots of the earlier films. *Friday the 13th Part 3* (1982) quickly establishes its interest in its 3-D effects with various objects pointing at the screen, a welcome distraction from the stereotypical teens who get together for a weekend at Crystal Lake and are killed by the waiting Jason, who here first dons his now-trademarked hockey mask. *Part 3* maintains the moral retribution of the first two films, killing those who smoke pot, have sex, or even *want* to have sex. Alas, Jason would be back for more, in the optimistically titled *Friday the 13th: The Final Chapter* (1984), in which the killer maims his way through six rambunctious teens on a vacation at Crystal Lake, only to find himself brought down by a preteen named Tommy (Corey Feldman), who has been studying his "case" and, after violently killing the killer, seems to usurp Jason's deadly impulses. His older sister remains the Final Girl, but Tommy becomes an outlet for the preservation of menace, reminding us that Jason was the product of trauma, and foreshadowing yet another return of the killer.

That return is *Friday the 13th Part 5: A New Beginning* (1985), in which Tommy (John Shepherd) has become a teenager, now haunted by the memory of Jason. Here we find that Jason is not *really* the killer after all, but actually the father of a murdered teen, whose psychosis has led to him killing more teens: the emphasis on the dangers of teen sexuality had thus shifted to a greater threat against the preservation of family. This concern for the family is carried over in the somewhat comical *Friday the 13th Part 6: Jason Lives* (1986), its title signaling the return of the "real" Jason. Now Tommy (Thom Mathews) accidentally brings Jason back to life, and thereafter becomes a much more determined and less ambiguous avenger of the *original* Jason, who is engaged in yet another killing spree that includes sexual teens but *not* children staying at Camp Crystal Lake—children thus seem to be an insulated bastion of innocence that Jason cannot violate. Tommy and his new girlfriend appear to eventually drown Jason in Crystal Lake, their unconsummated relationship thereby granting them the title of Final Couple, with the frightened children as their reward. Only those who honor Jason's power of terror and thus avoid sex can survive, revealing Jason as the ultimate oppressive, abusive parental authority figure, a teenager's true nightmare.

That notion is manifest even more explicitly in *Friday the 13th Part 7: The New Blood* (1988), which focuses on a psychokinetic teenager (shades of *Carrie*) who also inadvertently brings Jason back to life with her powers, just in time for him to kill a number of her sexually active friends. Tina (Lar Park Lincoln) is actually plagued by the memory of drowning her abusive father as a child, when she discovered her psychokinetic abilities, and the most compelling moment of the film occurs when Tina (with the help of her boyfriend) actually conjures her dead father out of Crystal Lake to pull Jason back in: the guilt of the original abuser is thus absolved by his role as a savior from a greater evil. While the teens continue to pay for their transgressions as before, leaving the Final Couple responsible to the end, the image of irresponsible adults such as Tina's dad and her manipulative therapist (who has been trying to exploit her powers for his research) has become more closely aligned with the menace that Jason represents, so that while teens are to blame for Jason's continual rebirths, the literal "sins of the father" have provided the true inspiration for both the killer's rampage and the heroine's revenge. (Similar issues connecting the killer with notions of parenthood were also being explored in the subgenre at this time in the *Nightmare on Elm Street* series).

The appearance of *Friday the 13th Part 8: Jason Takes Manhattan* in 1989 appeared to signal the end of the series, and at least did so in terms of its usual use of teenage protagonists. This installment is a particularly empty experience as Jason kills numerous teens on a cruise, although the film does make a tentative social statement when some of the teens find themselves in Manhattan and confronted by street thugs, whose demands of money are tame compared to Jason's terror. When the thugs kidnap one of the teens and inject her with drugs, Jason suddenly shows up and kills them, a unique instance of Jason actually (incidentally, perhaps) saving one of his erstwhile victims. Drugs, it would seem, are a greater evil to be avenged than simply killing teenagers. Once again, after Jason kills more victims, a teenage Final Couple survive to drown him, this time in toxic waste.

Part 8 would be the last *Friday* for four years until the dreadful *Jason Goes to Hell: The Final Friday* in 1993. With another optimistic title, this supposedly conclusive chapter in the series did not prominently feature teen characters, save three who are gratuitously killed by Jason early on, two in the act of boldly having sex without a condom, pointing to a '90s sense of irresponsible sexual activity that justifies their murder. However, the lead characters are nonetheless very youthful in appearance, once again embodying the "20-something teenager" emblematic of '90s films. Perhaps the one interesting element in the film comes in the last shot, when Jason's empty hockey mask is pulled into hell by the bladed hand of *A Nightmare on Elm Street*'s Freddy Krueger, a fitting postmodern cross-serial nod to horror fans and presumably a dual ending for both immortal screen teen killers (the *Final Nightmare* of the *Nightmare* series had appeared in 1991, although series originator Wes Craven himself produced a postmodern take on the series in 1994). As if there were no more teenagers for the aging Jason to kill, with this final image the slasher cycle seemed to close its most enduring franchise and visibly pass the mantle on to Craven's character, who not only appeared in *New Nightmare* in 1994 but became one of the many inspirations for the killers in Craven's 1996 film *Scream,* in which teenagers themselves take on a fresh generation of victims. Yet as this book goes to press, new productions of *Friday the 13th* (*Jason X,* 2002) and *A Nightmare on Elm Street* are scheduled for release, leaving open the opportunity for these immortal killers to terrorize the tougher teens of the twenty-first century.

The *Nightmare on Elm Street* Series

In 1984 established horror director Wes Craven introduced the last popular slasher series of the '80s (which lasted into the '90s), featuring a deformed killer with razor blades mounted to his hand. *A Nightmare on Elm Street* utilized many of the then-typical motifs in teen horror films—a seemingly indestructible killer stalks and brutally kills teenagers, especially those who have or want to have sex, avenging past violence against him—yet now the killer was not only more developed within the narrative, but his very existence was predicated on the fears and dreams of his teenage victims. The *Nightmare* series entertained the idea that teenagers had themselves brought Freddy Krueger, a notorious child murderer played by Robert Englund in all the films, back to "life" through their frightful nightmares, allowing the otherwise dead killer to cross over to a reality in which he could actually harm and kill more youth.

From the first film onward, the teen victims of Freddy had to learn how to control their own mental processes, particularly their fears and fantasies, in order to conquer and defeat the killer. As the series progressed, however, a variety of social issues became intricately connected to the killer and his victims: Freddy himself had been an abused child, the result of a sadistic rape (reminding us that evil adults breed monstrosities as children), and his young victims had to overcome their given problems (e.g., drug use, parental neglect, sexual aggression or confusion) on their own, lest they face his wrath, a wrath that was in the last instance wrought by the victim's own weakness. Judith Williamson added:

> In social terms it is possible to read Krueger as the unsavory working classes suppressed and fought off by the aspiring, middle-American parents who are presented as at best inadequate—alcoholic mothers and dictatorial fathers abound. Freddy is *their* victim even as their children, in a vicious cycle of effects, are his.[28]

This cyclical contest of power for teen characters was considerably different from the *Halloween* and *Friday the 13th* series, in which the protagonists spent more time eluding the alien killer than confronting their own familiar fears. In the *Nightmare* series, the true danger comes from within, and the classic teen achievement of higher self-esteem and confidence becomes the only effective weapon in avoiding destruction. These films tell teens that they must grow up smart and tough or else perish. Wes Craven himself called horror films a "boot camp for the psyche" and said that teens like horror films because they "put them under terrifying conditions and show that you can survive. You come out feeling better and stronger."[29] Craven must have also realized that only *certain* characters survive, and that their actions embody particularly admirable human qualities such as integrity, purity, intelligence, and loyalty—a veritable pledge for teen horror heroines and heroes.

The first *Nightmare on Elm Street* was perhaps the most typical of past slasher films, with its connection of sex and death, gradual stalking of teens who are brutally killed, and revelation of the killer avenging his past. On otherwise quiet Elm Street in Springwood, Ohio, a girl has a nightmare in which a man with a burned face and fingers with razors chases her through a boiler factory, and is later surprised to find that her friend Nancy (Heather Langenkamp) had a similar dream, as did her boyfriend and their friend Glen (Johnny Depp). The next night, after having wild sex with her boyfriend, the girl dreams of the same man and she is brutally murdered. Nancy then becomes the focus of the rest of the film as she continues having visions of the nightmare killer and his victims: while her cop father ineffectively works on the case, she realizes that she can confront the killer in her dreams and becomes determined to fight him. At one point, Nancy later takes a bubble bath in which she nods off and finds the killer pulling her under the water (a particularly

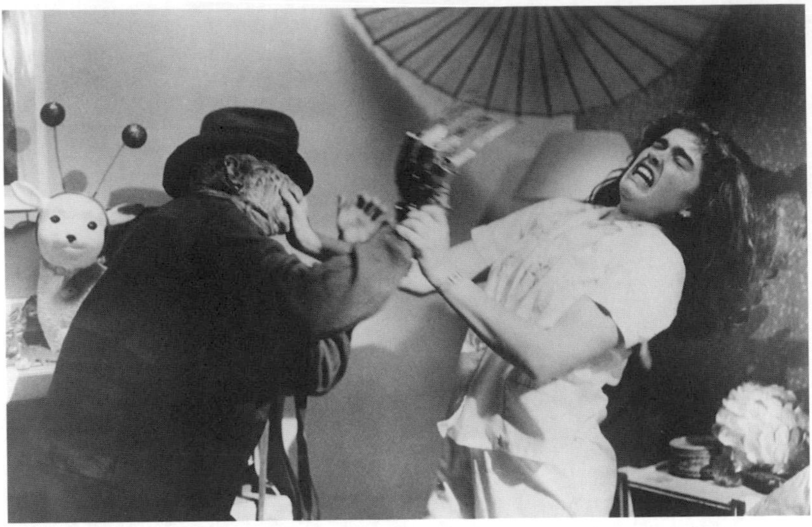

The Final Girl of *A Nightmare on Elm Street* (1984), Nancy (Heather Langenkamp), uses her ingenuity and determination to confront and conquer the psychic stalker Freddy Krueger (Robert Englund).

ominous shot of the razor hand reaching up between Nancy's naked legs provokes a tension of brutal virgin rape), yet she escapes his clutches and realizes that she must stay awake in order to avoid further attacks.

Nancy's mother, rapidly becoming an alcoholic, tells her that the man is Freddy Krueger, a local child murderer who was unjustly freed years before, and so she and other parents had set him on fire in a boiler factory. When the mother tells her, "He's dead because Mommy killed him," the connection of parental revenge and child victimization is clear: Nancy and her friends have been suffering the attacks of Freddy through their dreams because of their parents' repressed anger and guilt from killing Freddy. Or, as David Edelstein saw it, "the children are vulnerable to their nightmares because their drunken, divorced, and inattentive moms and dads have failed them. That's a reactionary message, but it's still the source of children's most powerful nightmares."[30] Douglas Rathgab proposes that the teens are more culpable: "Although the sins of the parents are clearly being visited upon the children, the children's sexual offenses provide more than enough horrorific justification in the film's moral scheme for their own victimization. Their mores have become somehow identified with Krueger's own sexual offense."[31] This is an issue that will however be challenged in the sequels (which Rathgab's 1991 article, oddly enough, does not discuss), as the teens' "sexual offenses" become morally ambiguous if not altogether displaced.

After many failed attempts, Nancy sets up one last trap to "catch" Freddy, trying to bring him out of her dream state into reality where he can again be destroyed, only Freddy seems to take the upper hand, calling on her disconnected phone and telling her, "I'm your boyfriend now," with a grotesque set of lips and a tongue forming on the mouthpiece and kissing her. This slimy sexual assault is contrasted with the obscure but bloody death at midnight of Glen, her actual boyfriend, who had fallen asleep instead of helping Nancy to capture Freddy. The irresponsible Glen thereby pays for his lack of dedication, while Nancy's growing strength is met with her subconscious fears of sexual violation. With Nancy literally locked behind bars in her own house, her drunken mom passed out in bed, and her dad investigating Glen's death across the street, she launches her prepared assault on Freddy, rigging her house with various booby traps and going to sleep to bring him back. Freddy nonetheless survives Nancy's weapons, captures her mother, and then tries to kill Nancy, until she tells him that she knows he's only a dream, and stands him down with demands to return her mother and friends. Such a show of conscious authority causes the monster to disappear, until the final scene, where Nancy has returned to a serene morning on which her mother sends her off to school with her friends, and they suddenly become trapped in the car as Freddy appears to grab her mother again. (Philip Kemp later claimed that this ending was added by producers to facilitate sequels.[32]) Despite this typical unresolved coda, *A Nightmare on Elm Street* offers perhaps the most powerful and resolute of female horror heroines in the teen genre: Final Girl Nancy insulates herself against the threats of the killer and the disbelief of her parents and successfully eliminates Freddy single-handedly, not by force but by sheer will.

The second film in the series, *A Nightmare on Elm Street 2: Freddy's Revenge* (1985), switched the gender of the protagonist and concentrated less on the hero's ultimate comprehension of the killer, addressing more so his troubled sense of sexuality and his "use" of Freddy to confront it.[33] (As with the *Halloween* and *Friday the 13th* series, the original director did not direct any of the sequels, with the exception that Wes Craven wrote and directed *New Nightmare,* the seventh in the series in 1994, and cowrote the third film.) Here Jesse (Mark Patton) fears Freddy has taken over his body, and his girlfriend works to convince him of her love, which ultimately allows him to free himself from his intimate union with Freddy; it is also a restoration of heterosexual order in the form of a Final Couple that finally returns Jesse to "normal" even though Freddy—born from Jesse's previously confused sexuality—has killed so many other normal teens. Perhaps Freddy's real revenge was simply to use Jesse as such a pawn, exploiting his sexual fears to carry out his more nefarious task of killing children who were about to become sexual.

The third film, *A Nightmare on Elm Street 3: Dream Warriors* (1987) takes a less individualistic approach toward sexuality and instead focuses on a group of different teenagers who all—save one—are virtually asexual in their pursuit of the physical power that they hope will allow them to destroy Freddy. A group of institutionalized "suicidal" teens, all of whom have been terrorized by Freddy in their dreams, now try a radical therapy approach to confront Freddy. Along the way, we learn that Freddy was the offspring of a nun in the 1940s who was kept in a tower and raped hundreds of times by inmates, "the bastard son of a hundred maniacs," thus explaining Freddy's pathology as the result of ultimate perverse sexuality. Meanwhile, as the teens create various hypnotic fantasies to empower themselves, Freddy continues his rampage against the weaker youth until the heroine of the first film, Nancy (Heather Langenkamp), who here plays a psychology researcher, is able to finally kill him so that three Final Teens survive, having conquered their deepest fears after Freddy is supposedly eliminated once and for all.

A Nightmare on Elm Street 4: The Dream Master (1988), which is arguably the most aesthetically accomplished film in the series, takes up with the surviving teens of the previous film: this time Freddy is revived and systematically kills these survivors, after which one of their friends, Alice (Lisa Wilcox), becomes the new heroine. By this point in the series, teen characters were being killed simply because they *knew* past victims, and the teens who are killed are less morally suspect than their predecessors, with no greater transgressions than intelligence and confidence, although perhaps these qualities are meant to be the very essence of what a child-killer like Freddy seeks to snuff out. The film ends with Alice harnessing her positive dream power and dressing up in a teen-styled samurai outfit to fight Freddy, from whom she demands the release of his victims who, rather than coming back to life, appear to leave Freddy's body as spirits sent to the heavens. Once again the series offers a puissant image of the Final Girl, although its shift in the murderer's motives is disturbing, if only because "good" kids are now being killed and not coming back, similar to the plight of Nancy at the end of the previous film.

By the late '80s, the character of Freddy Krueger had become a pop phenomenon, with an assertive marketing campaign of various products and a syndicated television show called "Freddy's Nightmares," which showcased changing stories in a format similar to the popular "Tales from the Darkside" series. In trying to induce youth culture to idolize and commercialize a child-killer whose victims were rapidly becoming more numerous and respectable, the series' producers may have covertly catered to a sense of masochistic self-loathing in teens at the time while outwardly amplifying Freddy's more acceptable contempt for authority and sarcastic wit (he delivers increasingly more one-liners in each film), although the next film in the series shifted focus again.

With *A Nightmare on Elm Street 5: The Dream Child* (1989) the series moved from moral lessons about teens' actions to rather metaphysical questions about life, particularly pondering whether the evil that Freddy represents is a product of nature or nurture. Alice (Lisa Wilcox) returns, now facing Freddy's mother, who has entered Alice's dreams to take Freddy back, presumably to his prebirth, preevil state, but Freddy refuses and launches a further assault on Alice and her friends. Alice becomes the object of Freddy's desire to have his own child, indicating his plan to produce another monster such as himself as well as his more implicit longing for sexual consummation with one of his victims. Alice, who's been impregnated by her now-dead boyfriend, knows that the fetus growing inside her has been exploited by Freddy to generate new dreams and may become evil like him, but rather than abort the baby, thereby killing the possibility of spawning another Freddy, Alice adamantly declares her choice to raise the baby herself. In a less fanciful film such an action could be taken as a testament to a pro-life stance, but here Alice uses her capacity to give birth as her defense against Freddy's supposed power, for if she can raise a "good" child then she can defeat Freddy once and for all. In a highly symbolic showdown, Alice violently pulls the Freddy fetus out of her body, an image of monstrous birth *and* abortion, and this mutant then enters Freddy's mother, where he is finally recontained in her womb. By concentrating on the birthing process, *The Dream Child* pushes its teen characters to a higher level of responsibility than before: they are no longer trying to save just themselves but their posterity. The film also posits, albeit rather weakly, that Freddy's evil is the result of subhuman mutation and can only be contained within a superhuman goodness, his mother the nun. The final image of Alice cooing over her new "good" baby is still a bit haunting back in the daily world where the teenager is faced with the challenge of raising a child alone, a child who is destined to be trouble, and thus perhaps a more realistic nightmare for teen girls than any offered by Freddy.

Freddy's Dead: The Final Nightmare (1991) retains this focus on parental responsibilities and their relation to Freddy's terror. After a group of abused teen mental patients are stalked and killed by Freddy, their therapist realizes that she was adopted and that Freddy is her real father: she had repressed her memories of her father killing her mother after she found his torture chamber where he killed children. As it turns out, Freddy was abused by his own adoptive father and took to slicing himself in the stomach to displace the pain (saying a line that could be a cynical anthem for teen angst, "If you can just stop feeling pain, you can start using it"), and thus the film advances the role of Freddy's abused development in addition to his evil conception to explain his pathology. Ultimately the therapist brings Freddy back into the human world and kills him, becoming the rare Final Girl who's not a teenager. The film actually raises sympathy for Freddy in its condemnation of all parental abuses and further removes the weight of responsibility from children themselves: the teens, their therapist, and Freddy are all by this point merely reacting to the acts of their parents in a sad attempt at self-preservation. The childless town of Springwood becomes a final symbol of parental irresponsibility, where the parents must forever face the horror of losing their children because they did not raise them right, an appealing image to the teenager's sense of revenge and anger at his or her family for not being appreciated enough.

The final film in the series, *Wes Craven's New Nightmare* (1994), is endlessly interesting but ironically of little value to this study since it does not prominently feature teenagers. The film is a self-reflexive study of Craven's own frustrations with the *Nightmare* franchise and, it would seem, the film industry in general. Heather Langenkamp returns playing herself, trying to move on from her association with the *Nightmare* films and raise her son, only she's being visited by Freddy in her dreams. She learns from the real producers of the series that Wes Craven is working on yet another sequel, which he tells her he must complete as a way of recapturing Freddy from his dangerously free role in American society. That sequel becomes the film we are watching, in which Heather has to fight Freddy to save her child, and in the end learns that she was simply a part of Craven's plot (literally) to "put Freddy back where he belongs."

The film thus speaks to Craven's reclaiming of the Freddy Krueger character and raises the obvious issue of why we so enjoy horror films: because of the cathartic release in seeing someone else survive terrors beyond our experience, a release that Craven is claiming we enjoy in real life as much as in movies. By jettisoning the teenagers who populated the previous six films, Craven opens his concerns to a wider audience, pointing to the possibility that two important changes had taken place between 1984 and 1994: the film industry became less dependent on depicting teens as a way to lure their masses to the box office, and the image of immoral, suffering teens in excessively horrific circumstances had become ultimately uninteresting, especially compared to the more realistic horrors that teens faced in nonhorror films of the early '90s. These changes would nonetheless reverse in the late-'90s youth cinema, due primarily to Craven's next teen horror film, *Scream,* in 1996.

The *Slumber Party Massacre* Trilogy

In 1982 a unique slasher series began when Amy Jones directed *Slumber Party Massacre* from feminist author Rita Mae Brown's script: the film launched the only teen horror series written and directed exclusively by women. However, despite what may have been attempts to critique, if not at least make ironic, the usual slasher formula of killing innocent female teens, the trilogy features rather standard slasher plots, gratuitous female (and only female) nudity, and the brutal killing of teenagers. Rex Reed quipped that all the first film proved was "that women can manufacture garbage that degrades and insults women just as greedily and speedily as men."[34] The first film was indeed the most standard: Trish's (Michele Michaels) parents go away for the weekend and she throws a slumber party for her girlfriends, who are systematically killed by an escaped maniac wielding a large power drill. Trish wonders if she should invite the new girl at school, Valerie (Robin Stille), but her conceited friend Diane (Gina Mari) discourages her. From the outset Valerie is thus designed to become the Final Girl, ostracized by the main group of hedonists and, as it turns out, responsible for babysitting her younger sister.

The killing begins at school that afternoon when, after an excessive scene of girls showering, the maniac kills a girl in the locker room, thereby transforming the previous scene of sexual titillation into one of arousing graphic violence. When the party begins at Trish's house that evening, the girls begin drinking beer and smoking dope while dutiful Valerie hangs out with her sister Courtney (Jennifer Meyers) next door. The girls are soon joined by two of their male friends who've been watching them and playing scary pranks, and with Trish's plan to have a "girls night" thus broken, Diane invites her boyfriend over, implying that she's been horny for him. This admission of sexual desire by Diane, who further wants to leave the party to have sex, leads to the first killings at the party when Diane finds her boyfriend's headless body in the garage and screams as the killer drills her (the phallic symbolism of his drill being obvious), which the girls inside cannot hear because they are blending drinks: Diane's "punishment" for her greater moral indiscretion—leaving her girlfriends to go have sex—is thus ignored by the girls engaging in a lesser indiscretion. The killer then goes through more of the party guests, and in a climactic showdown, Trish, Valerie, and Courtney (along with a concerned female gym teacher who shows up only to be killed) fight the maniac until Valerie lops off his drill bit with a machete—the castrating virgin—and rams him with her long blade. Perhaps what is most different about *Slumber Party Massacre* is its conclusion leaving three Final Girls, Valerie being the most standard, her younger sister Courtney being even more innocent, and Trish, sympathetic to Valerie and tougher than her girlfriends.

Along the way the film points to certain interesting frustrations for its female teens: Trish laments the loss of the old days before her girlfriends had boyfriends and speaks to a sense of female bonding that is obviously disrupted by the invasion of men (including the killer), whereas Valerie, in being isolated from her female cohort, takes solace in her role as big sister, a role that effectively keeps her alive. As in other slasher films, only the most moral characters live, but here those characters also embody levels of respectable femininity—loyal, strong, smart, attractive, innocent—that may have been consistent with Jones and Brown's intent. There's no mistake that the first two films in the series present a male killer who is actually *under*developed, with little background or motive to provide any insight to his actions, lest the killer become the "star" as he did in the major slasher series. Carrie Rickey notes, "There's something empathetic in the way Jones unfolds her story from the victim's point of view, never exulting in the psychotic power of the killer," although the mystique of that power seemed to justify the sequels in this and all of the other slasher series.[35]

Another distinction of the *Slumber Party Massacre* films is that in all three the killer actually dies, despite an unrealistic level of struggle, at the hands of the Final Girl(s). However, in the second film, simply titled *Slumber Party Massacre II* (1987), the killer is not human but rather—borrowing from *A Nightmare on Elm Street*—a dream product of Courtney (Crystal Bernard), the surviving sister from the first film who is now a 17-year-old virgin. She dreams about having sex with her boyfriend, although in the dream he turns into the psycho killer she has been seeing throughout the film. The connection between sex and death is thus made explicit, but much needs to be said about this hallucinatory killer: he is a leather-jacketed rock star with a spiked electric guitar, the neck of which turns into a drill, and he sings and dances when he later pursues Courtney and his other victims (this during the odd late-'80s phase of rock-and-horror films). The killer is obviously an expression of Courtney's deepest distorted desires, a rock-and-roll rebel who eventually kills her sexually active friends in humorous contempt via Courtney's dreams, thus implicating her for this violence produced by her sexual repression. Oddly enough, it is Courtney's later decision to have sex that brings into reality the killer, who then goes on to kill everyone else.

Courtney eventually corners the killer on a roof and attacks him with power tools and a blow torch, although she suddenly wakes up in bed with her boyfriend. For a moment the entire brutal episode seems to have been her postcoital nightmare vision—indicating her incredible guilt, shame, and terror at losing her virginity—but in the last instance Courtney has another nightmare image of the phallic drill bursting through the floor. Courtney has literally loosed and yet cannot seem completely to destroy the demon of her sexuality, which was the result of her original trauma in witnessing the deaths of her older sister's friends. The second film thus rather rationally posits that a traumatized teen girl confronting her entrance into sexual practice may indeed experience a displaced terror, although Courtney's created killer reveals a more systemic sexual crisis, signaling that her having sex will leave her further traumatized, alone, and psychotic. Sex does not yield death but dementia.

The third film in the series, *Slumber Party Massacre III* (1990), offers a far less intriguing plot than the first two films. Here the killer is revealed to be a college guy at the titular party, whose uncle molested him as a boy, resulting in his sexual dysfunction with girls. After much bloody mayhem, three girls eventually corner and kill the killer, one of them finally grabbing the ubiquitous power drill and driving it into him repeatedly, although these Final Girls remain essentially without identities. This film unfortunately attempts to explore the pathology behind the killer and in that way derails the female-oriented perspective of the first two films; the dead teens here are killed simply because masculine sexual deviance has produced masculine sexual impotence, which is redirected into a homicidal impulse triggered by the sexual advances of women. In that way, the girls are killed not so much for their own sexual desires but for their attempts to sexually please men, and perhaps that is the film's cautionary, if not reactionary, message. At any rate, no new women (or men) in Hollywood have come forth to continue the series.

Nonserial Slasher Films

Considering how many teen slasher films were released between 1980 and 1999—I count at least 50—the number that were *not* part of series is strikingly small, less than half. Of that number, the majority are obscure and largely not worth considering in depth, although I here incorporate a chronology of teen slasher films in that period to describe the cycle of the style outside of its more successful serial counterparts.

1981 was the banner year for the teen slasher film, with the first sequels to the *Halloween* and *Friday the 13th* films being released as well as the parody *Student Bodies* and three lesser-known films, *The Burning, Eyes of a Stranger,* and *Graduation Day,* all featuring a maniacal killer stalking and murdering teens. Nonserial teen slasher films then went out of vogue for the next few years as the cycle declined, producing sparse examples like *The Final Terror* in 1983 and *The Mutilator* in 1985. By 1986 the slasher cycle was finding renewed momentum, and the next few years were prolific indeed; that year saw the release of *Girls School Screamers* and a college variety of *Slumber Party Massacre* called *Sorority House Massacre* (which yielded a sequel in 1992, *Sorority House Massacre 2: Nighty Nightmare*), plus the mildly popular *The Hitcher*. Another 1986 slasher film was *Slaughter High,* in which an erstwhile nerd, now a mental patient due to the abuses he suffered from teen tormentors in high school, dreams of exacting his revenge against them—a film that is in many ways the literal "revenge of the nerd" that Jonathan Bernstein claimed as the motivation behind so many teen slasher films. *Slaughter High* is rare as a youth horror film that pits young people against each other; accordingly, there is no Final Girl, because no one is innocent.

1987 produced a slew of minor slasher films such as *Blood Lake, Hide and Go Shriek, The Last Slumber Party* (another film inspired by *Slumber Party Massacre*), *The Majorettes,* and *Night Screams,* and then 1988 saw the release of four sequels in slasher series as well as the notoriously titled *Bloody Pom Poms* (released on video as the less enticing *Cheerleader Camp*), which attempted to combine the fading formulas of the teen sex romp and the slasher film. After 1988 the slasher film continued to be produced mostly in series with the exception of obscure films like *Offerings* (1989), *The Invisible Maniac* (1990), and *Lunatic* (1991), and for five years after 1991 there were no nonserial teen slasher films.

Then in late 1996 Wes Craven released *Scream,* a genre-revising semisatirical slasher film met by great critical acclaim and financial success.[36] The scenario may initially seem familiar but the film is full of vital shifts in the slasher method. First, teenage Casey (Drew Barrymore) is terrorized on the phone by a voice that quizzes her with questions about her knowledge of teen horror films, and after she gives a wrong answer, the faceless killer eviscerates her boyfriend and then her. The film thereby immediately signals its intent to dissect the generic traditions of teen horror, and continues to do so through its introduction of classic characters. Sidney (Neve Campbell, with a Final Girl's masculine character name) is a virginal high school student recovering from the brutal rape and murder of her mother a year before and delicately warding off the sexual advances of her boyfriend Billy (Skeet Ulrich, looking much like Johnny Depp from Craven's first *Nightmare* film). Now Sidney's school and town have become gripped by the fear of a psycho killer on the loose, and her friends only exacerbate the tension: Stuart (Matthew Lillard) is obnoxious enough to joke about Casey's death even though he had dated her, and Randy (Jamie Kennedy) is a conspiracy theorist convinced that the killer is following "the rules" of slasher films. Only Sidney's friend Tatum (Rose McGowan) is sympathetic to the tensions she feels, especially since she begins to suspect that her mother's killer, Cotton Weary (Liev Schreiber), has escaped.

Sidney is next to be attacked by the killer, but she shows her mettle in fighting him off, and her suspicions point to Billy. Stuart soon holds a party at his house attended by a large group of students (who seemingly could care less that two of their classmates have just been murdered by an uncaught killer), during which Tatum is crushed in a garage door. While this is unbeknownst to Sidney, she decides to go against her better judgment and have sex with Billy to get over her "sexual anorexia," feeling that she can now lose her virginity since "This isn't a movie." Afterward, Sidney finally realizes that there are two killers, Billy and Stuart, who reveal that they framed Cotton Weary and killed Sidney's mother because she was sleeping with Billy's dad, a heavily contrived motive that nonetheless speaks to Billy's dual oedipal mania in killing the woman who broke up his family and then sleeping with the daughter of his father's lover (whom he also raped), as well as Stuart's domestic misogyny in killing his former girlfriend Casey and current girlfriend Tatum. Sidney then fights Billy in the same costume he had been using to kill everyone else, temporarily taking on the identity and the power of the killer herself, and later kills Stuart by smashing his head with a (symbolic) television. Surviving virgin Randy warns Sidney that the killer always comes back to life in slasher films, and when Billy makes one final lunge, Sidney shoots him in the head saying, "Not in my movie." This final statement offers an additional sense of potency to the Final Girl Sidney, who not only survives the loss of her virginity and kills the killer, but essentially lays claim to the entire film, taking no risk that the killer could become deified, unlike her female counterpart Nancy in *A Nightmare on Elm Street*.

Scream is significant for a variety of reasons, not the least of which is that it brings so much depth and attention to what had appeared to be a dead subgenre. The fact that *Scream* yielded a sequel within a year and became a trilogy within four years is testament to the film's financial success as well as its vivification of the slasher style, although the characters in the film, including the killer, mark a clear departure from their original inspirations. Billy and Stuart are actually teenagers themselves, killing other teenagers as well as parental authority figures, and despite their murder mania they are otherwise portrayed as rational, nonpsychotic (and thus ultimately vulnerable) human beings. Sidney is not killed for having sex, despite her great transgression of actually sleeping with the killer—the killer and rapist of her infidel mother—and she is left standing as a strong survivor of the terror with the one virgin left in the film, Randy, who is saved only by his knowledge of horror films (the rare Final Guy who is not romantically involved with the Final Girl). Craven remains rather indebted to his own postmodern notions of self-reflexivity (at one point Tatum tries to comfort Sidney by telling her she's not in a "Wes Carpenter" movie), and ends the last scene with a reporter, who also survived the bloodbath, doing a live shot from the site of the tragedy, signaling that the television media have become the purveyors of real horror in the years since the slasher film lost prominence.

Scream 2 (1997) was even more reflexive as a critique of horror sequels, right down to an early scene featuring college film students discussing the "best" movie sequels. The story again focuses on Sidney, who is now trying to move on from the traumas portrayed in the first film, and while the suspense builds quite effectively, the film is not as engaging as the original. After Sidney deals with her suspicions and torments over a new series of murders now that Cotton Weary is free from prison, the revelation of the killer is rather hokey: it is Billy's distraught mother, out for revenge. Again Sidney is able to dispatch the killer with the help of some surviving friends, but the sequel's statements on the genre, which are as bold as a scene in which two characters discuss the narrative *as* a movie plot, had already grown obvious and tired. This may explain why *Scream 3* (2000) was weaker still: all of the characters are now well past their teen years, and the film loses the very youthful innovations that made the original so successful. (Curiously enough, Sidney's promiscuous mother is yet again the inspiration for the killer—a son she gave up for adoption—and thus the whole series, like Craven's *Nightmare* series, is founded on the deeper sins of parents, the consequences of which children must endure.) We can at least be thankful if the third film is indeed the final installment, which is likely given the escalating budgets of the films and aging of the original cast, the presence of whom, unlike other slasher series, has proved vital to the success of the films.

Another popular slasher film appeared in 1997 with a less reflexive approach, *I Know What You Did Last Summer,* which was soon sequelized the following year as *I Still Know What You Did Last Summer.* In the first film, two graduating high school couples cover up their accidental killing of a pedestrian, and over the course of the next year their relationships quietly fade away until someone begins taunting them with notes alluding to their crime. This brings the teens back together, and the film does well to examine how their friendships have fallen prey to moral tensions around the accident and its repression, as well as social tensions around them moving on with their lives. However, the narrative focuses more on mounting menace: as they make various inaccurate assumptions about the identity of the note writer, the characters become the targets of increasingly disturbing pranks, and before long two of them are murdered. The stalker turns out to be the pedestrian himself, who survived the accident and is now out for revenge, yet a surviving Final Couple are able to elude his wrath and supposedly drown him in the ocean. The heroine, Julie (Jennifer Love Hewitt), at last returns to college, only a now-typical studio ending suggests that the killer is still alive, which obviously provides the foundation for the sequel. This next film finds Julie just leaving her teen years and taking off on a vacation with other college friends, where they are inevitably stalked by the same psychopath. The relative success of these two films would suggest that the slasher style is still thriving, yet their lack of generic revision—placing a strong heroine within yet another sadistic scare-fest—reveals how little slasher conventions have changed in the past generation, even if the moral issue of the stories has shifted to criminal guilt rather than sexual guilt. Increasingly media savvy youth will likely demand more sophisticated approaches to such established traditions, as Owen Gliberman noted: "The audience for movies like *I Still Know What You Did Last Summer* has become much, much smarter than the movies themselves."[37]

One can only wonder where the teen slasher film will go from here, and if its imaging of teens will continue in the knowing mode of *Scream,* with teenage killers and Final Girls (and Guys?) surviving their sexual initiations in a society where sex is no longer as scary as their peers. David Edelstein wrote in 1984:

> Slasher movies appeal to our most puritanical urges and also to our most adolescent; they offer bloody, purgative violence as a substitute for sexual uncertainty—terrorist tactics to restore the status quo. The expression is ghastly, but we should recognize the underlying cry. Like the exhortations of the Moral Majority, hack-'em-ups are aimed at people frightened of sexual freedom but also terribly interested in it—tense people who haven't resolved their inner contradictions. And given our culture, which prods relentlessly at their genitalia, it's no wonder they're tense.[38]

By the end of the 1990s, teenage sexuality had achieved more prominent discourse in American society, although it was no less the object of repression and oppression. This is perhaps why a horror film such as *Scream* still functioned in the '90s, and also why its Final Girl achieved the pyrrhic victory of living despite her sexual experience, the potential pleasure of which is vanquished by the evil intent of her partner. Teens will always struggle with their tensions and inner contradictions about sexuality, and yet they may become informed enough about it so that their access to it is no longer viewed with overwhelming fear. The necessary social restriction on sexual pleasure for teenagers may thus no longer be suited to films in which indestructible killers deliver the message (a change that *I Know What You Did Last Summer* implements) and may instead find its place in subgenres that more directly address the complexities and importance of the issue.

SUPERNATURAL MOVIES

A tradition of movies related to the supernatural goes back to the earliest days of cinema, although rarely did these films address teenagers (such examples as *The Ghost of Dragstrip Hollow* [1959] and *The Ghost in the Invisible Bikini* [1966] were few, even in the exploitation circuit). In fact, stories of the supernatural and occult did not become particularly popular in teen films until after the wane of the early-'80s slasher trend, and even then their narratives were wildly divergent. The box-office smash *Poltergeist* (1982) featured a family terrorized by unsettled spirits in their house, yet the role of its lone teen character, the eldest daughter, played by Dominique Donne, was rather undeveloped. Two years later the even more successful *Gremlins* featured Zach Galligan as a young adult character (actually in his early 20s) saddled with the terrifying invasion of little monsters launched from the mishandling of supposedly harmless teddy-bear creatures. Both films spawned further sequels and imitators, as did the college films *The Evil Dead* (1983), in which lurking spirits in the woods attack young victims in excessively gruesome ways, and *Ghoulies* (1985), which was itself an imitation of *Gremlins* with its title goblins creating icky havoc. However, the only notable supernatural teen film before 1987 was *Christine* in 1983, wherein an evil car seems to possess its young owner.

1987 then became the nascent year for supernatural teen films, although the three released that year were not very popular, nor were the three released in 1988 (*Beetlejuice* was a success that year, but its story concentrated primarily on the antics of its eponymous "bio-exorcist" and less upon the role of its rising teen star, Winona Ryder). Despite the lack of profit in this category, studios continued releasing supernatural teen films over the next decade, few of which drew much attention from audiences. The relatively consistent output of supernatural teen films since 1987 suggests a certain outlet being offered from the menace of the slasher films—teens in supernatural films tend to be smarter and less passive in their possession by spirits than the numerous cowering murder victims in slasher films—and it may also indicate an attempt by studios to capitalize on the public's interest in after-death experiences and ghosts.

The texts of most of these films, while offering a variety of explanations for their otherworldly machinations, tend to hinge upon relatively simple characterizations of teens who usually appeal, consciously or not, to the power of spirits and deviant deities for deliverance from their teen plights. Nerdy characters become tough and cool; disregarded teens become saviors; unpopular outcasts get noticed. In the end, the teens always realize that the power of dark forces is greater than they are, and usually they perish accordingly, although some films in the '90s pointed to teens more successfully harnessing such forces before their destruction.

Supernatural Films of the 1980s

Supernatural films deal with mysterious forces that possess people and compel them to commit various bizarre, usually murderous acts. A smaller number of supernatural films actually deal with the lethal acts of objects, such as two "evil car" movies of the '80s, *Christine* and *The Wraith* (1986), which examine how teenagers are affected by automotive apparitions: the latter film, which follows a car-spirit avenging the death of a teenager killed by nefarious street punks, was not widely seen, whereas the former film was a mild success and provided an important foundation in characterizations from which other supernatural youth films would grow.

Christine was adapted from Stephen King's novel about a demonic 1957 Plymouth Fury and was directed by John Carpenter of *Halloween* fame. The film is set in 1978 California and features a Faustian tale of a high school nerd, Arnie (Keith Gordon), paying too much money for the junky old car, spending an excessive amount of time bringing it back to its original form (a contrivance that is completely unrealistic), and then seemingly becoming controlled by it. Arnie and his friend Dennis (John Stockwell) are just starting their senior years of high school, and Dennis teases Arnie that this should be the year he gets laid, preferably with a girl. The irony of his statement is that since Arnie is unable to find "normal" sex, he has to buy it in the form of the car, which he lovingly refers to as "Christine" as he spends much time literally laboring over her body. Arnie gradually transforms from meek and accommodating—his first sign of rebellion is arguing with his overbearing parents that he's been a dutiful son and should be allowed to keep the car—to acting tough and dis-

In *Christine* (1983), Arnie (Keith Gordon) is shocked to find his beloved Plymouth Fury defiled by high school bullies. His girlfriend Leigh (Alexandra Paul) is only beginning to understand the supernatural powers of the car, which has apparently possessed Arnie.

interested in anything but the car. Apparently as a result of his transformation, he gains a highly coveted human girlfriend as well, the virginal Leigh (Alexandra Paul), who's such a contrast and a threat to Christine that the car tries to kill her, forcing Arnie to declare his devotion to the car over Leigh.

The film's imaging of Arnie and Dennis is rather unusual: Dennis is a popular jock at school who defends Arnie from auto shop thugs, and he does not envy Arnie for winning Leigh as much as he becomes concerned that Arnie is acting self-destructively, an unexpected portrait of a high school jock who's not only emotionally invested in a friend but a nerd friend moreover. Arnie's change is signaled by his upturned collars, doffing of his large glasses, and newly aggressive manner with his parents (as if the car has regressed him from '70s nerd to '50s rebel), and further by his dismissal of Dennis, who in an emotional scene actually cries over how Christine has affected Arnie. Referring to Wood's classic horror film argument, Sheila Johnston describes Arnie's metamorphosis as " 'the return of the repressed' which surfaces through the supernatural aspect of *Christine,* the disturbing side of masculinity normally glossed over in growing up movies," the opposite of which—a reassuring side of masculinity—can be said of Dennis.[39] The horrific parts of the film come when Christine chases down and kills Arnie's high school antagonists, who had also earlier broken into his garage and viciously destroyed the car, even shitting on the dashboard, whereupon the car seemed to "heal" herself. The vile "gang rape" of the car is thus the motivation for Arnie's revenge scenario, although Christine's connection to the demonic (the car has been killing passengers since it was first assembled) is the force that simultaneously restores her and keeps Arnie pathologically attached. In the climactic showdown, Dennis and Leigh join forces and crush the car with a bulldozer after it kills Arnie, although the film ends with a typical shot portending that the car may still be "alive." (Fortunately, there were no sequels.)

Christine offers a troubling notion of how far an outcast teen may go to gain respect and attention, although Arnie's culpability is supposedly alleviated by his "possession" by the feminine auto, as if a nerd could only gain such respect and attention through supernatural forces. The narrative offers little explanation for why this one car is so demonic, but in its examination of the relationship among the three main teenagers, the film's message becomes one about the pitfalls of artificial rebellion, if not more so about the dangers of neurotic devotion, which in this case is the result of Arnie's displaced sexual frustration. Before Christine kills him, Arnie tells Dennis that love has a voracious appetite that consumes everything around it unless you "feed it right," and Arnie says he has such a love for Christine. This pathetic and demented perspective on love as destruction is one high school nerd's rationalized attempt to explain his difference from his peers, a horrific product of adolescent social frustration at its worst.

Various demons also lurked behind the plots of late-'80s teen horror films such as *Night of the Demons, 976-EVIL,* and the handful of films about the supposedly dark powers of rock music. *Night of the Demons* (1987), while not theatrically or critically successful, nonetheless generated two sequels in the '90s, and all three films revolve around the haunted goings-on at an abandoned funeral parlor called Hull House, where in the first film two high school girls become "sexually possessed" and go on an erotic-homicidal rampage. *Night of the Demons 2* (1994) actually featured more-developed teen characters, who again become sexually possessed by the house demons, although this version is more direct in its equation of teen sexual desire with demonic possession: the titillating nudity of the film ultimately becomes terrifying, and the demons themselves are deceptively sexually inviting. The evil spirits returned again for the third film, which appeared in 1997 and did little to further the franchise, even if it maintained the theme of the series on the latent evils of female sexual domination. *976-EVIL* (1988) features a teenage boy who tries to transform from a wimpy nerd to a hip demon though an occult phone service, and like all youth who attempt to use supernatural forces to improve their personal life, the protagonist perishes accordingly. Not unlike *Christine,* this is a nerd transformation scenario gone bad, warning that if wimps do not accept the minimal appeal of their sensitivity and insight, then they will be damned in denying it for any greater power, which will only destroy them.[40]

The 1988 remake of *The Blob* combined teenage social tensions with extraterrestrial fears and government conspiracy theories. In this rare supernatural plot where the teen protagonists have no role in initiating the terror, juvenile delinquent Brian (Kevin Dillon) finds himself teamed up with previously snobby cheerleader Meg (Shawnee Smith) in fighting the oleaginous monster, the residue from a "meteorite" that is really a government experiment in chemical warfare gone mysteriously wrong.[41] After the blob begins consuming various people, the prim Meg actually defies her parents and seeks out Brian to ask for help, revealing her respect for his toughness and showing him that she means business by saying the word "shit." Brian and Meg eventually run into the clutches of a corrupt government biological team that is trying to control the blob and that views its victims as expendable test subjects.

Brian rushes to the rescue on his mighty motorcycle, while Meg realizes that the blob can only be stopped by being frozen and engages the locals to train gas fire extinguishers on it. Brian then hijacks a snow-making truck and drives it into the blob; only Meg becomes the hero when she loads the truck with a bomb, causing it to explode into ice crystals, thereby saving Brian and the entire town. The film's development of its teen characters is inconsistent—a stereotypical high school lothario becomes one of the first victims when he tries to take advantage of his blob-infested girlfriend—yet Meg's image as an indefatigable savior, of her new boyfriend and everyone else, is worth emphasizing, not only for the rarity of being a teen female action hero, but for her swift dismissal of her clean cheerleader image to become the intrepid avenger of the town's destruction. Meg and Brian make no pretensions to take on the government or the forces that set the blob on its rampage, nor is their devotion to each other excessively romantic or sanguine. In their determination to simply destroy the blob and save themselves, Meg and Brian become two of the most resourceful, smart, and ironically realistic teens in the entire horror subgenre.

Although the supernatural youth film subgenre became even more prolific over the next few years, the films were generally less visible. *Clown House* and *The Kiss* were made 1988, followed by *The Channeler, Teen Witch,* and *Girlfriend from Hell* in 1989, the latter of which features an outcast teen girl being turned into an insatiable vamp by the devil.

Supernatural Films of the 1990s

The supernatural youth film remained a consistent style of teen horror in the '90s despite the continually diffuse quality of its output during the decade. Obscure and familiar products continued to appear such as *Cthulhu Mansion* (1991), *Pet Sematary 2* (1992), *Teenage Exorcist* (1993), *Shrunken Heads* (1994), and *Black Circle Boys* (1997), while more prominent supernatural films remained quite intriguing. One of the best (and one of the best teen horror films in general) was the fascinating *Mirror, Mirror* in 1990.

Mirror, Mirror features unusually complex teen characters in Megan (Rainbow Harvest) and Nikki (Kristen Dattilo), who form a friendship after the recently relocated Megan enrolls in Nikki's cliquish private high school. Megan is an outcast from the start, wearing conspicuously gothic fashions, and when the established students tease her, the well-adjusted Nikki comes to her defense. Megan soon realizes that an old mirror left in her new house has the power to grant distorted wishes: she longs for her dead father, who returns only to decompose in front of her, and a rival at school develops a massive nose bleed as the mirror seems to bleed as well. What Megan wants most is not to have the mirror grant her wishes but to achieve them on her own, which is the very sense of power and confidence that she fails to muster. At one point Megan lures a boy to her through the mirror, but when he seems to reject her, she orders the mirror to take him away. She later conjures up the mirror's power to kill two more students, mistakenly believing this will impress Nikki, and Megan finally realizes that the mirror has grown out of her control as it leads her to kill her mother and Nikki's boyfriend, and eventually kills Megan herself. In a narrative twist, Nikki inadvertently wishes everything would return "to the way it was," and finds herself back in 1939, when the mirror first witnessed a woman killing her sister, who now turns out to be Nikki killing Megan, thereby continuing the cycle of murder that possessed the mirror in the first place.

Mirror, Mirror, like *976-EVIL* and other supernatural teen films, demonstrates the consequences of using mysterious forces to gain social acceptance. Megan initially believes that she can learn to control the mirror's power—a particularly potent scene shows her caressing the blood-dripping mirror as if it were a lover, pointing to the masturbatory narcissism that has arisen from her need to feel desired—but eventually the dark forces of the mirror, generated as they were by a generational hatred between sisters, corrupt her wishes. Megan's lack of faith in herself leads her to exploit the deceptive authority the mirror temporarily grants, and Nikki's distrust of Megan fuels the tragic tension between the two. Nikki tries to save Megan from the mirror's clutches only to find herself damned by her own desires for restoration, as if the mirror represents the lost sororal connection enacted by the original murder between the two 1939 sisters, a system of revenge in which the "good sister" destroys her less attractive counterpart. *Mirror, Mirror* portrays the tyranny of teen popularity in its image of Megan oppressed by both benevolent and malicious social forces, and ultimately posits that one's self-image is shaped less by true reflection than by social construction, as distorted as that image may be.[42]

Body Snatchers, a 1993 remake of the 1956 classic *Invasion of the Body Snatchers* (which had already been remade in 1978), uses a teenage girl as its moral and rational conscience, as she tries to evade the evil forces of the alien-infiltrated military which is harboring pods that erase one's identity and make everyone into the same type of automaton. John Powers observed that the film's "real subject is adolescent angst, the terror that the adult world will turn one's youthful uniqueness into a dull, quiescent middle-aged conformity," a viable reading that nonetheless requires a more complete historical perspective.[43] The 1950s story was read as a metaphor of McCarthy-era fears of communism; after *The Blob* in 1988, this *Body Snatchers* further invoked the paranoia of governmental conspiracies, so that the role of the lead teen is, if somewhat weakly, connected to the distrust of organized authority. Perhaps the film's most insightful point about its protagonist is her inability to fake the unemotional manner of the aliens—she is a genuinely sincere soul in a sea of posers. *Body Snatchers* is a fable of individuality in the face of overwhelming conformity, which in this context seems more a critique of the political status quo than a message to youth seeking their true selves.

The Faculty (1998) is another revision of the *Body Snatchers* scenario, this time with a group of unlikely teens banding together to resist the alien invaders who pose as their teachers and then their classmates. The film diligently employs the five school character types, and yet there are six teens: as it turns out, one of them is an alien, and the other youth must rely on their idiosyncratic qualities in surviving. Thus, the nerd provides necessary information, the popular girl supplies inspiring attitude, and in the narrative's oddest element, a smart delinquent develops the amphetamine that determines just who is an alien and who is human, so that for these teens doing drugs is their only means of showing just how "in" they are. Again, the threat to these youth is conformity, and they find themselves proudly upholding their senses of identity as they battle their way through the emotionless invaders until the nerd emerges as hero and destroys the mother monster, saving them all. Yet afterward, each of the characters find themselves on the verge of an unexpected transformation—the nerd has become a desired celebrity, the rebel girl has given up her "fake" lesbian identity to take up with the jock—and while this seems an homage to *The Breakfast Club,* it points to an interesting irony, since the teens' conquering of expansive evil has actually freed them from their previously restrictive roles, or conversely, through making them so acceptable, has rendered them even more conformist.

Whereas these two body-snatching scenarios appeared in films made five years apart, two 1996 films about Catholic school girls trying to master witchcraft appeared only months apart, as the low-budget *Little Witches* tried to capitalize on the notoriety of *The Craft,* which was certainly its superior.[44] In *The Craft,* Sarah (Robin Tunney) is a new teen in town, trying to make friends and recover from a suicide attempt. She meets Chris (Skeet Ulrich) at her Catholic prep school and warms to him, and he warns her about three girls who are looking for a fourth to join their minicoven, a contempt that Roger Ebert wryly questioned "since they have messy hair, slather on black lipstick, wear leather dog collars, smoke a lot, have rings piercing many of the penetrable parts of their bodies, sneer constantly, and, in short, look like normal, popular teenagers."[45] The nonetheless marginalized girls, who are led by Nancy (Fairuza Balk), befriend Sarah and tell her of their worship of a spirit who gives them their witchy powers. Sarah is initially reluctant to join despite her own obvious mystical talents, but she commits to the group after Chris spreads lies that she had sex with him, thereby establishing a galvanizing revenge scenario. As the story proceeds, each girl in the group is further revealed to have a certain personal problem: Nancy lives in squalor with her floozy mother and abusive stepfather, Bonnie (Neve Campbell) has burns covering much of her upper body that make her feel ugly, and Rachelle (Rachel True) is taunted by a popular girl at school who makes racist remarks about her. These dilemmas are meant to motivate the girls' turn to witchcraft, but as they systematically use the occult to eliminate these problems, their desire for more power corrupts them. Only Sarah, who does not need the "craft" to correct her personal misfortune, tries to maintain a safe distance: she puts a spell on Chris that makes him irrationally devoted to her and shows the other girls how they can levitate and, in a more cosmetic use of the power, change their facial features.

What seems like female bonding with the girls' wearing similar clothes and exchanging intimate stories becomes suspect as their occult powers yield more dramatic results: Rachelle's racist agitator loses her hair, Bonnie's scars heal, and Nancy's mean stepfather dies, leaving her and her mother a small fortune in life insurance. These changes fulfill what these characters have desired all along, but in true Faustian fashion, they do not guarantee happiness. Nancy becomes the most obsessed of the group and counters Sarah's growing concern, although after Sarah is attacked by Chris—his irrational devotion has turned him into a brutish rapist—Nancy reveals a more fundamental jealousy of her since Chris had previously rejected Nancy. In a scene that speaks to the dual tensions of good/evil and virgin/whore that the film sets up, Nancy tries to seduce Chris at a party in the form of Sarah: Chris desires the virginal Sarah, but Nancy cannot lure him to her aggressive carnality, resulting in Nancy "casting" him out of a window to his death. Despite this moralizing in the film—Nancy can never fully accept her true nature—Sarah nonetheless appeals to further occult powers as a way of leaving the group, "binding" Nancy from doing harm and invoking the spirit of her dead mother, who she realizes was a witch herself. This doesn't stop Nancy from enlisting Bonnie and Rachelle in a climactic assault on Sarah, in which Bonnie appears to be given back her scars, Rachelle loses her hair, and Nancy fights Sarah with violent spells and incantations. In the end, Bonnie and Rachelle are relieved of their powers and Nancy is confined to a mental hospital, leaving only Sarah with a sense of the craft, which seems more richly evidenced by her rejection of Bonnie and Rachelle's friendship than by her mental felling of a tree limb with a lightning bolt.

The Craft is as much a critique of the perfidy of school cliques as it is of witchcraft: Sarah simply wants friends, and at first the small group seems supportive and congenial, yet her role in showing the other girls how they can manipulate themselves to get what they want makes her responsible for the dangerous powers they harness. The girls lose sight of their own weaknesses and need for improvement when they see that they can "cure" their problems through superficial means—Bonnie, for instance, becomes a salacious tease as soon as her scars are gone—and in that way they lose their true identities in the fantasy roles they play. Nancy, with the most serious frustrations, suffers the most serious results, and only Sarah, who had previously come to better terms with her problems after her suicide attempt, is able to reject the temptation of abusing occult powers for selfish purposes. In this way *The Craft* undercuts its image of young female empowerment by its emphasis on self-acceptance.

The supernatural plot remained popular into the late '90s, evidenced most prominently by the well-received (if distant) *Carrie* sequel, *The Rage: Carrie 2* (1999), which again took up the story of a downtrodden teenage girl using her psychokinetic talents to avenge her mistreatment by villainous classmates. One important revision this film offers over its original is making the title character more wise and cynical about the behavior that is cast upon her, so that her vulnerability to the clique's scorn is less threatening, and her ultimate revenge against them is, consequently, less satisfying.

As in other styles of teen horror, youth who use the supernatural must not only have a sufficient motive for turning to and/or being victimized by mysterious forces, they must be afforded a greater authority or pride for surviving and rejecting those forces. Perhaps the greatest irony of teen occult stories then is their offering of an alternative explanation for the mysteries of the universe that is no less codified, rule-bound, and unreliable as the conventional forms of worship that the teens are resisting.

CONCLUSION

Like other successful genres, teen horror films achieved their greatest legitimacy through being satirized, first in the 1981 parodies *Student Bodies* and *Wacko,* and then in such productions as *Revenge of the Teenage Vixens from Outer Space* (1986), *Return to Horror High* (1987), and *There's Nothing Out There* (1990). Most recently, *Psycho Beach Party* (2000) and the incredibly successful *Scary Movie* (2000)—the latter of which lifted the original title for *Scream*—made a happy mockery out of old and new youth horror *and* sex film trends, with the long lapse in parodies signifying the culturally dormant period of the horror subgenre when such parodies would have been met with scant enthusiasm (and would have had few recognizable films to mine for their humor). At the end of the '90s, the subgenre had again seen a cyclical peak, which is now almost certain to decline as more nonteen thrillers become popular again, such as *The Blair Witch Project* (1999), *The Matrix* (1999), and *The Sixth Sense* (1999), all of which are also spoofed in *Scary Movie.*

There's Nothing Out There may have actually been the ultimate teen horror parody, written and directed by a college student named Rolfe Kanefsky who had spent his years of higher learning studying and challenging the practices of the entire horror genre. The film tells the story of teens spending spring break at a remote cabin who are systematically killed by a mysterious alien entity. In fact, main character Mike (Craig Peck), with his constant reminders to his friends of how teens like themselves are killed in similar situations in horror movies, seems to have been the direct inspiration for the Randy character in *Scream* six years later; he at least represents the parodic potential Wes Craven exploited in his film by having Randy mimic Mike from this little-seen low-budget prototype.

This film represents an appropriate stopping point for the films in this chapter, in which teens have been sadistically brutalized and have yet been expected to enjoy such a negative representation of themselves with masochistic abandon. Kanefsky himself was barely 20 when he wrote and directed *There's Nothing Out There,* a young man's attempt to "take back" the genre that he felt had so misrepresented youth that the only effective response was to turn the genre's conventions back upon themselves. Perhaps Kanefsky saw himself as the Mike character in his own film, warning his cohort against ignorance and gullibility, trying to make the experience of terror as informed and pleasurable as it could be for a population that had been asked to quiver and die so much at the hands of older filmmakers who told them that they would like the pain. For all of the lessons, entertainment, and provocation that the teen horror subgenre has brought to at least its core audience, few of its films have managed to combine the emotional intensity of fear with the fragile mysteries of entering adulthood and *also* gain respect or credibility with the public at large, despite the valuable, if extreme, portraits of teenagers that the subgenre presents.

5 YOUTH AND SCIENCE
Technology, Computers, Games

Compared to you, most people have the intellect of a carrot.
—PROFESSOR HATHAWAY TO TEEN PRODIGY MITCH IN *Real Genius*

A strange game. The only winning move is not to play.
—THE WAR GAMES COMPUTER IN *WarGames*

People have their good points.
—KYLE, COMPARING HIS GIRLFRIEND TO A ROBOT IN *Evolver*

Perhaps the most hybrid of youth film subgenres is the teen science film, which often combines elements of the school, horror, romance, and even delinquency subgenres, but which differs from those films because its use of science and fantasy yields distinct representations of youth that are not consistently found in those other subgenres. Youth in science films are sometimes the school nerd types who stumble into an adventure because of their keen curiosity, but rarely does that curiosity produce the social transformation that most nerds in school films achieve through fighting their nerd image. Sometimes science youth are tough and cynical teens who discover the value of humanity through a conflict with technology, although rarely do these kids commit any crimes or even push the boundaries of morality like most delinquents' conflicts with adult authority. Sometimes youth engaging in scientific exploits (who are predominantly white males) are also trying to work out romance, yet they rarely have time for sex. The representation of youth in science films occasionally indicates their special innocence or insight that is alien to adults and that provides youth with a new value for their perspective, and while this condition is also the case in many other youth films, in the science film the representation of youth hinges upon a specific combination of fresh intellect and naive insight; other subgenres only occasionally afford youth such a mental sophistication.

The image of youth in science films is always one of awe and fascination, on the part of both the protagonists and the adult perspectives that inform the films' production, always emphasizing the newness and surprising complexity—and hence mystery—of youth's involvement with science and technology. This sense of mystery is the most distinct and consistent generic element of youth science films, subsuming within this subgenre the mystery/thriller dimension of adult films (there are otherwise very few youth detective stories or murder mysteries) and replacing the intrigue of adult criminality with the intrigue of young adult curiosity.

Yet the youth science film does not necessarily borrow from the generic conventions of science fiction, if only because so many youth science films are built upon fairly plausible (if not probable) activities of most youth: the teens in these films discover the amazing capabilities of their new discoveries while engaging in typical youth excursions such as science fairs, summer camps, video games, and "playing around" with computers or media equipment. As in science fiction films, the protagonists encounter a strange new world in this subgenre, but these films tend to enlist their viewers in the possibility of this world occurring quite realistically in the present (although some movies employ unrealistic devices, and a few movies—such as *Solarbabies* and the *Back to the Future* films—are outright exceptions to this realism).

Some youth science films can even be viewed as threats or warnings alerting viewers of the potential dangers behind youth's exploration of science, but all of these films ultimately demonstrate that youth's access to and advancement of science can indeed serve a greater good. In that way, with the exception of the most fanciful films in this subgenre that could indeed be labeled science fiction, these films present a viable model for youth utilizing science in ways that their adult counterparts have not yet realized, and even the most fanciful films endorse a youth perspective on science that is somehow better for humanity at large. This model thus serves the interests of teens and adults alike.

THE THREE DIMENSIONS

The youth science subgenre is indeed the smallest of teen film subgenres, but its films divide into three separate plot dimensions determined by the *type* of science in which the characters are involved. One dimension of youth science films borrows some from science fiction and more from science fact, but still relies largely upon youth's unusual and occasionally dubious achievements in experimental endeavors. This dimension I call "simple science" since it is so often based upon reductions or distortions of scientific knowledge; examples include *Zapped* (1982), *Back to the Future* (1985, and sequels in 1989 and 1990), *Weird Science* (1985), *The Manhattan Project* (1986), and *October Sky* (1999). The second dimension of science films ups the ante of plausibility by incorporating the current technologies of computers and electronic games, which youth manipulate for pleasure or parental attention, such as *WarGames* (1983), *The Last Starfighter* (1984), *Arcade* (1993), and *Hackers* (1995). The third and most recently emerging dimension of youth science films involves young adults' access to media technologies, which, like computers, they also use to access new avenues of pleasure and self-expression, as in *Pump Up the Volume* (1990), *Wayne's World* (1992), *S.F.W.* (1995), and *Anarchy TV* (1997).

There is an interesting chronology of these different dimensions of youth science films over the past two decades. American political conditions often factor into simple science films, many of which incorporate subplots about corrupt government officials and scientists, such as *My Science Project* (1985), *Real Genius* (1985), and *The Manhattan Project*. Being thus time-bound, such examples gained popularity in the mid-'80s but disappeared by the end of the decade. Perhaps the increasing legitimacy of youth's access to computers and actual scientific knowledge signaled the end of this dimension, but the political tensions of the Cold War also fueled the fantasies of these films, as well as the computer films *WarGames* and *Defense Play* (1988).

In the dimension of computers and video games, the chronological shifts are not as distinct. Youth's use of computers in these films has become more confident but has not resulted in a higher output of examples. Considering the increasing media attention to children's use of computers (especially the Internet), the low number of films made in this dimension over the past 20 years is surprising. A few of these films are based on actual technologies that teens could indeed exploit, but some interject elements of fantasy (space travel, supernatural contact) to explain the characters' achievements, and all of them (save the teen sex romp *Joysticks*) point to a level of human interaction that these characters would be better off exploiting. This is the case from *WarGames* in 1983 to *Masterminds* in 1997.

The third dimension of youth science films, in which youth become involved in media production, only became prominent in the '90s, and has had a relatively low output; I thus omit a more complete analysis of these films.

However, media movies do demonstrate a set of concerns similar to those introduced in the computer films of the '80s: youth can utilize radio, video, and television for self-expression, but this use of technology can also be corruptive. Even the comic antics of *Wayne's World* and its sequel point to an exploitation of youth by corporate forces, led by adults who act young but who are ultimately more concerned with profits than pleasure or self-expression. While the radio technology utilized in *Pump Up the Volume* was available to youth for many years previously, the video technology in other youth media films only opened to consumers in the 1980s, and garnered faint interest in such productions as *I Was a Teenage TV Terrorist* (1987) and *S.F.W.*, even though these films speculate on how that technology—which '90s teens became exposed to as '80s children—helps young people to identify who they are. As with the minimal attention paid to youth in movies using computers, the paucity of films showing youth using media raises suspicions about Hollywood's reluctance to celebrate the empowering potential such technologies hold for young people. A recent example is the Oscar-winning *American Beauty* (1999), which portrayed its male teen protagonist's use of video as effectively neurotic, and only implied the liberatory expressive aspect of his digital camera.

Strikingly little research has been done on the depiction of science in youth films, despite the extensive writing that has been done on science fiction in general. (The "Wired" chapter from Bernstein's *Pretty in Pink,* the only source I found that evaluates youth science films as a subgenre, glosses over their social significance.) Considering not only the appeal and curiosity of these films, but the fact that youths' real-life involvement with science and technology is so often debated in the popular media, one can only wonder why researchers have not paid more attention to this issue. Quite likely the same ambiguous but certainly repressive forces that continue to restrict the production of youth science films to this day are responsible for the lack of serious study of these films. If adults begin to take seriously the power that youth are rapidly developing through their access to science and technology by depicting that access in films and validating it through research, they could aggravate their already explicit fears of an unmanageable, technically superior youth population.

SIMPLE SCIENCE

Films that appeal to teens' scientific curiosities offer some of the most energizing messages in youth cinema for their student viewers, enlisting (if not encouraging) the ambitions of intellectual success that children begin to develop when they are first asked what they want to do when they grow up. Often the mental complexity of these films is understandably minimal, with scientific terminology reduced to cool tech talk that usually cannot explain the complications of the films' plots, and in many cases the scientific principles under which the young characters work are either woefully misinformed or, more likely, simply indifferent to the realities of science. After all, these films are about fulfilling fantasies that often do not conform to concepts as rigid as laws of physics or nature, and the films portray their protagonists as smart enough or determined enough to overcome the limits of adult ideas and beliefs. In that way, most of these films cater to an image of youth that is based not only on a certain faith that adults do not exhibit, but on a certain wisdom as well.

There have been just over a dozen youth films in the past generation that explore how young people encounter and utilize science for purposes of self-discovery and identification, almost all of which were made between 1982 and 1990. The few films that employed at least somewhat rational scientific principles were generally made between 1984 and 1986, when the youth science film was at its apex: most of the films I locate in this dimension were made in that short time. In fact, Kim Newman even called "high-school science fiction" the "genre-of-the-year for 1985."[1] The reason for this is likely a combination of financial and social factors: the science-fantasy *E.T. The Extra-Terrestrial,* which featured a 10-year-old befriending a lovable alien, became the highest-grossing film of its time in 1982, and *Back to the Future* became a massively successful youth-themed time-travel hit in 1985. Hollywood studios must have realized the potential return on films that catered to both children's and adults' curiosities of the scientifically paranormal. Further, in the early '80s the thriving U.S. space shuttle program turned Americans' attention back to some of the previous generation's enthusiasm for space conquest and scientific progress, although these ambitions were severely traumatized by the *Challenger* disaster in 1986. The only visible films made since 1986 about youth utilizing rational principles of science (that is, outside of using computers, games, or media) have been *Race the Sun* (1996) and the '50s rocket-building tale *October Sky* (1999), neither of which were met with much attention.

Science in these films takes on one of two forms: the variety that attempts to appear rational, if radical, and the variety that casts science aside in the interest of more fanciful ideas. I proceed by dividing the simple science films accordingly.

Rational Science

The film that kicked off the "it could happen" premises of '80s simple science films, the 1984 sleeper *Kidco,* was actually less about science and more about business, and indeed, the film's populist youth message is so strong that young people could adopt its mythology for their own inspiration; there are few youth films in this entire study that are so literally supportive of preadult ingenuity and power. The story revolves around four siblings who develop and sell fertilizer from their farm to the local community, rising to rather immediate success but running into tax problems that they solve through their clever knowledge of soil science, economics, and law. *Kidco* demonstrates an unusually high level of confidence in its young characters, whose spirit to succeed is ultimately more important than their scientific or business acumen. This same attitude informs almost all of the other realist youth science movies that followed (exceptions being the barely seen video release *Twisted* [1985], and *Chopping Mall* [1986], a schlock horror spoof on rampant technology).

Another informed depiction of youth using science is in the 1985 film *Real Genius,* which opens with a rather high-tech demonstration of a secret government laser weapons system that a smarmy professor at a California polytechnic university is helping to develop with the research of his best students, unbeknownst to them. This plot device is rather cumbersome compared to the concerns of the 15-year-old main character, Mitch (Gabe Jarret), a genius who has been recruited by the professor straight out of his 10th-grade science fair, and who enrolls at the university filled with adolescent awe and anxiety about the bewildering potential surrounding him. That potential is best represented by the college-age Chris (Val Kilmer), a fellow prodigy who is one of the best minds at the school, even though he has learned to rebel against the academic elitism of his colleagues through serious partying. Mitch and Chris form a tenuous friendship: Mitch struggles to adapt to the fast pace of college life, feeling homesick and intimidated by his rowdy peers, and Chris inevitably exaggerates that sense of intimidation, both intellectually and emotionally. Mitch also becomes confused by his feelings for the supersmart, hyperkinetic Jordan (Michelle Meyrink), who comes on with an instant crush, made more bewildering by Mitch's lack of familiarity with relationships based on feelings instead of thoughts.

The film presents a clear indictment of the troubling connection between scholarly research and military-industrial exploitation (the laser being developed is intended to be strong enough to kill people from space), but *Real*

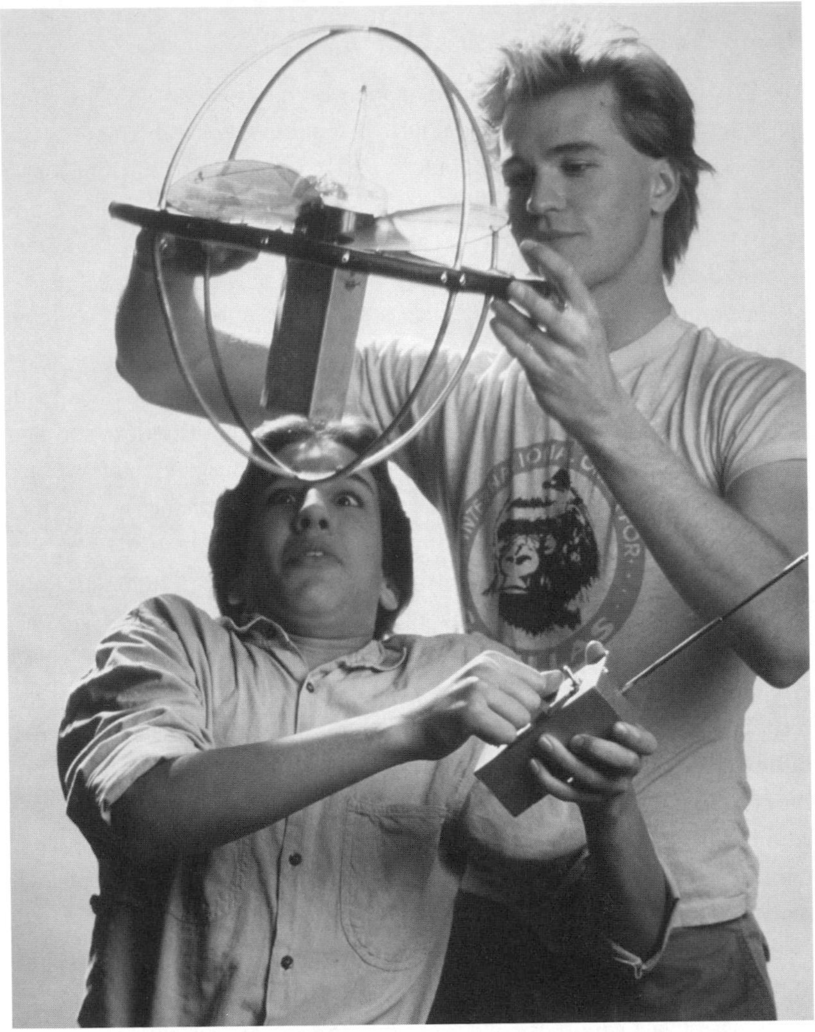

Adolescent whiz kid Mitch (Gabe Jarret, left) has a supreme understanding of science but is bewildered by partying prodigy Chris (Val Kilmer) in *Real Genius* (1985).

Genius spends more time contemplating the image problems faced by its genius characters. These students are not nearly so nerdy as their high school counterparts, with the clear exception of Mitch, whose clothes, awkwardness, and physical appearance remind us that despite his environment he is still a high school nerd, or as David Edelstein observed, "Mitch is stiff and sweet and unaffected. He's a mouth breather, a guy you pray will remember to swallow so he doesn't drool over his experiments."[2] Mitch and his colleagues are revealed to be the "real" geniuses of the film through their eventual realization that their talents are being corrupted; their youthful sagacity is brought out by their commitment to science for more pragmatic purposes, such as sabotaging the space laser to hit their professor's house, wherein they have positioned an enormous amount of popcorn, which then causes the house to explode in a burst of fluffy yet harmless puffed kernels.

Along the way, the young characters struggle with their advanced projects (offering a smattering of physics speak as they refine multimillion-dollar systems), stress over studying for finals, and ultimately accept that their smarts must be balanced by a zest for traditional pleasures, which is symbolized by the reclusive genius they discover living underneath the university who eventually uses his talents to win a contest so that he can wallow in consumer products and travel away in a motor home. *Real Genius* portrays the teen Mitch as one of the few complicated movie prodigies who is *not* determined to shed his intellectual image, who becomes accepted by his peers not only because he is smart but because he *learns* to have fun. His growing attraction to Jordan indicates his slow but certain ascent to a level of sexuality that is common among college students but has to be carefully negotiated for adolescents, a task at which Mitch genuinely succeeds. *Real Genius* presents the most plausible means by which a teen with the gifted curse of serious scientific comprehension can socially integrate with older students and retain a youthful, unembittered sense of discovery.

The plight of young scientist Paul (Christopher Collett) in the 1986 film *The Manhattan Project* involves similar adult-government conspiracies as *Real Genius,* although Paul's journey from the science fair to "saving the world" is far more literal and solitary, as he builds a nuclear bomb to demonstrate the imminent dangers of the technology. The film is thus a rare instance of youth using science to generate social change (although others do so with computers and media), even if its image of Paul as a teen with a message about technology is built upon his actual understanding and use of the very technology that he finds abhorrent. In that way, Paul is ironically aligned with his adult adversaries, and his otherwise delinquent application of science to achieve social awareness compromises his moral mission.

A far more problematic circumstance related to current technology arrived with the Twentieth Century–Fox release of *SpaceCamp* during the same week as *The Manhattan Project,* which the studio also produced. The timing could not have been much worse for the box office: just six months before its June 1986 premiere, the space shuttle *Challenger* exploded after liftoff, killing its entire crew. The film was shot the previous year at NASA's Space and Rocket Center in Alabama, where many young students had actually joined in camps to learn about and "experience" space exploration, and the film was clearly intended to join the growing list of youth science films that were appearing at the time, if not to capitalize specifically on youth interest in shuttle missions. By that summer of 1986, the space shuttle program was on indefinite hold, and many people—especially students, who had watched a schoolteacher die in the tragic accident—were not warm to the entertainment of watching five youths and a teacher being accidentally sent into space on a shuttle, thereafter fighting for their lives to pilot the ship back to Earth. Instead of advancing the simple science dimension, *SpaceCamp* effectively ended it.

The story borrows from *The Breakfast Club* by forcing together five contrasting young characters, who meet at the NASA Space Camp for a summer of educational excitement (they have all qualified for entrance through impressive academic records and interest in science). The oldest boy, Kevin (Tate Donovan), is an overconfident and aggressive rich kid, handling his sexual tensions with a girl colleague named Kathryn (Lea Thompson), who is ambitious but insecure; the remaining three are enterprising black teen Rudy (Larry B. Scott), who is given the mildly racist goal of opening fast-food franchises in space; a genius girl named Tish (Kelly Preston), who eschews her smarts through her garish outfits and makeup; and preteen prodigy Max (Leaf Phoenix), who the other kids tease for being so immature. After some failed training lessons, the five are elected to sit in a real space shuttle with their female instructor while ground control test-fires the ship's rockets. Unknown to them, a robot prototype, who had "befriended" Max, literally interprets his wish to be launched into space and overrides the ground control system, launching the five students and their teacher into orbit. The teacher initially has things under control and the students begin to enjoy their amazing journey, but the ship begins to run out of oxygen and the teacher gets trapped outside the shuttle, leaving the students to command the ship, work out many technical maneuvers, and save their teacher.

SpaceCamp, despite its forced attempt at a representative sampling of youth, does offer a dignified vision of teens using their brains while remaining conscious of their emotional crises. Of course the youth save the day (and their teacher), resulting in valuable identity lessons for all—Kevin learns to not be such a jerk, Kathryn gains confidence, Max earns respect—and the film develops these characters' epiphanies with sincerity. The film points out that

that the realities of science are incredibly complicated, and if youth are to achieve scientific know-how, they must be patient, hardworking, and willing to learn. In reflecting on the real-life shuttle disaster, David Sterritt wrote that *SpaceCamp,* "with its affection for the romance of space travel, and its message that youngsters always have a right to aspire to the stars, [is] a refreshing antidote to recent events."[3] How unfortunate then that just as films like *SpaceCamp, Real Genius,* and *Kidco* were beginning to demonstrate the realistic potential of youth to learn and use science—even while other films were demonstrating that potential in more fanciful terms—the dimension all but vanished. Perhaps the best evidence of this is *Beyond the Stars* (1989), which, despite starring the popular Christian Slater as a teenager who befriends astronaut Martin Sheen and becomes fascinated with lunar missions, had a restricted release and went largely unnoticed. The next significant films about youth and science would not be made until 1990, and they would still largely avoid issues about *learning* science, concentrating instead on computers, games, and media.

Only two films have been made about youth using rational scientific principles since 1986: *Race the Sun* in 1996 and *October Sky* in 1999, the first of which clearly indicated that the era of tech talk and scientific ingenuity marked by the mid-'80s films had evaporated, leaving only the spirit of youthful determination. *Race the Sun* is based on the true story of seven underachieving high school students from Hawai'i, who gain prominence in an international solar-powered car race across Australia. The film is unremarkable for its scant use of science, although its mid-'90s statement on race is curious (and reveals the significance of its title), since the students' inspiring teacher is African American and they are all native Hawai'ian—except for their leader, who is a white boy. The racial tensions of the plot are far more central than the students' brief foray into the science required to build their solar car, and they finish the grueling race in third place based on their physical persistence more than their intellect.

October Sky is at least a somewhat more scientifically minded story, perhaps because the source of its true story is two generations past, and thus its mentality is more sentimental and understandable for viewers. Homer Hickam (Jake Gyllenhaal) is a high school student in 1957 who decides to enter the field of rocketry amidst the humble squalor of his poor West Virginia coal mining town. The story gets some thrills out of Homer's rocket work, but the film is primarily a family drama, with Homer living in the shadow of his football star brother (like many other bright boys in American films, Homer tries to be athletic but fails), and living under the torment of his miner father, who would like to see his son taking up his coal career rather than dabbling in Sputnik-era aeronautics. Homer is not a born genius: he blows up all of his first rockets, even after he befriends class nerd Quentin (Chris Owen) and joins two other friends in building a launch pad on a distant hillside. But the boys have a predictably strong ally in their female science teacher Miss Riley (Laura Dern), who overcomes her own initial doubts to promote their efforts, and Homer is aided by his dad's coworkers at the mine, who help him forge various metal parts—everyone, it seems, wants to see Homer succeed in his odyssey except his father.

Despite their setbacks, the four boys work through various rocket prototypes and show further gumption by selling old railroad steel to fund their projects. Throughout, the narrative keeps the math and science involved in their plans at the margins, justified partly by the heroic Homer's deference to Quentin in understanding how their rockets work, until Homer begins learning more about such concepts as alcohol fuel and nozzle forms, and the boys hold their first successful launches. Unfortunately they are falsely accused of setting a forest fire with a runaway rocket and Homer's father is injured in an accident, so Homer agrees to drop his rocket plans and work in the mine to support his family. Adding to his anguish, Miss Riley is diagnosed with cancer, which further inspires Homer to clear his name from the fire incident through his diligent effort to learn trigonometry and explain his case to local officials. Homer returns to the rocket project with his friends and goes on to win the national science fair, earning college scholarships for his team and, in a touching conclusion, winning the restrained admiration of his father.

October Sky exemplifies well why simple science movies effectively faded away, not because it is unappealing (on the contrary, it is entirely heartwarming), but because it exposes its intimidation by the scientific principles its young protagonists master and instead concentrates on the more universal theme of needing parental love. This is a symptom of the inevitable approach Hollywood currently takes for its products, seeking wider audience profits compared to the more confidently teen-centric science films of the '80s. To its credit (and more so than *Race the Sun*), the film does portray the students using actual scientific methods and assertively learning to achieve their sapient goals, and on a general level, the film refreshingly "treats its teen-aged hero and his pals as distinctive, sentient human beings," as Susan Stark noted.[4] Yet the narrative's period setting and family turmoil neutralize the intellectual energy that the story is otherwise built upon, if only because the technology in question has been long since outdated and the family's influence is shown as disruptive to academic progress. The fact that the film was called "The Rocket Boys" during production (taken from the original title of Hickam's autobiography) and changed to the bland *October Sky* testifies to the studio's lack of faith in promoting a movie about science and youth, and regardless of the name change and the film's appeal, it was not popular at the box office. Nonetheless, the film does uphold many of the familiar traditions in representing teens involved with science: Homer gains authority through his endeavors and overcomes his lower-class liabilities, he is too busy working or studying to foster the crush a local girl develops on him, and his success shows adults the boundless potential of youth to learn and discover things their elders have begun to ignore.

Given the faithful adherence to these traditions by both *Race the Sun* and *October Sky,* and the fact that both films are ironically based on true stories using clear creative license, any future films about real youth using science will likely appear in a similar mold, carefully curtailing the acumen of their characters for the sake of amplifying more common dramatic qualities. The question remains if these films will also inadvertently curtail the very ambitions that compel youth to explore scientific ideas by continuing to make these ideas appear secondary to experiencing dramatic emotions.

Fantasy Science

The fanciful application of science to youth films produced an odd string of silly youth images in the 1980s. These films exploited typical teen anxieties such as dating, gaining popularity, and passing courses, while using a sci-fi aspect—combined with ubiquitous special effects—as a means of appealing to '80s science interests. The actual science that goes on in these films is understandably distorted if not entirely abstract, and these films accordingly offer rather extreme images of their young characters.

The excesses of the fantasy science category are best represented in its first '80s film, *Zapped,* a 1982 feature that oddly harks back to children's films of the '60s and '70s that featured youths with special mental powers (e.g., *The Computer Wore Tennis Shoes* [1969], *Now You See Him, Now You Don't* [1972], *Escape to Witch Mountain* [1975], *Return from Witch Mountain* [1978], and even the 1976 teen horror film *Carrie,* which the makers of *Zapped* intended to lightly parody), yet updating its formula to accommodate the then-current wave of teen sexploitation.[5] The story concerns two high school seniors, Barney (Scott Baio), a science whiz with inexplicably complete control of his own lab at school, and Peyton (Willie Aames), his oversexed and less thoughtful sidekick. Barney seems to be interested in testing the effects of alcohol on mice, but he and Peyton are also growing enormous marijuana plants in his lab. By chance Barney gives a mouse a concoction of beer and cannabis extract, which mysteriously gives the mouse telekinetic powers. He later knocks over a beaker of the special solution, inhales the fumes, and develops telekinetic powers himself—a true teen fantasy of the "beneficial" side effects of the two most popular youth drugs. Barney gradually realizes the extent of his powers as he causes maps to fall on a teacher during class, forces a girl's sweater to pop open, and makes toys in his room fly. Given Barney's supposed interest in science and the obvious potential of his telekinesis, he would be wise to investigate the composition of the mystery liquid and test it further, but the film's engagement with science ends when Barney and Peyton turn to using Barney's telekinesis for pranks and the procurement of girlfriends.

Zapped is one of the odd youth science films where the protagonists actually have sex: Peyton seduces prom queen Jane (Heather Thomas) after beating her boyfriend in a drinking contest, and Barney uses his telekinetic powers to bed Bernadette (Felice Schachter), a student reporter, on top of his lab table. This prolonged scene clearly demonstrates that the film is concentrated on the sexual more than the scientific (also evidenced by an unnecessary subplot in which the school principal has trysts with a teacher), and while Barney does exhibit a rather sincere interest in Bernadette, the film concludes with the inevitable prom where Barney uses his powers to rip off Jane's clothes, much to the delight of Peyton, and then rips off everyone else's clothes, resulting in much gratuitous nude mayhem.

Zapped thereby devolves into a sex farce, although the film does offer at least two interesting points of consideration for the fantasy science category. First, the meager use of "science" is to fulfill teen fantasies, not to respond to the perceived adult oppression that marks most other youth science films; the film clearly has little respect for science, but does demonstrate that using it (even unintentionally) can be fun. Second, Barney's caricatured parents present a paradigm that parents in many youth science films later follow: they don't understand their more intelligent child, and actually come to fear him (his mother even brings in priests to perform an exorcism). When parents are present in youth science films—which isn't very often—they tend to be baffled by and suspicious of their children, calling attention to the image of adult discomfort at the access youth have to science and technology.

1985 and 1986 were prolific years for the fantasy science category, just as they were for more realistic youth films. One of the biggest hits of the '80s was *Back to the Future,* released in July 1985 and followed the next month by *Weird Science* and *My Science Project* and in 1986 by *Solarbabies*. Despite its teen protagonist, *Back to the Future* was a typical Hollywood product designed to offer a visible cross-generational appeal in its story of 1980s boy Marty McFly (Michael J. Fox) being sent back to the 1950s. Unlike the usual smart science protagonists, Marty is scientific only by association, as his "Doctor" friend (Christopher Lloyd) handles the technology, leaving Marty to focus on pleasure-seeking consumption, since his greatest concerns are to play guitar at the prom, get back to his 1980s girlfriend after uniting his '50s-era parents, and enjoy more Pepsi. As David Denby put it, Marty "has the one thing every teenager wants—a superior experience of popular culture."[6] *Back to the Future* is less important for its portrayal of science or youth (indeed, most of the film is a period piece offering anachronistic mythological images of America in the '50s) than it is for its sheer success, which seemed to indicate that the combination of teens and pseudoscience—which thereby justified showy special effects—was a box-office treasure. This success is what the film's two sequels, and the other fantasy science films that followed, tried to exploit. Ironically, *Back to the Future,* which offered a very undeveloped depiction of contemporary youth, was the financial pinnacle of the science subgenre.

Weird Science was an appropriate title for the John Hughes film that followed his *Breakfast Club* from earlier in 1985. Anthony Michael Hall plays Gary, a 15-year-old who lusts after girls at school with his fellow nerdy friend Wyatt (Ilan Mitchell-Smith). Gary and Wyatt come up with a two-part idea to solve both their sexual and social problems: they design a "perfect woman" on their computer (while watching *Frankenstein,* no less), who comes to life during a freak electrical storm, and then they throw a huge party with their new creation, inviting everyone from school. The boys' design of adult "Lisa" (Kelly LeBrock) is a mixture of interesting data, described by Sheila Benson as "a computer-built dream woman with magical powers who can teach them self-confidence without involvement."[7] They feed their computer images of Playboy models and hook it up to a Barbie doll, but they also load in a vast amount of knowledge through a national internet system, since they want a voluptuous and smart woman who can fulfill their carnal *and* intellectual demands. Lisa's intelligence and social graces, as well as her sexuality, are then more than Gary and Wyatt know how to handle: they shower with her but are so intimidated by her (and possibly each other) that they leave their pants on, and later she takes them out for a wild night in Chicago but serves more as a chaperone to keep them out of trouble. (The only overt sexual contact that either of them has with Lisa is when she kisses Gary and grabs his ass, though he does wake up in her underwear.)

Once Lisa is designed in the first few minutes of *Weird Science,* the film pays less attention to further science, concentrating more on Lisa's role in building the teens' "self-confidence without involvement." Wyatt's parents are wealthy and never around, and he is taunted by a mean older brother, whom Lisa ultimately tames by turning him into a grotesque slime monster; Lisa likewise stands up to Gary's oppressive parents, pointing out that they don't love him or understand him. When Lisa uses her special powers to put together the huge party at Wyatt's house, she tries to show the boys how much everyone likes them for who they "really are," although Gary and Wyatt nonetheless attempt to incarnate another woman on their computer during the party, which accidentally results in a (phallic) nuclear missile rising up through the house (this is *weird* science). To teach the boys a lesson, Lisa brings in mutant motorcycle punks to crash the party and encourages Gary and Wyatt to make them leave, which they do, saving the party and gaining much respect from their peers. Gary and Wyatt thus quickly gain girlfriends and explain to Lisa that they don't need her anymore, and so she disappears and restores the otherwise destroyed house to normal.

Weird Science is both an example of the typical nerd transformation narrative common to many high school films and the sci-fi fantasy in which technology is ultimately shown to be a catalyst that makes the protagonists assert their human qualities and later abandon the technology. The film is thus an interesting generic hybrid, belonging also to the computer dimension of the youth science subgenre as well as the school and love/sex subgenres, although unlike the computer films (in which the technology is often similarly abandoned in the end), *Weird Science* incorporates broader scientific desires in the construction of its fantasy fiction, mixing issues of biology, chemistry, and electronics with pop psychology and the standard computer hacking. The protagonists in *Weird Science* do indeed gain self-worth through their crude experimentation, and their image as horny nerds is thereby transformed into that of confident, even arrogant young men—after all that Lisa has done for them, she remains a disposable commodity. Unfortunately, the sexist aspect of this fantasy drowns out the scientific.

The somewhat less sexist and somewhat more scientific film *My Science Project* premiered one week after *Weird Science,* but with much less critical and box-office attention, even though the film's image of disenchanted youth confronting mysteries ignored or misunderstood by adults (especially the government) is rather parallel to the last four youth fantasy science films of the '80s, *Flight of the Navigator, Solarbabies, Deadly Friend* (all 1986), and *Deadly Weapon* (1988). Like *My Science Project,* however, none of these films would garner nearly the same earnings or recognition as *Back to the Future* or *Weird Science,* indicating the waning popularity of the trend.

Deadly Friend offers the deepest commentary of these late-'80s science films, and is worth considering in more detail. The film is the horrific version of a teenage *Bride of Frankenstein,* and is not unlike *Weird Science* in its depiction of a boy creating the "perfect" girl. Paul (Matthew Labortreaux) is a 15-year-old prodigy on scholarship to a polytechnic university where he is involved in developing robotic technology. He has already built a helpful family robot called BB, who also defends Paul against local bullies and helps him to impress the pretty but abused girl next door, Sam (Kristy Swanson). BB is eventually gunned down by an angry neighbor, leaving Paul in shock, which is further compounded when Sam's father beats her so badly that she has a fatal brain hemorrhage. Working off of his unfulfilled attraction to Sam and his recent research in electrobiology, Paul and a friend steal Sam's body from the hospital and Paul implants BB's microchip into her brain.

In scenes that draw attention to the masculine power fantasy on which the film is built, Paul activates Sam by remote control and teaches her how to move, but in a surprising twist, Sam appears to still have her original conscience as well, and goes off to kill her father. Sam later kills the neighbor who destroyed BB, revealing that the prototype robot's "thoughts" are also running through her. Paul realizes that Sam has become dangerous and tries to shut her down, which he cannot do, apparently because her circuitry and chemistry have synthesized to give her autonomy (a temporary nod to feminist vengeance). Just as Sam appears to be reachieving her human nature, police gun her down because of her attacks. The unrepentant Paul then sneaks into a morgue to steal Sam's body again, only this time her skin peels away to reveal BB, who says, "Come with me, Paul," and kills him.

The potency myth of *Weird Science* is here turned into a nightmare, not only because Paul cannot control his creation, but further because the "good" scientist restored "life" to a woman who had been brutally killed and who responds with brutality herself. In many ways *Deadly Friend* is the typical nerd fantasy of an outcast gaining acceptance, and because the acceptance that Paul gains is so rigidly controllable, he becomes distraught by his lack of greater acceptance. Presumably Paul planned to fashion Sam into the girlfriend he never had, and to right the wrongs of her father, yet his high scientific knowledge, it would seem, is no match for a woman scorned. In the end, Paul must pay for his imitation of God by being destroyed by his own creation, only now in its original robotic form, again indicating that the very technology that allows us to manipulate (and simulate) life is also that which destroys it, including those people who manufacture and think they can master the technology. Paul's final union in death with his creation is a clear statement on the perversity of the human desire to control scientific mystique.

Until the appearance of more intelligent teens in *Hackers* and *Evolver* in 1995, for the nine years after 1986, when youth employed science in films (minimally and infrequently), they were portrayed as less astute and simply more "clever" or just lucky. This shift is certainly evident in the last three youth films that focused on fantasy science after 1986, all of which were sequels to previous hits: *Zapped Again,* and *Back to the Future Part II* and *Part III. Zapped Again,* the 1989 sequel to *Zapped,* does offer an interesting gender revision from the original: now the male protagonist is no longer a science whiz, but rather his female crush is more intelligent and enterprising, one of the first smart female teens to employ science in the subgenre, and the only one who expresses a proactive interest in the potential of developing science on a larger scale. Teen females in other '80s films always work in reaction to their male counterparts' ideas, and the more authoritative teen females of '90s science films use their brains to fight adult and peer oppression.

The *Back to the Future* franchise, as previously noted, was never founded on an image of youthful intelligence as much as it was on the adult nostalgia for an innocence since passed, and both sequels became less engaged in the complicated science fantasy of the original film and more on their ostentatious special effects. The series ended in 1990 with its third installment posing as a Western, as if the more scientific aspect of the fantasy could not be sustained. This lack of sustenance marks the entire cycle, since *Back to the Future Part III* is the last notable instance of Hollywood using a young adult actor in a science fantasy unrelated to computers or electronic games.[8]

GAMES AND COMPUTERS

Given the popular rise of arcade-style video games in the early 1980s, as well as their TV and personal computer counterparts, a crossover appeal in other media was inevitable. A number of pop songs related to video games were recorded in the early '80s, children's television programming began incorporating computers and games (in actual game shows and the drama series *Whiz Kids* from 1983–84), and many trade paperbacks emerged that promised to divulge the secrets of success to winning video games.

However, there were relatively few movies that capitalized on the game craze at its peak: *Tron* in 1982 was the most popular, although it featured adult characters, while *Joysticks* (1983) and *The Last Starfighter* (1984) are the only teen films that prominently featured video games in the '80s. By the time of *Arcade* in 1993 and *Brainscan* in 1994, the "video game" was no longer viewed in the pleasurable or even empowering mythology of 10 years earlier—the games had become dangerous. Perhaps the social image of video games as offering necessary outlets to angst-ridden youth had jaundiced into a paranoia arising from the games' exploitation of youth; perhaps studios assumed that young people already had so much enjoyable exposure to video games at home and in arcades that they would not pay to see them happily dramatized on the screen; perhaps the special effects excesses of *Tron*—which required a crew of hundreds of technicians—deterred studios with smaller budgets. In any case, youth access to computerized games in films of the '90s became more sensationally sinister.[9]

Whatever was the reason behind the general disinterest in game-oriented films may have also applied to computer-oriented films about youth, even though *WarGames* was a critical and financial success in the 1983 era of nuclear proliferation (and one of the very few youth films to be nominated for Oscars). There were other Cold War–themed movies such as *Red Dawn* (1984) and *Born American* (1986), which did not rely on the computer smarts of their teen protagonists, but *WarGames* remained the apex of the youth computer film, with only *Explorers* (1985) and the obscure *Defense Play* (1988) offering any other developed depictions of young people using computers in the '80s. This is especially ironic in the face of the increasing presence of personal computers in American homes throughout the '80s, and the increasing social concerns over what youth could do with them (as witnessed prominently in *WarGames* and satirized in *Ferris Bueller's Day Off* [1986], with the Matthew Broderick characters in both using their home computers to alter their school records).

Unlike the more science-oriented films previously detailed, the game and computer youth movies since 1980 have largely avoided science and have concentrated instead on the "real-life" adventures that teens discover as a result of an initial exploration of their computer or game curiosities. Hence, most of these films follow their protagonists on chases as they try to elude corrupt forces, and few of them delve into the intricate technical skills required to operate computers at the high level demanded by their plot contrivances. Like most of the science films, all of these films do ultimately provide a humanist message about abandoning technology for the sake of more holistic and wholesome human contact, eventually demonstrating the perfidious dangers posed by such otherwise beneficial machines and toys.

As with most youth films and the science subgenre in general, the game/computer film declined dramatically in the late '80s (only one between 1985 and 1991, *Defense Play* in 1988), and its overdue reemergence in the early '90s was predominantly the domain of low-budget and straight-to-video studios; even higher-end productions like *Hackers* (1995) and *Masterminds* (1997) proved to be box-office flops. This decline indicates that the social and studio interest in portraying teens using computers and games in films remains minimal, despite the extensive popular press coverage around issues of youths' access to computers, as exhibited by the high-profile kidnappings of teens via the Internet and the general failure of the Communications Decency Act of 1996 to control "cyberporn" and other Internet "offenses."

I divide the films in this section by their concentration on game or computer applications, labeling "game movies" as those that feature youth engaging in video, computer, or robotic technology in the pursuit of pleasure, and labeling "computer movies" as those that feature youth using computers to more experimental or investigative ends. Of course there is some overlap in notions of pleasure and experimentation, but for the most part game movies maintain a sense of competition based on the technology featured, while computer movies are most often focused on individuals' testing of—and escaping—technology.

Tech Games

The teen video game category got off to a dubious start with *Joysticks* in 1983, a film that attempted to capitalize on both the current social fascination with arcade games and the trend in explicit teen screen sexuality through its story of a recent high school graduate who defends his video arcade against angry locals and demonstrates his virility to girls with his mastery of games using his joystick. The only other teen video game movie of the '80s was the 1984 fantasy *The Last Starfighter,* which uses a video game merely as a plot device to demonstrate more elaborate teen ambitions. The story opens in a California trailer park community, where working-class Alex (Lance Guest) is hoping to get a loan to go to a good college and, as he says, "do something with my life other than going to 'City College' and getting drunk on weekends with my high school friends." The class tensions among these characters are different from most teen films, if only because they do not have nearby middle- or upper-class peers reminding them of their plight, and because Alex's recognition of his class position is meant to explain his displaced attention to a video game at a local convenience store. He does not stand out at school or in society, but he becomes so proficient at the game that one night the entire community comes out to see him break the high score, a feat he achieves in a fit of frustration after being notified that he has been rejected for his college loan.

The film's connection of working-class dreams with such otherwise impractical skills as playing video games is then amplified by Alex's sudden recruitment by space aliens who take him to their planet to defend their population against an enemy rebellion. The aliens, it turns out, had been using the Earth-based video game (actually called "Starfighter" and manufactured by Atari) to seek out the best fighters, and their confidence in Alex's skills provides an esteem he did not enjoy back home. After a battle in which all of the other planet's ships are destroyed by the enemy, Alex is left as the "last starfighter," and with the help of another alien—who is not a fighter—Alex uses his knowledge of the video game system to pilot his ship into enemy territory and destroy their entire fleet, working his way up through "levels of difficulty" that climax in a game-winning defeat of the main enemy base. Despite his victory, and a global celebration in his honor, Alex must then pursue the enemy leader, who escaped during the attack. Nonetheless, he makes a quick stop at Earth, where he tells his mom he's okay, receives the communal endorsement of the trailer park population, and picks up his initially reluctant girlfriend, who eventually realizes that a life in space fighting enemy aliens is more exciting than living in a trailer park.

While the actual video game element of *The Last Starfighter* is rather lessened compared to *Joysticks,* the film aims for a moral message that clearly attempts to connect youthful "video skills" to a higher purpose, indicating that these games are not only effective fantasy outlets for teens, but may possibly serve a more profound or even professional purpose. After all, a number of billionaires in the booming computer industry of the '90s were teen video game players in the '70s and '80s, and their skills in understanding those systems obviously served them well. *Joysticks* and *The Last Starfighter* certainly do not promise such opportunities, although the real-life success achieved by "nerd moguls" of the past generation may appear fateful by comparison.[10]

After many years during which the only video game movie to appear was the preteen *The Wizard* in 1989—the novelty of arcade and home video games having worn off by the mid-'80s—two movies in the early '90s featured young people using robotics and electronics, *And You Thought Your Parents Were Weird* (1991) and *Remote* (1993), although in both cases the youth involved seem to have little fun with their toys as "games," and neither film gained any significant attention.[11] A few other game movies of the '90s offer more involved commentaries on the use of electronic games by young people, and in each case the lessons learned cast a very suspicious light on these erstwhile technologies of pleasure that become weapons of destruction.

Arcade (1993) was the first youth movie since *Joysticks* to return to a video arcade set (the game in *The Last Starfighter* stood alone), only now the bright lights and wild spirit of early-'80s video fascination have been replaced by a dark and dank underground arena where cynical teens have grown unimpressed with the usual video offerings. The arcade is thus appropriately called "Dante's Inferno," and a video game executive shows up one day to demonstrate the prototype of a new interactive virtual reality machine called "Arcade." The contraption uses electric gloves for controls and a small eye screen within an enclosed booth, wherein the players must ascend through seven levels of dangerous tasks. The teens gathered at the arcade produce their best player to defeat the new game, and in a dramatic struggle with the machine he seems to disappear—it turns out that he's been sucked into the internal "reality" of the machine—yet despite this, the executive hands out prototype television versions of "Arcade" and asks the teens to test them at home. When the executive tells them, "You're the market share," the film points to a certain consumerist critique, while also employing the sci-fi trappings of the alternate "video reality," yet perhaps the most interesting youth aspect of the film is the relationship between its two leads, Alex (Megan Ward) and Nick (Peter Billingsley).

Alex is a teenage girl who blames herself for her mother's recent suicide; her father has become subsequently depressed, and she turns to her arcade friends for solace. However, she's also the smartest and strongest character of the group, who not only suspects that something is wrong with the "Arcade" game but who enlists Nick's help in investigating the company that produces it. All of Alex and Nick's friends become captives of the game, and when the two appeal to a programmer at the game company, he explains that the "learning" capacity of the game actually comes from the organic neural structure of a brain-dead child. Another moral critique is then offered through the final playing of the game as Nick and Alex venture into its internal reality to rescue their friends: the "voice" of the game tells them, "Our parents destroy us," and after Alex saves a small boy in a middle level—Nick lost the game earlier—the child later reveals that he is indeed the "brain" of the entire system, apparently angry and lonely after being sold to the game company by his capitalizing parents (we are also later told that his mother beat him to death). At last, Alex reaches the highest level of the game, where she defeats the machine and gains the release of her friends from its clutches.[12]

Arcade clearly comments on the potential harm, addiction, and oppression of home and arcade video game systems, tracing parental malevolence through teens' supposedly enjoyable access to video games that remain sources of *adult* irresponsibility. Yet the film's internal fantasy of Alex mastering the game in a symbolic gesture of overcoming her parents' faults—a parallel of the boy sold to the company—offers the first instance in the science subgenre of a female character outwitting her male counterpart (*Hackers* would be the second). Unlike the characters in *Hackers,* Alex and Nick don't even become romantically involved (she remains loyal to her boyfriend, impotently trapped inside the game), and her longing for resolution from her mother's suicide is achieved in virtually solitary terms as the game "voice" taunts her with threats of failure, reminding her that she failed to make her mother happy. *Arcade* itself thus taps into young female fears and insecurities, with a final image of the boy still lingering to taunt Alex, while offering a rare image of teen female determination through the otherwise male-dominated video game arena.

Like *Arcade,* the 1995 film *Evolver* clearly positions youth as the victims of adult exploitations of new technology. Here a teen computer whiz wins a robot that learns—or "evolves"—through higher levels of competition, only he eventually realizes that the machine was originally created by the military to kill in combat, and it begins murdering local teens. *Evolver* thus becomes a now-classic indictment of the adult military-industrial complex that, through its development of weapons, has wreaked havoc on youth. The semiromantic pairing of the protagonist with a feisty girlfriend continues the traditional casting pattern seen in *WarGames, Defense Play,* and *Arcade,* although the female characters in the '90s films have become more equal to the males in terms of computer skills and/or general ingenuity, and in this narrative the girl leans on the boy to turn away from his technological fascinations for the joys of human contact.

Where *The Last Starfighter, And You Thought Your Parents Were Weird, Remote,*

Arcade, and to a lesser extent *Brainscan* offer certain reconciliations for teens' familial and social problems through their use of tech games, the two films that lie at either end of the tech game chronology—*Joysticks* in 1983 and *Evolver* in 1995—are the two most occupied with their characters' sexual reconciliations. To be sure, *Joysticks* was produced in an era of lewd films exploiting teen sexuality, and *Evolver*'s sexual tones are quite tame by comparison, but the notion of a link between teen sex and technology somewhat problematizes the image of the brainiac, self-absorbed computer nerd featured as a caricature in nonscience films. The teens featured in tech game movies are not only more socially sophisticated and generally accepted compared to their counterparts in other youth subgenres, but their potential access to sexuality—albeit rarely manifested—indicates a level of specialized "potency" that distinguishes them further.

All of the tech game films demonstrate a consistent problematics of reliance on video/computer games for youth who use them to gain pleasure or self-esteem in lieu of learning through human interaction. These films point to the additional parental or social connection that youth using these devices are trying to discover, and always raise the concern that youth may turn away from their parents, peers, or even lovers in alliance with the "affections" they gain from these games. This issue is perhaps the most profound in all of these films, and it is an issue that is made even more complex in films concentrating specifically on youth and computers.

Computer Kids

The youth films featuring computers since 1980 comprise a sparse and eclectic vision of how youth may utilize the technology, in all cases demonstrating a special comprehension of how computers affect humanity on the part of teens as compared to adults. Nowhere is teens' special comprehension more evident than in the first and most popular of these films, *WarGames* (1983). The story follows David (Matthew Broderick), a smart but underachieving high school student with a home computer system that he uses for nothing more sinister than playing games and changing his grades. One day while playing with Jennifer (Ally Sheedy), his only apparent friend, they hack into a game company to play what they think is called "Global Thermonuclear War," not realizing that the system is hooked up to the national defense center at NORAD, where it simulates war games to test for military strategies. Military officials then witness a fake attack that they think is real—especially after replacing human personnel in missile silos with supposedly more reliable com-

David (Matthew Broderick) unwittingly takes on the U.S. military in *WarGames* (1983) when he tries to play a game through his modem. His friend Jennifer (Ally Sheedy) looks on in wonder, presumably astonished by the massive size of his computer system.

puters—and they eventually locate David as the sender of the simulation. Before he can clear his name and explain what happened, the game continues with an even larger simulation, sending the military spiraling toward a real nuclear war.

That David's role in the situation is effectively dismissed by the military leaders, who suspect that "the kid" must be working for the Soviets, is a sign of his authoritative incapacity, but the intrigue that surrounds him also signals an adult fear of youth accessing and mastering computer systems that they deem fail-safe: if a teenager can infiltrate the system, could "the enemy" do so as well? David further insults military intelligence by escaping from custody at NORAD and meeting up with Jennifer so that they can enlist the help of Dr. Falken (John Wood), a former government scientist who saw the destructive potential of his work. Falken designed the original war games program, and he returns with the two teens to NORAD for a final showdown with "Joshua"—the secret program that is running the simulation, named for his dead son (another link to the mystique of youthful understanding). Despite the military's concern that the country is being attacked, Falken takes Joshua through various simulations with David until the computer "learns" that no one can win a nuclear war. This lesson is thus brought about through the dead spirit of Falken's little boy, and by David's passionate appeal to the military leaders not to launch a counterattack until they can see that the game is not real. David, nor ostensibly anyone else, needs to be such a genius to realize the insanity of war, but the typical adult resistance to children's perspective in this case—especially in comparison to the initial cynicism of Falken—indicates that even unremarkable teens like David and Jennifer have less paranoid, more humane concerns for the world.

WarGames not only uses this demonstration of youthful insight for its political message, but further uses the social positioning of teens to entertain more general ideas about the use of computers by the public, at a time when many films were introducing computers in usually less technologically suspect adult narratives—as in *Superman 3* (1983), *Tin Man* (1983), *Electric Dreams* (1984), and *Prime Risk* (1984). David Denby comments on this trend in his review:

> Computer games require decisiveness but not imagination; their demand on your attention and coordination is extraordinary, their demand on your creativity practically nil. The great value of a computer as a character in a science-fiction movie is that it is relentless yet utterly logical. Thus a boy from the arcades like David is just as adept as the most experienced scientist in understanding a computer run amok. He's one of the video-age kids with reflexes honed by the machine.[13]

While Denby's comments about the lack of computer creativity may seem dated given the capacities of today's computers, his observation that a teen character such as David is ideally suited to demonstrate the rather uncanny democratizing of technology through computers reveals both the concern and fascination that adults have with their own use of computers. These human-made machines give people incredible capabilities, and the young are in the best position to take advantage of those capabilities, which may indeed make them smarter and happier if the machines don't corrupt them first with such "nonproductive" pleasures as playing games. As Denby implies, the generation of children who have grown up with home computers since the 1980s have been shaped by them and thus are able to use them in efficient and understanding ways, ways that may indeed seem foreign to the generation who invented the computers.

This issue is also at stake in *Defense Play* (1988), which has a plot rather similar to *WarGames* with just slightly older characters, in this case a high school senior who teams up with a potential girlfriend and discovers a secret government plan to develop remote-controlled miniature attack helicopters. Yet unlike *WarGames*, where the preparation for global war was exposed by youth as irrational, *Defense Play* uses youth to maintain the goal of "global defense"—the enemy is decidedly foreign and not ourselves—utilizing the teens' computer skills not to save humanity but to save the military's money and ambitions. Despite the timeliness of *Defense Play* and the general appeal of computers to youth, only one other youth-and-computer movie was released in the '80s, the rather fanciful *Explorers* (1985). Next to *Hackers* in 1995, *Explorers* is the most computer-literate of youth films, at least in its exposition where two friends work on circuit boards and programming schematics to create an energy source that allows them to travel through space.

Hackers (1995) is the first film of the '90s to return to the previously popular youth-computer theme, but its narrative is so dense and its characters so intense by comparison to past youth-computer films that it may well alienate the less computer-centric members of the young population (it drew small audiences during its well-publicized release). *Hackers* is a kinetic thrill ride, employing both the traditional boy-girl romantic pairing and a plot that pits its teen characters against adult corruption; in these ways the film is nothing new, but perhaps its overwrought attempt to portray the mercurial young computer culture demonstrates the difficulty current films have in addressing youths' access to computers, and further explains why studios have avoided producing films that would capitalize on this otherwise large and visible culture.

The story focuses on Dade (Jonny Lee Miller), who as a superhacker child was convicted of crashing international computer systems and ordered by the courts to avoid computers until he was 18; the film opens just after that birthday as Dade has settled into a new high school with a new handle, "Crash Override." The crowd of computer enthusiasts that Dade falls in with at school talk in a hyper lingo, but in place of drugs, sex, or music they talk about computers, dealing in discs and Internet passwords at gaudy nightclubs with a secrecy usually reserved for other traditional teen taboos. They are also multicultural like many other '90s teen ensemble casts: Dade becomes their unofficial white male leader, Ramone or "Phantom Phreak" (Renoly Santiago) is an energetic Latino, Paul or "Lord Nikon" (Laurence Mason) is a hip African American, Emmanuel or "Cereal Killer" (Matthew Lillard) is an oddball Jewish spaz, and Joey (Jesse Bradford) is still in braces and hoping to earn his real handle.

Dade becomes interested in their female friend, Kate or "Acid Burn" (Angelina Jolie), whom he realizes is an "elite" hacker one night when she interrupts his infiltration of a television programming system. Kate's role offers one of the few smart and ambitious images of teen females in the science subgenre, and of all of them she is definitely the most sexualized: her tight clothes, excessive makeup, and numerous make-out scenes with a dull boyfriend (whom she apparently uses for nothing but sex) give her less prominent computer skills an additional potency. Hence, she becomes an object of Dade's desire both on the level of intellectual competition (as when the two set up a hacking contest to see who's better) and in terms of alleviating his sensitive virginal status—he demands that if he wins the contest, she will abandon her leather pants and wear a dress on a date. This "prize" points to a male sexual tension that Maitland McDonagh finds most peculiar, given "the movie's sexual worldview, which is simultaneously infantile and fetishist. Boys wear rubber, lipstick, and spandex, but do not seem to have a sexual bone in their unmuscled bodies. Have these kids truly sublimated all their hormonal urges into massaging their keyboards?"[14] Indeed, the film seems to point to an altogether alternative or hybrid sexuality resulting from these characters' preoccupations with their computers, which Dade resists through his more traditional heterosexual conquest of Kate.

Outside of the usual "little crimes" that these hackers commit, they all dream of hacking a supercomputer system known as the Gibson, which Joey begins to do one night until his mother shuts off his computer. Such an intervention of adult authority is carried over in the characters' other attempts to explore their computer worlds, especially when Joey is arrested for hacking into the Gibson of a mineral company. As it turns out, "The Plague" (Fisher Stevens), the computer security director of the company, has been conspiring to scam millions of dollars from company accounts, but Joey's infiltration gathers so much attention that The Plague has to invent a virus that threatens to capsize five of the company's oil tankers. Dade and his cohort then find themselves on the side of exposing this conspiracy, saving the environment, and clearing their names—The Plague has convinced the FBI that the teens are responsible for the virus—and the film becomes a showdown between the corporate/legal system of the Plague and the social/creative contacts of the teens. Dade and Kate enlist the help of two other "elites," who gather the forces of other hackers all over the world in a climactic assault on the Gibson. Oddly enough, despite the film's abundance of tech talk, the narrative would have you believe that being a good hacker is simply a matter of fast typing and hard keypunching, as witnessed in the montage of aggressive physical moves that punctuate the ending. Here the film "steps into a profusion and confusion of techno-gadgetry which goes exponentially from the improbable to the impossible, the outrageous, the preposterous and the absurd," as Edwin Jahiel argued.[15] Within a video game format that is unlike any real computer system of the '90s, the teens use their cyberacrobatic flair to crash the Gibson and are vindicated. At last, Dade takes Kate on a date in her tight leather dress, and shows her how he has hacked the lighting systems of three buildings to spell out "Crash and Burn" (i.e., "Dade + Kate") on the skyline. After this dubious moment of high-tech romance, they finally kiss.[16]

Hackers offers such a bombastic, technocentric vision of youth (Dade even "thinks" in screen images and sound bites) that the teens have virtually no identity outside of their computers. Even their typical resistance to adult authority is based upon access to their computers, and the fact that three of the six teens seem to have no parents (and Kate's are barely mentioned) obviously motivates their interest in fighting the resistance of the "parent" computer, the Gibson. Computers and cops have thus taken the place of parents and teachers (despite many scenes in school, only once is a teacher shown), as if these youth have evolved beyond the dimension of normal teen rebellion. *Hackers* thus portrays the conflict for youth talented in these skills by resorting to a more general empathy that other youth might share, and thereby avoids more complicated explanations for their actions and thoughts. The teens in the film still win out over adults and save the day, and the boy and girl are still united.

Hackers is similar to other teen computer films in that the characters do become more humane through their technological conflict, although their motives to expose adult computer corruption are more selfish compared to *WarGames* and *Defense Play*: they don't expose the treachery of war or crime as much as they reveal the hedonism of a youth culture built upon entangled gratifications, using the complexity of laptops instead of drugs, the speed of the Internet instead of cars, and the pleasure of cracking codes instead of having sex. The film's image of computer youth in the '90s is the same as the thrill-seekers of past generations, only now their toys can literally change the world. Given the film's high exposure but small audience, this may be a level of responsibility that, while powerful, teens do not yet want to have thrust upon them.

Hesitation also marked the most recent film focusing on a teen computer expert, *Masterminds* (1997). Here the protagonist is a delinquent hacker who happens to witness a terrorist takeover of a private school, and while the movie at first portends to showcase his various computer skills, the hero spends most of his time outwitting the bad guys through his further knowledge of electronics and mechanics, and little time is spent on any actual use of computers. Once again, the potential dramatic device that computers could represent in youth films is cast aside, even though so many teens are undoubtedly excited by and engaged in computer use, and so many recent films about adults seem to celebrate computer concepts in their narratives, such as *Johnny Mnemonic* (1995), *The Net* (1995), *Mission: Impossible* (1996), *You've Got Mail* (1998), *Pi* (1998), *The Matrix* (1999), and *A.I.* (2001). *Masterminds* becomes another vision of the troubled kid who makes good through rising above and exposing the bad behavior of adults, a vision that most game/computer movies (and many delinquency movies) have always relied on, even though now technology plays an decreasingly important role.

CONCLUSION

Most of the films in this chapter point to a certain frustration experienced by youth in the face of "adult" control, in this case the control of knowledge or technology. The common crisis experienced by youth in most of these films involves their attempt to ascend to adult levels of authority granted through their knowledge of science and their access to materials that they are clearly beginning to gain at younger ages than in past generations. Perhaps what is being expressed most then is an *adult* anxiety about mental weakness signaled by teens' usurpation of their authority on these levels, and these films attempt to displace that anxiety back upon their young viewers, who are told that their confrontations with science, computers, and media will be arduous and confusing. Youth in these films are almost always allowed to demonstrate a certain competence and insight into the mysteries of contemporary phenomena, as long as they are made to realize the constraints on their abilities. This realization may be the somewhat cynical central message of this subgenre: already disempowered youth must work hard to gain an identity that they may ultimately not define and an authority that may ultimately be more limiting than liberating.

6 YOUTH IN LOVE AND HAVING SEX

I gave her my heart and she gave me a pen.

—LLOYD DOBLER, AFTER BEING DUMPED BY DIANE COURT IN *Say Anything . . .*

You realize we're all going to go to college as virgins. They probably have special dorms for people like us.

—JIM TO HIS BUDDIES IN *American Pie*

I felt like when she was being ripped out from inside of me that everything I loved about being young was being ripped out at the same time.

—DARCY, REFLECTING ON HER PREGNANCY IN *"For Keeps"*

Romantic longing and sexual curiosity take on heightened intensity and profundity for youth in the adolescent years. A large part of working through puberty to adulthood is the struggle to recognize and cope with the emotional and physiological changes that arrive with the onset of secondary sexual characteristics: young people develop crushes and question their sexual impulses as they witness their bodies changing, members of the opposite (and/or same) sex becoming more attractive, and their friends becoming more occupied with aspects of dating. Because adolescent sexuality is so confusing for those who experience it and is still difficult to be understood by those who have endured it, the topic provides ripe tension and drama for films about youth. Furthermore, because adolescent sexuality is a socially taboo topic—the threats of teen pregnancy and sexually transmitted diseases, adult tensions over pedophilia, and the general moral concern over how sex could "corrupt" youth, among other reasons—the subject becomes both a way of stimulating supposed prurient interests while also addressing the very oppression and repression of teen sexuality. This address could thus offer a certain liberation for the natural development of youth sexuality that is so often stunted by social codes, or it could exploit and even further suppress the exploration and acceptance of youth sexuality.

TRENDS IN THE SUBGENRE

Youth films that have depicted teens pursuing love and sex have offered a wide spectrum of perspectives for and about their subjects. Encountering sexual feelings and practices for the first time, young viewers are told, can be exciting and terrifying, fun and tragic. More often than not, the emphasis in youth films since 1980 has been on positive aspects of young love and negative aspects of young lust, often depending on the time period of the film. The major wave of teen sex romps in the early '80s was inaugurated by the Canadian film *Porky's* in 1981, which was about young men's pursuit of sexual hijinx in the '50s and aspired to be a simply more graphic updating of the nostalgic *American Graffiti* (1974) and, to a lesser extent, *Grease* (1978). All of these films were huge box-office hits, and all of them pointed to their adult directors' sentimental attachments to their own discoveries of sex (and love), which were apparently playful, humorous, and ultimately safe. If these films had concentrated on potentially negative aspects of teenage sexuality as later contemporary films would do, they would have likely failed to draw young audiences, who would have likely perceived them as preachy message movies: such failure was and remains the fate of most films that do depict negative aspects of teen sexuality, such as *Blue Denim* (1959), *Last Summer* (1969), *Class* (1983), *"For Keeps"* (1988), *Just Another Girl on the I.R.T.* (1993), *Fear* (1996), and *Lolita* (1998).

That teenage sexuality has often been depicted by Hollywood as tormented is not surprising, especially given its implicitly negative depictions in the horror genre, and the "need" for teens' anxieties about sex to be addressed (or occasionally alleviated) by the entertainment media, a need that translates into industry profits. However, youth films in the love/sex subgenre (a label I explain below) have since 1980 undoubtedly moved through particular trends that are not always consistent or progressive. After the sexual revolution of the '60s gave rise to the late-'70s disco era in which adults were encouraged to revel in a number of excesses, youth seemed to be pushed toward the same moral loosening. 1980 saw the taboo-breaking success of *The Blue*

Lagoon, a sexual-awakening story (which was itself a remake of a tamer 1949 British film) whose Edenic myth symbolized the fanciful discoveries of youth sexuality in subsequent '80s films. Two less successful 1980 films—*Foxes* and *Little Darlings,* the latter featuring two teen girls racing to lose their virginity—also raised the stakes of sexualized youth depictions. The success of these films seemed to indicate that audiences were ready, if not eager, for more explicit portraits of youth sexuality, and over the next few years, large and small studios alike flooded the market with depictions of teens' rowdy and occasionally educational forays into sexual practice, even if most of them failed to profit from their suggestive titles: *Private Lessons, Hot Bubblegum* (1981); *Fast Times at Ridgemont High* (1982); *Getting It On, My Tutor* (1983); *Screwballs, Hollywood Hot Tubs, Joy of Sex* (1984); *Pink Nights, Gimme an F!* (1985); and *Thinkin' Big* (1986). What was less prominent in the early '80s were depictions of youth dealing with the more romantic aspects of their burgeoning sexuality. Yet films that did just that by the mid-'80s became quite successful, and the relatively explicit youth sex trend waned with the appearance of more sensitive narratives, especially those written and/or directed by John Hughes, such as *Sixteen Candles* (1984), *Pretty in Pink* (1986), and *Some Kind of Wonderful* (1987), and non-Hughes productions like *Lucas, Seven Minutes in Heaven* (both 1986), *Can't Buy Me Love,* and *Square Dance* (both 1987).[1]

By the late '80s, when social discourses around AIDS had made youth sexuality an even greater concern and teenage pregnancies were on the rise (the number of unmarried pregnant teens increased by over 10 percent in just the five years from 1985 to 1990, to 1 out of every 10 girls), American youth films made a clear move away from the sexualized images of youth that dominated the screen in the early '80s and concentrated further on romantic presexual relationships among teens.[2] Period films harking back to more "innocent" eras for youth became increasingly popular—*Peggy Sue Got Married* (1986), *Dirty Dancing* (1987), *A Night in the Life of Jimmy Reardon* (1988), *Cry-Baby* (1990)—and in the case of the biggest youth film of the late '80s, *Dirty Dancing,* seemed to sublimate teenage sexual energy into safer, if nonetheless still erotic, outlets. A few films began to explore the more serious consequences of teenage sexual activity (*"For Keeps"* [1988] and *Immediate Family* [1989], both focused on teen pregnancy), although again such films tended to draw relatively smaller audiences.

In the early '90s the film industry largely continued to avoid or displace depictions of teenage sexuality (the brief "lambada" craze in early 1990 was an example of such deliberate displacement), and the technique of using period settings to do so became even more prominent (in 1991, six period youth love/sex films were released compared to four set in contemporary times). However, as the mid-'90s approached, some low-budget independent films began taking more direct and often serious approaches to teen sexuality (e.g., *Gas Food Lodging* [1992], *Just Another Girl on the I.R.T.* [1993], *Spanking the Monkey* [1994], *Art for Teachers of Children* [1995]), while nonconfrontational period romances remained safer for most studios (e.g., *Calendar Girl* [1993], *The Inkwell* [1994], *Circle of Friends* [1995], *That Thing You Do!* [1996], *Titanic* [1997]). The depiction of adolescent romance and sexuality in general had clearly become problematic in many '90s films, with a host of "dangerous deviants" appearing in films such as *The Crush* (1993), *Kids* (1995), *To Die For* (1995), *Fear* (1996), *Wild Things* (1997), *Cruel Intentions* (1999), and even a teen deviant trilogy, *Poison Ivy* (1992–97). As more American films in the mid-'90s made specific statements about youth love and sex than in the early '90s, their messages became rather pessimistic and cynical. This cynicism may have been emblematic of revived anxieties about youth sexuality in society at large, may have been the effort of the industry to appeal to teens' curious but serious concerns and fears about sexuality, may have been indicative of teens' own confusions about the increasingly sexualized culture in which they live, or most likely a combination of all these factors. As the '90s closed, films featuring young romance spoke to a revived notion of romantic destiny—the mega-successful *Titanic* (1997), *Can't Hardly Wait* (1998), *She's All That, 10 Things I Hate About You, Drive Me Crazy* (all 1999)—while most films featuring youth sexuality continued to be rather dark—*Johns* (1997), *Lolita, The Opposite of Sex* (both 1998), *Cruel Intentions, Election* (both 1999), *The Virgin Suicides* (2000). In both cases, love and sex films retained certain cautionary messages.

PATTERNS AND IMAGES

One generic pattern of youth love/sex films that becomes clear by the mid-'80s—and explains why I label the subgenre as such—is the division between narratives in which the attainment of love is more prominent and narratives in which the pursuit of sexual practice is the focus. While some characters in youth films after 1980 seem to pursue both love *and* sex, the vast majority are preoccupied with one goal or the other, and not both. In fact, in most youth love stories, sex is either not an issue or is experienced as a natural result of romantic achievement, whereas in most youth sex stories, love is either not an issue or is experienced as a natural result of sexual achievement. I thus divide my study accordingly into love stories and sex stories.

Within these two divisions, the sex story presents more experiential variety than the love story. In the youth love story, teens struggle to confirm their romantic feelings and secure a union in the face of an oppressive obstacle that must be overcome for the couple to either live happily ever after or realize that their union was not meant to be. Variety in the love story arises from the different obstacles that prevent the teens from realizing their romance; they are most often held apart by the codes of family expectations, and thus this approach constitutes the focus of my analysis. However, other social barriers such as age, race, or class differences may also impede young lovers: examples of the age conflict include *Sixteen Candles* (1984), *Man in the Moon* (1991), *Boys* (1996), and *Never Been Kissed* (1999); romantic racial differences have been examined less often, as in *China Girl* (1987), *Gas Food Lodging* (1992), *Bleeding Hearts* (1995), and *Save the Last Dance* (2001); class conflicts can be found in *Valley Girl* (1983), *Reckless* (1984), *Can't Buy Me Love* (1987), and all the John Hughes teen films of the mid-'80s (although such conflicts became notably scarce in '90s romances, at least until *Titanic*).

Variety in the sex story is founded on the different desires for youth to have sex, and occasionally on the consequences of those desires: when the narrative emphasis isn't on the simple quest to lose virginity, the characters find themselves confused over their sexual attraction to an adult or a member of the same sex, or they are left to deal with pregnancy or, in remarkably few cases, a sexually transmitted disease. I examine each of these topics except adult-teen pairings, all of which work on tensions about sexual responsibility and yet tend to be adamantly ambiguous in placing "blame" on both characters for their illicit desires; examples include *My Tutor* (1983), *Blame It on Rio* (1984), *Smooth Talk* (1985), *The Crush* (1993), *To Die For* (1995), *Election* (1999), and each of the three *Poison Ivy* movies.

The images of youth across romantic and sexual narratives of the past generation are actually quite diverse, although as in the school subgenre, a certain hierarchy of competence is established and enforced according to character types. Nerds usually have the most difficulty attaining love or sex, and popular teens most often struggle with a surplus of suitors and sexual opportunities that come their way. Romantic and sexual competence may have little relation to social stature in reality, but in youth films the characters' level of acceptance is integrally linked to their attractiveness, which is often (mis)taken as an index of sexual and amorous "skills." Some films challenge this notion, especially love stories, which often reveal that the most popular teens are self-centered or ignorant lovers and the less popular (because poorer, rebellious, unattractive, or different) teens are more affectionate, or at least more appreciative of affection.

An interesting discourse on youth empowerment is also presented in youth love/sex films. Less popular, less powerful teens sometimes achieve self-respect and acceptance through their romantic and sexual pursuits, and girls, ever the object of boys' desires, realize the power they can gain through carefully regulating boys' access to them. Few of these films could be called feminist, however, and are more often sexist in their portrayals of young women's exploitation by young men, or at least their formal imaging of girls' bodies, which are held up for voyeuristic pleasure by the male gaze in much greater proportion than the number of boys who are photographed for the opposite purpose. Many youth love/sex films tell young women to resist their image as sexual objects but in their telling objectify them all the same.

This chapter proceeds with an analysis of "family conflict" youth love films from 1980 to 1999 and then makes a point of comparison to those that focus on three prominent sexual topics: losing virginity (wherein I discuss the few mentions of sexually transmitted diseases), homosexuality, and pregnancy. There is some overlap within these divisions that is noted throughout, and there is further overlap with films in other subgenres that feature romantic or sexual experiences as a lesser aspect of their narrative; those that are important examples are also noted.

YOUTH IN LOVE

Essentially all drama is founded on conflict, and youth love stories are no exception. The classical romantic drama of "boy meets girl, boy loses girl, boy gets girl back" operates (with genders sometimes switched) in the youth film, although the reasons why the romantic relationship is threatened are always motivated by factors external to the characters. Rarely does a screen teen in love wrestle with personal notions of self-fulfillment or readiness to be in a relationship; rather, teens know their love is sure and true and simply have to overcome whatever *social* forces prevent them from expressing it and achieving reciprocity. These conflicts may be motivated by adults' doubts of and prohibitions against the success of young love, and they may demonstrate to youth the fallibility of emotional security; but like virtually all romantic stories, virtually all youth love films allow their characters at least the temporary fulfillment of their amorous ambitions.

Family Matters

From simple love advice to prearranged marriages, youth have witnessed their parents shaping, if not controlling, their romantic endeavors. Youth are often conditioned to evaluate potential lovers according to attractability scales dictated by their families, ranging from financial and social status to appearance and manners. While many youth are inevitably influenced by these familial codes, many also rebel against them, deliberately falling in love with and even marrying partners who clearly violate their family's hopes and expectations.

The family is also an index to larger social structures for youth. In loving outside of the family code, youth can assert an individuality that would otherwise be compromised by the generally conformist practices of heterosexual dating and the pursuit of marriage. In youth love films, the characters still want to find love and (usually) marriage, but they want to find it in their own ways and on their own terms, and going outside an established "acceptable" range is a way to verify that independence. In finding a romantic partner who is unacceptable to one's family, a young person achieves a level of social rebellion and personal fulfillment.

Youth films since 1980 that have employed the family as the oppressive mechanism to teen love have been fairly consistent in demonstrating that parents do *not* know best when it comes to young romance. Parents' often good intentions—to see their child married to a "proper" person—become a barrier to their children's more sincere insight that love is not based on propriety but rather on feelings. Sometimes parents ultimately capitulate to their children's desires, often remembering their own youthful ambitions for true love; some of these films feature teens trying to restore just such a perspective in parents who have grown cynical after being divorced or widowed. Parents who do not ultimately honor their child's romantic wishes always face losing their child altogether. Despite the powerful influence of the family, these films make it clear that young love outside the family is stronger, or at least more dedicated, than love for the family itself.

When *Endlesslove* appeared in 1981, its frank discussion of young sexuality was on the cusp of the new wave in teen sexual representation. As David Considine points out in *The Cinema of Adolescence,* after the controversial British film *Friends* in 1972 "encouraged the franker depiction of sexuality in American motion pictures" about youth, Hollywood products such as *Jeremy* (1973),

The Little Girl Who Lived Down the Lane (1977), and *Manhattan* (1979) portrayed increasingly sexually sophisticated teens, while *Taxi Driver* (1976) and *Pretty Baby* (1977) codified images of teenage prostitutes.[3] By the time of *Rich Kids* in 1979, the feigned marital harmony between two 12-year-olds—whose relationship is a rebellion against their self-absorbed divorced parents—demonstrated a rather involved level of sexuality for adolescents, especially since their contact fills the void of emotional intimacy left by their parents, and appears to represent a more mature psychological *and* sexual experience than their parents can sustain.

Unlike *Porky's* and the sex-centric films that followed it, *Endlesslove* combined the classic *Romeo and Juliet* story of forbidden young love and the growing presence of teen sexual activity to yield an image of young romance so potent that few other youth films took the issue seriously for the next five years. Most early-'80s youth love films after *Endlesslove* were comedies—exceptions included *Reckless* (1984), *Tuff Turf* (1985), and *Nickel Mountain* (1985)—and while this may not demonstrate a causal effect within the subgenre, the critical drubbing that *Endlesslove* received, and the fact that *Reckless, Tuff Turf,* and *Nickel Mountain* all failed to profit, must have been an influence on the industry. Only after the notable success of John Hughes's teen comedies and dramas from 1984 to 1987 did the industry start to release a few more serious teen love stories such as *Lucas* (1986), *Square Dance* (1987), and *China Girl* (1987).

Endlesslove is something of an updating and revision of *Splendor in the Grass* (1961) with the genders and circumstances switched. In *Splendor,* a teen girl ends up institutionalized apparently because of parental restrictions against her having sex; her sexual repression seems to literally drive her crazy. In *Endlesslove* a 17-year-old, David (Martin Hewitt), ends up institutionalized after having an apparently excessive sexual relationship with his 15-year-old girlfriend Jade (Brooke Shields), whose parents eventually prohibit her from seeing David. The family difference between these two is made clear from the start: David's wealthy parents are conservatively introverted, while Jade's parents are middle-class bohemians who are passionately active with their children.[4] Jade's previously permissive father realizes the extent of his daughter's intimacy with David and forbids her from having him over—he doesn't quash her having sex; he's just angry that she gets so little sleep. This quickly depresses David, and in a pathetic attempt at heroism he lights a small fire on Jade's porch, planning to rescue her and her family and thus demonstrate his worth, but the whole house burns down and the family barely escapes. David is then sent to a mental hospital, where his love for Jade borders on mania for the next two years. The family conflict is made more dramatic when David learns that both his and Jade's parents have split up after lengthy marriages—their love having led to the literal dissolution of their families—thereby showing, as Sheila Benson wrote, "the purity and strength of the kids' love versus the failure (corruption, abrogation of duty) of the parents."[5] *Endlesslove* further presents the parents as thoroughly culpable in the corruption of their children's romantic morals: David's parents simply don't understand him and can't help him, and Jade's parents' liberalism is revealed to be rather immoral itself when her mother tries to seduce David and her father finds his own younger girlfriend. Further, Jade's sexual confusion is only amplified by her father's sudden and serious possessiveness of her.

The film uses a strained contrivance to enact a final moral dilemma for the protagonists: after David is freed from the asylum and sets out to find Jade, her father is run over while chasing him. With her father's restrictions thus gone, Jade reluctantly goes to David and gives in to his aggressive plea for the renewal of their relationship, but her brother "rescues" her and turns David over to the police for his role in their father's death. The security of family remains tentatively in place, but the last scene of the film shows Jade going to visit David in jail after her mother tells her to find the love she "deserves." This ending questions whether David's devious love for Jade is indeed what she gets for not recognizing how problematic their relationship is. Jade ultimately makes the decision to return to David after his enactment of two tragedies that figuratively and literally destroyed her family, and given how little Jade has articulated any real passion for David throughout the film, *Endlesslove* shows this young woman returning to her vexatious lover for the same ambiguous reasons that attracted her to him in the first place. The mythology of inexplicable love, beyond the codes of family and society, is thus preserved.

That mythology is conveyed with less serious consequences in most youth love films, especially comedies like *Secret Admirer* (1985), which is built on a wild goose chase over a love letter written by a teenage girl that affects both her circle of friends and her parents, and *Nice Girls Don't Explode* (1987), a comic fable about a girl whose "pyrotechnic sexuality" is revealed to be a ploy by her mother to stop the daughter's natural urges. The film treats the clichéd image of the overbearing mother with obvious humor and levity, although this theme had been more often conveyed with devastating effects in youth dramas such as *Rebel Without a Cause* (1955), *The Restless Years* (1958), *Five Finger Exercise* (1962), and *Carrie* (1976). In fact, while many youth love films after

1980 feature overbearing fathers, only *Nice Girls Don't Explode* and few others—the black comedies *Trust* (1991) and *Welcome to the Dollhouse* (1996) among them—feature the excessively protective mother that threatened youth in previous generations, a sign that perhaps mothers are no longer perceived to have such power over their children. This may be most evidenced by the mother in *Gas Food Lodging* (1992), who attempts to keep her lascivious older daughter in line by threatening to kick her out of the house, only to have her leave on her own terms when she becomes pregnant.

Dirty Dancing (1987) and *She's Out of Control* (1989) also feature prohibitive fathers, yet an apparently more caring and ultimately more devious father is featured in *Say Anything...* (1989). One of the best-received youth films of the decade, *Say Anything...* is the story of just-graduated Lloyd Dobler (John Cusack), who rather impulsively decides to ask out Diane Court (Ione Skye), the pretty class valedictorian (a nonnerd intellectual), whom every other student has regarded as unattainable. Lloyd is quirky yet dependable, which is why he's the designated "keymaster" on his first date with the otherwise reclusive Diane at the school graduation party, and why Diane finds him so appealing. Roger Ebert, who was effusive in his praise of the film, explains its careful chemistry:

> The romance between Diane and Lloyd is intelligent and filled with that special curiosity that happens when two young people find each other not only attractive but interesting—when they sense they might actually be able to learn something useful from the other person. Lloyd has no career plans, no educational plans, no plans except to become a championship kick-boxer, and then, after he meets Diane, to support her because she is worthy of his dedication.[6]

However, her divorced and protective father, who appears to have been Diane's sole "friend" until Lloyd, soon grows concerned about her deepening romance with him, especially after Diane wins a coveted fellowship to study in England. Lloyd doesn't pose any direct threat to Diane's ambitions, and still her father, who clearly doesn't understand their level of intimacy, tells her to end their relationship before she leaves on her trip, and she complies, sinking Lloyd into a somber depression. The image of Lloyd outside Diane's window, holding his boom box over his head after their breakup and playing the song they heard when they lost their virginity to each other, has become an icon of teen romantic longing.

Lloyd (John Cusack) and Diane (Ione Skye) glow with the anticipation of true love in *Say Anything . . .* (1989).

The film is one of the few youth love stories to feature the protagonists successfully negotiating their own differences: the fact that Diane is clearly smarter and better off than Lloyd while Lloyd is more gregarious and humble is not a problem to them, just to Diane's dad. Diane's dad, however, is revealed to be embezzling funds from the nursing home that he operates, supposedly to support her future, and after she learns of her father's crime she turns on him, whereupon Lloyd thankfully takes her back. Jonathan Bernstein explains the moral that many youth may have derived from this, since the father's "stated crime was bilking the aged, but his implicit and far more heinous felonies were smothering his daughter with love and interfering in her romance with a cool dude."[7] The contrivance of this plot twist notwithstanding, the film's climax becomes a compelling emotional showdown between Lloyd and Diane's father, who ends up in jail and insists that Diane not to go England with her loyal boyfriend. Diane's devotion to her father is nonetheless completely shaken, and she invites Lloyd to go on the trip with her.

The final scene of *Say Anything . . .* is one of the rare moments in youth love films where the teen characters are happily united and facing a promising future together: on the plane waiting to leave for England, Lloyd holds the nervous Diane's hand and reassures her that they will be safe. Yet this ending also leaves open a certain ambiguity and tension about their destiny (critics have pointed to its similarity to *The Graduate* [1967]. The film is thus a parable not merely about the morality of devotion—Lloyd's is righteous while Diane's father's is selfish—but about the risks and rewards of romantic patience and loyalty. Despite Lloyd's pain at first being dumped by Diane, and his friends' advice that he should find another girlfriend, Lloyd recognizes in Diane a special quality founded not on her looks or popularity but on an emotional fulfillment rarely afforded to teens in films. The sophistication and maturity of their relationship is rare as well, and justifies the film's hopeful ending.

Youth love stories, as previously mentioned, took a decidedly different turn over the early '90s: fewer young romances reached the screen, and most of those that did began to reveal an increasing cynicism about the topic (as in *Trust, Gas Food Lodging,* and *Just Another Girl on the I.R.T.*), or else they softened the narrative concentration on the couple's success by introducing other dominant dramas (both "lambada" movies in 1990 did this, as did *Mystery Date* [1991], *What's Eating Gilbert Grape* [1993], and *Little Women* [1994]). However, the role of the family in youth love films of the '90s was no less prohibitive than in the '80s. While some '90s romances featured more supportive families, such as the period fantasy *Edward Scissorhands* (1990), the general attitude of parents toward their children's lovelorn ways was one of suspicion and sometimes scorn. *Clueless* in 1995 tried to make this attitude ironically humorous (not much unlike *She's Out of Control*), but more films at the time depicted the family in stern, even violent modes, with their children facing serious consequences, as in *Mad Love* (1995), *Fear* (1996), *William Shakespeare's Romeo + Juliet* (1996), and *Titanic* (1997).

Two comedies that balanced both irony and parental contempt were Hal Hartley's independent productions *The Unbelievable Truth* (1990) and *Trust* (1991). In the first film, Adrienne Shelly plays Audrey, an idiosyncratic high school senior who dumps her steady boyfriend and develops an interest in a 30-ish ex-convict she believes is a kindred spirit, leading to much family strife and a series of tense but often humorous confrontations. The fact that Audrey is not attracted to him for wealth and rescue from her working-class background is, as in most other youth films that present class as a barrier to romance, only realized after she becomes involved with a wealthier man and attempts to assimilate into a higher-class lifestyle. *The Unbelievable Truth,* like Hartley's next film, demonstrates not only that ambitions for wealth are corruptive, but that his young characters' relationships are necessarily founded on nonfinancial, mutually honest—albeit quirky—goals for leaving the confines of corruptive families.

Hartley's thesis on relationships continues in the richly textured *Trust,* so much so that he again cast Adrienne Shelly as a suburban high school senior looking to get away from her strange family. Shelly plays Maria, whose brash manner is so abrasive to her father that he keels over from a heart attack after she tells him she's pregnant by her boyfriend, prompting her mother Jean (Merritt Nelson) to tell Maria that she will have to devote her life to providing for her. Maria descends into a cowering depression that carries her far away from her previously consumptive and carefree style: she feels the contempt of her football-focused boyfriend, who blames her for getting pregnant, the guilt of "killing" her father, and the condemnation of her vengeful mother. Into her life walks Matthew (Martin Donovan), an even more depressive 20-something whose obsessive-compulsive working-class father hounds him constantly. Matthew has grown so disgusted with the world of capitalist technocracy that he quits his computer repair job, and despite his claims to love no one, he becomes instantly concerned with Maria's well-being after finding her drunk and despondent. These are even greater kindred spirits than the couple in *Unbelievable Truth:* what then becomes Maria's sudden change to dutiful daughter in pragmatic penance for her wanton past intertwines with Matthew's resolution to live his cynical life without upsetting his abusive father, and together they seem to reluctantly agree that life is founded on dour survival. J. Hoberman responded to the characters' plight:

> The emphasis on shame pushes *Trust* well beyond the discomfort zone of early John Hughes, but where *Trust* seems most adolescently heartfelt is in its vision of a nightmarish older generation. *Trust* is a kind of allegory about growing up in which children and the absence of children each produces its own form of misery.[8]

Maria and Matthew's destiny is pulled in the two directions that offer them either the preservation of their stoic suffering for the sake of familial calm or the opportunity to fulfill more ambiguous yet beneficial goals. Matthew proposes to move in with and get married to Maria to help her to raise the child, only soon their laborious and tedious days—they both take menial jobs and begin to argue—quickly aggravate the young couple's originally placid personalities. The possessive Jean, who has felt competitive with Matthew from the start, tries to exploit the couple's troubles and break them up, whereupon Maria, after much tribulation over the decision, has an abortion and tells Matthew that she doesn't want to marry him. What costs this couple their capacity to stay together then is not their lack of affection for each other but their attempt to conform to the familial standard handed down by their parents. At one point Matthew expresses the code by which essentially all familial romantic dramas operate: "A family is like a gun—you point it in the wrong direction and it could kill someone." Maria's decision to have the abortion and not start a family with Matthew (which topic I discuss further in a later section) is her liberation from the stark working-class ennui she sees ahead, and which she has already seen her divorced older sister endure. However, Matthew, on the wrong end of these family triangles and feeling completely dejected after learning of Maria's decision, finally decides to kill himself with the hand grenade he has morbidly carried throughout the film.

Trust, which is full of symbolic touches such as Maria wearing Matthew's dead mother's dress in recognition of his regressive desire to find a new family, ends with a wistful and obliquely optimistic denouement after Maria finds Matthew sitting with his unexploded grenade, which doesn't go off until she throws it away. While lying with Matthew after the explosion and with the police coming to take him away, Maria expresses the arbitrary nature of their relationship by telling Matthew that she cares for him just because he "happened to be there." Matthew then never takes his eyes off of Maria as he is carried off to jail, and the film ends with a shot of Maria gazing back at him, framed by two green traffic lights. Philip Strick observed the film's trajectory as such: "Logically, Maria kills her father at the start of the film and her unborn child at the end, leaving her free to put her glasses on in conscious assumption of scholarship while traffic lights suspended behind her indicate a clear road ahead."[9] For all of their intellectual wrestling with purpose and destiny—Maria and Matthew have many talks about the meaning of life and love, or the lack thereof—the young couple find themselves at a literal intersection in their lives that promises greater wisdom, if less certainty, than the bounded lifestyles of marriage and children that they forgo. Whatever decisions they make together or individually will be better than what their families had wrought in the small town of their youths.

Such sobering messages are present in other '90s youth love stories that followed, although two—*Cool as Ice* (1991) and *My Father the Hero* (1994)—used familial tensions about romance as mere plot devices for respectively younger and older star vehicles, in the former film for poser rapper Vanilla Ice, and in the latter for French star Gerard Depardieu. Serious approaches to familial influence on young love were more common, although *Clueless* (1995) did comically employ the device of the protective father, who is nonetheless so absorbed in his work that he doesn't notice or care about the growing attraction between his daughter and stepson. *Clueless* thereby offers an ironic critique of familial love, since Cher (Alicia Silverstone) finds her long-sought boyfriend right at home, a resolution that I have argued elsewhere infers "that the world of sexuality has become so difficult for teens to navigate that Cher's choice of her stepbrother for a boyfriend is completely rational despite its dilemmas."[10] More explicit family-related critiques of youth romance can be found in *Gas Food Lodging, What's Eating Gilbert Grape, Mad Love,* and two Shakespeare adaptations, *William Shakespeare's Romeo + Juliet* and *10 Things I Hate About You* (1999).

The most explicit and tense depiction of family relations impacting teen romance is in *Fear* (1996), which is something of an adolescent *Fatal Attraction*. Where other films have shown even irrational young love to be a sanctuary from problems, *Fear* offers up an antagonist who is himself crazy, and who uses his pathological devotion to terrorize the object of his affection. Nicole (Reese Witherspoon) is that object, a virginal high school student just beginning to explore the more deviant sides of youth culture—drinking, drugs, raves—much to the consternation of her father Steve (William Petersen), who lives with a relatively compassionate second wife. Nicole is only tamely rebellious, even though she is growing increasingly angry with her father's contradictory attempts to promote family activities and still be devoted to his work. When Nicole meets David (Mark Wahlberg) at a rave, he is the essence of tough-guy sweetness, rescuing her from a riot and respecting her resistance to anything more than kissing. He turns on even more charm when he meets Nicole's dad and stepmother, although Steve immediately senses something sinister in the young man. That suspicion inevitably leads Nicole to further defend David, and thus the film sets up its central conflict between paternal overprotection and romantic danger.

Immediately after Nicole consummates her relationship with David—in a scene that shows her as especially passive and unsure—he becomes an insecure lunatic, violently beating Nicole's friend Gary (Todd Caldecott) when he sees him hugging her, and smacking Nicole in the process. At first Nicole abandons David, ignoring his attempts at apology, but once her father suspects that David hit her and blames her for being irresponsible (a scolding that is made ironic by his discovery of a condom wrapper), she soon hears David's apology and takes him back. The stakes of resistance are clear: the more her father threatens her, the more Nicole seeks to find comfort in David. However, as if to verify paternal authority and wisdom over all, the film shows Nicole being further duped by David as her father learns of David's criminal past and confronts him directly, telling him to stay away from her. Nicole does not realize David's truly devious nature until she sees him violently grabbing her friend Margo (Alyssa Milano) at a party, ostensibly en route to raping her. David is then further incensed by Nicole's resistance to him and kills Gary and beats Margo. Steve finally boils over with rage and smashes up the house where David lives with four cretinous cronies, prompting the young gang to launch an all-out assault on Nicole and her family.

The climax of *Fear* makes the film's message about extrafamilial dangers dramatically graphic: Nicole and her family are temporarily safe from David's friends' rampage since architect Steve built the house to resist such an assault, only the safety of home is broken after Steve goes outside to confront David himself and winds up as a hostage to the hoodlums. While most of David's friends are dispatched by the fighting family, David himself kills his last surviving friend to be alone with Nicole, and then as he threatens to kill her father, she stabs him in the back, giving Steve the chance to throw David out of Nicole's bedroom window. The family, along with the traumatized Margo, are reunited after the harrowing ordeal, with the monstrous threat to family unity dead outside the house. *Fear* unfortunately carries out this preservative message through excessive violence against its young female cast, especially Margo, and posits that teenage girls will endure great abuse by young men in the service of attaining romantic ideals. *Fear* is ultimately reactionary in regard to its handling of Nicole's otherwise typical discovery of first love, for despite its pertinent warnings about deceptively attractive young men, it exploits female fears of masculine aggression, obsession, and devotion. The film's one concession to less-threatening masculinity, Gary, is killed, and given that "father knows best," Nicole is ultimately empowered only by his paternal authority, and remains a victim of the very love and affection she was seeking from men in the first place.[11]

In 1995 the schlock studio Troma released its rarely seen Romeo and Juliet story *Tromeo and Juliet,* a very '90s updating of the classic original tale of teen love rent asunder by family difference and oppression, this time incorporating copious doses of sex and violence. Another updating that was less prurient but almost as excessive was *William Shakespeare's Romeo + Juliet* the next year, a postmodern adaptation of the sixteenth-century play that is a quickly paced flashy commentary on contemporary media, capitalism, and law, still keeping the original drama's concerns with family relations that doom the star-crossed lovers. Leonardo DiCaprio plays Romeo and Claire Danes is Juliet, both actors delivering their Shakespearean lines against the backdrop of Verona Beach, an apparently Floridian setting wherein cultural clashes among whites, blacks, and Latinos parallel the class rivalry between the protagonists' families, the Montagues and Capulets. The young men of the rival families now battle with guns instead of swords, and an early fight scene staged at a gas station conjures up current urban crises of gang warfare.

But the story centers on the title characters, who meet at a lavish masquerade party where Juliet's parents are trying to interest her in the handsome Paris (Paul Rudd), a wealthy young businessman. Instead, the angel-costumed Juliet becomes immediately entranced by Romeo, her knight in faux armor. The teens are filled with the rush of attraction, yet realize that their opposing families—here made foes by corporate competition—will not allow their union. They quickly agree to a secret wedding with Father Laurence (Pete Postlethwaite), and after further fighting erupts between the Montague and Capulet youth, Romeo kills Juliet's cousin Tybalt (John Leguizamo), which forces Romeo to leave town. He nonetheless finds his way back to Juliet and they consummate their relationship, only to learn that Juliet's father has planned a hasty wedding for her and Paris. The suicidal Juliet turns to Father Laurence, and together they plan to fake her death so that afterward she can be reunited with Romeo. The news of this ruse fails to reach Romeo, and after a rousing race in which he fights his way to Juliet's unconscious body, believing she is dead, he takes poison to kill himself, prompting the arising Juliet to shoot herself in the head. The moral of the story is then pronounced by the presiding police officer, who chastises the families for allowing their mutual contempt to destroy their innocent children.

What was already a compelling play about the consequences of social hatred is here brought to the screen with an energetic illustration of unleashed romantic longing overcoming familial and cultural differences, only to fail in its attempt to transcend those conflicts. The contemporary updating suggests that the Romeo and Juliet of the 1500s are little different from teenagers today kept apart by intolerance and prejudice. Overall, many youth love films of the '90s took on a more desperate tone compared to the many '80s romantic comedies, including those profiled here as well as *Lisa* (1990), *Alan & Naomi* (1992), *Foreign Student* (1994), *Boys* (1996), *Welcome to the Dollhouse* (1996), *Niagara, Niagara* (1998), and *She's All That* (1999). The family remains the foremost site of youthful romantic obstacles, and the appearance of *Romeo + Juliet* in the mid-'90s signals the film industry's understanding of that dilemma—and its continuing romantic appeal—to young audiences. The somber message of the movie is nonetheless the most pessimistic of any youth love/sex film, and is perhaps only so due to its historic source; vilifying family in contemporary terms is easily permissible when the inspiration is more than 400 years old. Yet more-recent period films such as *Titanic, The Ice Storm* (1998), and *The Virgin Suicides* (2000) and contemporary-set films such as *Anywhere but Here* (1999) and *American Beauty* (1999) further portray the family as a destructive force in teens' romantic-sexual development. If the image of family-tormented youth in future films becomes even more critical and lethal, then these late-'90s films may be seen as turning points in that representation.

YOUTH HAVING SEX

The sexual development and practice of young people has been a topic of concern and fascination for centuries, both to youth, who themselves have much to learn and appreciate, and to adults and parents, who recall their discoveries of sexuality with both nostalgia and alarm, thereby treating these facts of life with alternating doses of sensitivity and hyperbole. Most people have their first shared sexual experiences (intercourse or otherwise) in their teen years, and so youth films are likely sites for the discussion and dramatization of sexual explorations. Yet while many youth films from 1980 to 1999 featured teens engaging in sexual practices, the majority were decidedly negative in their portrayals, demonstrating the complications of sex, as well as the disappointments, confusions, and potential dangers. Youth in these films find themselves involved in sexual activities in one form or another, whether intercourse, foreplay, or the basic negotiation of sexual preferences, and like the youth love film, the majority of these narratives could be characterized as comedies, although they also tend to take seriously the stakes of sex.

Losing Virginity

The most common plot of youth sex films throughout the early 1980s was the quest of teens to lose their virginity. First sex is a classic rite of passage for young adults, especially as adolescence brings with it the hormonal and physical changes that instill suddenly strong sexual impulses in teens. For both genders, sexual practice is often a signifier of adulthood, because with it comes a level of intimacy and responsibility beyond the experience of children; however, like children, most sexually active teens are still learning to handle their increasing senses of potency, obligation, and maturity, all of which are components of sexuality even though many teens are unprepared for how these aspects of adulthood will change them. The 1969 film *Last Summer* may be the best example of how unresolved virginal tensions can lead to unexpected moral consequences: the idyllic arrangement of two teen boys and a teen girl is disrupted when a second teen girl tries to befriend them, ultimately resulting in the three original friends raping the newcomer. Such excessive reactions would be rare in subsequent youth films, perhaps since teens themselves often avoid paying to see such harsh possibilities.

Before the era of AIDS, the most serious consequences of teen sexual practice were pregnancy, venereal disease, and emotional distress. While AIDS was recognized in 1981, its capacity to be spread by heterosexual contact was not clear until the mid-'80s, and not coincidentally, there was a dramatic decline in the number of youth films featuring the loss of virginity after 1986. In fact, with the exception of the parodic *Virgin High* in 1990, the youth sex-quest film stopped production altogether from 1986 to the mid-'90s; then when *Kids* appeared in 1995, the previously playful loss of virginity was portrayed as sinister and as reviled as any crime, although like the depiction of much youth criminality, it also retained a cachet of rebellion. Over the following few years, with social concerns about AIDS being marginalized in the United States, teenage sexual activity found its way back to the screen in less threatening but more mature ways. Few of the early-'80s tales of losing virginity featured any of the potential medical consequences of sex, but most of them did weave emotional issues with the curiosity of their characters. To most of the teens in these films, sex was a new dark continent to be explored, and most of them faced certain fears and frustrations in that exploration, and, at least until *Kids*, the vast majority prevailed with some level of happiness. Nonetheless, few of these films could be said to have capriciously promoted sex for the population they were directed to, if only because the sex act itself was so rarely portrayed in as pleasurable terms as its anticipation.

The 1980 film *Little Darlings* made the sex-quest plot explicit: two teenage girls at summer camp compete to see who can lose her virginity first. One girl lies about having sex with an adult counselor, while the other is greatly aggrieved when she actually has sex with a teenage boy; the film, like most others after it, reveals the disappointments of first sex for many teens. The next year the more successful *Porky's* further capitalized on the group pursuit of first sex from the male perspective, albeit removed to the 1950s. The title of another 1981 film, *Goin' All the Way*, suggested the salacious manner in which most of the losing-virginity sagas would operate; the story revolves around a high school senior who cannot seem to convince his girlfriend to have sex with him. After much wrangling, some of which is admittedly heartfelt, the boy convinces the girl of his love for her, and she is so thrilled that she finally "goes all the way" with him. Her systematic process of deciding to lose her virginity is a narrative paradigm common to all "good" girls in youth sex films: boys always want to have sex and must learn to control their urges, but moral girls are so anguished by their sexual thoughts and impulses as to ensure their resistance to boys' urges, granting them a certain sense of power via the denial of mutual satisfaction. Like many other youth sex films to follow, *Goin' All the Way* ends with the suspense-relieving consummation of the protagonists' relationship, wherein the loss of virginity and *not* the sex act provides the ultimate resolution for both teens' tensions, even though the characters remain clearly confused and overwhelmed by sex, a condition that is typical of virtually all youth sex films.

The sex-quest film came into its own in American youth cinema of the 1980s with the very successful *Fast Times at Ridgemont High* in 1982. The film takes on high school life in broad terms, and thus sex is merely one aspect of the narrative's matrix, even if the sexual development of Stacy (Jennifer Jason Leigh) is a dominant plotline. First she decides to lose her virginity to a man in his 20s—she tells him she's 19 when she's really 15—and then later has casual 10-second sex with the slimy Mike (Robert Romanus); in both cases, her enjoyment of the experience is fleeting if existent. Stacy bears the further brunt of her disappointing sexual initiations when she finds herself pregnant and decides to have an abortion. Sex comes with a definite price for the spacey Stacy, who thinks nothing of birth control, although David Denby accurately notes that while "Stacy and her friends are shucking off their clothes before they've explored friendship or the pleasures of courtship or romance," this theme is "developed satirically, not as a moral judgment."[12] Such satire is carried on in the loss of virginity for Mark (Brian Backer), which is opposite to Stacy's—more arduous and less consequential. Mark, working against but confirming his nerdy image, takes Stacy out on a formal dinner date and forgets his wallet. He is even more awkward when they return to her house and she tries to seduce him. Yet Mark is the one character who, by the film's end, does not have sex and seems best off for it: Mike is despised, Stacy is dejected, and her oversexed best friend is ultimately left alone as well. Stacy, having had her fill of troubling sexual experiences, agrees to proceed patiently with Mark, portending that this approach will be the best for both of them, and thus Mark's virginal status is rendered more reassuring rather than frustrating.

The title of *The Last American Virgin* (1982) is both humorous and, within the context of the film's bleak narrative, ominous. Gary (Lawrence Monoson) and his two buddies Rick (Steve Antin), a good-looking stud, and David (Joe Rubbo), a rotund jovial goof, are three teenagers eager for their first sexual experiences. Rick is a smooth operator compared to shy Gary, which becomes a big problem for him when Rick wins the heart of Karen (Diane Franklin), for whom Gary pines away throughout the entire film. Gary is one of the most sympathetic and sensitive characters in any teen sex-quest film: he has the same raging urges as other young males and still appears genuinely conflicted over his affection for Karen, yet he ultimately resists his friends' forays into quickly losing their virginity. When Rick convinces three teen girls to join him and his two friends for a little party, Gary is not only left with the "least attractive" girl but ungraciously fumbles when he tries to make out with her. After more frustration, Gary tries to lure Rick away from Karen by taking his friends to a prostitute, and he denies himself another opportunity to lose his virginity (although all three boys do develop crabs). What Gary wants more than sex, unlike his cohorts, is love. The film is certainly filled with plenty of bawdy sex scenes, though, and plays up masculine sexual aggression, as when Rick proudly announces that he has deflowered Karen. This upsets Gary visibly, and after Rick arrogantly refuses to help Karen when she becomes pregnant, Gary becomes even more angry with Rick, and devotes his Christmas vacation to helping her get an abortion.

The last section of the film then becomes surprisingly depressing. Gary scrambles to raise the money for Karen's abortion and hides her away during her recovery, after which he finally tells her he has been in love with her all along. Gary assumes that he has proven himself to her enough to secure their romance, but he soon finds Karen back in the arms of the lecherous Rick. The final shot of the film is Gary driving away into the night, crying—and still a virgin.[13] For all the work the film has done in portraying the virtue of Gary's patience and understanding, this conclusion declares that he has been a fool to invest so much in Karen, and on a larger scale suggests that waiting for the "right person" to lose one's virginity to is a damaging ambition. Like so many youth love/sex films, the division between love and sex is thus enforced—the two rarely occur in the same relationship. *The Last American Virgin* becomes a warning to youth against the pursuit of sex, which leads to disease, pregnancy, and the loss of friends, and the pursuit of love, which is unpredictable and unrewarding.[14]

1982 also saw the release of the period film *Losin' It,* whose provocative title was indicative of the increasingly direct sexual marketing of youth films at the time. *Losin' It* is perhaps most notable for featuring Tom Cruise in his first starring role, within a group of four boys who travel to Mexico to alleviate their virginity, although Cruise would find even greater visibility as a frustrated virgin later in 1983 when he starred in *Risky Business*, one of the highest-grossing youth films of the decade. The latter story uses the by-then classic device of a teenager's parents going away on a trip, leaving high school senior Joel (Cruise) alone at home. First Joel does little more than dance around in his underwear and sample his dad's scotch, until the increasing pressure of his friends—who tease him for his lack of prowess and spontaneity—makes him sexually insecure. As one buddy famously advises him, "Say 'what the fuck.' If you can't say it, you can't do it." The enterprising Joel knows that he should concentrate on his schoolwork, but he breaks down and calls a young prostitute named Lana (Rebecca DeMornay), who promptly fulfills his carnal curiosities.

The film parallels Joel's ambitions to become a successful capitalist with his venture into the world of sexuality: after Lana steals his mother's prized crystal egg in payment for her services, Joel rescues her from her maniacal pimp Guido (Joe Pantoliano) to make a deal for the egg. Lana suggests that he can get the egg back and make even more money if he were to hook up his rich friends with her prostitute colleagues, a proposal that Joel at first resists but soon finds a necessity after he crashes his father's expensive car, an "accident" that Lana appears to have caused. Joel thus learns that the exchange of sex for property is a potentially lucrative business and has no shame in taking advantage of his friends, from whom he immediately gains respect and admiration. Lana helps Joel set up his house as a one-night brothel, and even provides special accommodations for a college interviewer from Princeton, only the business goes sour the next day when Guido comes to collect for the services of his "employees." Joel madly scrambles to rectify the situation and succeeds in the nick of time, getting back the egg and furniture that Guido had stolen from him, gaining acceptance to Princeton, and cleaning the house just before his parents return. In a final scene, Joel demonstrates his newfound savvy and sophistication to Lana by teasing her that she'll now have to pay *him* to be his girlfriend, thereby shifting the economic power of sexual value onto himself, and more so by implying that he wants to continue his prostitution service in college, revealing his dubious perspective in which he has become a "proper pimp." David Denby observed that when "Joel surmounts his sex and career anxieties by turning himself into a pimp," it is "presented without irony or a hint of criticism, as a triumph of free enterprise."[15]

Risky Business accommodates its losing-virginity agenda within the first third of the story, following Joel through his role as virginity-ender for the young male population around him. Joel's own sexual activity is thus less relevant to the narrative than his selling of sex, and he gains his sense of acceptance and authority accordingly, such as when he coolly pitches his service to a diverse range of young men he meets. That Joel is a salesman of commodified women is obvious, as he claims to be selling "experience" to his eager clients, who see no problem or danger with having sex for money (again, early enough that AIDS was not considered an issue, although other diseases were still prominent) and are happy to lose their virginity with complete strangers, and moreover, with the same complete strangers to whom their friends are also losing theirs. *Risky Business* thus pitches the morality of young men especially low, and makes Joel's misogynist sex business an acceptable sign of his financial acumen—he earns far more money for his "project" than do his fellow aspiring classmates—even if Guido takes back his profits. Joel can be viewed as the teen baron of Reagan-era capitalist exploitation, which is justified by the gratification it provides to the masses, and his image as a slick, successful dealer is an explicit inspiration for young men to continue the tradition of patriarchal economic practice. With such an endorsement being rendered so entertaining by the comic style of the film, Joel's coming-of-age is more a celebration of his daring business education than a questioning of the licentious methods by which it is achieved.

Other sexual adventures followed in teen films after the sleeper success of *Risky Business,* introducing mildly diverse variations. Products such as *Private Lessons* (1981), *Class* (1983), and *My Tutor* (1983) offered the services of older women to teenage boys seeking sexual initiation. *Private School* (1983), *Joy of Sex* (1984), and *Paradise Motel* (1985) enlisted larger groups of friends who help each other find sex, which was also the case in *Hot Moves* (1984), a film that provided the now archetypal plot of boys taking an oath to lose their virginity by a certain deadline. The sex cycle started showing some signs of change by 1985, when the most successful sex quest was *The Sure Thing,* a film about college students who show a certain level of maturity over their predecessors. Further evidence would also come that year with *Once Bitten,* a horror comedy in which a sexually frustrated teen (played by a young Jim Carrey) is doubly relieved of his virginity, first metaphorically through the not-quite-sexual blood suckings of a lady vampire, and then literally through his girlfriend, who must finally have sex with him to save him from the virgin-hungry vampiress. The film thus fantastically makes losing virginity a matter of life and death, or on another level, hints that if teens wait too long to have sex they will be susceptible to monstrous consequences. Yet when the protagonists consummate their relationship in a coffin, the film tacitly hints at the increasingly morbid notions of youth sex that would prevail in the later '80s and '90s as the threat of AIDS became more prominent and did indeed make sex for some a matter of life and death.

A low-budget soft-porn youth film called *The Big Bet* (1986) then became not only one of the most offensive portrayals of teen sexual activity among the many of the '80s, but effectively its death knell. Chris (Lance Sloane) becomes attracted to new girl at school Beth (Kimberly Evenson), yet is so insecure that he bets a rival that he can have sex with her within 10 days, a tactic apparently meant to inspire him in pursuing Beth and win him praise among the cool kids at school. The narrative uses a recurring device in which Chris fantasizes about having sex with numerous naked women, including his attractive older neighbor, and with each new fantasy he becomes progressively frustrated at his inability to bed Beth, despite his variously preposterous efforts. What then appears to be a possible sign of Chris's respect for Beth—he begins to feel guilty for making her the object of a bet—is completely compromised when he gets mad at her and becomes so distraught that he runs off and has sex with his suddenly willing neighbor. The idea that the older woman teaches Chris "how to make love" caters to a primal male fantasy, but far more depraved than this Oedipal fiction is Beth's sudden forgiving of Chris after he beats up his rival at school. Beth is supposedly so turned on by Chris's show of masculine violence and so flippant about her objectification by Chris and all the other boys (who have also placed bets on her having sex) that she becomes the sexual aggressor, inviting Chris to take her on the living room floor. The story appears to end right there, with the sexual conquest thus reached, until the end credits continue the tale: we see Chris and Beth graduate and later happily have a child. The still images do not suggest how long this process takes, yet it remains an odd recuperation of an otherwise irredeemably macho scenario. This ending suggests that the inevitable pregnancy of Beth justifies Chris's reprehensible treatment of her, as if creating a family nullifies the tension over her role as a mere sex toy—he must love her if they are staying together.

The Big Bet was little seen in theaters but definitely represents the worst of its kind: an unfunny, unfeeling, and ultimately deceptive teen sexploitation movie that further maligned the image of youth. Given that these kinds of products had become so common by the mid-'80s, teenagers may have grown insulted at such insensitive stories, although considering how many the film industry made in the first seven years of the '80s—at least 25—the industry's sudden cessation of these films in 1986 remains intriguing. With the more sincere sexual portrayals of teens in John Hughes's films of the mid-'80s becoming more popular, the pornographic quality of a teen-oriented film like *The Big Bet* may have signaled to studios the paucity of options left in portraying teenage sexual discovery in explicit terms.[16]

As noted in the horror chapter, after a genre has become codified and recognized, it can be and often is parodied. In the case of the teen sex-quest film, studios may have felt that parodies were unnecessary since the films tended to be so comical already, but one example did appear in 1990, the laboriously humorless *Virgin High*. The story is familiar: a high school student tries to convince his prudish girlfriend to have sex with him, only her father sends her off to a Catholic boarding school, which the protagonist and his buddies spend the rest of the story trying to infiltrate. *Virgin High* knows enough about the subgenre it is satirizing, but fails to make the oddities and inanities of the teen sex-quest film at all funny or interesting. Sex is still immoral and self-destructive, even though guys want nothing but and girls ultimately surrender to it; the desire for teens to have sex cannot be stopped by any force, be it parental, religious, or geographic.

Five more years elapsed in which the teen sex-quest film appeared to have vanished. Even though teenage characters in some youth films continued to have sex, the narrative emphasis on sexual conquest was not prominent in these films like it had been in the early to mid-'80s; the family-friendly *Mermaids* (1990) and the anachronistic *Return to the Blue Lagoon* (1991) were both evidence of this, as their sexually curious teen characters moved within the more sensually subtle confines of PG-13 ratings. Then, the appearance of Larry Clark's *Kids* in 1995 presented a radical revision of the teen sex-quest story, a feigned documentary approach to not only youth sexuality but general delinquency, drug use, and sexually transmitted disease. The film revolves around two teen boys, Telly (Leo Fitzpatrick) and Casper (Justin Pierce), the first of whom begins the film's day-in-the-life of debauchery by deflowering an apparently pubescent girl while the other is drinking the first of many 40-ounce beers. Telly prides himself on being a "virgin surgeon" who pursues particularly young girls, and on this day his goal is to have two of them. He waxes philosophical on the powerful significance he feels in being so many girls' first sex partner: to him, the conquest of virgins—all of whom he abandons after having sex with them—is more than a sign of his masculine prowess; it is the very means by which he gains identity. The few girls who are presented in the film are less developed characters, but as an early dialogue scene shows, they are just as sexually excitable as the boys who pursue them. The one conspicuous exception is Jennie (Chloe Sevigny), who reveals that she only ever had sex one time, with Telly, and discovers soon thereafter that he has infected her with HIV. The film's narrative thus becomes something of a picaresque journey for Jennie as she tries to find Telly before he infects another girl by the end of the day.

Despite Jennie's presence in the story and the one dialogue scene offered between girls, *Kids* never offers a balance or reprieve from its objectified positioning of young women, and is ultimately boldly exploitative of its entire young cast. Critics made much of the fact that the script was written by Harmony Korine when he was just 19, and perhaps he was making a statement on the difficulty girls face in dealing with urban boys today, for he appears himself as a friendly nerd who meets Jennie at a rave and, with empty consolations, forces her to take a drug that he insists will make her feel better. By the end of the film, Jennie finds Telly but doesn't bother to stop him when she sees he is having sex with yet another virgin, and she is so stoned that she cannot even protest when Casper later rapes her, a scene made all the more brutal by the sustained filming of it for over two minutes. As I have written elsewhere, "[T]he film cheaply offers a false empowerment for its female characters, who initially appear confident in their knowledge and appropriation of sex, and who are ultimately victimized by it. The film is not merely sexist or patriarchal, it endorses an understanding of youth sexuality that is degrading for both genders."[17]

The ribald search for hedonistic pleasure that permeates *Kids*—all of its young characters are looking for beer, drugs, sex, and/or the next party—is based on its distinctly masculinist perspective, or as bell hooks claimed in more assertive terms, "What is being exploited is precisely and solely a spectacle of teenage sexuality that has been shaped and informed by patriarchal attitudes."[18] *Kids* does not make sexuality for youth appear effortless; however, the film's one-dimensional perspective—that is, that boys are dogs and girls are not much better—denies the psychological intricacy of the issue. The main, if singular, consequence of sexuality in *Kids* is the potential spread of HIV, a serious issue to be sure, but Telly's habitual practice of deflowering virgins, for instance, is left on the moral surface. The main lesson of *Kids*—that sex can be deadly—is never realized on-screen. The film concludes with Telly visibly infecting another girl with HIV and reciting in a voiceover, "When you're young, not much matters. . . . Sometimes when you're young, the only place to go is inside. That's just it—fucking is what I love. Take that away from me and I really got nothing." This ending may be meant as further ironic commentary on the fact that Telly is likely to die from his fucking practices, except he is never forced to confront them. As Owen Gliberman said, "We never get to see if the little son of a bitch has a soul after all."[19]

The perspective on youth sexuality offered by *Kids* is incomplete and misogynistic, although within the context of so many vilified images of teen sexuality in the '90s, the film can appear to be merely marking a moment in the cultural zeitgeist. Very much like *Teenage Crime Wave* and other extreme portraits of the "youth threat" in the 1950s, *Kids* attempts to inflame the otherwise serious conditions of youth sexual practice by celebrating the unbridled decadence and anomie of ignorant antiheroes like Telly and Casper, and in that way is similar to the basest of the teen sex comedies of the early '80s. Tom Doherty rightly said, "*Kids* can probably be best described as an ethnographic film on urban teen subculture for an art-house crowd ready to be appalled at what's the matter with kids today."[20] The fact that *Kids* portrays the working class instead of the middle or upper class and that it directly addresses the issue of HIV-AIDS (as little as it actually *informs* about it) does not nullify the film's reactionary approach of depicting youth sexuality as dangerous and deviant, beyond being devoid of any real pleasure.

Portrayals of teen sex in other '90s youth films are not quite as pessimistic or condescending, although it is usually shown to be distinctly more problematic than it was in the '80s, and instances of "first sex" are depicted far less often since teenagers tend to be either virgins for the entire film or sexually experienced before the start of the story. The first case persisted in films such as *Clueless* (1995), *Welcome to the Dollhouse* (1996), *Trojan War* (1997), and *Never Been Kissed* (1999), while the second case was evident in films like *Hackers* (1995), *Girls Town* (1996), *Wild Things* (1997), *The Opposite of Sex* (1998), and *10 Things I Hate About You* (1999). Even films that did continue to feature deflowering scenes, such as *Titanic* (1997), *Can't Hardly Wait* (1998), *The Rage: Carrie 2* (1999), and *The Virgin Suicides* (2000), featured the fated moment as solemn and sincere, quite a remove from the silly and lascivious nature of teen sex scenes in the more immature early '80s.

Two 1999 films then offered bipolar revisions of the teen sex-quest film, the first more aligned with the sinister quality of *Kids* and the second an almost nostalgic return to the sex romps of the '80s. *Cruel Intentions* is a young updating of *Dangerous Liaisons,* in which the wealthy roué Sebastian (Ryan

The virginal and luckless Jim (Jason Biggs) is chagrined in *American Pie* (1999) when his parents find him masturbating while watching a porno channel (his sock aid is concealed by the pillow).

Phillipe) makes a wager with his sexually alluring stepsister Kathryn (Sarah Michelle Gellar) that he will be able to bed down proud virgin Annette (Reese Witherspoon).[21] The film plays with ripe sexual tension between the step-siblings—Kathryn will allow Sebastian to do "anything" he wants to her if he wins the bet—and the contemptible rich kids are portrayed as unbearably selfish and venal. However, Sebastian finds himself unexpectedly falling in love with the endearing Annette, and even though he does succeed in stealing her prized virginity, he ultimately becomes more concerned with the preservation of their relationship. The resolution of the story then speaks to the moral consequences of the characters' villainous use of sex: Sebastian is killed in a car accident and Kathryn is exposed in front of her entire school as the vindictive phony that she is. These character assassinations, both literal and symbolic, arise from treating sexual conquest in such a ruthless way.

The sexual conquests of the characters in *American Pie* are not only more light-hearted, but they are also in many ways redemptive. The plot is lifted straight out of the early '80s, with four male high school seniors making a pact to lose their virginity. Jim (Jason Biggs) emerges as the main character, an inexperienced bumbler humbled by his parents' discovery of him masturbating with a sock, which is actually less embarrassing than his later use of a warm apple pie. He joins his friends for a party where they each anticipate some level of sexual activity, a longing that brings nothing but dejected frustration, and convinces them to pledge allegiance to having sex before the prom, a mere few weeks away.

Given this objective, the story could easily emulate the excessive concupiscence of the '80s films it echoes (as it certainly raises the level of gross bodily-fluid gags), yet the film often handles the libidinous boys' travails in an honest, believable fashion. There are some unrealistic sexist moments, such as when Jim invites attractive exchange student Nadia (Shannon Elizabeth) to his house, with the ulterior motive of seducing her while his friends watch over an Internet feed, which would publicly verify his virility. First, Jim steps out to join his buddies in a communal orgy of voyeurism as they watch Nadia undress in his bedroom, where she happens to find one of his porn magazines and impulsively decides to masturbate in front of the hidden camera. This scenario then becomes even more improbable when Jim returns and Nadia invites him to fondle her, but as if countering his "visual conquest" of her with his deeper insecurity, her simple contact causes him to prematurely ejaculate. Such twists mark the film's sense of balance, for the boys realize that their horny desires will take them nowhere, and the girls they pursue want more than to be chased: they want a level of affection and attention not accorded to teen girls in most previous sex comedies, or as Jonathan Foreman made the comparison, "[T]he girls in *American Pie* are much more than life-support systems for breasts."[22]

Thus, as Kevin (Thomas Ian Nicholas) tries to convince his girlfriend Vicky (Tara Reid) to go all the way, he realizes that he needs to make their foreplay more pleasurable *to her*. He then learns to practice other sexual techniques (including oral approaches detailed in a secret "sex bible"), which help to both encourage Vicky's interest and convince her of his devotion; more significantly, this further promotes the attainment of a girl's orgasm as a plot point in teen films. The jock "Oz" (Chris Klein) woos a girl by joining a jazz choir, risking his reputation and his place on the lacrosse team, only to discover his talents as a singer as well as his own sensitivity, making him all the more endearing to her. And refined dork Finch (Eddie Kaye Thomas), who pays a female friend to spread rumors of his potency—in an effort to "buy" a sexual identity after fearing he will never earn his own—decides to give up on dating his classmates, only to find himself seduced by a friend's randy mother.

Alas, the hapless Jim has the toughest luck of the bunch, since he ends up with a nerdy date at the senior prom and little prospect of losing his virginity, until she shows him the carnal carnivore she really is, resulting in the boy being used for sex by the girl, another twist that is recuperated by his eventual pride in being so used. In fact, as the boys move toward their climactic first times, they each earn a modicum of self-esteem by rising above their initially base impulses and learning to treat the self-assured girls with respect, so that all of their eventual sex scenes are rendered tender and/or humorous, and furthermore, they are all ultimately celebratory, a phenomenon that had been minimized in American youth films for over a decade.[23] Perhaps the common acceptance of safe sex (which is clearly practiced in the film) and the refreshing sense of confident *female* sexual pleasure that the film promotes signal further changes in the film industry's attitudes toward teen sex. As Owen Gliberman noted, "It reflects a major shift in contemporary teen culture that the girls in *American Pie* are as hip to sex as the boys."[24]

As of this writing, however, the majority of youth sex in cinema remains problematic, and whether *American Pie* (and its successful 2001 sequel) represent a return of the romp or even an inauguration of more balanced, meaningful depictions of carnal education remains to be seen. A film like *Coming Soon* (1999) offers both good and bad news in this regard: the film is an even more girl-focused comedy about losing virginity and, more prominently, about girls' efforts to achieve orgasm. Yet due to the film's extolling of young women's sexual satisfaction, it garnered an NC-17 rating in its initial release, leading to considerable distribution problems. *American Pie* became a huge hit after being reedited from its NC-17 to an R; the more sensitive *Coming Soon,* without the support of a major studio, faded to video, where few teens saw its healthy gender inversion of the sex-quest plot. The same double standard that promoted female sexual practice while denying female sexual pleasure in earlier youth films may thus still be a disruptive factor in bringing more realistic and positive depictions of teenage sexuality to American movies.

Homosexuality

Teenage homosexuality (and bisexuality) in American cinema up to the 1990s was handled in often vague if not symbolic terms, and when it was handled, the characters in question were almost always troubled and trying to deny their nonheterosexual impulses, lest they face the consequence of ridicule, condemnation, or even death. In David Considine's examination of homosexual youth depictions, he discusses the ostracizing of thinly coded gay characters in '50s films such as *Rebel Without a Cause* and *Tea and Sympathy,* pointing out that European films dealt with the issue of adolescent homosexuality more often and more confidently. By the time of *Ode to Billy Joe* in 1976, Hollywood appeared still uneasy with the queer youth concept, for the fleeting homosexual encounter of the title character results in his suicide. Considine cites the 1980 film *Happy Birthday, Gemini* as "a quantum leap forward in Hollywood's treatment of adolescent homosexuality," where a father supports his 20-year-old son's questioning of his sexual preference.[25]

Considine goes on to list a number of adult gay and lesbian characters in films of the '80s, but his enthusiasm for the progressive potential of *Happy Birthday, Gemini* appears optimistic, since images of queer youth were rare in American cinema at the time. For instance, another 1980 youth film, *Fame*, featured only one gay character within the relatively high homosexual population of the New York School for Performing Arts, who is handled sympathetically through the film's implication that, as Considine himself points out, "he is doomed to a loveless life of unhappiness."[26] Kevin Bacon played a teen hustler in the obscure film *Forty Deuce* (1982), in which his character tries to finance a heroin deal by selling a runaway boy, a plot that obviously does not offer an appealing image of young gay males. In *The Celluloid Closet*, Vito Russo provides commentary on two other obscure and troubling films featuring gay teens: *Abuse* (1982), the story of a gay boy who falls in love with a filmmaker who is studying how the child is brutalized by his parents, and *The Boys Next Door* (1986), in which a repressed teen becomes so tormented over his latent homosexuality that he becomes homicidal.[27] A rather underdeveloped gay teen appears at the end of *Torch Song Trilogy* (1988) as the adopted son of the lead character, and queer issues do surface for protagonists in a select few other '80s films such as *A Nightmare on Elm Street 2* and *Vision Quest* (both 1985). Perhaps the clearest sign of tension over homosexual youth in American films of the '80s was in *Less than Zero* (1987), featuring the deemphasized practice of a young male prostitute who became more sexually ambiguous in his translation from page to screen.

An argument could be made that young people typically do not openly question their sexuality until their college or post-teen years, and more so, that the very notion remains a threat to the established heterosexual majority, especially for young people whose impressionability is very much a concern for conservative parents.[28] Another potential problem with the depiction of youth homosexuality may be the already popular perception of teens as oversexed, and therefore being gay or lesbian at such a young age could appear more sexually irresponsible, a concern that may have been more acute in the early AIDS era. This of course unfairly shifts the emphasis of same-sex relationships to the sexual and away from the romantic, yet most queer youth depictions in the '90s tended to deal with tensions around both sexual experience and romantic longing, or in other words, the same tensions that heterosexual teens are shown dealing with in other films. Ironically, as concerns over AIDS and gay rights legislation increased in the '90s, the number of homosexual characters in American films, both youth and adult, increased, sometimes in stereotypically negative roles, but generally in a more positive light.

In 1991 gay director Gus Van Sant turned two of the '80s heterosexual heartthrobs into young hustlers in *My Own Private Idaho,* a film clearly directed at an adult audience that still provided the most complete exploration of young homosexuality in American films up to that time. River Phoenix and Keanu Reeves play narcoleptic Mike and forsaken rich stud Scott, respectively; the characters become involved in a far-reaching search for Mike's mother, during which Scott takes up with a young woman and abandons his previously gay ways. The characters are at the fringe of their teen years—both are around 20—while a number of older and some younger gay characters populate the story, which employs a very loose adaptation of Shakespeare's *Henry IV, Part 1*. The film is sometimes difficult to appreciate as a drama of young gay life, if only because its conspicuous stylization renders its often poignant characterizations rather esoteric. Mike's narcolepsy is analogous to his ongoing sexual crisis in which he is effectively resisting heterosexuality—when he is picked up by a rich woman and gets excited, he falls asleep—where Scott's heterosexual destiny comments on the influence of wealth in negotiating sexual practice, since his father's inheritance and upper-class background appear to directly carry him away from his temporarily alternative lifestyle.

A sweet if sad affection exists between Mike and Scott that speaks to the certain complication of being a young homosexual, yielding a particular sympathy for same-sex attraction among youth. Scott will only have sex with men for money, while Mike longs for a shared love with Scott that remains unrequited. Scott appears to recognize Mike's interest but cannot manifest the level of emotion needed to actually *love* another man like Mike loves him, and thus the film points to a crucial difference between gayness as a sexual practice and as a way of life. Scott's inheritance from his famed father is one not only of money but of the very tradition that is heterosexuality, whereas Mike is left at the end of the film on his apparently endless search for a waking comfort that is, in the context of the film and of American culture, simply not available to most young gay men.

The gender-bender comedy *Just One of the Guys* (1985) had glancingly considered the complications of same-sex attraction for teens, but eight years later its essential opposite, *Just One of the Girls* (1993), demonstrated a certain shift in directly dealing with the homosexual tensions of its plot. The unisexually named Chris (Corey Haim) is a 16-year-old who dresses as a girl to avoid the taunts of local bully Kurt (Cam Bancroft), and as fate would have it, Kurt becomes attracted to this new "girl" at school. After Chris finally reveals himself as a boy in front of the entire school, Kurt's buddies tease him that he must be gay, and that he should beat up Chris to prove that he's not. In an unexpected show of tolerance and homosocial camaraderie, Chris immediately allows Kurt to hit him, knowing that he won't, and both boys shake hands. *Just One of the Girls* does not feature any homosexual characters, but it does entertain many issues about homosexual attraction and gender relations among teens. Kurt's lack of being able to explain his love for the "female" Chris speaks to the common mythology of young love—that it is powerful and inexplicable—while it also blurs the distinction between hetero- and homosexual attraction, since Chris looks rather the same in both forms and has the same social qualities. The fact that Kurt cannot "win" Chris in female or male form despite his own overmasculinized performance leads to his difficult recognition of his own vulnerabilities, which include desiring a masculine girl. The film's lack of restoring heterosexual normalcy—Chris is still left alone, despite his crush on Kurt's sister—is a further sign of its suggestion that youth attractions may be motivated by homo- or bisexual impulses, and that such impulses are understandable, at least under certain circumstances.[29]

A film that boldly paints its teen characters as homosexual regardless of circumstance is *Totally Fucked Up* (1994; the film was marketed as *Totally F***ed Up,* but its unexpurgated title is spoken as a front credit by one of the main characters). The film showcases a thriving yet endangered young queer population, and remains to date the most complete depiction of a queer teen ensemble. Directed with a nod to formal experimentation by young gay filmmaker Gregg Araki, the story follows six homosexual friends through 15 segments, a conscious homage to the approach used by Jean-Luc Godard in his famous youth film, *Masculin-Féminin* (1966), which Randy Gener comments upon by calling the characters "the postpunk children of MTV and HIV," since "Marx is dead and Coca-Cola is a cliché."[30] Appropriately, the film deals with a number of masculine and feminine gender issues for young people, although more so than in other youth portrayals, the characters' lives in *Totally Fucked Up* revolve around their sexual activities. Steven (Gilbert Luna) and Deric (Lance May) are interracial lovers; Steven is an aspiring film student who is making a video documentary about his gay friends, including the mopey Andy (James

Duval), confident Tommy (Roko Belic), and lesbian partners Michele (Susan Behshid) and Patricia (Jenee Gill). The group openly talks about their sexual experiences and desires, sharing a comfort with each other that demonstrates their security and loyalty: they discuss their cynicism and fantasies about romance, elaborate on their idols (all heterosexual movie stars who they suspect are gay, such as Tom Cruise), believe that AIDS is a government conspiracy, and sometimes even masturbate together (while watching porn, or at a party, where the girls ask the guys to ejaculate into a bowl so they can try artificial insemination with a turkey baster).

The narrative begins (and Araki clearly signals it as such) when Andy meets and slowly falls in love with a young man and Steven cheats on Deric with another guy, leading Deric to leave him; worse yet, he is later beaten up by gay-bashers. Tommy's parents realize that he is gay and throw him out of the house (no parents actually appear in the film). Michele and Patricia, who are the least developed characters, face no turmoil like the boys; Tony Rayns argues that "the girls are all too clearly present for PC reasons of balance and solidarity, but the only problems Araki can think of giving them are those of shopping and prospective lesbian parenting; most of the time they are there only as confidantes for the screwed-up boys."[31] Steven tries to apologize to Deric for his indiscretion, and the loyal friends bond when Deric is beaten, but the film makes its clearest statement after Andy's boyfriend leaves him for another guy, sending him into a depression that leads to his suicide.

The film actually begins with a statistic that 30 percent of teenage suicides are homosexuals, and with this ending the film somberly portrays its otherwise fun-loving and pleasure-seeking characters as tragically tormented. The image of Andy falling into his wealthy parents' pool and drowning is a statement on the indifference of class to alleviate the "teen angst" that the film portends in its subtitle. Still, *Totally Fucked Up* remains a balanced, normalizing image of teen homosexuality, depicting its characters as afflicted with many of the same dilemmas as all youth—parental and relationship problems, boring jobs, drugs, sexual curiosities, career anxieties—which are made more pressurizing by the fact that they live in a generally homophobic society that does not tolerate one common aspect of their identities, their sexual preferences. Kevin Thomas points out that none of the characters are presented "as gay stereotypes but rather as indistinguishable in dress and mannerisms from other L.A. teenagers. (Only one of the actors is actually gay.) The irony is that if any of these young men had been even slightly obviously homosexual, they might have developed lots more resiliency."[32]

This is a point worth interrogating, for it is not sustained in the depiction of homosexual teens in following films: overtly homosexual youth may show signs of resolve but are nonetheless vulnerable to attack, and youth who are either more subtle in their "queerness" or still questioning their sexuality are no less tough and no more vulnerable. Thomas's claim about *Totally Fucked Up* does not apply so well to the lesbian characters, nor to Tommy, whose confidence seems rooted, perhaps not ironically, in his buff jock body and good looks, and other films would explore how issues like appearance and class indeed complicate characters' handling of their homosexuality. In fact, the only prominent queer teen images after *Totally Fucked Up* were of lesbian characters, raising the question whether young male homosexuality is generally more difficult to depict—or more culturally problematic—than young female homosexuality. Four other films about gay boys in the late '90s received little attention: *The Delta* (1997) explores the life of a sexually undecided teenager whose relationship with an Afro-Vietnamese immigrant leads, inadvertently, to a random murder; *The Toilers and the Wayfarers* (1997) is a mild drama about a cast-off German American teen coming to terms with his emerging homosexuality and cultural identity; *Johns* (1997) is the bleak tale of a teenage hustler who falls in love with a 20-something hustler and learns the dangers of working the streets; and in the excellent *Edge of Seventeen* (1999), an '80s teen faces the complexities of coming to terms with his attraction to men and coming out to his girlfriend and his mother.

Two mid-'90s independent films about young lesbians were somewhat more visible, and depicted the topic as relatively normalized. Edwin Jahiel rightly observed of *The Incredibly True Adventure of Two Girls in Love* (1994) that "lesbianism here is treated in a natural, matter-of-fact way, with not even a soupçon of self-consciousness, preaching or defensiveness."[33] Randy Dean (Laurel Holloman) is a high school senior who fancies herself a rebel like James Dean—tough, removed, cool, and also like the real Dean, gay. The locals mostly think of Randy as some kind of alienated tomboy: she wears primarily masculine clothes, sports a short haircut, and promotes a brash attitude. She has a kissing affair going with a married woman, but her only friend appears to be Frank (Nelson Rodriguez), a geeky gay classmate who is as equally disinterested in fulfilling social norms, although he is not as actively rebellious as Randy. The story concentrates on Randy's brewing relationship with Evie (Nicole Parker), an attractive and popular girl at her school who Randy develops a sensitive crush on. Despite knowing the problems that could arise, Randy carefully pursues Evie, and to her relief Evie (who has just broken up with her whiny boyfriend) is receptive to her advances.

The film makes Evie's reciprocal attraction to Randy rather effortless. The two characters have clear differences—Evie lives with her wealthy mother and Randy lives with her working-class lesbian aunt and her girlfriend; Evie is well-read and intellectual while Randy struggles in her studies; Evie is black, Randy white (the interracial and cross-class relationships between queer characters in youth films suggests that their sexual tolerance carries over to racial and class tolerance); Randy is confident in her sexual preference, and Evie is just starting to question hers—but these differences are cast aside in their mutual attraction. When Randy reveals her interest in Evie, she even tells Evie how dangerous the situation could become, but romantic Evie throws that caution to the wind. The film thus portrays Evie's choice of Randy as part of the natural sexual development of a teenager, marked by the usual excitement and confusion that characterize young heterosexual relationships. In many ways this may appear idealistic, yet the film never raises the stakes for these characters so high that the long-term repercussions of their acts are seriously questioned. (An end credit implies that the story is the semiautobiographical account of filmmaker Maria Maggenti, who apparently wanted to keep the story within the realm of comfortable plausibility.) The film concludes with another classic rite of passage for teens, when Evie invites Randy to her house for a weekend while her mom is away: the two concoct a messy dinner, get drunk, and make love—the first time either actually has sex with another woman. Evie's mom catches them, however, and a chaotic chase ensues in which various characters end up cornering the two girls at a motel, who agree to emerge after they swear to love each other forever.

To be sure, *Incredibly True Adventure* is full of significant issues about the troubles of being young and queer: locals taunt Randy constantly, and Evie's friends reject her when she reveals she's in love with Randy. Yet the film is filled just as much with otherwise typical teen torments: first love, school trouble, overbearing parents, the uncertain future. Like *Totally Fucked Up,* the film makes clear that homosexual youth have much in common with their heterosexual counterparts, but by leaving Evie's sexual identity ambiguously bisexual, and by eschewing excessive drama, the film presents an even more neutral portrait of queer youth, whose sexuality is only one part of their identity and not their defining quality.[34]

Another examination of young lesbianism is offered in *All Over Me* (1996). Where the conflicts in *Incredibly True Adventure* primarily revolve around the characters' choice of a same-sex partner, here the homosexual issue itself is less conflictive and more subtle. Claude (Alison Folland) is a 15-year-old growing up in Hell's Kitchen, trying to finish 10th grade and enjoy the summer with her best friend Ellen (Tara Subkoff), with whom she plays guitar in hopes of forming a rock band. Claude has doubts about her weight and appearance, especially in comparison to waifish Ellen, and still the two clearly have a physically comfortable intimacy with each other: they fake fucking in front of a fun-house mirror for laughs, and after Ellen loses her virginity to her new boyfriend Mark (Cole Hauser), Claude invites her to show her how it felt, whereupon the two girls tenderly hump and kiss. The occurrence of this scene just after Ellen has first had sex with a man is significant, if only because it signals the apparent end of the intimacy that Claude and Ellen have shared and marks the beginning of Claude's futile attempt to save Ellen from Mark's mean, macho clutches. Each girl tells the other she loves her, but Claude is almost masochistically devoted to Ellen, helping her through a series of bad drug experiences and fights with Mark. Such devotion nonetheless shifts the power in the relationship from Ellen to Claude, and as Nell Bernstein noted, "Claude isn't quite sure who she wants to be yet, but you can see a more certain self straining to break through, and it makes her beautiful."[35]

The plot takes its most dramatic turn when one of Claude's gay friends is killed by the homophobic Mark, and another of her gay friends warns that she could be next, pointing to her emergent homosexual leanings, which she soon thereafter declares further by going to a club and picking up a cute riot grrrl guitarist named Lucy (Leisha Hailey). Claude's shift of affection to Lucy is gradual: she tries to remain loyal to Ellen but becomes disgusted by her self-destructive behavior with Mark, urging her to tell the police of his role in the murder. Ellen's protection of Mark is simply too much for Claude to bear—after all, he killed her friend and stole her girlfriend—and in the end Claude herself turns Mark in. In poignant closing shots, Claude practices guitar with the more talented and receptive Lucy and then kisses her in public, providing a social recognition of her lesbian identity, and Ellen sees Claude burying a coin that her murdered friend had given her, symbolically putting to rest that darker, more confusing part of her life.

While Claude does struggle in her relationships with Ellen and Lucy, her choice of both of them as potential partners is not disputed in itself, save by the bigoted Mark. *All Over Me* simply portrays Ellen as a more insecure, selfish, and inappropriate partner for Claude, not solely on the grounds of her heterosexuality—which remains in question—but because of her abusive, morally irresponsible (in)actions. In that way the film is very much like other youth love stories, deemphasizing the pursuit of sex and focusing on the protagonist's search for a compatible partner. Perhaps with *All Over Me* American youth cinema witnesses the integration of homosexual teen characters into plots that further normalize queer lifestyles and depict queerness as one of many qualities that youth may encounter on their path to adulthood (as in the more recent *Election*), and do so within the guise of other generic styles, in this case a murder drama.[36] For Ellen, the queer issue remains distressing and uncertain, while Claude handles her homosexuality quite confidently by the end of the film, and is apparently better for getting away from the bad influence of Ellen; the story is picaresque but not preachy, showcasing a possible homosexual scenario for youth without exploiting it through mystique or alienation.

Given this handful of queer youth roles in films of the '90s, teenage homosexuality has become somewhat more acceptable, and its often sensitive, nonextreme representation provides an image of queer youth as increasingly accepted, striving for identity like all young people, on their own terms. Yet for this representation to become most actualized, Hollywood will need to produce more films featuring homosexual and bisexual teens in otherwise everyday roles, something the industry seems to be some distance from achieving, even after the Oscar-winning *Boys Don't Cry* (1999) drew further attention to nonstraight sexuality issues for youth. More recently the witty and sincere *But I'm a Cheerleader* (2000) openly challenged homophobia and offered queer teens support, while at the same time *Scary Movie* (2000) still indulged in tired clichés about teens' sexual confusion. The progress that has been made in depicting queer youth in diverse and realistic ways may indeed be further neutralized by stereotypical representations, at least until dominant American culture is able to accept nonheterosexual people.

Pregnancy

Despite the relative frequency with which teenage pregnancies occur in reality, in youth films teen pregnancies have been rare and have typically followed a particular pattern. In films before the legalization of abortion in 1973, virtually all "illegitimate" pregnancies resulted in the mother giving birth, often in a "special hospital" for unwed mothers, who would then give the baby up for adoption. Teen mothers would go away for a while to have the baby and then return to the fold of home and school without discussing the event, lest the taboo affect the girl as well as her family. A variation of this is presented in *Blue Denim* (1959), in which a teenage girl becomes pregnant by her boyfriend, who raises the money for her to have an abortion, and only minutes before the dreaded clandestine event she is saved by both the boy's father and her own. Toward the end of the film, the girl is sent away to have the child in secrecy; the boy goes after her—against the wishes of his parents, who think he is throwing his life away—so that they may sustain a family of their own and live happily ever after.

Pregnancy in youth films after 1980 was first handled by having the girls go to abortion clinics for legal, safe abortions. There were often emotional and moral issues raised by these situations, but the legality and availability of abortion, and more so its discretion, kept the pregnant characters from facing the consequences of going to term and having a child. This was the case in films such as *The Last American Virgin* (1982), *Fast Times at Ridgemont High* (1982), and *Teachers* (1984).[37] Yet these depictions only persisted in the early '80s; by the late '80s, with abortion becoming an ever more controversial topic, and publicized scandals involving teen pregnancies and risky adoptive parenting, the few films that did depict teen pregnancy showed their characters having the child (even the potentially monstrous titular offspring in *A Nightmare on Elm Street 5: The Dream Child* in 1989). In the teen pregnancy films of the '90s, most of the characters decide to have their babies and two decide to raise them themselves despite their lack of income. This change in images of teen pregnancy may be indicative of a certain conservative influence on American films after the more sexually liberal era of the early '80s, although it is worth noting that most of the '90s films in which girls have their babies were written and directed by women, who were perhaps promoting the positive possibilities of actually having a child rather than the by-then assumed freedom of choice in aborting it.

In *Fast Times,* the narrative tone of Stacy's predicament is not condemning or condescending, even though her relatively uneventful abortion is perhaps a bit too emotionally casual: she's more upset that Mike fails to help her than that she's aborting a child after only two sexual contacts. By my research, this is the first positive depiction of teen abortion in American youth cinema, at least positive in as much as Stacy has the procedure done at a legal clinic, suffers no apparent pain, and is happier for having it done. In *Last American Virgin,* Karen's need for an abortion is seized upon by Gary as an opportunity to declare his love for her, even though he is not the father. Gary is effectively trying to show Karen that he can be caring and affectionate through accommodating her in her time of crisis, only she returns to her despicable boyfriend at the end, leaving Gary as a mere tool for her to help endure the abortion. Gary's lack of having sex makes his realization even more pathetic, and the film thus shows abortion in a strikingly cavalier light. The matter is taken somewhat more seriously in *Teachers* when student Diane (Laura Dern) becomes pregnant to an unscrupulous gym teacher. Another teacher's role in helping Diane have an abortion—he takes her to a clinic and keeps the secret about his colleague—is then questioned from the perspective of how much a teacher should assist a student in her personal life. The issue of whether or not Diane should have the baby is not raised, nor is her moral culpability in maintaining the affair that led to her pregnancy.

By 1988, *"For Keeps"* presented an entirely different image of teenage pregnancy. Darcy (Molly Ringwald) and Stan (Randall Batinkoff) are high school sweethearts just beginning to have intercourse.[38] Darcy has ambitions to become a newspaper editor, and Stan is gunning for a scholarship to Cal Tech, but their futures are thrown into jeopardy when Darcy realizes she is pregnant. When their parents find out, Darcy's single mother pushes her to have an abortion while Stan's parents insist that she have the baby and put it up for adoption, shutting out Darcy and Stan's eventual plan of having the child. The tone of the film is decidedly comic, at least at first: the parents are portrayed as bumbling and detached from their children's own interests, much like those in John Hughes's films, and most of the tension between the families is portrayed satirically. What Darcy and Stan begin to realize is that they have developed a certain autonomy in making their decision to keep the baby, and they move into a squalid apartment determined to have their child and show their parents that they can subsist on their meager income. The film thereby plays to a middle class mythology for youth, who resist their parents' humble privilege to stake out their own.

One of the most compelling aspects of Darcy and Stan's relationship is how nonsexual they are: their sixth and last sexual experience results in the pregnancy, as if to demonstrate that pregnancy is possible with minimal effort and despite taking precautions (Darcy was on the pill). Darcy doesn't even see Stan naked until after they're living together, an improbable scenario perhaps meant to demonstrate their previous innocence; as Janet Hawken further claimed, "[T]he lack of sex—or rather sex within a once-in-a-lifetime monogamous relationship—is another lesson for post-AIDS youth."[39] Ironically, the moment that Darcy does see Stan naked, he proposes to her—as if they had never considered marriage an option before—and they run off to an ersatz ceremony at a strange chapel. The rest of the film portrays the problems with having and raising a child as teenagers: the couple is constantly struggling for money, Darcy is forced to drop out of school and becomes depressed, Stan begins to drink and almost has an affair. Stan is otherwise a remarkably well adjusted young father, caring for the baby while Darcy is postpartum, and rejecting his coveted scholarship so that they can stay together. Darcy, however, realizes that their youthful dreams are being destroyed, and fakes a fight with Stan to demand a "divorce" (their marriage wasn't legal) and convince him to go to Cal Tech.

By this point the film has presented Darcy as the more irresponsible of the two, until her sacrificial gesture of turning away Stan reveals her apparent pragmatic altruism: she plans to live with her mother and get a job so that at least Stan can have the future he wanted. However, the film sells out its own foreboding of teen parenting with a saccharine happy ending in which Stan secures scholarships for both of them to attend college locally and Darcy accepts his proposal to get married again, this time for real. For all of its demonstrations of the difficulties of pregnancy and child raising, *"For Keeps"* preserves the romantic ideal of love conquering all obstacles, holding out to youth the very fantasy that many believe is possible under such daunting circumstances. Roger Ebert wryly noted that the movie lacks "a notice at the end advising teenagers that for every young couple like this one, there are a thousand broken hearts."[40] This is because the film is a conservative recuperation of nuclear family values and tradition for two young people who temporarily threaten to have a premature family outside of legal wedlock and almost break up that family for their own interests, sustained by a deceptive dream of personal and parental success.

Immediate Family (1989) presents a teenage girl's pregnancy from a deliberately adult point of view (it has a distinct "ripped-from-the-headlines" feel to it, given the similar "Baby M" controversy of the previous year). Linda (Glenn Close) and Michael (James Woods) are a well-off 30-something couple who cannot have children, so they enter into an open adoption with impoverished young Lucy (Mary Stuart Masterson), who has a relatively loyal boyfriend in Sam (Kevin Dillon). The open adoption procedure means that the married couple gets to know the mother of their child and support her through the pregnancy, which makes for a certain bonding at first that becomes all the more painful when Lucy decides to keep her baby. Like *"For Keeps",* this film shows teenage parenting to be arduous and symptomatic of a white-trash destiny, but it does not alleviate that condition with a happy ending for the teen. Rather, the happy ending is shifted to the older couple: after trying to raise the child with Sam and running into expected financial difficulties, Lucy emotionally turns over the baby to Linda and Michael, saying she's not ready to be a mom. Then, over an essentially upbeat montage, the baby grows up healthy and happy as Lucy receives updates from Linda and Michael; she is now attending beauty school and still seeing Sam, with no apparent plans for marriage or children.

The two teens in *Immediate Family* are not portrayed unsympathetically, although an unmistakable class critique is implicit in the narrative's resolution: Lucy and Sam are simply not wealthy enough to raise a child like Linda and Michael can, even though the "adults" seem so aloof and superficial compared to the spirited and tough teens. Lucy's admission of being unprepared to raise a child is honest, and appears to be based as much on her lack of money as on her need for more maturity to handle such a responsibility. This seems to be a responsible message itself, yet the film simply inverts the conservative perspective of *"For Keeps"* so that family values are sustained in the older characters, becoming a corrective of the "Baby M" case in which the infertile parents were forced to give their adopted child to its real mother. Within the context of working-class struggle and inferiority that the film presents, its message is "that in spite of biology, certain people should have children and others (the lumpen) shouldn't," as David Edelstein argues.[41] The younger characters in this case are able to abandon the seriousness of their decision to keep the baby by getting rid of it after a trial basis, thereby commodifying the child—a notion made explicit in the adoption selection process—and depicting the teens as conscious of the burden that a child represents and shirking away from it accordingly.

Trust (1991) was the first youth film in six years to feature a teenager having an abortion, after careful thought about her future with a brooding new boyfriend who isn't the father of the child. Maria's decision does not come easily, and after foreseeing the hardships ahead, she has the abortion on her own rather than taking Matthew's offer of marriage, thus preserving her freedom. An interesting political aspect of the film is the depiction of protesters outside the abortion clinic—nowhere to be seen in the '80s films—and a hardened but caring nurse who works there. In a touching moment, Maria describes to the nurse how she thinks her impregnating estranged ex-boyfriend saw her—as collective body parts for his sexual pleasure, dejectedly summing up the considerably different consequences of pregnancy for girls than boys. *Gas Food Lodging* (1992) also features a pregnant teenager abandoned by her lover, only Trudi (Ione Skye) has the child. In somewhat similar fashion to past tradition, she drops out of school and goes away from home to give birth, and once she moves away the attention of the story focuses more on her younger sister. The film's ending suggests that Trudi will stay away from home after giving the child up for adoption, and portends that she has a hard life ahead of her, however different from her mother, who kept and raised Trudi when she herself was a young woman.

Just Another Girl on the I.R.T. (1993) presents Chantel (Ariyan Johnson), a street-tough, academically smart Brooklyn 11th grader filled with racial pride. The film follows her through what could have been another uneventful high school year, until she becomes pregnant by her boyfriend. For all of Chantel's ambition and intelligence, she cannot decide what to do about her pregnancy. At first her boyfriend offers her money for an abortion, which is eventually ruled out as an option after she hesitates for too long. She then tries to ignore and hide her condition by dressing up in baggy clothes. When she eventually does give birth at her boyfriend's apartment, the film shows her labor pain with graphic intensity, made all the more unsettling by her decision to abandon the newborn immediately thereafter. However, her boyfriend, who was supposed to leave the infant in a garbage bag, is struck by his conscience and saves the child, encouraging Chantel to help raise the baby properly with his help. In the last scene, she declares her plans to be a good mother while she pursues her career goals. Like so many other rebellious teens, Chantel has the requisite issues and problems with authority that empower her resistance to conformity, and thus her new role seems to come to her naturally. Jami Bernard found a deeper political parallel in this role:

> Chantel is smart, quick, opinionated, and can mow down the competition with her big mouth. But on the subway, and outside her own insulated world, she is perceived by the rest of society as either invisible or a nuisance—just as black women have been depicted for the most part in all movies, including those made by black men.[42]

Indeed, since this African American female rebel personification is essentially unique in youth films, one can easily criticize the film's less-than-positive message about its protagonist. But the question of why such an otherwise aware and assertive girl would become so desperate as to commit infanticide demands closer consideration, if only because the film *is* calling attention to the difference between the academic and social struggles of high school and the more ambiguous and consequential struggles of adult life, which Chantel is not ready to face. Chantel is in her insular element mouth-

Chantel (Ariyan Johnson) is self-assured until she has to contemplate the dilemma of her pregnancy in *Just Another Girl on the I.R.T.* (1993).

ing back to her teachers and talking trash with her girlfriends, but no teenager, regardless of race, is ready to handle the independence and responsibilities of parenthood—or so the film initially seems to stress. With its ending, *Just Another Girl* then implies that while the transition to adulthood is tough, one simply has to live up to it, and thus Chantel, as David Denby observed, "manages to triumph without losing or learning anything."[43] The narrative contrasts Chantel's strong will and rebelliousness with her overwhelming confusion and lack of moral direction brought on by the pregnancy, and while rationality prevails, the film paints an ultimately questionable portrait of the very desperation that many real youth face in the same situation (as witnessed by the number of reported real-life incidents of teens killing their newborns), for which there is no clear resolution.

Manny and Lo (1996) offers a quite unconventional teen pregnancy tale. 16-year-old Lo (Aleksa Palladino) and her younger sister Manny (Scarlett Johansson) are on the run from their different foster parents so they can be together, when one day Lo, who has occasional unsafe sex with boys she meets on the road, discovers that she's pregnant. Lo is refused by an abortion clinic because she has carried the pregnancy for too long, so she and Manny stumble upon the idea of kidnapping a knowledgeable maternity store worker, Elaine

(Mary Kay Place), who happens to be shielding some secrets of her own. The girls take Elaine to a mountain cabin they've invaded and slowly reveal to her their expectation of having her help deliver Lo's baby. At first Elaine is indignant toward the girls, but after she realizes Lo's needs she agrees to help her, putting Elaine in a complex maternal role—to Lo, her unborn baby, and the mother-longing Manny—which had been denied her earlier in life when she found she was unable to have children herself.

Elaine's devotion to the girls then becomes unexpectedly maniacal: when the cabin's owner returns, Elaine secretly ties him up in a barn so as not to ruin the fulfillment of her new identity. Upon learning this, Lo becomes suspicious of Elaine and abandons her, moving on with Manny until her labor sets in, whereupon Manny takes Lo back to Elaine, who remains not far from where they left her, waiting and willing to deliver Lo's baby. During the preceding confrontation, Lo challenges Manny if she wants to stay with Elaine, since she has clearly developed an affection for her, but the younger sister stays with her blood. This gesture of family preservation is then given further emphasis at the end, with Elaine apparently staying with the two girls after Lo's delivery, as if she will carry on her affirming familial matriarchy. Lo's reluctance to deal with her pregnancy is indicative of her need to keep moving, and given their fugitive status, Lo's mobility and already parental care of Manny preclude her from being able to raise a child. Yet Manny's less nervous wisdom prevails, for both girls' greatest need is for just such a family arrangement that Elaine and a new child offer. The ending suggests that the characters' lives have been difficult enough on their own, and will be better if they stay together.

Gas Food Lodging, Just Another Girl on the I.R.T., and *Manny and Lo* were made by women, showing the increased presence of female filmmakers in youth cinema, and the changing perspectives on attitudes toward youth pregnancy. By the '90s the issue was no longer so simple as an uneventful abortion or a fanciful salvation: the protagonists in these films all remain unmarried and facing a life of struggle ahead, but they are determined to persevere.[44] Such is also the case with Dedee (Christina Ricci) in the male-made *Opposite of Sex* (1998), who decides to have her baby and give it to her gay brother and partner so that she can still work out the issues of her complicated life, and with the abandoned Novalee (Natalie Portman) in *Where the Heart Is* (2000), who finds a supportive community of odd characters to help her raise her child after she famously gives birth in a store, one of whom she eventually does marry. These depictions give their young women a noble sense of strength, achieved after overcoming their troubling pregnancies, and change the image of teenage pregnancy itself from degrading to potentially empowering.[45] The assumed misfortune of being an unmarried teen mother is alleviated to celebrate independent female capability and solidarity.

CONCLUSION

Where youth in school films struggle for identity in their educational surroundings and delinquents do so through rebellion, youth in love/sex movies inadvertently discover their identities through their pursuits of romance and sexual pleasure. In love stories, youth strive to find the other who will make them significant, the other who will give them a sense of purpose and meaning, who will complete who they are. In sex stories, even when sex is disappointing and dull, youth seek affirmation of their desirability and fulfillment of their desire. In most cases, however, these goals go unfulfilled or are compromised.

The image of youth in love/sex films from 1980 to 1999 changed from melodramatic and carefree to serious and concerned, and also exposed an increasing vilification of young sexuality. The processes of falling in love and losing virginity became ever more complex in the era of AIDS (although still remarkably few youth love/sex films address the topic), and the general dominance of negative youth depictions in the '90s reflected social tensions around teen promiscuity and irresponsibility, not to mention hedonism. Yet unlike rebellion and even education, youth must continue to learn the customs of love and sex to ensure the survival of humanity, and perhaps that authority presents a threatening notion of youth power to adult filmmakers. For as wondrous and pleasurable as love and sex are, youth are frequently reminded through films how disheartening and deflating the experiences can be, far more so than adult-oriented films about the same issues, as if young people need to develop a healthy cynicism about romance in order to prevent them from expecting too much of it.

7 CONCLUSION
Youth Cinema at the Millennium

There have been two primary goals of this study: to examine how the image of youth developed in American cinema during the last generation of the twentieth century, and to demonstrate that such an examination must be founded on an analysis of various generic conventions pertaining to films about youth. I will speak to this second aim first, since it has been more implicit.

One of my arguments that has been established from the start is that depictions of teenagers in cinema are characterized by and rely upon certain generic elements, for many of the same reasons that all films are produced within certain generic traditions and styles. The generic identification of a given movie makes it more marketable by the film industry and thus conditions a set of expectations in its audience, yielding a codified system of standards that producers, critics, and viewers employ in evaluating a film's quality. A film is generally considered to be most appealing when it dynamically fulfills the codes of its genre, and perhaps more so when it integrates past codes with newly introduced ones, developing further genres and subgenres in an evolutionary cycle.

When a given social population is portrayed through existing and emerging genres, a consequential set of standards and expectations is developed over time by the film industry and the audience. The population in question is depicted as acting within a certain range of behaviors and having a limited number of concerns. In this way character paradigms are generated, easily identifiable figures who have a perceived—if not necessarily representative—connection to their real-life referents. Genres of human types are thereby formed.

These character types are most fruitfully studied within an analysis of the generic styles of the films in which they appear. Because these types cross over and intertwine with more than one genre, yet retain a certain coherence within the genres in which they are portrayed, certain subgenres emerge, as do further categories within those subgenres. The generic traditions of horror that some youth films work under, for instance, are integrated with certain concerns and conventions of youth cinema as its own genre, producing a hybrid set of combinative plot elements, narrative motifs, and styles of representation that make the "youth horror film" a specific subgenre unto itself. Then, within that subgenre, further subgeneric categories of the horror film can be located, such as the slasher film and the zombie film, and how youth are portrayed in relation to these styles is generally indicative of larger issues of youth representation.

Another example may better illustrate the point. Within youth delinquency films, a spectrum of delinquent styles is utilized, spanning a range of moral concerns and actual types of rebellion. Within each of these styles, which borrow from other generic traditions (such as the beach movie, musicals, family dramas, and crime stories), clear processes of representing youth are discernible in relation to that style's conventions. The dance-loving youth, for example, win respect by engaging everyone else in dancing; the children of bad parents fight for their parents' love, with mixed results; tough girls struggle for an identity free from patriarchal and age-based discriminations. The diversity of delinquency in films about teenagers is indicative not only of the diverse motivations and means of delinquency of teenagers in reality, but also of the many different *identities* of youth that are represented by these films.

Given that diversity, within the delinquency subgenre and others, the method of studying these films must necessarily be as inclusive as possible. This inclusiveness has been a major methodological campaign of my research. Many genre researchers select films in a hit-or-miss fashion, rendering their analysis arbitrary or assumptive. Thus I took the position that I would address as many films as were relevant within each youth subgenre, giving additional attention to films that merited it.

This procedure of course raised a new set of problems as it alleviated old ones. First and foremost, I could not see *all* of the films within each subgenre, since some were simply unavailable. In trying to make comprehensive claims about individual subgenres, I thus found myself still relying on certain assumptions, which I tried to resolve by at least reading about the films that I could not view. This aspect of the research was humbling, and exposed another dilemma in current film research, the lack of access to all texts. Rarely do contemporary literary scholars ever suffer to locate recent books or magazines, but many films continue to be difficult if not impossible to find, even in today's video/digital movie climate. I inevitably had to accept the limitations of access placed on me by available distribution sources, although I know that given time, many of the titles that I have thus far been unable to locate may become available for viewing and incorporated into a future study. Partially as a consequence of these limitations, and more so as a symptom of personal bias, I also found myself inevitably giving more attention to the films that I enjoyed the most and found the most significant, which in many ways seems appropriate, but begs the question of how subjectively a film's "merit" is determined.

Another problem with my approach was that by trying to be so comprehensive, I initially developed an overambitious set of "rules" that I thought these films followed, which is a classic flaw of much genre research. Despite the similarities of films within each subgenre, they were made by different studios under different conditions and over time, and are thus not as rule-bound as other phenomena of film history (such as the use of certain equipment). Genre study is indeed an inexact science, regardless of how exact we scholars would like to make it. I have attempted to be as precise as possible while still appreciating that the codes and patterns I am studying are quite malleable and arguable. I have worked from the most informed foundation possible, both in terms of my knowledge of the films I have studied and my curiosities about the films I have not.

I believe that such a foundation is required for any serious genre study. The genre researcher must strive for maximum comprehensiveness while developing an analytically reliable understanding of the films in question. Research can still focus on particular aspects of a genre, such as its aesthetic style or plot development, but these aspects must be studied against as inclusive a background as possible—even when limits imposed by publishers prevent full discussion of all aspects and examples in the text. This background can only be achieved by studying the maximum number of films within that genre, and the social, industrial, and/or aesthetic conditions under which they were released. My subject has been the image of youth between the ages of 12 and 20 in American films released between 1980 and 1999; in studying that subject I have incorporated an understanding of youth trends, public politics, and film industry operations during that same time. I do not feel that my study is nearly as far-reaching as it could be, but given my particular focus on the generic development of youth images, I feel that I have covered an optimal number of relevant examples and contextual issues.

This book further reveals the difficulty of doing social representation research within film studies. Mine is but one perspective on the vast array of films about youth, and I am no longer a member of the audience to whom these films are directed. I bring to my analysis a bundle of personal experiences that influence even my most rigidly objective readings (if indeed any reading can be objective). My tacit effort as a social image researcher has been to recognize and minimize the influences of my past that limit me from understanding social experiences that are not similar to my own. To assume that films can aid me in that goal is treacherous, since they are the already limited representations of an elite industry that is maintained largely by the dominant interests of culture. Finding a space in which to consider these films that is both subjectively reflective *and* socially responsible is thus remarkably difficult, yet again, by considering the widest range of examples against the most inclusive set of contextual issues does take us further in producing an informed analysis. The truth will remain that regardless of how informed a social researcher is, the research will always be imbued with the problematics of her or his personal ideological positions.

In terms of studying youth, these problematics are especially crucial to remember. Essentially all academic researchers have passed their teenage years, and are no longer able to view themselves as part of the youth population. This factor is an advantage in terms of maintaining one's distance from the subject being studied, and presumably ensures a certain amount of wisdom gained past the teen years. Yet, all too often, youth films are viewed and studied by adult critics in a manner that is condescending toward their themes as well as their characters. Even some scholars who have written seriously about youth films, such as Armond White, Jon Lewis, Thomas Leitch, and Jonathan Bernstein, seem to hold many of the films they study in contempt, if not also the teens who view them. Scholars like David Considine, Carol Clover, Thomas Doherty, and Vicky Lebeau have demonstrated that the youth film can be studied seriously within various legitimate academic frames without positioning youth—characters or viewers—as necessarily inferior subjects.

Youth films, as has been argued throughout this book, reveal an enormous amount about who we are, and despite their limitations, they are just as cinematically rich—in terms of aesthetics, politics, and social imaging—as the dominant cinema that is about adults. In fact, given their limitations, and the assumptions that are often made about them, American youth films in the late twentieth century depicted a generally diverse and most often positive image of teenagers. In most cases, youth are portrayed as stoic, resilient, strong, inquisitive, hopeful, and/or creative. Consider how many different types of characters have been introduced in the various subgenres of youth cinema during this time, and the variety of themes that these characters have addressed. Virtually all real-life teen experiences are available in youth films, albeit some with much more prominence than others. The increasing roles for teenage girls and African Americans, while not without problems, have been a progressive change over the white male dominance of teen films up to the 1980s (although such dominance persists).

Still, many images and themes have yet to be covered, or covered adequately, in American youth cinema. Girls are still not represented with the same frequency as boys. The number of noncriminal roles for African American and Latino/a characters remains shamefully small. Teenage problems with drugs, depression, and divorce have received relatively little attention. Pregnancy, abortion, and parenting in youth films are far rarer than they are in real life. The incidence of sexually transmitted diseases among youth has been virtually ignored. The fact that more teens are entering college than ever before, and facing changing pressures accordingly, has not been reflected in recent youth films. The crucial use of computers and technology by youth in identifying themselves and learning about the world has been remarkably underrepresented. The wide involvement of youth in community and religious organizations is virtually never shown. Youth rarely have political affiliations, even if they have clearly political ideas.

What was covered in youth films from 1980 to 1999, from a generic and representational perspective, is the following (Appendix A provides a chronological filmography of youth films that relate to these trends):

Of the five basic school characters, the intellectual nerd is still transforming to a higher degree of acceptance, the delinquent has become more complexly affected, the rebel has more reasons to revolt, the popular student has become more vulnerable, and jocks are less visible. The nerd character remains subject to humiliation by his or her peers, yet most nerds in school films succeed in proclaiming a sense of self-identity and assurance that other characters do not, and gain their acceptance through proud perseverance. Delinquents in school films have become less culpable for their behavior, since films about them have pointed to an increasing array of social and educational sources for their misguided behavior. Likewise, rebels are more aware of their surroundings and the oppositions they face, and usually address ever more serious issues. Popular students, whom youth films have traditionally derided for their wide acceptance, have been shown struggling with many of the same identity issues as their less accepted counterparts. And athletes, while having no less prominence in real American high schools, have dwindled in school films as their screen image has also become one of greater sincerity and sympathy.

Within the delinquency subgenre, as with the delinquent school character, there are now more reasons for youth to rebel, and more means with which to do so. The most visible shift within this subgenre has been in its moral addresses toward its characters: many delinquency films of the early to mid-'80s made deviance look fun and ultimately harmless, but by the early '90s the dominant image of youth delinquency was the dangerous African American hoodlum, an image that has since diminished. Delinquency by the mid-'90s incorporated a broader moral spectrum, and this tended to neutralize the potency of youth rebellion accordingly, with the appearance of many "endearing animal" and "bad parent" depictions that showed teens affably fighting larger issues about their rights over against many downright angry youth fighting for their rights to express that anger. The delinquency subgenre offered the clearest developments in the depiction of female and minority youth as well, under usually positive but sometimes negative terms.

The youth horror subgenre is barely hanging on to what is left of its tradition, and seems only able to do so by critiquing its past. The boom that buoyed the youth horror film in the early '80s lasted only a few years, and while numerous similar films continued to be made, their popularity and impact diminished. Nonetheless, these films are very revealing of youth issues on a metaphoric level, pointing to shifts in concerns about sexuality, drug use, spirituality, and social oppression. The teenage characters in these films have become more authoritative and less victimized by the forces of evil that they confront, to the point that a number of youth horror films by the '90s had become reflexive and revisionist.

Science films, despite the dominant role that technology now plays in the lives of today's youth, have all but disappeared. The novelty of youth using computers has worn off, and yet the greater access youth have to computers has not generated more narratives depicting youth using them. Youth involved in other science and technology fields have also lost their place in recent youth movies after having a prominent role in the early to mid-'80s. Radio and video, which teens continue to have greater exposure to at home and in schools, remain uncommon sights in youth films. The power that youth develop through these devices and fields may explain why they have been less represented by filmmakers, as the most common image of youth employing science in the '90s shows them failing to use it properly or master it as they expected.

Films about youth falling in love and having sex are perhaps the most difficult to categorize. During the early '80s, when the abundance of teen sex films reveled in the liberation of portraying the sexually adventurous teenager, young romance was the exception. But by the mid-'80s, after the sex stories had become so routine and social concerns over teen pregnancy, AIDS, and other sexually transmitted diseases rendered the teen sex-quest film unpalatable, youth began finding love again. Love and sex are generally available to all teenagers, and have been used as a democratizing force in youth films. In the '90s, an increasing variety of teen romantic and sexual experiences were represented: interracial, homosexual, passionate, dysfunctional, dangerous, liberating. The "threats" of young love and sex are as present as ever, but youth have been given more credit for handling their affairs, and '90s films implicitly offered greater rewards (and punishments) for teens' amorous pursuits than the sex act itself.

Overall, American youth films in the late twentieth century depicted teenagers as an increasingly self-aware and insightful group, who are still learning much about life and about who they are, and who are usually doing so with energy and intelligence. This generally positive depiction has not prevented a number of films from vilifying youth or representing them as irresponsible and stupid, yet these films are the exception. Most often, even within condemning films, at least one teenage character retains some sense of integrity or morality. An argument can be made that adult filmmakers are only producing such images of youth to appeal to young audiences who patronize the films, and that these images are based on the social realities and fantasies of most youth, or else the films would not find an audience. This argument helps explain the decline of many styles of youth film, such as the horror and sex-quest films. Why other realistic conditions like those listed above have yet to be depicted more often is due to a complicated series of reasons, ranging from simple conservatism on the part of the film industry to a potentially more sinister concern that youth (or even adults) cannot handle seeing all of their realities incorporated into the entertainment of going to the movies. If this latter possibility is true, it speaks to the film industry's failure to give youth enough credit for handling a more complete range of narratives about themselves.

As stated in the introduction, a split image of youth has been presented in American films since the 1950s: good kids and bad kids. Youth films at the end of the twentieth century questioned that traditional bifurcation and problematized the image of youth having inherent values. By giving youth

Sara (Julia Stiles) and Derek (Sean Patrick Thomas) in *Save the Last Dance* (2001) represent ambitious and harmonious teens who work hard to overcome personal problems and succeed in their goals. The American film industry would do well to produce many more images of youth like this.

more diverse powers of self-identification, recent youth films have placed more responsibility on their protagonists to deal with their ascent through adolescence, an ascent that can take any number of directions en route to maturity. With the formation of the Generation X identity in the '90s, young people were told that the path to adulthood is longer and less secure than ever before, and that they must resist the temptation to "slack" lest they remain in a state of permanent adolescence. Most youth films of the '90s further encouraged such resistance.

An effect that may arise from efforts to avoid the Generation X label is increased pressure on young people to succeed, or more so, to become wary of being young and suspicious of others who are. An emerging conflict in many recent youth films has been between characters who are ambitious and energetic and those who are not. Given that many youth will inevitably face confusions and doubts as they navigate their way to adulthood, those who are less secure may become objects of ridicule. A backlash to the Generation X paradigm could easily emerge in the first youth generation of the twenty-first century, who like past generations will want to disentangle themselves from the outdated identity of their predecessors, and who may do so by taking on ever more radical means of promoting new identities.[1] This movement could ultimately be a positive motivating force for many youth, but it may leave some behind. The slacker of the future may be treated with the contempt of young criminals today.

Films about youth will of necessity continue to cater to adolescent (and adult) fantasies and interests, and will most likely continue to do so through the subgeneric modes of representing youth that have been established over the past generation. The science subgenre might actually be revived as the integration of technology in teens' lives becomes an unavoidable part of their representation, although if the integration is that complete, a separate subgenre may no longer be distinct. Horror films will most likely continue to reconsider their appeal to youth, relying on the increasing awareness of young viewers to appreciate being scared. Love and sex films will continue to thrive, becoming more romantic and risqué as youth gain access to previously taboo information and engage in morally questionable behavior at increasingly younger ages. The school film is likely to remain relatively unchanged, although its division of character types may further blur and overlap. The greatest change in any youth subgenre will almost certainly come from depictions of delinquency, which have seen considerable change and diversification in the past generation. Styles of rebellion will continue to come and go, and all the while youth will continue to become more conscious of their reasons for rebelling and, perhaps, become more effective at it.

Any future study of the image of youth in cinema should continue to trace these subgeneric divisions and their developments, and should expand to an even more complete sampling of relevant films and explore possibly new subgenres. Greater access to film availability through digital technology should eventually allow for the inclusion of virtually all youth films, and will demand more extensive analysis than that which can be offered here. Contextualizing youth films within social and cultural conditions will continue to be vitally important to understanding how the images of youth are generated by cinema, and with the growing presence of youth on television, the Internet, and in music, future studies of youth representation will likely take on multimedia perspectives. Above all, a certain support and sympathy for youth must be the foundation for studying their media representations, at least so long as they remain excluded from the systems that generate their representations. Again, the access youth have to technology will not only change their senses of identity, but it should provide them with the means to take greater control over the production of their images, which will be a radical development indeed.

This book has been an attempt to show how images of youth in American cinema at the turn of the millennium are evolving, and its main argument has been that adolescent depictions are becoming increasingly complex, dynamic, and revealing. My intention has been to direct greater attention to the study of youth as a social group in media, and to lend legitimacy to that endeavor by demonstrating how sophisticated are the ways that youth have been portrayed. As purveyors of a global culture, we must be especially concerned with how we tell youth who they are, since their impressionability allows them to utilize a wide range of images that can induce them both to achieve greatness and to falter in despair. As succeeding generations of young people become the adults of each tomorrow, the media that define them will be largely responsible for their roles in the world. We can only hope that media making will continue to become an increasingly democratic and accessible process, and that those people who create media in the future will respect and celebrate all of the discoveries, anxieties, opportunities, pains, wonders, and joys of what it means to be young.

APPENDIX A
Filmography of Youth Films, 1980–2001

The following films constitute the universe of American films about youth released (theatrically or straight-to-video) in the last 20-plus years of the twentieth century. All of these films were evaluated for inclusion in this study. A few films on this list are arguably not youth oriented, but are included here because they feature characters aged 12 to 20. Films about college-age characters are not included unless they feature precollege characters as well.

1980

The Apple
The Blue Lagoon
Carny
Fade to Black
Fame
Foxes
The Great Santini
Happy Birthday, Gemini
Hot T-Shirts
Idolmaker
Little Darlings
Mother's Day
My Bodyguard
Ordinary People
Out of the Blue
Times Square
Up the Academy
The Watcher in the Woods

1981

Blood Beach
The Burning
Carbon Copy
Choices
The Chosen
The Dark End of the Street
Endlesslove
Eyes of a Stranger
Fear No Evil
Four Friends
Friday the 13th Part 2
The Funhouse
Goin' All the Way
Graduation Day
Halloween 2
Hollywood High 2
Hot Bubblegum
Ladies and Gentlemen, The Fabulous Stains
Midnight
Night Crossing

Only When I Laugh
Private Lessons
Student Bodies
Sweet 16
Taps
Wacko

1982

Abuse
American Taboo
Beach House
The Beast Within
Class of 1984
Diner
The Escape Artist
Fast Times at Ridgemont High
Forty Deuce
Friday the 13th Part 3
Grease 2
Homework
I Ought to Be in Pictures
The Last American Virgin
Liar's Moon
The Slayer
Slumber Party Massacre
Split Image
Tex
Zapped

1983

All the Right Moves
Angelo, My Love
Baby It's You
Bad Boys
Boogey Man 2
Christine
Class
Death Wish Club
The Final Terror
First Turn On
Getting It On
I Am the Cheese
Joysticks
Lords of Discipline
The Loveless
My Tutor
The Outsiders
Private School
The Prodigal
Risky Business
Rumble Fish
Running Hot
Savage Streets
Sleepaway Camp
Snow: The Movie
Valley Girl
WarGames
Wild Pony
Wild Style

1984

Alphabet City
Angel
Bad Girls' Dormitory
Beat Street
Birdy
Blame It on Rio
Children of the Corn
Delinquent School Girls
Delivery Boys
Fatal Games
Firstborn
The Flamingo Kid
Footloose
Friday the 13th: The Final Chapter
Grandview, U.S.A.
Hadley's Rebellion
Hard Choices
Hollywood Hot Tubs
Hot Dog . . . The Movie
Hot Moves
Joy of Sex

The Karate Kid
Kidco
The Last Starfighter
Lovelines
Making the Grade
Meatballs 2
A Nightmare on Elm Street
Night of the Comet
No Small Affair
Nothing Lasts Forever
Oddballs
Old Enough
Private Resort
Racing with the Moon
Reckless
Red Dawn
Repo Man
Scarred
Screwballs
Sharma and Beyond
Sixteen Candles
The Stone Boy
Stranger than Paradise
Suburbia
Surfacing
Surf II
Teachers
Thrillkill
Where the Boys Are '84
The Wild Life

1985

Alien Dead
Avenging Angel
Back to the Future
Better Off Dead
The Boys Next Door
The Breakfast Club
Cave Girl
Cheerleaders' Wild Weekend
Claws
Club Life
Evils of the Night
Explorers
Fast Forward
Friday the 13th Part 5: A New Beginning
Fright Night
Gimme an F!
Girls Just Want to Have Fun
Goonies
Heaven Help Us
Heavenly Kid
The Hills Have Eyes Part 2
Hot Chili
Hot Resort
Joey
The Journey of Natty Gann
Just One of the Guys
The Legend of Billie Jean
Mask
Mischief
The Mutilator
My Science Project
The New Kids
Nickel Mountain
A Nightmare on Elm Street Part 2: Freddy's Revenge
Odd Birds
Once Bitten
Out of Control
Paradise Motel
Pink Nights
Real Genius
Return of the Living Dead
Screen Test
Secret Admirer
Silver Bullet
Smooth Talk
Snowballing
Sylvester
Teen Wolf
That Was Then, This Is Now
Tomboy
Tuff Turf
The Vals
Vision Quest

Weird Science
Young Sherlock Holmes
The Zoo Gang

1986

At Close Range
The Big Bet
Blue Velvet
Born American
Brighton Beach Memoirs
Chopping Mall
Class of Nuke 'Em High
Critters
Dangerously Close
Deadly Friend
Desert Bloom
Dutch Treat
Ferris Bueller's Day Off
Fire with Fire
Flight of the Navigator
Friday the 13th Part 6: Jason Lives
Girls School Screamers
Hell High
The Hitcher
Hoosiers
Iron Eagle
The Karate Kid, Part II
Kidnapped
Labyrinth
Lucas
The Manhattan Project
Nightmare Weekend
One Crazy Summer
Out of Bounds
Peggy Sue Got Married
Platoon
Playing for Keeps
Pretty in Pink
Quicksilver
Rad
Radioactive Dreams
Revenge of the Teenage Vixens from Outer Space
Running Mates
Scream for Help
Seven Minutes in Heaven
Slaughter High
Solarbabies
Something Special
SpaceCamp
Spookies
Stand by Me
Thinkin' Big
Thrashin'
3:15
Trick or Treat
Twisted
Wildcats
Wired to Kill
The Worst Witch
Youngblood
Zero Boys
Zombie Nightmare

1987

Adventures in Babysitting
Amazing Grace and Chuck
Back to the Beach
La Bamba
Beyond Innocence
Big Town
Blood Lake
Bloodspell
Can't Buy Me Love
China Girl
The Curse
Dirty Dancing
Doom Asylum
Gaby: A True Story
The Gate
Grotesque
Hangmen
Hell on the Battleground
Hide and Go Shriek

Hiding Out
Hot Pursuit
In the Mood
I Was a Teenage TV Terrorist
I Was a Teenage Zombie
The Kindred
The Last Slumber Party
Less than Zero
Light of Day
Like Father, Like Son
The Lost Boys
Maid to Order
The Majorettes
Masters of the Universe
Meatballs 3
The Monster Squad
Morgan Stewart's Coming Home
My Little Girl
Nice Girls Don't Explode
A Nightmare on Elm Street 3: Dream Warriors
Night of the Demons
Night Screams
North Shore
O.C. & Stiggs
Pretty Smart
The Principal
Red Nights
Return to Horror High
River's Edge
Slaughterhouse
Slumber Party Massacre II
Some Kind of Wonderful
Square Dance
Stacking
Summer Camp Nightmare
Summer School
Sweet Lorraine
Terminal Entry
Terror Squad
Three for the Road
Three O'Clock High
A Tiger's Tale
Undercover
Welcome to 18
White Water Summer
Witchboard
The Wraith
Zombie High

1988

The Abomination
Aloha Summer
Apprentice to Murder
The Beat
Big
Black Roses
The Blob
Bloody Pom Poms
Bulldance
Cannibal Campout
The Chocolate War
Clown House
Colors
Critters 2: The Main Course
Curfew
Cutting Class
Dakota
Death by Dialogue
Defense Play
Doin' Time on Planet Earth
Dudes
18 Again!
"For Keeps"
Friday the 13th Part 7: The New Blood
Girls Riot
The Gold and Glory
The Great Outdoors
Hairspray
Halloween 4: The Return of Michael Myers
Hollow Gate
The "In" Crowd
The Invisible Kid
The Islander
Johnny Be Good
Kansas

The Kiss
Leader of the Band
License to Drive
Little Nikita
Lone Wolf
Lurkers
Madame Sousatzka
My Best Friend Is a Vampire
Mystic Pizza
The Night Before
A Night in the Life of Jimmy Reardon
A Nightmare on Elm Street 4: The Dream Master
976-EVIL
1969
Nowhere to Run
Permanent Record
Phantasm II
Phantom Brother
Pin
Plain Clothes
Prince of Pennsylvania
Rebel High
The Rescue
Return of the Living Dead Part II
Running on Empty
Salsa
Satisfaction
A Secret Space
Senior Week
Sister, Sister
Sleepaway Camp II: Unhappy Campers
Stand and Deliver
Stones of Death
Student Affairs
Teen Alien
Teen Vamp
Valentino Returns
Vice Versa
Voyage of the Rock Aliens
Watchers
Waxwork
The Wizard of Loneliness
Wizards of the Lost Kingdom II
Young Guns

1989

Back to the Future Part II
Beverly Hills Brats
Beware: Children at Play
Beyond the Stars
Bill and Ted's Excellent Adventure
Blueberry Hill
Buried Alive
Buying Time
Catch Me If You Can
Cemetery High
The Channeler
C.H.U.D. II: Bud the Chud
Dad
Deadly Innocence
Dead Poets Society
Dream a Little Dream
Far from Home
Flesh Eating Mothers
The Fly 2
Friday the 13th 8: Jason Takes Manhattan
Girlfriend from Hell
Gleaming the Cube
The Gumshoe Kid
Halloween 5: The Revenge of Michael Myers
Heathers
Hitz
How I Got into College
Immediate Family
In Country
The Karate Kid III
Kinjite: Forbidden Subjects
Lean on Me
Lost Angels
Misplaced
Monster High
Morgan's Cake

My Mom's a Werewolf
A Nightmare on Elm Street 5: The Dream Child
Night Visitor
Offerings
Parenthood
Personal Choice
Pet Sematary
Rooftops
Say Anything . . .
See You in the Morning
Shag
She's Out of Control
Sing
Sleepaway Camp III: Teenage Wasteland
Staying Together
Stuff Stephanie in the Incinerator
Survival Quest
Teen Witch
Troop Beverly Hills
True Blood
Twister
Uncle Buck
War Party
Witchcraft II: The Temptress
Zapped Again

1990

Alligator Eyes
Backstreet Dreams
Back to the Future Part III
Blood Games
The Cellar
Class of 1999
Coupe de Ville
Courage Mountain
Cry-Baby
A Cry in the Wild
Dead Girls
Diving In
Edward Scissorhands
Feelin' Screwy
The Forbidden Dance
Harley
House Party
The Invisible Maniac
Kid
Lambada
Lena's Holiday
Lisa
Lord of the Flies
Mad About You
Mermaids
Mirror, Mirror
The Natural History of Parking Lots
Night Life
Pump Up the Volume
Riding the Edge
Rockula
Slumber Party Massacre III
Soultaker
Stella
Streets
There's Nothing Out There
Think Big
The Unbelievable Truth
Virgin High
Watchers 2
Welcome Home, Roxy Carmichael
The Willies
Young Guns II

1991

Across the Tracks
All I Want for Christmas
An American Summer
And You Thought Your Parents Were Weird
Bill and Ted's Bogus Journey
Billy Bathgate
Book of Love
Boyz N the Hood
Child's Play 3

Class Act
Class of Fear
Class of Nuke 'Em High Part II: Subhumanoid Meltdown
Convicts
Cool as Ice
Cthulhu Mansion
December
Dogfight
Don't Tell Mom the Babysitter's Dead
Dutch
Family Prayers
Fast Getaway
Freddy's Dead: The Final Nightmare
Goin' to Chicago
Hangin' with the Homeboys
The Haunting of Morella
Heaven Is a Playground
If Looks Could Kill
Infinity
Livin' Large
Lunatic
Man in the Moon
My Own Private Idaho
Mystery Date
No Secrets
The People Under the Stairs
Popcorn
Prayer of the Rollerboys
Rambling Rose
Raw Nerve
Return to the Blue Lagoon
Rock 'n' Roll High School Forever
Shout
Society
Sounds of Silence
Straight Out of Brooklyn
Toy Soldiers
Trust
Up Against the Wall
White Fang
Wild Hearts Can't Be Broken

1992

Adventures in Dinosaur City
Alan & Naomi
Big Girls Don't Cry . . . They Get Even
Body Waves
Brutal Fury
Buffy the Vampire Slayer
Children of the Corn II: The Final Sacrifice
Children of the Night
Critters 3
Critters 4
Crossing the Bridge
Dark Horse
Dr. Giggles
Encino Man
Forever Young
Gas Food Lodging
Gate II: The Temptress
Gladiator
Hold Me, Thrill Me, Kiss Me
Johnny Suede
Journey to Spirit Island
Juice
Ladybugs
Magic Kid
Meatballs 4
Miracle Beach
My Grandpa Is a Vampire
Newsies
Pet Sematary 2
Poison Ivy
The Power of One
A River Runs Through It
Sarafina!
Scent of a Woman
School Ties
Sleepwalkers
South Central
Terminal Bliss
There Goes My Baby
This Is My Life
3 Ninjas
Twin Peaks: Fire Walk with Me

Wayne's World
Where the Day Takes You
Who Shot Pat?
Wild Orchid II: Two Shades of Blue
Zebrahead

1993

Airborne
An Ambush of Ghosts
American Heart
Arcade
Body Snatchers
A Bronx Tale
Calendar Girl
The Crush
The Day My Parents Ran Away
Dazed and Confused
The Double O Kid
Dream Date
A Far Off Place
Free Willy
Guncrazy
Jack the Bear
Jailbait
Jason Goes to Hell: The Final Friday
Just Another Girl on the I.R.T.
Just One of the Girls
Kalifornia
King of the Hill
Last Action Hero
The Liar's Club
The Man Without a Face
Matinee
Menace II Society
My Boyfriend's Back
Nukie
112th and Central
Only the Strong
Ordinary Magic
Pocket Ninjas
Remote
Rescue Me
Return of the Living Dead 3
Rich in Love
The Sandlot
The Seventh Coin
Showdown
Sidekicks
Sister Act 2: Back in the Habit
The Skateboard Kid
Surf Ninjas
Swing Kids
Tainted Blood
Teenage Bonnie and Klepto Clyde
Teenage Exorcist
Test Tube Teens from the Year 2000
That Night
This Boy's Life
3 Ninjas Knuckle Up
Ticks
Trauma
Unbecoming Age
Warlock: The Armageddon
Watchers 3
Wayne's World 2
Weekend at Bernie's II
What's Eating Gilbert Grape
White Wolves: A Cry in the Wild II

1994

Above the Rim
Brainscan
The Browning Version
Camp Nowhere
Class of Nuke 'Em High 3: The Good, the Bad and the Subhumanoid
Crooklyn
A Dangerous Place
Double Dragon
Dream a Little Dream 2
Ernest Goes to School
Foreign Student
Fresh
Fun

Holy Matrimony
Imaginary Crimes
The Incredibly True Adventure of Two Girls in Love
The Inkwell
Lassie
Little Women
Magic Kid II
Milk Money
Mirror, Mirror 2: Raven Dance
Mi Vida Loca
Mod Fuck Explosion
Mortal Danger
My Father the Hero
My Girl 2
Natural Born Killers
The Next Karate Kid
Night of the Demons 2
Phantasm III: Lord of the Dead
A Pig's Tale
Pumpkinhead II: Blood Wings
Richie Rich
Rudyard Kipling's The Jungle Book
Safe Passage
Season of Change
Shrunken Heads
The Skateboard Kid 2
Spanking the Monkey
Spitfire
The Stoned Age
Tammy and the T-Rex
3 Ninjas Kick Back
Totally Fucked Up
The War
Wes Craven's New Nightmare
White Fang 2: Myth of the White Wolf
Windrunner

1995

Angus
Animal Room
The Babysitter
The Baby-Sitter's Club
The Basketball Diaries
Big Bully
Billy Madison
Bleeding Hearts
Born to Be Wild
A Boy Called Hate
The Brady Bunch Movie
The Break
Breaking Free
Captain Nuke and the Bomber Boys
Casper
Children of the Corn III: Urban Harvest
Circle of Friends
Clockers
Clueless
Dangerous Minds
Dead Beat
Demolition High
Don't Be a Menace to South Central While Drinking Your Juice in the Hood
Evolver
Fall Time
Far from Home: The Adventures of Yellow Dog
Free Willy 2: The Adventure Home
Gold Diggers: The Secret of Bear Mountain
Hackers
The Indian in the Cupboard
A Kid in King Arthur's Court
Kids
A Little Princess
The Love Lesson
Mad Love
Mighty Morphin Power Rangers: The Movie
Mr. Holland's Opus
Mommy
Monster Mash: The Movie
My Antonia
National Lampoon's Senior Trip
The Neon Bible
New Jersey Drive
Now and Then
Poison Ivy 2: Lily

Powder
The Power Within
Pros and Cons of Breathing
Raging Angels
Rift
S.F.W.
Tales from the Hood
Tall Tale
To Die For
Tom and Huck
Tromeo and Juliet
True Crime
Unstrung Heroes
White Wolves II: Legend of the Wild
A Young Connecticut Yankee in King Arthur's Court

1996

Address Unknown
Alaska
All Over Me
American Buffalo
Before and After
Boys
Children of the Corn IV: The Gathering
The Craft
The Crucible
The Doom Generation
Double Play
Father's Day
Fear
First Kid
5 Dark Souls
Flipper
Fly Away Home
Foxfire
Freeway
Galgameth
Girls Town
High School High
House Arrest
Illtown
Johns
Little Witches
Lunch Time Special
Magenta
Manny and Lo
Marvin's Room
Mirror, Mirror 3: The Voyeur
Mommy 2: Mommy's Day
Mrs. Winterbourne
My Uncle: The Alien
The Offering
The Paper Brigade
Parallel Sons
Phat Beach
Provocateur
Race the Sun
Ripe
Scream
Sleepers
Sometimes They Come Back . . . Again
Sticks and Stones
The Substitute
Sunchaser
Sunset Park
Telling Lies in America
That Thing You Do!
Tiger Heart
To Gillian on Her 37th Birthday
Welcome to the Dollhouse
White Squall
William Shakespeare's Romeo + Juliet
Wish upon a Star

1997

Air Bud
Anarchy TV
Black Circle Boys
Born Bad
Buck and the Magic Bracelet
Campfire Tales
Cries of Silence
The Delta

Eight Days a Week
Eye of God
Free Willy 3: The Rescue
Good Burger
Gummo
Hurricane Streets
I Know What You Did Last Summer
Little Boy Blue
Lover Girl
Masterminds
Night of the Demons 3
Nowhere
187
Poison Ivy: The New Seduction
Ronnie and Julie
Scream 2
Somebody Is Waiting
Squeeze
Star Kid
Teenage Catgirls in Heat
That Darn Cat
Timeless
Titanic
The Toilers and the Wayfarers
Trading Favors
Trojan War
Warriors of Virtue
Wild America
Wild Things
Young Hercules

1998

Air Bud: Golden Receiver
American History X
Another Day in Paradise
Apt Pupil
Billboard Dad
Bloodsuckers
Buffalo '66
Can't Hardly Wait
Children of the Corn V: Fields of Terror
Cry of the White Wolf
Dancer, Texas Pop. 81
Disturbing Behavior
Eden
The Faculty
Frankenstein Reborn
Halloween H_2O
He Got Game
The Ice Storm
If I Die Before I Wake
I Still Know What You Did Last Summer
Little Men
Lolita
Niagara, Niagara
Nowhere to Go
The Opposite of Sex
Past Perfect
Pecker
Pleasantville
P.U.N.K.S.
Ricochet River
Ringmaster
Rushmore
17 & Under
Slums of Beverly Hills
Small Soldiers
A Soldier's Daughter Never Cries
Starship Troopers
Strangeland
Superstar
Talisman
3 Ninjas: High Noon at Mega Mountain
200 Cigarettes
Whatever
Wicked
Wilbur Falls
Wrestling with Alligators
Yellow

1999

The Adventures of Sebastian Cole
American Beauty
American Pie

American Virgin
Anywhere but Here
Arthur's Quest
Best Laid Plans
Blue Ridge Fall
Boys Don't Cry
Brokedown Palace
Cash Crop
Children of the Corn 666: Isaac's Return
Cider House Rules
Coming Soon
Coyotes
Cruel Intentions
Deal of a Lifetime
Desert Blue
Detroit Rock City
Dick
Drive Me Crazy
Drop Dead Gorgeous
Edge of Seventeen
Election
Fortune Cookie
Freeway II: Confessions of a Trickbaby
Getting to Know You
Girl, Interrupted
Go
Idle Hands
Jawbreaker
Joe the King
The Joyriders
Just Looking
The Last Best Sunday
Liberty Heights
Light It Up
The Mod Squad
Munchies
Never Been Kissed
October Sky
Outside Providence
Passport to Paris
Phantom Town
Polish Wedding
The Prince and the Surfer
Pups
The Rage: Carrie 2
She's All That
Six Ways to Sunday
Sweet Jane
Teaching Mrs. Tingle
10 Things I Hate About You
Trash
Trippin'
Tumbleweeds
Varsity Blues
Whiteboys
The Winslow Boy

2000

Air Bud: World Pup
All I Wanna Do
Almost Famous
Black and White
Boricua's Bond
Bring It On
The Bumblebee Flies Anyway
But I'm a Cheerleader
Center Stage
Cherry Falls
Crime and Punishment in Suburbia
The Dream Catcher
Final Destination
Finding Forrester
George Washington
Girlfight
Here on Earth
The Hi-Line
The Journey of Jared Price
Just Looking
Living the Life
Mad About Mambo
Our Lips Are Sealed
Psycho Beach Party
Remember the Titans
Scary Movie
Shriek If You Know What I Did Last Friday the 13th

Skipped Parts
The Smokers
Snow Day
Terror Tract
The Tic Code
Tigerland
Traffic
The Vault
The Virgin Suicides
Walking Across Egypt
Whatever It Takes
Where the Heart Is
Wildflowers

2001

Baby Boy
Bully
Cheaters
Children of the Corn: Revelation
Children on Their Birthdays
Close Call
Come Together
crazy/beautiful
Donnie Darko
18
Flossin
Get over It
Ghost World
The Glass House
Hedwig and the Angry Inch
Igby Goes Down
Jacked
Josie and the Pussycats
L.I.E.
Life as a House
Max Keeble's Big Move
Mockingbird Don't Sing
My First Mister
The New Guy
Nikita Blues
Not Another Teen Movie
O
Our Song
The Princess Diaries
Purgatory House
Riders
Riding in Cars with Boys
Save the Last Dance
Sugar and Spice
Wet Hot American Summer
Winning London
The Young Girl and the Monsoon

APPENDIX B
Subjective Superlative Lists

As a way of closing this lengthy study, I offer the following lists of various subjective categories for the youth films I have examined from 1980 to 1999. These lists are meant to be entertaining as well as informative. All titles are in alphabetical order.

MOST ENJOYABLE FILMS

American Pie
The Brady Bunch Movie
Can't Hardly Wait
Clueless
Ferris Bueller's Day Off
Fly Away Home
Heathers
House Party
The Incredibly True Adventure of Two Girls in Love
Lucas
Man in the Moon
Real Genius
Risky Business
Say Anything . . .

LEAST ENJOYABLE

Anywhere but Here
The Babysitter
Boys
Children of the Corn
The Doom Generation
Endlesslove
Every *Friday the 13th* movie
Gummo
Johnny Be Good
Lolita
O.C. & Stiggs
Sing
Terminal Bliss
Twin Peaks: Fire Walk with Me

MOST AESTHETICALLY AMBITIOUS

American Beauty
The Chocolate War
Fresh
Fun
Gas Food Lodging
Go
Mirror, Mirror
My Own Private Idaho
A Nightmare on Elm Street 4: The Dream Master
Pleasantville
Ripe
Rushmore
S.F.W.
Spanking the Monkey

Three O'Clock High
Titanic
Totally Fucked Up
Welcome to the Dollhouse
William Shakespeare's Romeo + Juliet

MOST CINEMATICALLY INEPT

The Beat
The Big Bet
Gummo
The Hitcher
Hot Dog . . . The Movie
Joysticks
Out of Control
The Principal
Private Lessons
Private School
Revenge of the Teenage Vixens from Outer Space
Sing
Teen Wolf
Terminal Bliss
True Crime

MOST BIZARRE

Apt Pupil
Born American
Dangerously Close
Dudes
The Doom Generation
Freeway
Jawbreaker
Little Witches
Night of the Comet
Nowhere
Pecker
Powder
The Rescue
Society
Starship Troopers
Twin Peaks: Fire Walk with Me

MOST UNEXPECTEDLY INTRIGUING

Amazing Grace and Chuck
Arcade
Black Roses
Bleeding Hearts
Coming Soon
Deadly Friend
Evolver
Foxfire
Getting to Know You
Just One of the Girls
Kidco
Lambada
Legend of Billie Jean
Light It Up
Niagara, Niagara
The Opposite of Sex
No Secrets
Return of the Living Dead 3
Sleepaway Camp
Square Dance
Squeeze
Suburbia

BEST / WORST TITLES

And You Thought Your Parents Were Weird
Bloody Pom Poms
Chopping Mall
Don't Be a Menace to South Central While Drinking Your Juice in the Hood
Don't Tell Mom the Babysitter's Dead
Gimme an F!
Hide and Go Shriek
I Was a Teenage TV Terrorist
The Last American Virgin
Mod Fuck Explosion
My Best Friend Is a Vampire
My Grandpa Is a Vampire
My Mom's a Werewolf
My Uncle: The Alien
Nice Girls Don't Explode

Revenge of the Teenage Vixens from Outer Space
Shriek If You Know What I Did Last Friday the 13th
Stuff Stephanie in the Incinerator
Teenage Bonnie and Klepto Clyde
Teenage Catgirls in Heat
Test Tube Teens from the Year 2000
Trojan War
Tromeo and Juliet

MOST POSITIVE REPRESENTATIONS OF YOUTH

Alaska
Amazing Grace and Chuck
Angus
Fly Away Home
Dakota
Edge of Seventeen
Kidco
Lucas
Mask
My Little Girl
October Sky
Pump Up the Volume
Race the Sun
Say Anything . . .
Stand and Deliver
WarGames

MOST NEGATIVE REPRESENTATIONS OF YOUTH

Class of 1984
Cruel Intentions
The Crush
Dangerously Close
Gummo
Kids
The Liar's Club
Lord of the Flies
Nowhere
187
Out of Control
The Rage: Carrie 2
River's Edge
The Substitute
Twisted

MOST INFLUENTIAL TO OTHER YOUTH FILMS

Boyz N the Hood
The Breakfast Club
Dangerous Minds
Fast Times at Ridgemont High
Footloose
Free Willy
Heathers
The Karate Kid
A Nightmare on Elm Street
Risky Business
Scream
Sixteen Candles
SpaceCamp
WarGames

MY PERSONAL FAVORITES

The Breakfast Club
The Chocolate War
Election
The Faculty
Fun
Heathers
Lucas
Mirror, Mirror
Pump Up the Volume
Say Anything . . .
Spanking the Monkey
Trust
Welcome to the Dollhouse
William Shakespeare's Romeo + Juliet

NOTES

CHAPTER 1. INTRODUCTION: THE CINEMATIC IMAGE OF YOUTH

1. See Thomas Doherty, *Teenagers and Teenpics: The Juvenilization of American Movies in the 1950s* (Boston: Unwin Hyman, 1988), 1–16.

2. In my 1998 dissertation at the University of Massachusetts ("Generation Multiplex: The Image of Youth in American Cinema, 1981–1996"), I analyze hundreds more films than can be included here, and provide more analyses of some specific teen subgenre categories that are here minimized to brief descriptions for the sake of space and concision.

3. Kenneth Keniston, "Youth: A 'New' Stage of Life," in *Youth and Culture: A Human-Development Approach,* ed. Hazel V. Kraemer (Monterey, Calif.: Brooks/Cole Publishing, 1974), 103.

4. A classic example of the moral concerns raised about children's exposure to movies in the early twentieth century is Jane Addams's "The House of Dreams" from her book *The Spirit of Youth and the City Streets* (1909), reprinted in *The Movies in Our Midst: Documents in the Cultural History of Film in America,* ed. Gerald Mast (Chicago: University of Chicago Press, 1982), 72–78.

A plethora of studies claiming the negative influence of movies on children then appeared throughout the 1920s and 1930s, including the infamous Payne Fund studies, although rarely did these analyses consider the image of youth presented in film, being more concerned with how youth could emulate supposedly immoral behaviors of adults on screen. These studies were conducted and published during a wave of moral panics that led to the foundation of the Motion Picture Production Code in 1930 and an overall crackdown on the moral looseness or ambiguity of American films. Nonetheless, many of these studies used often dubious methods and made often spurious claims. See Alice Mitchell, *Children and Movies* (Chicago: University of Chicago Press, 1929); Ruth Peterson and L. L. Thurstone, *Motion Pictures and the Social Attitudes of Children* (New York: Macmillan, 1933); Herbert Blumer and Philip Hauser, *Movies, Delinquency, and Crime* (New York: Macmillan, 1933); Wendell Dysinger and Christian Ruckmick, *The Emotional Responses of Children to the Motion Picture Situation* (New York: Macmillan, 1933); Henry James Forman, *Our Movie Made Children* (New York: Macmillan, 1933); P. G.

Cressey and F. M. Thrasher, *Boys, Movies, and City Streets* (New York: Macmillan, 1934); and Richard Ford, *Children in the Cinema* (London: George Allen and Unwin, 1939).

For a contemporary analysis of these studies and the attitudes that fueled them, see Garth S. Jowett, Ian C. Jarvie, and Kathryn H. Fuller, eds., *Children and the Movies: Media Influence and the Payne Fund Controversy* (New York: Cambridge University Press, 1996). See also Georganne Scheiner, *Signifying Female Adolescence: Film Representations and Fans, 1920–1950* (Westport, Conn.: Praeger, 2000).

5. See William S. Loiry, *The Impact of Youth: A History of Children and Youth with Recommendations for the Future* (Sarasota, Fla.: Loiry Publishing House, 1984), 135; and Christine Griffin, *Representations of Youth: The Study of Youth and Adolescence in Britain and America* (Cambridge, England: Polity Press, 1993), 18–23.

6. The actual Paramount ruling can be found in *United States* v. *Paramount Pictures, Inc.*, 334 U.S. 131, 166 (1948).

7. The "Miracle Decision" is 1952 U.S. Supreme Court *Burstyn* v. *Wilson*, 343 U.S. 495.

8. For an account of these films, see Alan Betrock, *The I Was a Teenage Juvenile Delinquent Rock 'n' Roll Horror Beach Party Movie Book: A Complete Guide to the Teen Exploitation Film, 1954–1969* (New York: St. Martin's Press, 1986).

9. See Geoffrey T. Holtz, *Welcome to the Jungle: The Why behind "Generation X"* (New York: St. Martin's Griffin, 1995), 69–70.

10. Janet Weeks, "Hollywood Is Seeing Teen," *USA Today*, Dec. 22, 1997, D1. See also Leonard Klady and Dan Cox, "Media Taps into Zit-geist," *Variety*, Feb. 22–28, 1999, 1, in which Klady provides a "Teen Screen Time Line" from 1955 to 1998 that testifies to the decline in teen films during the late '80s—he mentions no "key events in the life of juve pics" from 1984 to 1992, the longest gap in the 43 years he covers. This otherwise fallow period nonetheless contained such significant films as *The Breakfast Club* (1985), *Dirty Dancing* (1987), *Say Anything . . .*, *Heathers* (both 1989), and *Boyz N the Hood* (1991).

11. Chris Nashawaty, "The New Teen Age," *Entertainment Weekly*, Nov. 14, 1997, 24–35. See also Thomas Hine, "TV's Teen-Agers: An Insecure, World-Weary Lot," *New York Times*, Oct. 26, 1997, sec. 2, 1; Michael Krantz, "The Bard of Gen-Y," *Time*, Dec. 15, 1997, 105; Mark Sinker, "Youth," *Sight and Sound* 8, no. 6 (June 1998): 5–7; Josh Young, "They're All That," *Entertainment Weekly*, Mar. 12, 1999, 20–29; two articles both called "High School Confidential," one by Veronica Chambers and Yahlin Chang, in *Newsweek*, Mar. 1, 1999, 62–64, and the other by David Denby, in *The New Yorker*, May 31, 1999, 94–98; Stephanie Zacharek, "There's Something about Teenage Comedy . . . ," *Sight and Sound* 9, no. 12 (Dec. 1999): 20–22; Kay Dickinson, "Pop, Speed, and the 'MTV Aesthetic' in Recent Teen Films," *Scope* (2001), online at http://www.nottingham.ac.uk/film/journal/articles/pop-speed-and-mtv/htm.

12. Molly Haskell, *From Reverence to Rape: The Treatment of Women in the Movies* (New York: Holt, Rinehart and Winston, 1974); Thomas Cripps, *Slow Fade to Black: The Negro in American Film, 1900–1942* (London: Oxford University Press, 1977); Siegfried Kracauer, *From Caligari to Hitler: A Psychological History of the German Film* (Princeton: Princeton University Press, 1957).

13. Ralph Friar and Natasha Friar, *The Only Good Indian: The Hollywood Gospel* (New

York: Drama Book Specialists, 1972); Lester Friedman, *The Jewish Image in American Film* (Secaucus, N.J.: Citadel Press, 1987); Martin Norden, *Cinema of Isolation: A History of Physical Disability in the Movies* (New Brunswick, N.J.: Rutgers University Press, 1994).

14. Paul Willemen, "Presentation," in Stephen Neale, *Genre* (London: British Film Institute, 1983), 1.

15. Robin Wood, "Ideology, Genre, Auteur," reprinted from *Film Comment* 13, no. 1 (1977), in *Film Genre Reader II,* ed. Barry Keith Grant (Austin: University of Texas Press, 1995), 62.

16. Rick Altman, "A Semantic/Syntactic Approach to Film Genre," reprinted from slightly different form in *Cinema Journal* 23, no. 3 (1984), in Grant, ed., *Film Genre Reader II,* 26–40. Also see Altman's *Film/Genre* (London: British Film Institute, 1999).

17. Paul Schrader, "Notes on Film Noir," *Film Comment* 8, no. 1 (1972): 8–13; Jim Kitses, *Horizons West* (Bloomington: Indiana University Press, 1970); Jane Feuer, *The Hollywood Musical* (Bloomington: Indiana University Press, 1982); Rick Altman, *The American Film Musical* (Bloomington: Indiana University Press, 1987) and Rick Altman, ed., *Genre: The Musical* (London: Routlege and Kegan Paul, 1980).

18. Stuart M. Kaminsky, *American Film Genres,* 2nd ed. (Chicago: Nelson-Hall, 1985), 1–20.

19. Andrew Tudor, "Genre," in *Theories of Film* (New York: Viking Press, 1973), 131–50; reprinted in Grant, *Film Genre Reader II,* 4.

20. Ibid., 5.

21. Steve Neale, "Questions of Genre," *Screen* 31, no. 1 (spring 1990): 45–66; reprinted in Grant, *Film Genre Reader II,* 174. See Neale's further arguments about genre in his *Genre and Hollywood* (London: Routledge, 2000).

22. Thomas Schatz, *Hollywood Genres: Formulas, Filmmaking, and the Studio System* (New York: Random House, 1981), 3.

23. Janet Staiger, "Hybrid or Inbred: The Purity Hypothesis and Hollywood Genre History," *Film Criticism* 22, no. 1 (fall 1997): 6.

24. In addition to the new Altman (1999) and Neale (2000) texts mentioned above (notes 16, 21), see Torben Grodal, *Moving Pictures: A New Theory of Film Genres, Feelings, and Cognition* (New York: Oxford University Press, 1997); Nick Browne, ed., *Refiguring American Film Genres: History and Theory* (Berkeley: University of California Press, 1998); and Wheeler Winston Dixon, ed., *Film Genre 2000: New Critical Essays* (Albany: State University Press of New York, 2000).

25. Daniel Lopez, *Films by Genre: 775 Categories, Styles, Trends, and Movements Defined, with a Filmography for Each* (Jefferson, N.C.: McFarland and Company, 1993), 331.

26. Ibid., 332.

27. Ibid., 390.

28. *The Moving Image Genre-Form Guide,* comp. Brian Taves (chair), Judi Hoffman, Karen Lund, Library of Congress Motion Picture/Broadcasting/Recorded Sound Division report, Feb. 12, 1997. My thanks to Brian Taves for providing me with this report.

29. *Moving Image Genre-Form Guide,* 60.

30. See Wiley Lee Umphlett, *The Movies Go to College: Hollywood and the World of the*

College-Life Film (Rutherford, N.J.: Fairleigh Dickinson University Press, 1984), and David Hinton, *Celluloid Ivy: Higher Education in the Movies, 1960–1990* (Metuchen, N.J.: Scarecrow, 1994).

31. For an interesting examination of teen images in period films, see Lesley Speed, "Tuesday's Gone: The Nostalgic Teen Film," *Journal of Popular Film and Television* 25, no. 1 (fall 1998).

32. G. Stanley Hall, *Adolescence: Its Psychology and Its Relations to Physiology, Anthropology, Sociology, Sex, Crime, Religion, and Education* (New York: D. Appleton & Company, 1904). Scholars who in some way or another credit Hall with "discovering" adolesence are Johan Fornas in "Youth, Culture and Modernity," in *Youth Culture in Late Modernity,* ed. Johan Fornas and Goran Bolin (London: Sage, 1995), 5; Griffin, 11; and John R. Gillis in *Youth and History: Tradition and Change in European Age Relations, 1770–Present* (New York: Academic Press, 1981), 118.

33. Griffin, 18–26.

34. Robert Havighurst traced developmental ascents through adolescence to adulthood in *Developmental Tasks and Education* (New York: Longman and Co., 1948). Jean Piaget's contribution, among others, was a theory of cognitive development during adolescence in *The Growth of Logical Thinking* (New York: Basic Books, 1958), written with Barbel Inhelder. Erik Erikson mapped out psychological development according to age, in which adolescence was a stage for young people to negotiate their ego identity to achieve adulthood, which he discussed in books such as *The Challenge of Youth* (Garden City, N.Y.: Anchor Books, 1963) and *Identity, Youth, and Crisis* (New York: W. W. Norton, 1968). D. W. Winnicott proposed a variety of theories about the roles of play in child development in *The Child, the Family, and the Outside World* (Baltimore: Penguin, 1964) and *Playing and Reality* (New York: Tavistock Publications, 1971). Anna Freud was an advocate of children's rights based on her psychological research, which is collected in *Beyond the Best Interests of the Child* (New York: Free Press, 1979), written with Joseph Goldstein and Albert Solnit, and *A Child Analysis with Anna Freud* by Peter Heller (Madison, Conn.: International Universities Press, 1990). David Considine also discusses these and other adolescent research developments in his dissertation, *The Depiction of Adolescent Sexuality in Motion Pictures: 1930–1980,* 8–18. See also Morton Hunt, *The Story of Psychology* (New York: Doubleday, 1993), 350–95.

35. Kenneth Keniston, *Youth and Dissent* (New York: Harcourt Brace, 1960).

36. Philippe Aries, *Centuries of Childhood: A Social History of Family Life* (New York: Random House, 1962).

37. James Coleman, *The Adolescent Society: The Social Life of the Teenager and Its Impact on Education* (New York: Free Press of Glencoe, 1961); Stuart Hall and Tony Jefferson, eds., *Resistance through Rituals: Youth Subcultures in Post-war Britain* (London: Hutchinson, 1976); Angela McRobbie, *Feminism and Youth Culture: From "Jackie" to "Just Seventeen"* (London: Macmillan, 1991); Dick Hebdige, *Subculture: The Meaning of Style* (London: Methuen, 1979), and *Hiding in the Light* (London: Methuen, 1993).

38. Griffin, 196–214.

39. Geoffrey Pearson, *Hooligan: A History of Respectable Fears* (New York: Schocken

Books, 1983); Jon Lewis, *The Road to Romance and Ruin: Teen Films and Youth Culture* (New York: Routledge, 1992).

40. Grace Palladino, *Teenagers: An American History* (New York: Basic Books, 1996). Michael Barson and Steven Heller offer a somewhat sensational approach to teen history in *Teenage Confidential: An Illustrated History of the American Teen* (San Francisco: Chronicle Books, 1998). Also see Lucy Rollin's interesting *Twentieth-Century Teen Culture by the Decades: A Reference Guide* (Westport, Conn.: Greenwood Press, 1999).

41. Loiry, 223–45.

42. Douglas Coupland, *Generation X: Tales for an Accelerated Culture* (New York: St. Martin's Press, 1991). Perhaps the most personal examination of the emergent 20-something population can be found in the unique oral history written by Michael Lee Cohen, *The Twenty-Something American Dream: A Cross-Country Quest for a Generation* (New York: Dutton, 1993). See also David M. Gross and Sophfronia Scott, "Proceeding with Caution," *Time*, July 16, 1990, 56–62.

43. This elongation of youth, or more specifically the delay of adulthood, is discussed in broader social terms in "The Rocky Road to Adulthood," by Marcia Mogelonsky, *American Demographics* 18, no. 5 (May 1996): 26–35, 56.

44. Susan Littwin, *The Postponed Generation: Why America's Grown-Up Kids Are Growing Up Later* (New York: Morrow, 1986). Barbara Schneider and David Stevenson have conducted an extensive longitudinal study that questions the Generation X notion of youth in *The Ambitious Generation: America's Teenagers, Motivated but Directionless* (New Haven: Yale University Press, 2000).

45. Karen Ritchie, *Marketing to Generation X* (New York: Lexington Books, 1995).

46. Weeks, D1.

47. Mary Pipher, *Reviving Ophelia: Saving the Selves of Adolescent Girls* (New York: Ballantine, 1994).

48. David M. Considine, *The Cinema of Adolescence* (Jefferson, N.C.: McFarland, 1985).

49. Considine, *Cinema of Adolescence*, 9.

50. Lewis, 1–8.

51. Timothy Shary, "The Teen Film and Its Methods of Study." *Journal of Popular Film and Television* 25, no. 1 (spring 1997): 38–45.

52. Lewis, 3.

53. Ibid., 2.

54. Ibid., 150.

55. Armond White, "Kidpix," *Film Comment* 21, no. 4 (Aug. 1985): 9–16; Kathy Merlock Jackson, *Images of Children in American Film: A Sociocultural Analysis* (Metuchen, N.J.: Scarecrow Press, 1986); Thomas Leitch, "The World According to Teenpix," *Literature Film Quarterly* 20, no. 1 (Jan. 1992): 43–48; Randall Clark, *At a Theater or Drive-In Near You: The History, Culture, and Politics of the American Exploitation Film* (New York: Garland Publishing, 1995); Wheeler Winston Dixon, "'Fighting and Violence and Everything, That's Always Cool': Teen Films in the 1990s," in *Film Genre 2000*, 125–42; and Steve Neale, "Teenpics," in *Genre and Hollywood*, 118–25. See also Molly Haskell, "Teen Power," *Scenario* 5, no. 2 (1999) and the "Teenpics" section of *The Cinema Book* (1999). While the

articles tend not to concern the movies discussed here, issue no. 48 of *The Velvet Light Trap* (2001) on "Children, Teens, and the Media" offers evidence of the diverse research currently being written on preadult media.

Harvey Roy Greenberg offers a brief reflection on filmic images of youth in his article "On the McMovie: Less Is Less at the Simplex," in which he describes a subjectively defined category of films he calls "McMovies" that cater to simplified tastes and mentalities. Within this category he locates a number of teen films, and since his project is a larger psychoanalytic reading of culture through cinema, he concludes with the self-fulfilling statement that "Many McMovies about adolescents are informed by *a radically simplistic view of pubertal and postpubertal development*" (in *Screen Memories: Hollywood Cinema on the Psychoanalytic Couch* [New York: Columbia University Press, 1993], 195; emphasis in original). This is a good point, although like many critics, Greenberg does not explore the range of youth cinema that would be required to prove—and in many instances would disprove—his claim.

56. Murray Pomerance and John Sakeris, eds., *Pictures of a Generation on Hold: Selected Papers* (Toronto: Media Studies Working Group, 1996); Murray Pomerance and Frances Gateward, eds., *Sugar, Spice, and Everything Nice: Cinemas of Girlhood* (Detroit: Wayne State University Press, 2002).

57. Jonathan Bernstein, *Pretty in Pink: The Golden Age of Teenage Movies* (New York: St. Martin's Griffin, 1997).

58. Ruth M. Goldstein and Edith Zornow, *The Screen Image of Youth: Movies about Children and Adolescents* (Metuchen, N.J.: Scarecrow Press, 1980); Vincent Canby, "Stop Kidding Around," *New York Times,* July 23, 1972, sec. 3, 1.

CHAPTER 2: YOUTH IN SCHOOL

1. Jonathan Bernstein, *Pretty in Pink: The Golden Age of Teenage Movies* (New York: St. Martin's Griffin, 1997), 158.

2. "Popularity" in this case, as in most others, is somewhat subjectively measured, although my research and experiences support the claim that *The Breakfast Club* and *Heathers* were undoubtedly the most seen and influential school films between 1985 and 1990 (and along with *Say Anything . . .* and *Dirty Dancing,* the most popular teen films of this time in general). Yet to demonstrate the specious value of box-office earnings as an indicator of popularity—and to explain why I use them sparingly to support social/aesthetic claims—*Breakfast Club* earned $38.1 million in its U.S. theatrical release compared to the floplike numbers of *Heathers*—only $1.1 million. The latter film became much more successful on cable and video, and has seen further recognition through VHS and DVD rereleases, making an assessment of its true audience reach more difficult to determine. Further, reports of domestic box-office earnings often vary widely from source to source, and grosses can still be based on faulty approximations (even at the studio level); to this day, debate persists over distributors and studios inflating their earnings numbers, while straight-to-video films have essentially no way to measure their viewers, despite their potential impact.

Unless otherwise noted, all box-office figures in this book are based on U.S. theatrical earnings and are gathered from *The Internet Movie Database,* online at http://www.imdb.com.

3. *Lucas* review, Joseph Gelmis, *Newsday,* Mar. 28, 1986, Part III, 5.

4. Three increasingly inconspicuous sequels followed, which effectively offered more of the same: *Revenge of the Nerds 2: Nerds in Paradise* (1987), *Revenge of the Nerds 3: The Next Generation* (1992), and *Revenge of the Nerds 4: Nerds in Love* (1994), which was made for TV.

5. *The Breakfast Club* review, David Denby, *New York,* Feb. 18, 1985, 95.

6. *Lucas* review, David Edelstein, *Village Voice,* Apr. 15, 1986, 64.

7. *Lucas* review, David Denby, *New York,* Apr. 28, 1986, 93.

8. Some critics pointed out that the film, which was directed by convicted child molester Victor Salva, also speaks to the tensions of pedophilia.

9. *Class Act* review, David Denby, *New York,* June 22, 1992, 56.

10. *Class Act* review, Jami Bernard, *New York Post,* June 5, 1992, 25.

11. There is apparently an argument as to whether Dawn is 11 or 12 years old. Many reviews list her as 11, but most American school students do not start seventh grade until the age of 12. I include *Welcome to the Dollhouse* because it is about junior high school and clearly addresses school issues.

12. *Welcome to the Dollhouse* review, Lisa Schwarzbaum, *Entertainment Weekly,* May 31, 1996, 43.

13. *She's All That* review, Jane Ganahl, *San Francisco Examiner,* Jan. 29, 1999, D3.

14. *The Breakfast Club* review, David Edelstein, *Village Voice,* Feb. 26, 1985, 52.

15. The screenwriter of *Tuff Turf,* who is listed as "Jette Rinck," likely used a pseudonym: this is the same name as the James Dean character in *Giant* (1956).

16. *Tuff Turf* review, Michael Wilmington, *Los Angeles Times,* Jan. 11, 1985, Calendar, 15.

17. An obscure spoof of high school delinquency movies is *Student Confidential* (1987), in which four students go bad under the influence of a corrupt millionaire.

18. The director of *Class of 1984,* Mark Lester, was also responsible for *Truck Stop Women* and *Roller Boogie,* so his possible foray into docudrama is questionable indeed.

19. *Lean on Me* review, Charles Epstein, *Films in Review* (June–July 1989): 361.

20. The sequel, *Class of 1999 II: The Substitute* (1993), lacks the gangs and grand sociopolitical gestures of the first film, and becomes a violent contest between bad students and a sadistic teacher posing as an android. What the film illogically omits from the original is the near-futuristic image of schools overrun by organized delinquents—in fact, the students' presence in the film is quite small—and its already empty statement on youth violence is cast aside as all culpability for violence and delinquency is passed on to teachers, leaving the students conspicuously unmotivated in raising the trouble that their teachers are trying to eradicate.

21. *Lambada* (1990) showcases a typical "inspiring teacher" role and, like *Stand and Deliver* and *Lean on Me,* also features an ethnic group of successful underachievers, yet its concerns lay with an idealized vision of education based on racial tolerance (through dance) rather than combating delinquency.

22. Jeannette Sloniowski, "A Cross-Border Study of the Teen Genre: The Case of John N. Smith," *Journal of Popular Film and Television* 25, no. 3 (fall 1997): 132.

23. The film has had three made-for-TV or video sequels, all starring Treat Williams in the title role: *The Substitute 2: School's Out* (1998) did little to improve upon the original; *The Subsitute 3* (1999), while slightly more popular thanks to a wider video release, was no more significant; the fourth film was unnumbered as *The Substitute: Failure Is Not an Option* (2000).

24. *All I Wanna Do* is only one of many youth period films set in 1963, the year of Kennedy's assassination, which seems to mark the division of the prosperous post–World War II '50s from the cynical Vietnam War '60s (many more youth films take place in 1962 and 1964). Also set in 1963 are *Coupe de Ville, Dirty Dancing, The Flamingo Kid, Hoosiers, Mermaids,* and *Shag*.

25. *Rushmore* review, Kevin Courrier, *Box Office Magazine,* online at http://www.boxoff.com.

26. James C. McKelly offers a comparative reading of the rebel aspects of *Heathers* and *Rebel Without a Cause* in "Youth Cinema and the Culture of Rebellion: *Heathers* and the *Rebel* Archetype," in *Pictures of a Generation on Hold: Selected Papers,* ed. Murray Pomerance and John Sakeris (Toronto: Media Studies Working Group, 1996).

27. The film plays somewhat like *The Breakfast Club* in its plot of confined students who bond over their shared problems, a connection that is made clever by the casting of Judd Nelson as the students' favorite teacher. However, the 1985 film clearly showed the class and power issues that divided the students through the school caste system, and there is no similar division here. Further, these students' problems are far more pressing (though perhaps less common) than those of *The Breakfast Club* kids.

28. *Light It Up* review, Mick LaSalle, *San Francisco Chronicle,* Nov. 10, 1999, E4.

29. *Clueless* review, Owen Gliberman, *Entertainment Weekly,* July 28, 1995, 42.

30. *Election* review, Cindy Fuchs, *Philadelphia City Paper,* online at http://www.citypaper.net. See also Annie Nocenti, "Adapting and Directing *Election:* A Talk with Alexander Payne and Jim Taylor," *Scenario* 5, no. 2 (1999): 104–9, 189–90.

31. Stephen Holden, "A New Rule: The Beautiful Are the Bad," *New York Times,* Feb. 28, 1999, 13. David Denby also addressed this issue in his perceptive but sometimes stereotypical "High School Confidential."

32. Oddly enough, one of the highest-earning youth sports films of the 1980s was *Wildcats,* in which the teen characters were secondary to the star draw of Goldie Hawn—the film made $26.3 million at the box office. However, as any polling of '80s youth will reveal, *Wildcats* left far less of an impression than films like *All the Right Moves* and *Vision Quest*. By the '90s, youth sports films were still earning low numbers, such as $8.8 million for *The Next Karate Kid* and $10 million for *Sunset Park,* only by this point the films were indeed leaving smaller impressions.

33. The Disney studio in the mid-'90s began releasing a number of youth-themed sports films after the success of its 1992 children's film *The Mighty Ducks,* one of which was the baseball fantasy remake *Angels in the Outfield* (1994) and others of which included the martial arts franchise of *3 Ninjas* (1992–98), peewee football comedy *Little*

Giants (1994), weight-loss fitness-camp comedy *Heavyweights* (1994), soccer comedy *The Big Green* (1996), and two sequels to *The Mighty Ducks, D2* and *D3*, in 1994 and 1996. Films from other studios in this same vein included the baseball comedies *Rookie of the Year* (1993) and *Little Big League* (1994) and the military academy comedy *Major Payne* (1995). While some of these films featured some teenage characters, most are excluded from the present study because they are primarily about preteens and most are not about school sports; further, these films were clearly made to appeal to a preteen audience and do not consider the representation of youth that this study examines.

34. *Vision Quest* review, David Edelstein, *Village Voice,* Feb. 26, 1985, 52.

35. *Varsity Blues* grossed $52.9 million at the box office.

36. *Varsity Blues* review, Owen Gliberman, *Entertainment Weekly,* Jan. 22, 1999, 72.

CHAPTER 3: DELINQUENT YOUTH

1. See James Alan Fox, *Trends in Juvenile Violence: A Report to the United States Attorney General on Current and Future Rates of Juvenile Offending* (Washington, D.C.: Bureau of Justice Statistics, U.S. Department of Justice, 1996) and more importantly, Fox, *Trends in Juvenile Violence: 1997 Update* (Washington, D.C.: Bureau of Justice Statistics, U.S. Department of Justice, 1998). See also *Indicators of School Crime and Safety, 1999* (Washington, D.C.: U.S. Department of Education and U.S. Department of Justice, Oct. 1999).

2. *Juice* review, Anne Billson, *New Statesman and Society,* Aug. 28, 1992, 28.

3. *Beat Street* review, J. Hoberman, *Village Voice,* June 19, 1984, 53.

4. *Footloose* review, Donald Greig, *Monthly Film Bulletin,* Apr. 1984, 116.

5. *Dirty Dancing* grossed $63 million in its initial 1987 release, and earned about $1 million more in its 10th-anniversary release in 1997.

6. *Salsa* (1988) is steeped in passion as well, although it isn't a film about teenagers per se, since the main characters are just over 20. The film is a curious preview of Hollywood's attempt to capitalize on Latin music and dance with the lambada movies two years later, displacing sexual and ethnic tensions into its titular dance form.

7. *Dirty Dancing* review, Roger Ebert, *Chicago Sun Times,* Aug. 21, 1987, C1.

8. The cancellation of the long-running popular television dance program *American Bandstand* in 1989 would be further evidence that media-based teen dancing would decline in the 1990s.

9. There were two other aquatic animal films released in the mid-'90s that are not suited to the present study: *Andre* (1994), about a young girl's relationship with a seal; and *Magic in the Water* (1995), about a "bad dad" who becomes possessed by a mythical whalelike creature that teaches him how to love his kids better—very much in keeping with the theme of problem parents so prominent in '90s films.

10. *Free Willy* grossed $77.7 million at the box office.

11. *Free Willy* review, Hal Hinson, *Washington Post,* July 14, 1993, D1.

12. *Lord of the Flies* review, Gary Giddins, *Village Voice,* Mar. 20, 1990, 66.

13. *Red Dawn* review, Lenny Rubenstein, *Cineaste* 13, no. 4 (1984): 41.

14. *Red Dawn* was the first film to test the MPAA's new PG-13 rating, which was designed to accommodate a higher level of violence and sex in movies that high school students could attend without their parents.

15. *Red Dawn* review, David Denby, *New York,* Aug. 20, 1984, 90.

16. *Iron Eagle* review, J. Hoberman, *Village Voice,* Feb. 11, 1986, 56. Hoberman's review is rich with political commentary, including a comparison of the current spate of military films with pornography, claiming that the Soviet government had itself labeled the new combat films "war-nography."

17. Peggy Orenstein, "The Movies Discover the Teen-Age Girl," *New York Times,* Aug. 11, 1996, sec. 2, 1.

18. Ibid., 20.

19. *Angel* review, Stanley Crouch, *Village Voice,* Feb. 7, 1984, 56.

20. *The Legend of Billie Jean* review, David Edelstein, *Village Voice,* July 23, 1985, 56.

21. *Mi Vida Loca* review, Kevin Thomas, *Los Angeles Times,* July 22, 1994, Calendar, 4.

22. *Mi Vida Loca* review, Leslie Felperin, *Sight and Sound* 5, no. 4 (Apr. 1995): 48.

23. *Girls Town* review, Emanuel Levy, *Variety,* Jan. 29, 1996, 77.

24. *Girls Town* review, Phil Riley, *Motion Picture Guide Annual 1997,* 146.

25. *Girls Town* review, Levy, 77.

26. Bernard Weinraub, "Who's Lining Up at Box Office? Lots and Lots of Girls." *New York Times,* Feb. 23, 1998, B4.

27. Shirley Clarke's underground classic *The Cool World* (1963) was an exception—it provided a harsh portrait of a teen ghetto gang seriously involved in crime—yet its harshness may have been the very factor that prevented it from receiving wider distribution. See Donald Bogle, *Toms, Coons, Mulattoes, Mammies, and Bucks: An Interpretive History of Blacks in American Films,* new expanded edition (New York: Continuum, 1989), 200–201.

28. Ed Guerrero, *Framing Blackness: The African American Image in Film* (Philadelphia: Temple University Press, 1993), 182. S. Craig Watkins refers to this trend as the "ghetto action film cycle" in his book *Representing: Hip Hop Culture and the Production of Black Cinema* (Chicago: University of Chicago Press, 1998); however, he does not use the term to distinguish such nonteen action films as *New Jack City* from teen movies. He does concur that the cycle ran from 1991 to 1995.

29. Jacquie Jones, "The New Ghetto Aesthetic." *Wide Angle* 13, no. 3–4 (July–Oct. 1991): 33.

30. Ibid., 43.

31. One film about African American youth that could arguably be claimed to be part of this cycle was *Squeeze* in 1997, about three young teens on the verge of adopting delinquent lifestyles. However, the story's focus on the characters' psychological experiences and their as-yet minor criminality do not enlist it within the same tradition as the early-'90s films.

32. In their feature review, John Leland and Lynda Wright describe how Rich was forced by a Brooklyn drug dealer to coordinate shooting the film according to his rules, and thus struck a deal for "security" on the set. The dealer, a teenager whom Rich had grown up with, died before the film premiered. *Straight Out of Brooklyn* review, *Newsweek,* May 27, 1991, 58.

33. See Mark Becker, "Exhibitors Warm Up to 'Boyz' of Summer" and "Stepping Up Cinema Security," *Variety,* July 22, 1991, 1 and 13. Singleton defends the film, and its marketing, in Alan Light, "Not Just One of the Boyz," *Rolling Stone,* Sept. 5, 1991, 74–75.

34. A rather similar phenomenon, both in terms of violence at screenings and media outcries over a youth delinquency film, occurred in 1979 during the release of the urban gang movie *The Warriors.* Details in Mark Thomas McGee and R. J. Robertson, *The J.D. Films: Juvenile Delinquency in the Movies* (Jefferson, N.C.: McFarland, 1982), 153–54.

35. *Boyz N the Hood* review, Jack Mathews, *Newsday,* July 12, 1991, part 2, 60.

36. Paula Massood, "Mapping the Hood: The Genealogy of City Space in *Boyz N the Hood* and *Menace II Society," Cinema Journal* 35, no. 2 (winter 1996): 94.

37. Guerrero, 189.

38. Two other films appeared in 1992 that were somewhat a part of the trend in African American youth crime films, but do not properly belong in this category. *Zebrahead* was more formally a study of interracial dating, and its small amount of violence, while speaking to the volatility of racial tensions, does not enlist it within the same subgeneric classification as the films above. *South Central* is another compelling film about the plight of urban blacks, but its main character is an adult ex-convict who returns to his family in an effort to keep his 10-year-old son from the life of crime that derailed him as a younger man. The film continues the message of the need for strong paternal guidance in young black men's lives, although within the confines of this study it does not qualify as a youth film.

39. Murray Forman, in his article *"The 'Hood Took Me Under:* Urban Geographies of Danger in New Black Cinema," notes that "the rise of a discourse locating the danger-ridden hood as a realm of authentic black identity and experience also invalidates a substantial segment of black culture and black experience that exists in other rural and suburban locales and cultural milieux" (in *Pictures of a Generation on Hold: Selected Papers,* ed. Murray Pomerance and John Sakeris [Toronto: Media Studies Working Group, 1996], 50). Paula Massood also discusses the urban typography of these films in "Mapping the Hood" (see note 36).

40. *Menace II Society* review, Peter Rainer, *Los Angeles Times,* May 26, 1993, Calendar, 1.

41. *Menace II Society* review, Paula Massood, *Cineaste* 20, no. 2 (1993): 44.

42. *Menace II Society* review, David Denby, *New York,* May 31, 1993, 54.

43. An interesting film using the basketball theme that is not very much about youth or crime but is worth citing all the same is *Heaven Is a Playground* from 1991. The film is based on the true story of a white sports writer who studied public basketball courts, here relocated from New York to Chicago, where hopeful African American youth aspire to college scholarships under the tutelage of a black freelance scout. The scout is joined in his efforts by a lawyer (the sports writer of the original story) who helps him negotiate a professional contract for his adopted son, a successful college player. Tragedy strikes when the scout's son dies from a cocaine overdose, but the scout manages to forge on, inspiring more young players. What is most compelling about the existence of this film—which had limited theatrical release—is that its positive image of the proud, noncriminal African American male youth who play basketball was lost in the attention paid to the more violent and distraught depictions of male African Ameri-

cans in crime films of the same time. The film can been seen as somewhat condescending in that it is told from the perspective of a white lawyer, and again the youth in the film are not very well developed, yet the film remains an important exception in the representation of African American youth in the early '90s.

44. *Clockers* review, James Berardinelli, online at http://www.movie-reviews.colossus.net/movies/c/clockers.html.

45. To his credit, John Singleton did follow up *Boyz N the Hood* with a drama about a 20-something black woman affected by the murder of her boyfriend, *Poetic Justice* (1993), although critics viewed the film as a pretentious attempt by Singleton to address the sexism of *Boyz,* and audiences gave the film a lukewarm reception as well. His next film, *Higher Learning* (1994), dealt with male and female college-age characters in an even more pretentious examination of racism, sexism, classism, and homophobia.

46. Robyn Wiegman discusses similar gender issues in "Feminism, 'The Boyz,' and Other Matters Regarding the Male," in *Screening the Male: Exploring Masculinities in Hollywood Cinema,* ed. Steven Cohan and Ina Rae Hark (New York: Routledge, 1993).

CHAPTER 4: THE YOUTH HORROR FILM

1. David Cook, *A History of Narrative Film,* 3rd ed. (New York: W. W. Norton, 1996), 945.

2. See Shelly Stamp-Lindsey, "Horror, Femininity, and Carrie's Monstrous Puberty," *Journal of Film and Video* 43, no. 4 (winter 1991): 33–44.

3. Carol Clover, *Men, Women, and Chain Saws: Gender in the Modern Horror Film* (Princeton: Princeton University Press, 1992), 35.

4. Cook, 944.

5. Cook claims that *Halloween* "returned sixty million dollars on an eight-hundred-thousand-dollar investment" (ibid., 945).

6. *Student Bodies* begins with this caption: "Last year 26 horror films were released. None of them lost money."

7. Chris Nashawaty, "Oh, the Horror," *Entertainment Weekly,* Jan. 17, 1997, 8.

8. Clover, 5.

9. Ibid., 35.

10. Ibid., 40.

11. Vera Dika, *Games of Terror:* Halloween, Friday the 13th, *and the Films of the Stalker Cycle* (Toronto: Associated University Presses, 1990).

12. Clover had published her original article on the Final Girl in 1987.

13. Dika, 55.

14. Ibid.

15. Ibid., 56.

16. Ibid., 57.

17. Robin Wood, "Introduction to the American Horror Film," in *The American Nightmare,* ed. Robin Wood and Richard Lippe (Toronto: Festival of Festivals, 1979).

18. Ibid., 167.

19. Ibid., 170.

20. Barry Sapolsky and Fred Molitor, "Content Trends in Contemporary Horror Films," in *Horror Films: Current Research on Audience Preferences and Reactions,* ed. James B. Weaver and Ron Tamborini (Mahwah, N.J.: Lawrence Erlbaum Associates, 1996).

21. Ibid., 46.

22. Jonathan Bernstein, *Pretty in Pink: The Golden Age of Teenage Movies* (New York: St. Martin's Griffin, 1997), 34.

23. Ibid., 37.

24. Ibid., 35.

25. Less relevant to youth cinema but worth consulting for recent horror film research are Isabel Pinedo's "Postmodern Elements of the Contemporary Horror Film" and Scott R. Olson's "College Course File on Horror," both in a "Film Genres" edition of the *Journal of Film and Video* 48, no. 1–2 (spring–summer 1996). Also, see Mark Edmundson, *Nightmare on Elm Street: Angels, Sadomasochism, and the Culture of the Gothic* (Cambridge: Harvard University Press, 1997), which considers the gothic traditions of horror in film and literature from a wide range of cultural influences. In *Laughing Screaming: Modern Hollywood Horror and Comedy* (New York: Columbia University Press, 1994), William Paul examines the "gross-out" influences of a number of youth horror films and comedies.

26. Bernstein also singles out "the blob movie," although I subsume this category within the "supernatural" heading since his one example—*The Blob,* 1988—does not constitute a style unto itself.

27. *Friday the 13th: The Final Chapter* review, David Edelstein, *Village Voice,* Apr. 24, 1984, 57.

28. *A Nightmare on Elm Street 3: Dream Warriors* review, Judith Williamson, *New Statesman,* Dec. 11, 1987, 24.

29. *A Nightmare on Elm Street* review, David Sterritt, *Christian Science Monitor,* Nov. 28, 1984, 34.

30. *A Nightmare on Elm Street* review, David Edelstein, *Village Voice,* Nov. 20, 1984, 55.

31. Douglas Rathgab, "Bogeyman from the Id," *Journal of Popular Film and Television* 19, no. 1 (spring 1991): 41. See also Jonathan Markovitz, "Female Paranoia as Survival Skill: Reason or Pathology in *A Nightmare on Elm Street?" Quarterly Review of Film and Video* 17, no. 3 (2000): 211–20.

32. *Freddy's Dead* review, Philip Kemp, *Sight and Sound* 2, no. 2 (Feb. 1992): 45.

33. As with the *Halloween* and *Friday the 13th* series, the original director did not direct any of the sequels, although Wes Craven did write and direct *New Nightmare,* the seventh in the series in 1994, and was a cowriter on the third film.

34. *Slumber Party Massacre* review, Rex Reed, *New York Post,* Nov. 12, 1982, 45.

35. *Slumber Party Massacre* review, Carrie Rickey, *Village Voice,* Nov. 30, 1982, 62.

36. The *Scream* films have earned more as a trilogy than other franchises have grossed as 7–9 film series (although *A Nightmare on Elm Street* may have earned higher *merchandizing* figures through product development). *Scream* earned $103 million in its 1996–97 release, *Scream 2* earned $101.3 million within the next year, and *Scream 3*

earned $89.1 million at the box office in 2000, making these the highest-grossing teen horror films of all time. Not far behind is another teen horror film, *I Know What You Did Last Summer,* which grossed over $70 million domestically in 1997.

37. *I Still Know What You Did Last Summer* review, Owen Gliberman, *Entertainment Weekly,* Nov. 20, 1998, 94.

38. *Friday the 13th: The Final Chapter* review, David Edelstein, *Village Voice,* Apr. 24, 1984, 57.

39. *Christine* review, Sheila Johnston, *Monthly Film Bulletin,* Mar. 1984, 77.

40. The film had a sequel in 1991 with *976-EVIL: The Astral Factor,* which did not feature teen characters.

41. At least two critics found this revelation to be connotative of AIDS: Michael Wilmington in the *Los Angeles Times,* Aug. 5, 1988, Calendar, 10; and Julian Petley in *Monthly Film Bulletin* (June 1989), 170.

42. The original film was less intriguingly sequalized in 1994 with *Mirror, Mirror 2: Raven Dance,* in which a teenage girl and her brother become victims of the mirror, and then *Mirror, Mirror 3: The Voyeur* in 1995 and *Mirror, Mirror 4: Reflection* in 2000, both of which are so obscure as to be unavailable for viewing.

43. *Body Snatchers* review, John Powers, *New York,* Feb. 21, 1994, 48.

44. The cinematic depiction of teen witches in the two 1996 films stands in stark contrast to the mildly successful late-'90s television show *Sabrina: The Teenage Witch,* where the main character's association with the supernatural is portrayed in still mystical but altogether positive ways. While not a witch, the same could be said of the heroine in TV's *Buffy the Vampire Slayer.*

45. *The Craft* review, Roger Ebert, *Chicago Sun Times,* May 10, 1996, C1.

CHAPTER 5: YOUTH AND SCIENCE

1. *My Science Project* review, Kim Newman, *Monthly Film Bulletin,* Aug. 1986, 249.

2. *Real Genius* review, David Edelstein, *Village Voice,* Aug. 13, 1985, 54.

3. *SpaceCamp* review, David Sterritt, *Christian Science Monitor,* June 6, 1986, 25.

4. *October Sky* review, Susan Stark, *Detroit News,* Feb. 19, 1999, E1.

5. *Zapped* review, Joseph Gelmis, *Newsday,* Aug. 27, 1982, part 2, 9.

6. *Back to the Future* review, David Denby, *New York,* July 15, 1985, 64.

7. *Weird Science* review, Sheila Benson, *Los Angeles Times,* Aug. 2, 1985, Calendar, 1

8. A handful of obscure youth films in the late '90s were still engaged in some level of scientific fantasy, such as *Star Kid* (1997), *P.U.N.K.S.* (1998), and *Phantom Town* (1999).

9. *Tron, Krull* (1983), all three *Star Wars* movies, and other fantasy films became the inspiration for arcade games in the early '80s, a trend that was reversed in the '90s with the release of several films inspired by video games—*Super Mario Brothers* (1993), *Street Fighter* (1994), *Double Dragon* (1994), and *Mortal Kombat* (1995), *Mortal Kombat: Annihilation* (1997), and *Wing Commander* (1999)—although almost all failed to perform at the box office, indicating that the young audiences to which they were directed were then disinterested in filmic representations of these otherwise massively popular video

games. More recently in 2001 *Tomb Raider* was a huge hit while *Final Fantasy: The Spirits Within* (which actually *looks* like a video game with its computer graphics) was a financial failure, indicating that the media industry is still seeking a way to synergistically combine movies and games.

10. Denis Wood offers an interesting mythological reading of *The Last Starfighter* in "No Place for a Kid: Critical Commentary on *The Last Starfighter*," *Journal of Popular Film and Television* 14, no. 1 (spring 1986).

11. *The Wizard* is an odd combination of *Rain Man* (1988) and *Tommy* (1975) with a traumatized nine-year-old video game savant being taken to Las Vegas by his older brother for a massive contest, complete with many intradiegetic advertisements for the increasingly popular Nintendo game system.

12. All of the "internal reality" scenes of the game are shot on video, providing a visually different texture that capitalizes on the phenomenological intensity of video compared to the filmed scenes. See my article on this topic, "Present Personal Truths: The Alternative Phenomenology of Video in *I've Heard the Mermaids Singing*," *Wide Angle* 15, no. 3 (July 1993): 37–56.

13. *WarGames* review, David Denby, *New York,* June 6, 1983, 84.

14. *Hackers* review, Maitland McDonagh, *Motion Picture Guide Annual 1996,* 145.

15. *Hackers* review, Edwin Jahiel, *Movie Reviews by Edwin Jahiel* (n.d.), online at http://www.prairienet.org/ejahiel/reviews.htm.

16. *Hackers* and a number of "Generation X" films in the mid-'90s oddly begin or end on the roofs of urban buildings: *Reality Bites, Floundering* (1994), *Empire Records* (1995), and *If Lucy Fell* (1996), which ends atop the Brooklyn Bridge; a number of other mid-'90s youth and Gen-X films feature rooftop or penthouse sets in their climaxes: *Shaking the Tree* (1992), *Amongst Friends, Remote* (both 1993), *Radio Inside* (1994), *Kids* (1995), and *The Substitute* (1996). These scenes usually make for spectacular aerial shots, but their commonality to otherwise diverse narratives may indicate a symbolism of "teetering" since most of these films leave their characters literally up in the air.

CHAPTER 6: YOUTH IN LOVE AND HAVING SEX

1. For an interesting examination of male sexuality in the youth films of John Hughes, see Marianne H. Whatley, "Raging Hormones and Powerful Cars: The Construction of Men's Sexuality in School Sex Education and Popular Adolescent Films," *Journal of Education* 170, no. 3 (1988): 100–121.

2. National Center for Health Statistics; Centers for Disease Control; cited in *The Adolescent and Young Adult Fact Book* by the Children's Defense Fund (Washington, D.C., 1991).

3. David M. Considine, *The Cinema of Adolescence* (Jefferson, N.C.: McFarland, 1985), 262. *The Last Picture Show* (1971), a more popular American film in release around the same time as *Friends,* was also a factor in the increasingly sexualized image of youth.

4. Director Franco Zeffirelli, who filmed the famous version of *Romeo and Juliet* in 1968, took advantage of loosening moral codes to show his young protagonists in

lengthy nude lovemaking sessions, all without any form of birth control, including one scene in which David is shown coming to an ostentatious orgasm.

5. *Endless love* review, Sheila Benson, *Los Angeles Times,* July 17, 1981, Calendar, 14.

6. *Say Anything*... review, Roger Ebert, *Chicago Sun Times,* Apr. 14, 1989, C1.

7. Jonathan Bernstein, *Pretty in Pink: The Golden Age of Teenage Movies* (New York: St. Martin's Griffin, 1997), 105.

8. *Trust* review, J. Hoberman, *Village Voice,* July 30, 1991, 53.

9. *Trust* review, Philip Strick, *Sight and Sound* 1, no. 9 (Sept. 1991): 53.

10. Timothy Shary, "The Only Place to Go Is Inside: Confusions of Sexuality and Class in *Clueless* and *Kids,*" in *Pictures of a Generation on Hold: Selected Papers,* ed. Murray Pomerance and John Sakeris (Toronto: Media Studies Working Group, 1996), 162.

11. Lisa Schwarzbaum commented on the release of *Fear* and *The Craft* in theaters and on video at the same time in a review titled "Demonic Youth," in which she noted "the conservatism of big-studio teen movies, now and forever," as "oh-so-sophisticated products of Hollywood" (*Entertainment Weekly,* Oct. 11, 1996, 99).

12. *Fast Times at Ridgemont High* review, David Denby, *New York,* Sept. 27, 1982, 50.

13. Jonathan Bernstein sarcastically comments on this ending: "No American movie would have a more down-beat climax till the advent of the similarly stomach-churning *Seven*" (25).

14. The director of *The Last American Virgin,* Boaz Davidson, attained prominence in the early '80s with his "Lemon Popsicle" series from Israel, produced by the Cannon company's Menahem Golan and Yorum Globus. Jonathan Bernstein provides some background on the connection between the "Lemon Popsicle" films and *Virgin:* "Though largely unseen in America, these movies (threadbare titillation set in the fifties, executed in a style that aimed for Porky's but achieved Benny Hill), packed European cinemas, largely on the backs of TV-advertised soundtrack albums stuffed to the gills with early days rock 'n' roll standards. . . . Boaz Davidson used its components—sex-seeking stud, shy guy and gutbucket—as the basis for *The Last American Virgin.* But there the similarities end" (22). Bernstein does not name the films in the series, but according to *Halliwell's Filmgoer's and Video Viewer's Companion* (10th ed., 1993, 214), after the original *Lemon Popsicle* film in 1981, Cannon rushed Davidson into production on *Going Steady* and *Hot Bubblegum* within the next year, by which time the series was labeled, and then Davidson went on to make the fourth film in the series, *Private Popsicle,* just after *Virgin,* in 1982. Information on subsequent films is difficult to clarify, although I have come across *Young Love: Lemon Popsicle 7,* which was made in 1987. The fact that these films were ignored in America but nonetheless were made with largely the same intentions as other American teen sex films of the time—and were so successful in Europe—raises the possibility that the increasingly sexual representation of youth in the '80s was a more global phenomenon, an investigation of which demands further study.

15. *Risky Business* review, David Denby, *New York,* Aug. 22, 1983, 62.

16. One unusual postteen sex-quest film after 1986 was *The Allnighter* (1987), in which a sexually desperate female brainiac searches for a man to satisfy her before she graduates from college, and settles on an available neighbor just moments before commencement. Critics panned the film, including Leonard Maltin, who succinctly expressed why

such films had become anachronistic when he called it "grotesque in the AIDS era" (*Leonard Maltin's Movie and Video Guide, 1999 Edition* [New York: Penguin], 26). Perhaps the truly last moanings of the '80s teen sex comedies came from the Canadian film industry, which produced *The Virgin Queen of St. Francis High* in 1988, although it attained virtually zero visibility; the film followed in the cycle of "big bet" plots with its story of a teen who wagers that he can bed down his high school's most conspicuous virgin beauty. The few reviews I have been able to find of this film are also uniformly negative.

17. Shary, "Only Place to Go," 160.

18. bell hooks, "White Light," *Sight and Sound* 6, no. 5 (May 1996): 10.

19. Owen Gliberman, "Bold before Their Time," *Entertainment Weekly,* July 21, 1995, 47.

20. Thomas Doherty, "Clueless Kids," *Cineaste* 21, no. 4 (1995): 15.

21. For a revealing discussion of moral and literary issues in *Cruel Intentions,* see Bruce Newman, "Can't Read the Classic? See the Teen Movie," *New York Times,* Feb. 28, 1999, 13. After an abortive attempt to adapt the original film into a TV series called *Manchester Prep,* the Fox network gave the show's pilot to TriStar, which released it as a video feature entitled *Cruel Intentions 2* in 2000.

22. *American Pie* review, Jonathan Foreman, *New York Post,* July 16, 1999, 33.

23. A revealing irony about the cast of *American Pie* is that many of the male actors were so religious that they were initially concerned about the moral implications of their roles, which they ultimately found to be compatible with their beliefs by the time the film went into production. See Rebecca Ascher-Walsh, "Virgin Territory," *Entertainment Weekly on Campus,* Apr. 1999, 10–12.

24. *American Pie* review, Owen Gliberman, *Entertainment Weekly,* July 16, 1999, 44.

25. Considine, *Cinema of Adolescence,* 242.

26. Ibid.

27. Vito Russo offers some of the only thorough coverage of *Abuse* in *The Celluloid Closet: Homosexuality in the Movies,* rev. ed. (New York: Harper and Row, 1987), 273–74; see also 260–61.

28. Significant images of youth questioning their sexuality are contained in the work of Sadie Benning, who as a teenager in the late 1980s began making technically crude but aesthetically rich pixelvision videos of lesbian life experiences, such as *Welcome to Normal, Me and Rubyfruit,* and *Jollies,* which have since become landmark texts of young lesbian representation. See Mia Carter, "The Politics of Pleasure: Cross-Cultural Autobiographic Performance in the Video Works of Sadie Benning," *Signs: A Journal of Women in Culture and Society* 23, no. 3 (1998): 745–69.

29. *This Boy's Life* (1993), which is set in the late '50s, introduces a gay teenage boy with a subtle crush on the protagonist, and while his role is rather small, the film reminds us that young same-sexual attraction is not a contemporary phenomenon.

30. *Totally F***ed Up* review, Randy Gener, *Village Voice,* Oct. 11, 1994, 74.

31. *Totally F***ed Up* review, Tony Rayns, *Sight and Sound* 5, no. 2 (Feb. 1995): 55.

32. *Totally F***ed Up* review, Kevin Thomas, *Los Angeles Times,* Nov. 2, 1994, Calendar, 4.

33. *The Incredibly True Adventure of Two Girls in Love* review, Edwin Jahiel, *Movie Reviews by Edwin Jahiel* (n.d.), online at http://www.prairienet.org/ejahiel/reviews.htm.

34. *Parallel Sons* (1995) features an intriguing story about a black teenager coming to grips with his African American identity while he ministers to a wounded black criminal and develops an attraction to him, but this film is unavailable for viewing.

35. *All Over Me* review, Nell Bernstein, online at http://www.salon.com, Apr. 27, 1997.

36. The 1996 short feature *Hide and Seek,* by avant-garde filmmaker Su Friedrich, testifies to this as well. The narrative considers the development of lesbian youth through narrative and documentary styles, depicting a 12-year-old girl coming to terms with her sexual identity in the 1960s.

37. *Nickel Mountain* (1985) features a teenage girl who becomes pregnant and has the child, but this unusual and obscure film was not indicative of other teen depictions at the time.

38. Speaking in 1988, at the effective end of Molly Ringwald's career playing teenagers, Roger Ebert astutely pointed out her—and John Hughes's—influence on youth films of the '80s: "The movies of Molly Ringwald have been responsible for a revolution in the way Hollywood regards teenagers. Before Ringwald (and her mentor, John Hughes) there were only horny teenagers, dead teenagers, teenage vampires and psychotic crack-ups" (*"For Keeps"* review, *New York Post,* Jan. 15, 1988, 27). Ebert's description refers to the increasing senses of sincerity and compassion that were characteristic of many youth films in the mid- to late '80s, and further intimates the subgeneric changes that would mark the more complex youth films of the era.

39. *"For Keeps"* review, Janet Hawken, *Monthly Film Bulletin,* June 1988, 174.

40. *"For Keeps"* review, Roger Ebert, *New York Post,* Jan. 15, 1988, 27.

41. *Immediate Family* review, David Edelstein, *New York Post,* Oct. 27, 1989, 21.

42. *Just Another Girl on the I.R.T.* review, Jami Bernard, *New York Post,* Mar. 19, 1993, 29.

43. *Just Another Girl on the I.R.T.* review, David Denby, *New York,* Apr. 5, 1993, 60.

44. The mistaken-identity comedy *Mrs. Winterbourne* (1996) features Ricki Lake as a pregnant 18-year-old who has her baby early in the film. As with her pregnant character in *Cry-Baby* (1990), the focus on the pregnancy is relatively minimal.

45. This revision of teenage pregnancy is even visible in the farcical *Sugar and Spice* (2001), in which a cheerleading captain unexpectedly becomes pregnant, then moves in with her teenage boyfriend, and takes a job to save for the baby. When her cheerleading friends realize her financial predicament, they agree to rob a bank, thereby turning one friend's supposed trouble into a windfall for the whole group. Pregnancy in this case is not only positive but profitable, and makes the cheerleaders more popular than ever before.

CHAPTER 7: CONCLUSION: YOUTH CINEMA AT THE MILLENNIUM

1. There may already be a backlash to the heavy visibility of youth imagery and marketing of the late '90s, as twenty-first-century teenagers confront their commodification by media outlets hungry for their money. See Josh Wolk, "Pop Goes the Teen Boom?" *Entertainment Weekly,* June 8, 2001, 26–35.

BIBLIOGRAPHY

YOUTH IN CINEMA/MEDIA

Addams, Jane. "The House of Dreams." In *The Spirit of Youth and the City Streets*. 1909. Reprinted in *The Movies in Our Midst: Documents in the Cultural History of Film in America,* edited by Gerald Mast. Chicago: University of Chicago Press, 1982.

Bernstein, Jonathan. *Pretty in Pink: The Golden Age of Teenage Movies*. New York: St. Martin's Griffin, 1997.

Betrock, Alan. *The I Was a Teenage Juvenile Delinquent Rock 'n' Roll Horror Beach Party Movie Book: A Complete Guide to the Teen Exploitation Film, 1954–1969*. New York: St. Martin's Press, 1986.

Blumer, Herbert, and Philip Hauser. *Movies, Delinquency, and Crime*. New York: Macmillan, 1933.

Carter, Mia. "The Politics of Pleasure: Cross-Cultural Autobiographic Performance in the Video Works of Sadie Benning." *Signs: A Journal of Women in Culture and Society* 23, no. 3 (1998): 745–69.

Chambers, Veronica, and Yahlin Chang. "High School Confidential." *Newsweek,* Mar. 1, 1999, 62–64.

Considine, David M. *The Cinema of Adolescence*. Jefferson, N.C.: McFarland, 1985.

———. *The Depiction of Adolescent Sexuality in Motion Pictures: 1930–1980*. Dissertation, University of Wisconsin, Madison.

Cressey, P. G., and F. M. Thrasher. *Boys, Movies, and City Streets*. New York: Macmillan, 1934.

Crichton, Sarah. "Off the Beach Blanket and Into the Bedroom." *Ms. Magazine,* June 1985, 90–91.

Dalton, Mary. *The Hollywood Curriculum: Teachers and Teaching in the Movies*. New York: Peter Lang, 1999.

Denby, David. "High School Confidential." *New Yorker,* May 31, 1999, 94–98.

Dickinson, Kay. "Pop, Speed, and the 'MTV Aesthetic' in Recent Teen Films." *Scope* (2001). Online at http://www.nottingham.ac.uk/film/journal/articles/pop-speed-and-mtv .htm.

Dixon, Wheeler Winston. "'Fighting and Violence and Everything, That's Always Cool': Teen Films in the 1990s." In *Film Genre 2000: New Critical Essays,* edited by Wheeler Winston Dixon, 125–42. Albany: State University Press of New York, 2000.

Doherty, Thomas. "Clueless Kids." *Cineaste* 21, no. 4 (1995): 15–17.

———. *Teenagers and Teenpics: The Juvenilization of American Movies in the 1950s*. Boston: Unwin Hyman, 1988.

Dysinger, Wendell, and Christian Ruckmick. *The Emotional Responses of Children to the Motion Picture Situation*. New York: Macmillan, 1933.

Ford, Richard. *Children in the Cinema*. London: George Allen and Unwin, 1939.

Forman, Henry James. *Our Movie Made Children*. New York: Macmillan, 1933.

Goldstein, Ruth M., and Edith Zornow. *The Screen Image of Youth: Movies about Children and Adolescents*. Metuchen, N.J.: Scarecrow Press, 1980.

Haskell, Molly. "Teen Power." *Scenario* 5, no. 2 (1999).

Hine, Thomas. "TV's Teen-Agers: An Insecure, World-Weary Lot." *New York Times*, Oct. 26, 1997, sec. 2, 1.

Hinton, David. *Celluloid Ivy: Higher Education in the Movies, 1960–1990*. Metuchen, N.J.: Scarecrow, 1994.

hooks, bell. "White Light." *Sight and Sound* 6, no. 5 (May 1996): 9–12.

Jackson, Kathy Merlock. *Images of Children in American Film: A Sociocultural Analysis*. Metuchen, N.J.: Scarecrow Press, 1986.

Jowett, Garth S., and Ian C. Jarvie, and Kathryn H. Fuller, eds. *Children and the Movies: Media Influence and the Payne Fund Controversy*. New York: Cambridge University Press, 1996.

Kearney, Mary. "Girls Just Wanna Have *Fun?*: Female Avengers in '90s Teenpics." In *Pictures of a Generation on Hold: Selected Papers*, edited by Murray Pomerance and John Sakeris, 97–106. Toronto: Media Studies Working Group, 1996.

Klady, Leonard, and Dan Cox. "Media Taps into Zit-geist." *Variety*, Feb. 22–28, 1999, 1.

Krantz, Michael. "The Bard of Gen-Y." *Time*, Dec. 15, 1997, 105.

Leitch, Thomas. "The World According to Teenpix." *Literature Film Quarterly* 20, no. 1 (Jan. 1992): 43–48.

Lewis, Jon. *The Road to Romance and Ruin: Teen Films and Youth Culture*. New York: Routledge, 1992.

McGee, Mark Thomas, and R. J. Robertson. *The J.D. Films: Juvenile Delinquency in the Movies*. Jefferson, N.C.: McFarland, 1982.

McKelly, James C. "Youth Cinema and the Culture of Rebellion: *Heathers* and the *Rebel* Archetype." In Pomerance and Sakeris, eds., 107–14.

Markovitz, Jonathan. "Female Paranoia as Survival Skill: Reason or Pathology in *A Nightmare on Elm Street?*" *Quarterly Review of Film and Video* 17, no. 3 (2000): 211–20.

Massood, Paula. "Mapping the Hood: The Genealogy of City Space in *Boyz N the Hood* and *Menace II Society*." *Cinema Journal* 35, no. 2 (winter 1996): 85–97.

Mitchell, Alice. *Children and Movies*. Chicago: University of Chicago Press, 1929.

Moraites, Maria. "The American High School Experience: A Cinematic View from the 1980s." Ph.D. diss., Loyola University Chicago, 1997.

Nashawaty, Chris. "The New Teen Age." *Entertainment Weekly*, Nov. 14, 1997, 24–35.

Nocenti, Annie. "Adapting and Directing *Election:* A Talk with Alexander Payne and Jim Taylor." *Scenario* 5, no. 2 (1999): 104–9, 189–90.

Orenstein, Peggy. "The Movies Discover the Teen-Age Girl." *New York Times*, Aug. 11, 1996, sec. 2, 1.

Perlman, Marc. *Youth Rebellion Movies*. Minneapolis, MN: Lerner Publications, 1993.

Peterson, Ruth, and L. L. Thurstone. *Motion Pictures and the Social Attitudes of Children*. New York: Macmillan, 1933.

Pomerance, Murray, and Frances Gateward, eds. *Sugar, Spice, and Everything Nice: Contemporary Cinemas of Girlhood*. Detroit: Wayne State University Press, 2002.

Pomerance, Murray, and John Sakeris, eds. *Pictures of a Generation on Hold: Selected Papers*. Toronto: Media Studies Working Group, 1996.

Rapping, Elayne. "Hollywood's Youth Cult Films." *Cineaste* 16, no. 1–2 (1988): 14–19.

Rathgab, Douglas. "Bogeyman from the Id." *Journal of Popular Film and Television* 19, no. 1 (spring 1991): 36–43.

Scheiner, Georganne. *Signifying Female Adolescence: Film Representations and Fans, 1920–1950*. Westport, Conn.: Praeger, 2000.

Shary, Timothy. "Angry Young Women: The Emergence of the 'Tough Girl' Image in American Teen Films." *Post Script* 19, no. 2 (winter/spring 2000).

———. "Film Genres and the Cinematic Image of Youth—A College Course File." *Journal of Film and Video* 53, no. 4 (winter 2002).

———. "Generation Multiplex: The Image of Youth in American Cinema, 1981–1996." Ph.D. diss., University of Massachusetts, 1998.

———. "The Only Place to Go Is Inside: Confusions of Sexuality and Class in *Clueless* and *Kids*." In Pomerance and Sakeris, 157–66.

———. "Reification and Loss in Postmodern Puberty: The Cultural Logic of Fredric Jameson and American Youth Movies." In *Postmodernism and Cinema,* edited by Cristina Degli-Esposti. Providence: Berghahn Books, 1998.

———. "The Teen Film and Its Methods of Study." *Journal of Popular Film and Television* 25, no. 1 (spring 1997): 38–45.

Sinclair, Marianne. *Hollywood Lolitas: The Nymphet Syndrome in the Movies*. New York: Holt, 1988.

Sinker, Mark. "Youth." *Sight and Sound* 8, no. 6 (June 1998): 5–7.

Sloniowski, Jeannette. "A Cross-Border Study of the Teen Genre: The Case of John N. Smith." *Journal of Popular Film and Television* 25, no. 3 (fall 1997): 130–37.

Smith, Gavin. "Pensees: Pretty Vacant in Pink." *Film Comment* 23, no. 4 (July–Aug. 1987): 70–77.

Snyder, Scott. "Movie Portrayals of Juvenile Delinquency: Part 1—Epidemiology and Criminology." *Adolescence* 30, no. 117 (spring 1995): 53–64.

———. "Movie Portrayals of Juvenile Delinquency: Part 2—Sociology and Psychology." *Adolescence* 30, no. 118 (summer 1995): 325–37.

———. "Movies and Juvenile Delinquency: An Overview." *Adolescence* 26, no. 101 (spring 1991): 121–32.

Speed, Lesley. "Tuesday's Gone: The Nostalgic Teen Film." *Journal of Popular Film and Television* 25, no. 1 (fall 1998).

Stamp-Lindsey, Shelly. "Horror, Femininity, and Carrie's Monstrous Puberty." *Journal of Film and Video* 43, no. 4 (winter 1991): 33–44.

Stoehling, Richard. *From* Rock Around the Clock *to* The Trip: *The Truth about Teen Movies*. San Francisco: Straight Arrow, 1969.

Umphlett, Wiley Lee. *The Movies Go to College: Hollywood and the World of the College-Life Film*. Rutherford, N.J.: Fairleigh Dickinson University Press, 1984.

Wartella, Ellen, and Byron Reeves. "Historical Trends in Research on Children and the Media, 1900–1960." *Journal of Communication* 35, no. 2 (1985): 118–33.

Weeks, Janet. "Hollywood Is Seeing Teen." *USA Today,* Dec. 22, 1997, D1.

Weinraub, Bernard. "Who's Lining Up at Box Office? Lots and Lots of Girls." *New York Times,* Feb. 23, 1998, B4.

Whatley, Marianne H. "Raging Hormones and Powerful Cars: The Construction of Men's Sexuality in School Sex Education and Popular Adolescent Films." *Journal of Education* 170, no. 3 (1988): 100–121.

White, Armond. "Kidpix." *Film Comment* 21, no. 4 (Aug. 1985): 9–16.

Wiegman, Robyn. "Feminism, 'The Boyz,' and Other Matters Regarding the Male." In *Screening the Male: Exploring Masculinities in Hollywood Cinema,* edited by Steven Cohan and Ina Rae Hark. New York: Routledge, 1993.

Wood, Denis. "No Place for a Kid: Critical Commentary on *The Last Starfighter.*" *Journal of Popular Film and Television* 14, no. 1 (spring 1986): 52–63.

Zacharek, Stephanie. "There's Something About Teenage Comedy . . ." *Sight and Sound* 9, no. 12 (Dec. 1999): 20–22.

ADOLESCENT DEVELOPMENT

Aries, Philippe. *Centuries of Childhood: A Social History of Family Life*. New York: Random House, 1962.

Coleman, James. *The Adolescent Society: The Social Life of the Teenager and Its Impact on Education*. New York: Free Press of Glencoe, 1961.

Erikson, Erik. *The Challenge of Youth*. Garden City, N.Y.: Anchor Books, 1963.

———. *Identity, Youth, and Crisis*. New York: W. W. Norton, 1968.

Freud, Anna, Joseph Goldstein, and Albert Solnit. *Beyond the Best Interests of the Child*. New York: Free Press, 1979.

Gillis, John R. *Youth and History: Tradition and Change in European Age Relations, 1770–Present*. New York: Academic Press, 1981.

Hall, G. Stanley. *Adolescence: Its Psychology and Its Relations to Physiology, Anthropology, Sociology, Sex, Crime, Religion, and Education*. New York: D. Appleton & Company, 1904.

Havighurst, Robert. *Developmental Tasks and Education.* New York: Longman and Co., 1948.

Heller, Peter. *A Child Analysis with Anna Freud.* Madison, Conn.: International Universities Press, 1990.

Keniston, Kenneth. *Youth and Dissent*. New York: Harcourt Brace, 1960.

———. "Youth: A 'New' Stage of Life." In *Youth and Culture: A Human-Development Approach,* edited by Hazel V. Kraemer. Monterey, Calif.: Brooks/Cole Publishing, 1974.

Piaget, Jean, and Barbel Inhelder. *The Growth of Logical Thinking*. New York: Basic Books, 1958.

Winnicott, D. W. *The Child, the Family, and the Outside World.* Baltimore: Penguin, 1964.
———. *Playing and Reality.* New York: Tavistock Publications, 1971.

CONTEMPORARY YOUTH

Acland, Charles. *Youth, Murder, Spectacle: The Cultural Politics of "Youth in Crisis".* Boulder, Colo.: Westview Press, 1995.
Barson, Michael, and Steven Heller. *Teenage Confidential: An Illustrated History of the American Teen.* San Francisco: Chronicle Books, 1998.
Cohen, Michael Lee. *The Twenty-Something American Dream: A Cross-Country Quest for a Generation.* New York: Dutton, 1993.
Coupland, Douglas. *Generation X: Tales for an Accelerated Culture.* New York: St. Martin's Press, 1991.
Epstein, Jonathan, ed. *Youth Culture: Identity in a Postmodern World.* Oxford: Blackwell, 1998.
Fornas, Johan, and Goran Bolin, eds. *Youth Culture in Late Modernity.* London: Sage, 1995.
Fox, James Alan. *Trends in Juvenile Violence: A Report to the United States Attorney General on Current and Future Rates of Juvenile Offending.* Washington, D.C.: Bureau of Justice Statistics, U.S. Department of Justice, 1996.
———. *Trends in Juvenile Violence: 1997 Update.* Washington, D.C.: Bureau of Justice Statistics, U.S. Department of Justice, 1998.
Gaines, Donna. *Teenage Wasteland: Suburbia's Dead End Kids.* New York: Pantheon Books, 1991.
Griffin, Christine. *Representations of Youth: The Study of Youth and Adolescence in Britain and America.* Cambridge, England: Polity Press, 1993.
Hall, Stuart, and Tony Jefferson, eds. *Resistance through Rituals: Youth Subcultures in Postwar Britain.* London: Hutchinson, 1976.
Hebdige, Dick. *Hiding in the Light.* London: Methuen, 1993.
———. *Subculture: The Meaning of Style.* London: Methuen, 1979.
Holtz, Geoffrey T. *Welcome to the Jungle: The Why behind "Generation X."* New York: St. Martin's Griffin, 1995.
Johnston, Lloyd D., Jerald G. Bachman, and Patrick M. O'Malley. *Monitoring the Future: Questionnaire Responses from the Nation's High School Seniors 1995.* Ann Arbor, Mich.: Survey Research Center, Institute for Social Research, 1997.
Littwin, Susan. *The Postponed Generation: Why America's Grown-Up Kids Are Growing Up Later.* New York: Morrow, 1986.
Loiry, William S. *The Impact of Youth: A History of Children and Youth with Recommendations for the Future.* Sarasota, Fla.: Loiry Publishing House, 1984.
McRobbie, Angela. *Feminism and Youth Culture: From "Jackie" to "Just Seventeen."* London: Macmillan, 1991.
Mogelonsky, Marcia. "The Rocky Road to Adulthood." *American Demographics* 18, no. 5 (May 1996): 26–35.
Palladino, Grace. *Teenagers: An American History.* New York: Basic Books, 1996.

Pearson, Geoffrey. *Hooligan: A History of Respectable Fears*. New York: Schocken Books, 1983.

Pipher, Mary. *Reviving Ophelia: Saving the Selves of Adolescent Girls*. New York: Ballantine Books, 1994.

Ritchie, Karen. *Marketing to Generation X*. New York: Lexington Books, 1995.

Rollin, Lucy. *Twentieth-Century Teen Culture by the Decades: A Reference Guide*. Westport, Conn.: Greenwood Press, 1999.

Schneider, Barbara, and David Stevenson. *The Ambitious Generation: America's Teenagers, Motivated but Directionless*. New Haven: Yale University Press, 2000.

Wyn, Johanna, and Rob White. *Rethinking Youth*. London: Sage Publications, 1997.

SOCIAL REPRESENTATION IN FILM

Bogle, Donald. *Toms, Coons, Mulattoes, Mammies, and Bucks: An Interpretive History of Blacks in American Films*. New expanded edition. New York: Continuum, 1989.

Charney, Mark. "'It's a Cold World Out There': Redefining the Family in Contemporary American Film." In *Beyond the Stars V: Themes and Ideologies in American Popular Film*, edited by Paul Loukides and Linda Fuller. Bowling Green, Ohio: Bowling Green State University Press, 1996.

Cortés, Carlos. "Hollywood Interracial Love: Social Taboo as Screen Titillation." In *Beyond the Stars II: Plot Conventions in American Popular Film*, edited by Paul Loukides and Linda Fuller. Bowling Green, Ohio: Bowling Green State University Press, 1991.

Cripps, Thomas. *Slow Fade to Black: The Negro in American Film, 1900–1942*. London: Oxford University Press, 1977.

Forman, Murray. "*The 'Hood Took Me Under:* Urban Geographies of Danger in New Black Cinema." In Pomerance and Sakeris, 45–56.

Friar, Ralph, and Natasha Friar. *The Only Good Indian: The Hollywood Gospel*. New York: Drama Book Specialists, 1972.

Friedman, Lester. *The Jewish Image in American Film*. Secaucus, N.J.: Citadel Press, 1987.

Grady, Dennis. "From *Reefer Madness* to *Freddy's Dead:* The Portrayal of Marijuana Use in Motion Pictures." In *Beyond the Stars III: The Material World in the American Popular Film*, edited by Paul Loukides and Linda K. Fuller. Bowling Green, Ohio: Bowling Green State University Press, 1993.

Greenberg, Harvey Roy. *Screen Memories: Hollywood Cinema on the Psychoanalytic Couch*. New York: Columbia University Press, 1993.

Guerrero, Ed. *Framing Blackness: The African American Image in Film*. Philadelphia: Temple University Press, 1993.

Haskell, Molly. *From Reverence to Rape: The Treatment of Women in the Movies*. New York: Holt, Rinehart and Winston, 1974.

Jones, Jacquie. "The New Ghetto Aesthetic." *Wide Angle* 13, no. 3–4 (July–Oct. 1991): 32–43.

Kracauer, Siegfried. *From Caligari to Hitler: A Psychological History of the German Film*. Princeton: Princeton University Press, 1957.

Lebeau, Vicky. *Lost Angels: Psychoanalysis and Cinema*. New York: Routledge, 1995.

Lehman, Peter. *Running Scared: Masculinity and the Representation of the Male Body*. Philadelphia: Temple University Press, 1993.

Morella, Joe. *Rebels: The Rebel Hero in Films*. New York: Citadel, 1971.

Norden, Martin. *Cinema of Isolation: A History of Physical Disability in the Movies*. New Brunswick, N.J.: Rutgers University Press, 1994.

Russo, Vito. *The Celluloid Closet: Homosexuality in the Movies*. Revised edition. New York: Harper and Row, 1987.

Traube, Elizabeth. *Dreaming Identities: Class, Gender, and Generation in 1980s Hollywood Movies*. Boulder, Colo.: Westview Press, 1992.

Watkins, S. Craig. *Representing: Hip Hop Culture and the Production of Black Cinema*. Chicago: University of Chicago Press, 1998.

Weaver, James B., and Ron Tamborini, eds. *Horror Films: Current Research on Audience Preferences and Reactions*. Mahwah, N.J.: Lawrence Erlbaum Associates, 1996.

Wexman, Virginia Wright. *Creating the Couple: Love, Marriage, and Hollywood Performance*. Princeton: Princeton University Press, 1993.

FILM GENRES

Altman, Rick. *The American Film Musical*. Bloomington: Indiana University Press, 1987.

———. *Film/Genre*. London: British Film Institute, 1999.

———. "A Semantic/Syntactic Approach to Film Genre." Reprinted from *Cinema Journal* 23, no. 3 (1984). In *Film Genre Reader II,* edited by Barry Keith Grant, 26–40. Austin: University of Texas Press, 1995.

———, ed. *Genre: The Musical*. London: Routlege and Kegan Paul, 1980.

Browne, Nick, ed. *Refiguring American Film Genres: History and Theory*. Berkeley: University of California Press, 1998.

Cantor, Joanne, and Mary Beth Oliver. "Developmental Differences in Responses to Horror." In Weaver and Tamborini, 67–85.

Cavell, Stanley. *Pursuits of Happiness: The Hollywood Comedy of Remarriage*. Cambridge: Harvard University Press, 1981.

Clark, Randall. *At a Theater or Drive-In Near You: The History, Culture, and Politics of the American Exploitation Film*. New York: Garland Publishing, 1995.

Clover, Carol. *Men, Women, and Chain Saws: Gender in the Modern Horror Film*. Princeton: Princeton University Press, 1992.

Dika, Vera. *Games of Terror:* Halloween, Friday the 13th, *and the Films of the Stalker Cycle*. Toronto: Associated University Presses, 1990.

Dixon, Wheeler Winston, ed. *Film Genre 2000: New Critical Essays*. Albany: State University Press of New York, 2000.

Edmundson, Mark. *Nightmare on Elm Street: Angels, Sadomasochism, and the Culture of the Gothic*. Cambridge: Harvard University Press, 1997.

Feuer, Jane. *The Hollywood Musical*. Bloomington: Indiana University Press, 1982.

Grant, Barry Keith. "Rich and Strange: The Yuppie Horror Film." *Journal of Film and Video* 48, no. 1–2 (1996): 4–16.

———, ed. *The Dread of Difference: Gender and the Horror Film*. Austin: University of Texas Press, 1996.

———, ed. *Film Genre Reader II*. Austin: University of Texas Press, 1995.

Grodal, Torben. *Moving Pictures: A New Theory of Film Genres, Feelings, and Cognition*. New York: Oxford University Press, 1997.

Kaminsky, Stuart M. *American Film Genres*. 2nd ed. Chicago: Nelson-Hall, 1985.

Kitses, Jim. *Horizons West*. Bloomington: Indiana University Press, 1970.

Lopez, Daniel. *Films by Genre: 775 Categories, Styles, Trends, and Movements Defined, with a Filmography for Each*. Jefferson, N.C.: McFarland and Company, 1993.

The Moving Image Genre-Form Guide. Compiled by Brian Taves (chair), Judi Hoffman, and Karen Lund. Library of Congress Motion Picture/Broadcasting/Recorded Sound Division report, Feb. 12, 1997.

Neale, Stephen. *Genre*. London: British Film Institute, 1983.

Neale, Steve. *Genre and Hollywood*. London: Routledge, 2000.

———. "Questions of Genre." *Screen* 31, no. 1 (spring 1990): 45–66. Reprinted in Grant, ed., *Film Genre Reader II*, 159–83.

Olson, Scott R. "College Course File on Horror." *Journal of Film and Video* 48, no. 1–2 (spring–summer 1996): 67–79.

Paul, William. *Laughing Screaming: Modern Hollywood Horror and Comedy*. New York: Columbia University Press, 1994.

Pinedo, Isabel. "Postmodern Elements of the Contemporary Horror Film." *Journal of Film and Video* 48, no. 1–2 (spring–summer 1996): 17–31.

Reed, Joseph. *American Scenarios: The Uses of Film Genre*. Middletown, Conn.: Wesleyan University Press, 1989.

Sapolsky, Barry, and Fred Molitor. "Content Trends in Contemporary Horror Films." In Weaver and Tamborini, 35–52.

Schatz, Thomas. *Hollywood Genres: Formulas, Filmmaking, and the Studio System*. New York: Random House, 1981.

Schrader, Paul. "Notes on Film Noir." *Film Comment* 8, no. 1 (1972): 8–13.

Staiger, Janet. "Hybrid or Inbred: The Purity Hypothesis and Hollywood Genre History." *Film Criticism* 22, no. 1 (fall 1997): 5–20.

Tudor, Andrew. "Genre." In *Theories of Film*. New York: Viking Press, 1973. 131–50. Reprinted in Grant, *Film Genre Reader II*, 3–10.

Willemen, Paul. "Presentation." In *Genre*, edited by Stephen Neale, 1–4. London: British Film Institute, 1983.

Williams, Tony. "Trying to Survive on the Darker Side: 1980s Family Horror." In Grant, ed., *Dread of Difference*, 113–37.

Wood, Robin. "Introduction to the American Horror Film." In *The American Nightmare*, edited by Robin Wood and Richard Lippe. Toronto: Festival of Festivals, 1979.

Wood, Robin. "Ideology, Genre, Auteur." Reprinted from *Film Comment* 13, no. 1. In Grant, *Film Genre Reader II*, 59–73.

INDEX

Aames, Willie, 192
abortion, 159, 221–222, 228–229, 246–248, 250, 252–253, 259. *See also* pregnancy
Above the Rim (1994), 131–132
abuse, 102, 112, 117, 120–121, 126, 140, 153–154, 160, 163, 195, 201, 221, 223–224, 239, 245, 289n.8
Abuse (1982), 239, 299n.27
Aces: Iron Eagle 3 (1992), 104
Addams, Jane, 283n.4
adolescence, 1–2, 17, 19–20, 37, 78, 96, 286n.34, 287n.55. *See also* psychology of youth
Adventures in Babysitting (1987), 84
African American crime dramas, 9, 59, 81–82, 85, 118, 122–135, 149, 292n.28, 293n.38
African American youth, 10, 30, 37–38, 46, 48, 50, 59, 65, 71, 76, 77, 86–88, 120, 122–135, 205, 251, 259–260, 292n.31, 293n.39, 293n.43, 300n.34. *See also* race issues
A.I. (2001), ix, xi, 208
AIDS, 9, 142, 211, 227, 231–232, 235, 239–240, 242, 248, 254, 261, 296n.41, 298n.16. *See also* HIV; sexually transmitted disease
Airborne (1993), 84
Air Bud trilogy, 96
Alan & Naomi (1992), 225
Alaska (1996), 103
alcoholism. *See* drugs, alcohol
All Fall Down (1962), 4
Alliance for a Media Literate America, x
All I Wanna Do (2000), 53, 290n.24
Allnighter, The (1987), 298n.16
All Over Me (1996), 122, 244–246
All the Right Moves (1983), 74, 290n.32
Almost Famous (2000), 85
Aloha Summer (1988), 84
Altman, Rick, 13
Amazing Grace and Chuck (1987), 84
American Bandstand television show, 291n.8
American Beauty (1999), 85, 183, 226
American Graffiti (1973), 210
American Heart (1993), 84
American History X (1998), 9, 85
American Pie (1999), 33, 209, 236–238, 299n.23
American Summer (1991), 84
Amongst Friends (1993), 297n.16
Anarchy TV (1997), 182
Anders, Alison, 119
Andre (1994), 291n.9
And You Thought Your Parents Were Weird (1991), 200–201
Angels in the Outfield (1994), 290n.33
angst, 4–5, 27, 50, 57, 160, 174, 197, 242
Angel trilogy, 111; *Angel* (1984), 113–114; *Angel 3: The Final Chapter* (1988), 114. See also *Avenging Angel*

Angus (1995), 29, 37
animal adventure films, 82, 94–99, 260, 291n.9
Animal House (1978), 7
Antin, Steve, 229
Anywhere but Here (1999), 226
Apt Pupil (1998), 141
Araki, Gregg, 241
Arcade (1993), 8, 182, 197, 200–202
Aries, Philippe, 20
Art for Teachers of Children (1995), 212
artistic youth, 40, 51, 53, 55, 60, 74, 87–88, 237, 245
Astin, Sean, 100
At Close Range (1986), 85
athletes, 9, 32, 36–37, 52, 63, 68, 69–78, 96, 131, 170–171, 175, 190, 259–260; female, 70–72; male, *31*, 72–78, 113, 237, 243. *See also* basketball; football; martial arts; wrestling
automobiles and youth, 3, 84, 169–172, *170*
Avalon, Frankie, 5
Avenging Angel (1985), 114
Aviles, Angel, 118

Backer, Brian, 34, 228
Back to the Future (1985), 181–182, 184, 193
Back to the Future Part II (1989), 196
Back to the Future Part III (1990), 196
Bacon, Kevin, 88–*89,* 100, 239
Bad Boys (1983), 85
Bad Girls' Dormitory (1984), 112
Baio, Scott, 191
Balk, Fairuza, 176
Bancroft, Cam, 241
Barrymore, Drew, 116, 165
Bartholomew, Freddie, 3
basketball, 69, 72, 76, 78, 131–132, 293n.43. *See also* athletes
Batinkoff, Randall, 248
Beach House (1982), 84
beach movies, 2, 5, 16, 82, 84, 256
Beach Party (1963), 5
Beat, The (1988), 35, 44
Beat Street (1984), 82, 87–88
Beatty, Warren, 30
Beetlejuice (1987), 169
Behshid, Susan, 242
Belic, Roko, 242
Benji films, 95
Benning, Sadie, 299n.28
Benson, Robbie, 6
Benson, Sheila, 193, 217
Berardinelli, James, 133
Bernard, Crystal, 162
Bernard, Jami, 38, 251
Bernstein, Jonathan, 24, 28, 146–147, 164, 183, 219, 258, 295n.26
Bernstein, Nell, 245
Best Man, The (1999), 124
Beverly Hills 90210 television show, 30
Beyond the Stars (1989), 189
Big (1988), 83
Big Bet, The (1986), 232–233
Big Green, The (1996), 290n.33
Biggs, Jason, 236
Bill and Ted's Bogus Journey (1991), 56
Bill and Ted's Excellent Adventure (1989), 29, 56
Billingsley, Peter, 200
Billson, Anne, 87
bisexuality of youth. *See* homosexuality of youth
Black and White (2000), 85
Black Beauty (1994), 95
Blackboard Jungle (1955), 4, 27, 45, 82
Black Circle Boys (1997), 173
Black Roses (1988), 147
Black Stallion, The (1979), 95
Black Stallion Returns, The (1983), 95
black youth. *See* African American youth; race issues
Blair, Linda, 112
Blair Witch Project, The (1999), 178
Blame It on Rio (1984), 213
Bleeding Hearts (1995), 213

Blob, The (1958), 138
Blob, The (1988), 172–173, 175, 295n.26
Blood Lake (1987), 164
Bloody Pom Poms (1988), 164
Blossom television show, 30
Blue Chips (1994), 70
Blue Denim (1959), 4, 210, 246–247
Blue Lagoon, The (1980), 7, 210–211
body images of youth, 22, *31*, 34, 37–40, 64, 73, 100, 245, 250
Body Rock (1984), 87
Body Snatchers (1993), 174–175
Born American (1986), 106–107, 197
Born to Be Wild (1995), 96–97
Borrego, Jessie, 118
box-office earnings, 288n.2
boys: delinquency, 37, 41–50; masculine identity, 36, 39, 43, 62, 71–78, 106–110, 117, 130, 143, 171, 195, 232–233, 237, 241; sexuality, 34, 36–37, 73, 206, 231, 240
Boys (1996), 213, 225
Boys Don't Cry (1999), 246
Boys Next Door, The (1986), 239
Boyz N the Hood (1991), 80, 81, 123, 125, *127*–129, 130, 133–134, 284n.10, 293n.33, 294n.45
Bradford, Jesse, 205
Brady Bunch Movie, The (1995), 62, 68
brains. *See* nerds
Brainscan (1994), 197, 202
Brando, Marlon, 4
Brat Pack, 10, 29
break dancing, 86–88, 94
Break, The (1995), 76
Breakfast Club, The (1985), 9, 26, 28–29, *31*, 34–35, 43, 50–52, 62–64, 68, 69, 72, 175, 188, 193, 284n.10, 288n.2, 290n.27
Breakin' (1984), 87
Breakin' Through (1984), 87
Breakin' 2: Electric Boogaloo (1985), 87
Bride of Frankenstein, The (1935), 195
Bring It On (2000), 71
Broderick, Matthew, 67, 197, 202–*203*
Broken Blossoms (1919), 3
Brothers, The (2001), 124
Brown, Rita Mae, 161
Brutal Fury (1992), 117
Buffy the Vampire Slayer (1992), 59, 62, 65
Buffy the Vampire Slayer television show, 10, 30, 296n.44
Burning, The (1981), 164
But I'm a Cheerleader (2000), 246

Caldecott, Todd, 223
Calendar Girl (1993), 212
Calhoun, Rory, 113
Campbell, Neve, 165, 176
Canby, Vincent, 25
Can't Buy Me Love (1987), 35–36, 62, 68, 211, 213
Can't Hardly Wait (1998), 10, 29, 37, 40, 41, 69, 72, 212, 235
capoeira, 76, 91. *See also* martial arts
Captain January (1924), 3
Carnegie Council on Adolescent Development, x
Carpenter, John, 139, 170
Carrey, Jim, 231
Carrie (1976), 30, 138–139, 153, 177, 191, 217. See also *Rage: Carrie 2, The*
cars. *See* automobiles and youth
Carter, Thomas, 94
Catholic youth, 53, 54, 175
Cavalieri, Michael, 70
Center Stage (2000), 93–94
Channeler, The (1989), 173
Chardiet, Jon, 87
Charlie's Angels (2000), 122
Cheerleader Camp (1988), 164. See also *Bloody Pom Poms,* 164
cheerleaders, 71, 172–173, 246, 300n.45
Cherry Falls (2000), 141
Chestnut, Morris, 129
Children of the Corn franchise, 141, 147
China Girl (1987), 9, 85, 213, 216
Chlumsky, Anna, 102

Chocolate War, The (1988), 51, 54, 55
Choices (1981), 74
Chong, Rae Dawn, 87
Chopping Mall (1986), 185
Christine (1983), 169–172, *170*
Circle of Friends (1995), 212
City Across the River (1949), 5, 27
Clark, Joe, 46–47
Clark, Larry, 233
Clark, Randall, 24
Clarke, Shirley, 292n.27
Class (1983), 35–36, 210, 231
Class Act (1991), 33, 37, 41, 43, 123
class issues, 1, 33–34, 36–39, 41, 43–44, 47, 50, 55, 59, 61, 63, 65, 73–74, 81–82, 85–88, 90–91, 93, 116, 120, 123, 125–126, 128, 135, 155, 176, 191, 198–199, 213, 215–216, 220–222, 235, 240, 242–244, 248–250, 290n.27. *See also* economy, effects on youth; employment of youth
Class of 1984 (1982), 9, 41–42, 45, 289n.18
Class of 1999 (1990), 42, 47–48
Class of 1999 II: The Substitute (1993), 289n.20
cliques. *See* secret societies
Clockers (1995), 124, 132–134
Close, Glenn, 249
Clover, Carol, 139, 143, 258
Clown House (1988), 173
Clueless (1995), 10, 29–30, 62, 65–67, *66*, 111, 220, 222–223, 235
Coburn, David, 106
Cold War, 8, 11, 101, 103–110, 182, 197, 203
Coleman, James, 20
college, 3, 7, 17–18, 22, 28, 34, 60, 70, 73–75, 77–78, 128–129, 166–167, 185–187, 190, 198, 230, 249, 259, 285n.30, 294n.45
Collett, Christopher, 187
Columbine (Colorado) high school murders, 42, 60
comedies, romantic, 8, 36, 142, 211, 217
comedies, sexual, 6–8, 16, 28–29, 142, 148, 164, 191–192, 198, 211
Coming Soon (1999), 238
Communications Decency Act of 1996, 198
computers and youth, 8, 37, 181–183, 193–194, 196–198, 202–208, 221, 259–260. *See also* Internet
Computer Wore Tennis Shoes, The (1969), 191
conformity, 40, 50, 52, 56–57, 61, 101–102, 174–175, 215
Conrad, Chris, 71
conservative politics, x, 20
Considine, David, ix–xi, 16–17, 22–23, 215, 238–239, 258, 286n.34
Coogan, Jackie, 3
Cook, Rachel Leigh, 39
Cool and the Crazy, The (1958), 51
Cool as Ice (1991), 222
Cooley High (1975), 123
Cool World, The (1963), 292n.27
Coup de Ville (1990), 290n.24
Coupland, Douglas, 21
Craft, The (1996), 122, 175–176, 298n.11
Crain, Jeanne, 4
Craven, Wes, 154–155, 157, 160–161, 165–167, 178, 295n.33
crazy/beautiful, x
Crime and Punishment in Suburbia (2000), 122
criminality of youth, 4, 9–10, 41–45, 49, 50, 57, 59–60, 80–83, 85, 111, 117–118, 122–135, 142, 167, 180–181, 206–207, 224, 227, 245, 292n.27, 300n.45. *See also* drugs; murder; punishment of youth; rape
Cripps, Thomas, 12
Crouch, Stanley, 113
Crowe, Cameron, 31
Cruel Intentions (1999), 30, 212, 235–236, 299n.21
Cruel Intentions 2 (2000), 299n.21. See also *Manchester Prep*

Cruise, Tom, 53, 74, 230, 242
Crush, The (1993), 212, 213
Cry-Baby (1990), 91, 211, 300n.44
Cry in the Wild/White Wolves franchise, 100
Cthulhu Mansion (1991), 173
cultural studies, 20–21
Curtis, Jamie Lee, 140, 149, 151
Cusack, John, 218–*219*

dancing and youth, 6, 256, 289n.21, 291n.8; as deviance, 9, 82, 86–94. *See also* break dancing; lambada; music and youth; proms; raves
Danes, Claire, 224
Dangerous Liaisons (1988), 235
Dangerously Close (1986), 44, 117
Dangerous Minds (1995), 10, 29, 42, 47–48, 76
Daniels, Jeff, 97
Dark Horse (1992), 95
Darro, Frankie, 3
Dash, Stacey, 65, *66*
Date With Judy, A (1948), 4
Dattilo, Kristen, 173
David and Lisa (1962), 52
Davidson, Boaz, 298n.14
Davis, Guy, 87
Dawson, Rosario, 59
Dawson's Creek television show, 10, 77
Day After, The (1983), 106
Day My Parents Ran Away, The (1993), 85
Dazed and Confused (1993), 84
Dead End Kids films, 3, 82
Deadly Friend (1986), 195–196
Deadly Weapon (1988), 195
Dead Poets Society (1989), 29–30, 53
Dean, James, 4–*5*, 28, 30, 56, 243, 289n.15
Defense Play (1988), 104, 182, 197–198, 201, 204–205, 207
deflowering, 229, 232, 233–234, 244, 245. *See also* virginity
delinquency, 5, 37, 39, 50, 56, 63, 80–136, 172, 175, 233, 256, 289n.20, 292n.31; in school, 4, 9, 27–28, *31*, 32, 41–50, 259; as a youth film subgenre, 8–9, 80–86, 256, 260, 263. *See also* African American crime dramas; animal adventure films; criminality of youth; dancing and youth, dance as deviance; drugs and youth; "harmless mischief" films; patriotic purpose films; runaways; tough girls; wilderness survival films
Delinquent School Girls (1984), 112
Delivery Boys (1984), 87
Delta, The (1997), 243
Delta Force (1986), 107
DeMornay, Rebecca, 230
Denby, David, 34, 36, 38, 106, 131, 193, 204, 228, 230, 252
Depardieu, Gerard, 222
Depp, Johnny, 155, 165
Dern, Laura, 190, 248
Detroit Rock City (1999), 84
De Wilde, Brandon, 4
DiCaprio, Leonardo, 224
Dick (1999), 122
Dika, Vera, 144, 147–148
Dillon, Kevin, 109, 172, 249
Dillon, Matt, 28
Dirty Dancing (1987), 80, 90–91, 93–94, 211, 218, 284n.10, 288n.2, 290n.24, 291n.5
disabled youth, 74, 95, 150, 152, 176, 240
Disney studio, 290n.33
Disturbing Behavior (1998), 69, 122
Diving In (1990), 75
Dixon, Wheeler Winston, 24
Doherty, Thomas, 18, 112, 235, 258
Dole, Bob, ix
Donne, Dominique, 168
Donnie Darko (2001), xiii
Donovan, Martin, 221
Donovan, Tate, 188
Don't Be a Menace to South Central While Drinking Your Juice in the Hood (1995), 124

Don't Tell Mom the Babysitter's Dead (1991), 9
Doom Generation, The (1996), 85
Doran, Ann, *5*
dorks. *See* nerds
Do the Right Thing (1989), 123
Double Dragon (1994), 296n.9
Downey, Robert, Jr., 43
Drive Me Crazy (1999), 212
drugs and youth, x, 3, 29, 45–49, 76, 85, 90, 111, 117–118, 125–126, 128, 130, 132–135, 142, 148–149, 153, 155, 175, 223, 233–234, 239, 242, 245, 259–260, 292n.32, 293n.43; alcohol, 3–4, 37, 77, 120, 132, 161–162, 192, 221, 223, 230, 233–234, 244, 249; marijuana, 35, 51, 63, 120, 152, 161, 192; tobacco, xi
Durbin, Deanna, 3
Durham, Steve, 106
Dutton, Charles S., 131
Duval, James, 241–242
Dylan, Bob, 48

East Side Kids films, 82
Easy Rider (1969), 6
Ebert, Roger, 91, 175–176, 218, 249, 300n.38
ecological themes in youth films, 98–99
economy: effects on youth, 4, 19, 21, 116, 135, 185, 230–231, 242, 248–250, 262. *See also* class
Edelstein, David, 36, 43, 73, 148–149, 156, 168, 186, 250
Edge of Seventeen (1999), 243
education of youth. *See* school, as an educational site
Edward Scissorhands (1990), 220
Election (1999), 29–30, 65, 67, 72, 110, 212, 213, 246, 290n.30
Electric Dreams (1984), 204
Elizabeth, Shannon, 237
Ellis, Aunjanue, 120
Emma (Jane Austen), 65
Empire Records (1995), 297n.16
employment of youth, 21, 87
Encino Man (1992), 59, 62
Endlesslove (1981), 7, 28, 215–217
Englund, Robert, 154, *156*
ephebiphobia. *See* fear of youth
Epstein, Charles, 46–47
Erikson, Erik, 20, 286n.34
Escape to Witch Mountain (1975), 191
Estevez, Emilio, 29, *31*, 52, 72
E.T. The Extra-Terrestrial (1982), 8, 184
Evenson, Kimberly, 232
Evil Dead, The (1983), 169
Evolver (1995), 8, 180, 196, 201–202
Exorcist, The (1973), 112, 138–139
exploitation films, 5, 16, 28, 111–114, 139, 168, 232
Explorers (1985), 197, 205
Eyes of a Stranger (1981), 164

Faculty, The (1998), 10, 29, 41, 50, 69, 137, 175
Fame (1980), 51, 86, 90, 239
families and youth, 4, 96–99, 103, 105–106, 109, 123, 132–134, 139, 149–152, 165, 176, 189, 202, 214–226, 253; dysfunctional families, 3, 96, 126, 216–217. *See also* fathers in youth films; mothers in youth films; parents' relationship to youth
Far From Home (1989), 116–117
Far From Home: The Adventures of Yellow Dog (1995), 95
Far Off Place, A (1993), 103
fashions among youth, 19, 29, *31*, 33–34, 38, 52, 61, 63, 65, *66*, 67, 114–116, 173, 176, 243
Fast and the Furious, The, x
Fast Forward (1985), 82, 87
Fast Times at Ridgemont High (1982), 7, 28–29, 30–31, 34, 51–52, 69, 72, 211, 228, 247
Fatal Attraction (1997), 223
fathers in youth films, 43, 53, 72, 78, 88, 97–98, 102, 105–110, 125, 128–131,

133–134, 152–153, 173, 190, 218–219, 221–224
Fear (1996), 210, 212, 220, 223–224, 298n.11
fear of youth (ephebiphobia), 4. *See also* youth, power of
Feldman, Corey, 152
Felicity television show, 94
femininity. *See* girls, feminine identity
feminism, 33, 67–69, 120–121. *See also* gender issues
Ferris Bueller's Day Off (1986), 9, 62, 84, 197
Feuer, Jane, 13
Final Couple, 150, 152–153, 158, 167
Final Fantasy: The Spirits Within (2001), 296n.9
Final Girl(s), 139, 143–144, 149–150, 152, *156*, 157–158, 160–163, 165–168
Final Terror (1983), 164
Fire with Fire (1986), 85
First Amendment, x, 4
First Turn-On, The (1983), 7
Fishburne, Larry, 128
Fitzpatrick, Leo, 233
Five Finger Exercise (1962), 217
Flamingo Kid, The (1984), 290n.24
Flashdance (1983), 90
Flight of the Navigator (1986), 195
Flipper (1996), 96
Floundering (1994), 297n.16
Fly Away Home (1996), 80, 97–98
Focus on the Family, x
Folland, Alison, 245
football, 36, 53, 54, 57, 69, 71, 72, 74, 76–77, 129, 189, 221, 290n.33. *See also* athletes
Footloose (1984), 88–90, *89*, 91, 94
Forbidden Dance, The (1990), 82, 86, 88, 92–93
Foreign Student (1994), 225
"For Keeps" (1988), 209, 210–211, 248–250
Forty Deuce (1982), 239
Foster, Jodie, 6
Fox, Michael J., 193
Foxes (1980), 28, 85, 112, 211
Foxfire (1996), 119–120
Frankenstein (1931), 193
Franklin, Diane, 229
Freddy's Dead: The Final Nightmare (1991), 160
Freddy's Nightmares television show, 159
Freeman, Morgan, 46
Freeway (1996), 119–120
Free Willy (1993), 96–97
Free Willy 2: The Adventure Home (1995), 97
Free Willy 3: The Rescue (1997), 97
Fresh (1994), 132–134
Freud, Anna, 20, 286n.34
Friar, Ralph, and Natasha, 12
Friday (1995), 124
Friday the 13th series, 150, 151–154, 155, 157, 164; *Friday the 13th* (1980), 7, 140–141, 148, 151; *Friday the 13th Part II* (1981), 151–152; *Friday the 13th Part 3* (1982), 152; *Friday the 13th: The Final Chapter* (1984), 152; *Friday the 13th Part 5: A New Beginning* (1985), 152; *Friday the 13th Part 6: Jason Lives* (1986), 137, 152–153; *Friday the 13th Part 7: The New Blood* (1988), 153; *Friday the 13th Part 8: Jason Takes Manhattan* (1989), 153. See also *Jason Goes to Hell: The Final Friday*; *Jason X*
Friedman, Lester, 12
Friedrich, Su, 300n.36
Friends (1972), 215, 297n.3
Fuchs, Cindy, 67
Fun (1994), 117–118
Funicello, Annette, 5
Furrh, Chris, 100

Galligan, Zach, 168
games in youth films, 106, 182, 196–202. *See also* athletes; video games
Ganahl, Jane, 40

gangs, 43–46, 85, 112, 129–130. *See also* criminality of youth; secret societies
Garland, Judy, 3
Gas Food Lodging (1992), 212, 213, 218, 220, 223, 250–251, 253
Gate, The (1987), 147
Gateward, Frances, 24
gayness. *See* homosexuality
Gedrick, Jason, 107
geeks. *See* nerds
Gellar, Sarah Michelle, 30, 236
Gelmis, Joseph, 32
gender issues, 12, 33, 38–39, 50, 62, 85–86, 91, 97, 106, 110–122, 124, 134–135, 137, 143–146, 165, 194, 196, 241. *See also* boys; feminism; girls; sexuality of youth
Gener, Randy, 241
Generation X, 21–22, 262–263, 287n.44, 297n.16. *See also* 20-somethings
genre issues: methodology, xiii, 11–19, 22–23, 85, 144, 146, 256–257; theory, 12–16, 255, 285n.24. *See also* subgenres of youth films; youth film as a genre
George Washington (2000), xiii
Getting It On (1983), 7, 211
Getty, Balthazar, 100
Ghost in the Invisible Bikini, The (1966), 168
Ghost of Dragstrip Hollow, The (1959), 168
Ghost World (2001), xiii, 122
Ghoulies (1985), 169
Giant (1956), 289n.15
Giddins, Gary, 101
Gidget films, 5
Gill, Jenee, 242
Gilliard, Lawrence, Jr., 126
Gimme an F! (1985), 211
Girlfight (2000), 71, 122
Girlfriend from Hell (1989), 173
Girl on a Chain Gang (1965), 112
girls: delinquency, 116–117, 119, 122; feminine identity, 22, 38–40, 62, 71, 91, 97–98, 103, 110–122, 143–144, 162, 195–196, 254, 259; sexuality, 33, 39, 52, 70–71, 119, 172, 206, 214, 234, 237–238, 244. *See also* popularity, effects on girls; tough girls
Girls Just Want to Have Fun (1985), 90
Girls School Screamers (1986), 164
Girls Town (1996), 10, 120–121, 235
Gish, Lillian, 2–3
Gladiator (1992), 85
Gliberman, Owen, 65, 77, 167, 235, 238
Go (1999), 85, 122
Godard, Jean-Luc, 241
Goin' All the Way (1981), 7, 227
Going Steady (1982), 298n.14
Gold Diggers: The Secret of Bear Mountain (1995), 102
Goldstein, Ruth, 25
Good Burger (1997), 84
Gooding, Cuba, Jr., *127*–128
Gordon, Keith, *170*
Gossett, Louis, Jr., 107, 110
Grace, Anna, 120
Graduate, The (1967), 220
Graduation Day (1981), 164
Grant, Leon, 87
Granville, Bonita, 3
Grease (1978), 7, 139, 210
Great Depression, 3
Green, Kerri, 36
Greene, Lisa-Gabrielle, 117
Greig, Donald, 90
Gremlins (1984), 168–169
Grey, Jennifer, 90
Guerrero, Ed, 123, 130
Guest, Lance, 198
guns in youth films, 41, 44–45, 76, 104, 107, 113–114, 119, 130, 133, 225
Gyllenhaal, Jake, 189

Hackers (1995), 33, 182, 196, 198, 201, 205–207, 235, 297n.16
Hadley's Rebellion (1984), 72
Hailey, Leisha, 245

Haim, Corey, 36, 241
Hairspray (1988), 91
Hall, Anthony Michael, 29, *31*, 34–35, 193
Hall, G. Stanley, 19–20
Hall, Stuart, 20–21
Halloween series, 149–151, 155, 157, 164; *Halloween* (1978), 7, 139–141, 143, 148, 149, 170, 294n.5; *Halloween II* (1981), 149; *Halloween III: Season of the Witch* (1983), 149; *Halloween 4: The Return of Michael Myers* (1988), 149; *Halloween 5: The Revenge of Michael Myers* (1989), 150; *Halloween: The Curse of Michael Myers* (1995), 150; *Halloween H20* (1998), 151; *Halloween: Resurrection* (2002), 151
Hangin' with the Homeboys (1991), 125
Hangmen (1987), 109
Happy Birthday, Gemini (1980), 239
Hardin, Melora, 92
"harmless mischief" films, 9, 84, 135
Harnos, Christina, 109
Harris, Bruklin, 120
Harris, Danielle, 150
Hartley, Hal, 220–221
Harvest, Rainbow, 173
Haskell, Molly, 12
Hauser, Cole, 245
Havighurst, Robert, 20, 286n.34
Hawken, Janet, 248
Hawn, Goldie, 290n.32
Hays Office, 3
Heathers (1989), 9, 26, 29, 33–34, 50, 56, 63–65, *64*, 67, 69, 72, 284n.10, 288n.2, 290n.26
Heaven Help Us (1985), 53
Heaven Is a Playground (1991), 293n.43
Heavyweights (1994), 290n.33
Hebdige, Dick, 20–21
He Got Game (1998), 78
Hell on the Battleground (1987), 109
Hewitt, Jennifer Love, 167
Hewitt, Martin, 216
Hickam, Homer, 189–191
Hide and Go Shriek (1987), 164
Hide and Seek (1996), 300n.36
Higher Learning (1994), 294n.45
high school. *See* school
High School Confidential! (1958), 5, 51
High School High (1996), 42, 49, 124
Hinson, Hal, 96
hip-hop and rap music, 48, 82, 86–88, 123
Hispanic youth. *See* Latino/a youth
Hitcher, The (1986), 164
HIV, 234–235, 241. *See also* AIDS; sexually transmitted disease
Hoberman, J., 108, 221
Holden, Stephen, 68
Holloman, Laurel, 243
Hollywood, 1–6, 8, 10, 21, 29, 42, 50, 86
Hollywood Hot Tubs (1984), 211
Holtz, Geoffrey T., 22
homophobia, 72
homosexuality of youth, 4, 9, 59, 66, 68, 73, 157–158, 175, 214, 238–246, 261, 299n.29, 300nn.34,36
hooks, bell, 234
Hoop Dreams (1994), 124, 132
Hoosiers (1986), 72, 290n.24
horror as a youth film subgenre, 6–8, 137–179, 210, 231, 256, 260, 263, 295n.25. *See also* Final Couple; Final Girl(s); mutants; occult topics; rock-and-roll music, as part of horror plots; sexuality of youth, connected to death; slasher/stalker films; supernatural movies; vampires; zombies
Horse Whisperer, The (1998), 95
Hot Bubblegum (1981), 211, 298n.14
Hot Dog . . . The Movie (1984), 84
Hot Moves (1984), 231
House Arrest (1996), 83, 85
House Party series, 123; *House Party* (1990), 84
Howell, C. Thomas, *105*
How I Got into College (1989), 35
Hud (1963), 4
Hughes, Albert and Allen, 129–131

Hughes, John, 9, 63, 193, 211, 213, 216, 221, 233, 248, 297n.1, 300n.38
Hurricane Streets (1997), 85
Hutton, Timothy, 53

I Am the Cheese (1983), 85
Ice, Vanilla, 222
Ice Storm, The (1998), 226
Ice-T, 125
Idle Hands (1999), 147
If Lucy Fell (1996), 297n.16
I Know What You Did Last Summer (1997), 30, 141, 167–168, 295n.36. See also *I Still Know What You Did Last Summer*
Immediate Family (1989), 211, 249–250
incest, 67, 223, 236
Incredibly True Adventure of Two Girls in Love, The (1994), 111, 243–244
independent films, 28, 139, 178, 198, 212, 220
I Never Promised You a Rose Garden (1977), 52, 112
Inkwell, The (1994), 212
International Velvet (1978), 95
Internet, 10, 60, 182, 193, 198, 205, 207, 237, 263. *See also* computers
interracial teen couples, 92, 94, 213, 241, 244, 261, 293n.38
Invasion of the Body Snatchers (1956), 174
Invisible Maniac (1990), 164
Iron Eagle (1986), 104, 107–109. See also *Aces: Iron Eagle 3*
Ironside, Michael, 70
I Still Know What You Did Last Summer (1998), 167
I Was a Teenage TV Terrorist (1987), 183
I Was a Teenage Werewolf (1957), 138

Jackson, Kathy Merlock, 24
Jahiel, Edwin, 207, 243
Jarret, Gabe, 185–*186*
Jason Goes to Hell: The Final Friday (1993), 153–154
Jason X (2002), 154
Jasper, Frank, 73
Jawbreaker (1999), 65, 67
Jaws (1975), 139
Jeremy (1973), 215
Jewish youth, 53, 91, 205
Joan of Arc, *115*–116
jocks. *See* athletes
Johansson, Scarlett, 252
Johnny Be Good (1988), 75
Johnny Mnemonic (1995), 208
Johns (1997), 212, 243
Johnson, Ariyan, 251–*252*
Johnson, LouAnne, 47–48
Johnston, Sheila, 171
Jolie, Angelina, 206
Jollies (1990), 299n.28
Jones, Amy, 161
Jones, Jacquie, 123–124, 134
Joy of Sex (1984), 7, 29, 211, 231
Joysticks (1983), 182, 197–198, 199, 202
Juice (1992), 129–130, 131, 134
junior high school. *See* school
Just Another Girl on the I.R.T. (1993), 50, 59, 135, 210, 212, 220, 251–*252*, 253
Just One of the Girls (1993), 241
Just One of the Guys (1985), 62, 68, 240

Kaminsky, Stuart, 13
Kanefsky, Rolfe, 178
Karate Kid series, 70
Keitel, Harvey, 133
Keith, David, 102
Kemp, Philip, 157
Keniston, Kenneth, 20
Kennedy, Jamie, 165
Kid, The (1921), 3
Kid and Play, 37, 123. *See also* Martin, Christopher; Reid, Christopher
Kidco (1984), 185, 189
Kids (1995), x, 9–10, 212, 227, 233–235, 297n.16
Killing Mrs. Tingle. See *Teaching Mrs. Tingle*
Kilmer, Val, 185–*186*
King, Perry, 45

King, Stephen, 139, 170
Kiss, The (1988), 173
Kitses, Jim, 13
Klein, Chris, 237
Korine, Harmony, 234
Korsmo, Charlie, 37
Kracauer, Siegfried, 12
Krull (1983), 296n.9
Krush Groove (1985), 87
Kubrick, Stanley, ix

Labortreaux, Matthew, 195
Ladies and Gentlemen, The Fabulous Stains (1981), 112
Ladybugs (1992), 70
Lake, Ricki, 300n.44
lambada, 82, 86, 92–93, 211, 220, 291n.6
Lambada (1990), 82, 86, 88, 92–93, 289n.21
Langenkamp, Heather, 155–*156,* 158, 160
Lassie (1994), 96
Lassie films, 95
Last American Virgin, The (1982), 7, 228–229, 247–248, 298n.14
Last Picture Show, The (1971), 297n.3
Last Slumber Party, The (1987), 164
Last Starfighter, The (1984), 182, 197, 198–201, 297n.10
Last Summer (1969), 210, 227
Last Time Out (1994), 70
Latino/a youth, 46, 48, 50, 60, 82, 86–88, 92, 118–119, 120, 125, 135, 205, 259, 291n.6. *See also* race issues
law. *See* police
Lean on Me (1989), 29–30, 41, 45–48, 289n.21
Learning Tree, The (1969), 123
Lebeau, Vicky, 258
LeBrock, Kelly, 193
Lee, Spike, 123, 124, 132–133
Legend of Billie Jean, The (1986), 114–116, *115*
Leguizamo, John, 225
Leigh, Jennifer Jason, 228
Leitch, Thomas, 24, 258
"Lemon Popsicle" films, 298n.14
lesbians. *See* homosexuality
Less Than Zero (1987), 85, 239
Lester, Mark, 289n.18
Levy, Emanuel, 121
Lewis, Herschell Gordon, 138
Lewis, Jon, 21, 23–24, 258
Liar's Club, The (1993), 85
License to Drive (1988), 84
L.I.E. (2001), xiii
Lieberman, Joe, ix
Light It Up (1999), 26, 41, 50, 59–60
Lillard, Matthew, 165, 205
Lincoln, Lar Park, 153
Lindo, Delroy, 132
Lisa (1990), 225
Little Big League (1994), 290n.33
Little Darlings (1980), 28, 211, 227
Little Giants (1994), 290n.33
Little Girl Who Lived Down the Lane, The (1977), 216
Little Nikita (1988), 109
Little Witches (1996), 175
Little Women (1949), 4
Little Women (1994), 220
Littwin, Susan, 22
Lloyd, Christopher, 193
Lolita (1998), 210, 212
London, Jack, 95
Long, Nia, 128
Lopez, Daniel, 16
Lopez, Magali, 118
Lopez, Seidy, 118
Lord of the Flies (1963), 100
Lord of the Flies (1990), 100–102
Lord of the Flies (William Golding), 100
Losin' It (1983), 7, 29, 229
Lost Boys, The (1987), 147
love. *See* romance and youth; sexuality of youth
Love, Pee Wee, 133
Love and Basketball, 71
Lowe, Rob, 29

Lucas (1986), 9, 28, 32–33, 35–36, 69, 72, 211, 216
Luna, Gilbert, 241
Lunatic (1991), 164
Lynn, Carrie, 64

Mabius, Eric, 39
Macchio, Ralph, 70
Mad About Mambo (2000), 94
Mad Love (1995), 220, 223
Maggenti, Maria, 244
Magic in the Water (1995), 291n.9
Majorettes, The (1987), 164
Major Payne (1995), 290n.33
Making the Grade (1984), 88
Manchester Prep television show, 299n.21
Manhattan (1979), 216
Manhattan Project, The (1986), 8, 182, 187
Man in the Moon, The (1991), 213
Manny and Lo (1996), 252–253
Margie (1946), 4
Mari, Gina, 161
Marjorie Morningstar (1958), 4
Mark, Marky. *See* Wahlberg, Mark
marketing to youth, ix, 22, 29–30, 86, 92, 159, 161, 200, 229, 255, 261, 300n.1
marriage of youth, 3, 215, 221–222, 248–250, 253
Marron, Marlo, 119
martial arts, 47, 69–71, 75–76, 109, 158, 290n.33. *See also* athletes; capoeira
Martin, Christopher, 37
Masculin-Féminin (1966), 241
masculinity. *See* boys, masculine identity
Mason, Laurence, 205
Massood, Paula, 129–130
Masterminds (1997), 182, 198, 207–208
Masterson, Mary Stuart, 249
masturbation, 174, 236–237, 242
Mathews, Jack, 128
Mathews, Thom, 152
Matrix, The (1999), 178, 208
Mattarazo, Heather, 1, 38
May, Lance, 241
McCarthy, Andrew, 29
McDonagh, Maitland, 206
McGee, Mark Thomas, 18
McGowan, Rose, 165
McKay, Jim, 121, 122
McRobbie, Angela, 20
Me and Rubyfruit (1989), 299n.28
Meatballs (1979), 7
media (at large): effects on youth, ix–xi, 3, 128, 264, 283n.4; representation of youth, xiii, 1, 10–11, 82, 98, 114, 123, 166, 182, 210, 255–264, 279–282, 287n.55, 300n.1; use by youth, 2, 51, 57–59, 60, 87, 96, 114, 123, 126, 181–183, 241, 260. *See also* marketing to youth
media literacy, x–xi
Medved, Michael, x
Menace II Society (1993), 129–131, 133–134
Mermaids (1990), 233, 290n.24
Meyers, Jennifer, 161
Meyrink, Michelle, 185
Michaels, Michele, 161
middle school. *See* school
Mighty Ducks, The (1992), 290n.33
Mighty Ducks D2 (1994), 290n.33
Mighty Ducks D3 (1996), 290n.33
Milano, Alyssa, 224
military, 47, 53–54, 70, 76, 100–101, 103–110, 119, 174, 185–187, 199, 201–205, 292n.16. *See also* war
Miller, Jonny Lee, 205
"Miracle Decision," 4
Mirror, Mirror (1990), 173–174
Mirror, Mirror 2: Raven Dance (1994), 296n.42
Mirror, Mirror 3: The Voyeur (1995), 296n.42
Mirror, Mirror 4: Reflection (2000), 296n.42
Missing in Action (1984), 107
Mission: Impossible (1996), 208
Misty (1961), 95

Mitchell-Smith, Ilan, 54, 193
Mi Vida Loca (1994), 118–119, 135
Modine, Matthew, 73
Mod Squad, The (1999), 122
Moesha television show, 10
Molitor, Fred, 146
Monoson, Lawrence, 229
Moore, Dickie, 3
morals of youth, ix, 3–5, 7–9, 19–21, 40, 41, 67–68, 78, 80–86, 102, 125, 134, 140, 142–143, 145, 148, 157–159, 161, 167, 176, 180, 187, 208, 210, 212, 231, 236, 246–247, 251–252, 256, 260–262, 283n.4, 297n.4, 299n.21, 299n.23
Morita, Noriyuki "Pat," 70
Mortal Kombat (1995), 296n.9
Mortal Kombat: Annihilation (1997), 296n.9
mothers in youth films, 5, 43, 54, 98, 151, 159, 165, 167, 217–218, 221, 237, 251–254
Motion Picture Association of America (MPAA). *See* ratings of movies
Mrs. Winterbourne (1996), 300n.44
multiplex movie theaters, 6, 19, 142
murder, 44–45, 49, 57, 60, 67, 87, 109, 113, 117–119, 128–130, 132, 139, 146, 149, 151, 163, 165–167, 169, 174, 201, 221, 224, 239, 243, 245, 251–252
Murphy, Brittany, 65, *66*
music and youth, 7, 29, 87, 108, 135, 141, 196, 218, 245, 263. *See also* dancing and youth; hip-hop and rap music; raves; rock-and-roll music
Mutilator, The (1985), 164
My Bodyguard (1980), 42
My Crazy Life. See *Mi Vida Loca*
My Fair Lady (1964), 37
My Father the Hero (1994), 222
My Friend Flicka (1943), 95
My Little Girl (1987), 116
My Own Private Idaho (1991), 240
My Science Project (1985), 33, 182, 193, 194–195
Mystery Date (1991), 220
My Tutor (1983), 211, 213, 231

National Media Education Conference, x
National Telemedia Council, x
National Velvet (1944), 95
Native American youth, 75
Neale, Steve, 13, 24
Nelson, Judd, 29, *31*, 43, 125, 290n.27
Nelson, Merritt, 221
nerds, 9, *31*, 32–40, 41, 55, *64*, 72, 146, 164, 169–171, 172, 175, 180, 185–187, 190, 193–195, 199, 202, 213, 228, 234, 237, 243, 259
Net, The (1995), 208
Never Been Kissed (1999), 10, 69, 213, 235
New Jack City (1991), 125, 128, 292n.28
New Jersey Drive (1995), 124, 132, 134
Newman, Kim, 184
New Nightmare. See *Wes Craven's New Nightmare*
Newsies (1992), 93
Next Karate Kid, The (1994), 70–71, 76, 290n.32
Niagara, Niagara (1998), 85, 225
Nice Girls Don't Explode (1987), 217–218
Nicholas, Thomas Ian, 237
Nickel Mountain (1985), 216, 300n.37
Night in the Life of Jimmy Reardon, A (1988), 211
Nightmare on Elm Street series, 150, 153, 154–161, 167, 295n.36; *A Nightmare on Elm Street* (1984), 140–141, 148, 155–157, *156*, 162, 165–166, 295n.31; *A Nightmare on Elm Street 2: Freddy's Revenge* (1985), 157–158, 239; *A Nightmare on Elm Street 3: Dream Warriors* (1987), 158; *A Nightmare on Elm Street 4: The Dream Master* (1988), 33, 142, 158; *A Nightmare on Elm Street 5: The Dream Child* (1989), 159, 247. See also *Freddy's Dead: The Final Nightmare*; *Freddy's Nightmares* television show; *Wes Craven's New Nightmare*

Night of the Demons (1987), 172
Night of the Demons 2 (1994), 172
Night Screams (1987), 164
976-EVIL (1988), 172, 174
976-EVIL: The Astral Factor (1991), 296n.40
Norden, Martin, 12
Norris, Chuck, 107
Norris, Mike, 106–107
No Secrets (1991), 117
Not Another Teen Movie (2001), xiii
Now You See Him, Now You Don't (1972), 191
nuclear war, 8, 106, 187, 197, 203–204
nudity of youth in films, 8, 28, 75, 161, 172, 192, 232, 248, 297n.4

Oates, Joyce Carol, 120
occult topics, 141, 147, 150, 168–177, 296n.44. *See also* horror
October Sky (1999), 182, 184, 189–191
Ode to Billy Joe (1976), 238–239
Offerings (1989), 164
Once Bitten (1985), 231–232
O'Neal, Ron, 125
O'Neal, Tatum, 6
187 (1997), 42, 49
Only the Strong (1993), 70, 76, 91
Opposite of Sex, The (1998), 121, 212, 235, 253
Ordinary People (1980), 85
Orenstein, Peggy, 111
orgasm, 152, 228, 237, 297n.4; female orgasm, 237, 238
Oscars (Academy Awards), 197
Osment, Haley Joel, ix
Our Gang films, 3
Our Song (2001), xiii, 122
Out of Control (1985), 99
Outside Providence (1999), 53
Over the Edge (1979), 28, 51
Owen, Chris, 190

Palladino, Aleksa, 252
Palladino, Grace, 21
Pantoliano, Joe, 230
Paquin, Anna, 97
Paradise Motel (1985), 231
Parallel Sons (1995), 300n.34
"Paramount Case," 4
parenting by teens. *See* pregnancy
parents' relationship to youth, ix, xi, 43, 52, 58–59, 80, 82–84, 85, 89, 97, 113–114, 135, 145–146, 153, 155–156, 160, 170, 190, 192, 194, 200–201, 207, 215, 217, 222, 242, 244, 248, 256, 260. *See also* families and youth; fathers in youth films; mothers in youth films
Parker, Nicole, 243
parodies, xiii, 49, 51, 65, 69, 91, 124, 178, 191, 233
Party of Five television show, 10
patriotic purpose films, 85, 103–110. *See also* Reagan era
Patton, Mark, 157
Paul, Alexandra, *170*–171
Pay It Forward (2000), x
Payne Fund studies, 283n.4
Pearson, Geoffrey, 21
Peck, Craig, 178
Peck, J. Eddie, 92
Peggy, Baby, 3
Peggy Sue Got Married (1986), 211
Penn, Christopher, 88
Penn, Sean, 51, 53
People Under the Stairs, The (1991), 141
Permanent Record (1988), 56
Persian Gulf War, 21, 110
Petersen, William, 223
Pet Sematary 2 (1992), 173
Peyton Place (1957), 5
Pfeiffer, Michelle, 47
Pfifer, Mekhi, 132
Phantom Town (1999), 296n.8
Phat Beach (1996), 84
Phillipe, Ryan, 235–236
Phoenix, Leaf (Joaquin), 188
Phoenix, River, 240
Pi (1998), 208

Piaget, Jean, 20, 286n.34
Pickford, Mary, 2–3
Pierce, Justin, 233
Pinkett, Jada, 130
Pink Nights (1985), 211
Pipher, Mary, 22
Pipoly, Daniel, 100
Place, Mary Kay, 253
Platinum High School (1960), 51
Platoon (1986), 104, 109
Plummer, Glenn, 130
Poetic Justice (1993), 294n.45
Poison Ivy series, 212, 213
police, 44–45, 59–60, 125, 128, 131–133, 135, 149–150, 155, 206–207
Pollyanna (1920), 3
Poltergeist (1982), 168
Pomerance, Murray, 24
popular culture, xiii, 7, 193. *See also* youth, culture of
popularity, 9, 26–27, *31*–32, 34, 37, 61–69, 77, 213–214, 259; effects on girls, 40, 57, 63–69, 174–175, 177, 300n.45
Porky's (1981), 7, 28, 210, 216, 227
Portman, Natalie, 253
Postlethwaite, Pete, 225
Powder (1995), 29, 37, 42
Powell, Jane, 4
Powers, John, 174
Power Within, The (1995), 76
pregnancy, 9, 21, 59, 74, 87, 113, 118–119, 120, 121, 130, 150, 159, 209, 211, 213, 214, 218, 221, 227–229, 232, 242, 246–254, 259, 261, 300n.37, 300n.44, 300n.45. *See also* abortion
prep(aratory) school, 43, 52–55, 72, 175
Presley, Elvis, 86
Preston, Kelly, 188
Pretty Baby (1977), 114, 216
Pretty in Pink (1986), 9, 33, 211
Price, Marc, 109
Prime Risk (1984), 204
Princess Diaries, The (2001), xiii
Principal, The (1987), 28, 41, 45–46
Prinze, Freddie, Jr., 39
Private Lessons (1981), 211, 231
Private Popsicle (1982), 298n.14
Private Resort (1984), 84
Private School (1983), 9, 29, 231
Program, The (1993), 70
Prom Night series, 141; *Prom Night* (1980), 140
proms, 39, 52, 65, 71, 88–90, 192, 193, 237
prostitution, 113–114, 216, 229, 230–231, 239–240, 243
Psycho Beach Party (2000), 178
psychology of youth, 20, 22, 32, 38, 43–44, 50–52, 57, 61, 63, 81, 112, 153–155, 158–160, 163–165, 174, 177, 183, 192, 199, 202, 216–217, 221–224, 242, 249, 259, 286n.34, 287n.55, 292n.31. *See also* adolescence
Pump Up the Volume (1990), 29, 42, 50–51, 56–59, *58*, 182–183
punishment of youth, 35, 37, 43, 55, 60, 119, 128, 134, 162, 205, 217. *See also* criminality of youth
punk culture, 45, 112, 194
P.U.N.K.S. (1998), 296n.8
Pups (1999), 85
Pygmalion, 39

queer youth. *See* homosexuality of youth

race issues, 12, 38, 46, 48, 50, 59–60, 76, 81–82, 85–88, 91–94, 106, 108, 121, 122–135, 176, 188, 189, 205, 251–252, 289n.21, 293n.39. *See also* African American youth, Asian American youth, Latino/a youth
Race the Sun (1996), 184, 189–191
Rad (1986), 84
Radio Inside (1994), 297n.16
Rage: Carrie 2, The (1999), 122, 177, 235
Rainer, Peter, 130
Rain Man (1988), 297n.11
Rambo: First Blood Part II (1985), 104
Ramones, 51

rape, 39, 45, 70, 112, 114, 117, 120–121, 154, 156, 158, 165–166, 171, 176, 227, 234
rap music. *See* hip-hop and rap music
Rathgab, Douglas, 156
ratings of movies, 5–6, 75, 141–142, 233, 238, 292n.14
raves, 93, 223, 234
Raymond, Usher, 59
Rayns, Tony, 242
Reagan era (1981-1989), 20–21, 29, 85, 103, 107, 110, 142, 231
Real Genius (1985), 8, 180, 182, 185–187, *186,* 189
Reality Bites (1994), 21, 297n.16
rebels and rebellion, 4, 6, 9, 30–*31,* 32–33, 44, 50–61, 80–83, 86, 88–90, 111–112, 116, 121, 125, 171, 175, 207, 227, 256, 259–260, 263
Rebel Without a Cause (1955), 4–*5,* 27, 30, 43–44, 82, 90, 217, 238, 290n.26
Reckless (1984), 213, 216
Red Dawn (1984), 104–106, *105,* 107–108, 197
Red Pony (1949), 95
Red Stallion (1947), 95
Reed, Rex, 161
Reefer Madness (1936), 5
Reeves, Keanu, 55, 240
Reform School Girl (1957), 112
Reid, Christopher, 37
Reid, Tara, 237
religion and youth, 53–54, 88–90, 138, 175, 177, 192, 259–260, 299n.23
Remember the Titans (2000), 78
Remote (1993), 200–201, 297n.16
Rescue, The (1988), 109
Restless Years, The (1958), 4, 217
Return from Witch Mountain (1978), 191
Return of the Living Dead trilogy, 141, 147
Return to Horror High (1987), 178
Return to the Blue Lagoon (1991), 233
Revenge of the Nerds (1984), 34
Revenge of the Nerds 2: Nerds in Paradise (1987), 289n.4
Revenge of the Nerds 3: The Next Generation (1992), 289n.4
Revenge of the Nerds 4: Nerds in Love (1994), 289n.4
Revenge of the Teenage Vixens from Outer Space (1986), 178
Reynolds, Joyce, 3
Ricci, Christina, 102, 121, 253
Rich, Matty, 126, 292n.32
Ri'chard, Robert, 59
Richards, Kim, 43
Rich Kids (1979), 7, 216
Richter, Jason James, 96
Rickey, Carrie, 162
Riley, Phil, 121
Ringwald, Molly, 29, *31,* 52, 63, 248, 300n.38
Ripe (1996), 119–120
Risky Business (1983), 9, 230–231
Ritchie, Karen, 22
River's Edge (1987), 85
Robertson, R. J., 18
rock-and-roll music, 4–5, 51, 57, 86, 116; as part of horror plots, 141, 147, 162–163; in rock movies, 5, 16, 51
Rock Around the Clock (1956), 86
Rock, Pretty Baby (1956), 4
Rock 'n' Roll High School (1979), 51
Rock 'n' Roll High School Forever (1991), 51
Rodriguez, Nelson, 243
Roller Boogie (1979), 289n.18
romance and youth, 171–172, 202, 205, 212, 214–226; age differences as a conflict in, 39, 213, 220; family conflicts in, 8, 215–226; first love, 2, 97, 209, 214, 244; as a youth film subgenre, 8, 94, 261, 263. *See also* interracial teen couples; parents' relationship to youth; sexuality of youth
romantic comedies. *See* comedies, romantic
Romanus, Robert, 34, 228
Romeo and Juliet (Shakespeare), 8, 216

Romeo and Juliet (1968), 297n.4
Romeo and Juliet (1996). See *William Shakespeare's Romeo + Juliet* (1996)
Romero, George, 138
Rooftops (1989), 82, 88, 91
Rookie of the Year (1993), 290n.33
Rooney, Mickey, 3
R.P.M. (1970), 6
Rubbo, Joe, 229
Rubenstein, Lenny, 105
Rudd, Paul, *66,* 225
Rudy (1993), 70
Rumble Fish (1983), 85
runaways, 39, 81, 85, 95, 119–120, 239
Rushmore (1998), 29, 54–55
Russell, Keri, 94
Russo, Vito, 239
Ryder, Winona, 36, 56, *64,* 169

Sabrina: The Teenage Witch television show, 296n.44
Salsa (1988), 291n.6
Salva, Victor, 289n.8
Santiago, Renoly, 205
Sapolsky, Barry, 146
Satcher, David (Surgeon General), x–xi
Satisfaction (1988), 116
Saturday Night Fever (1977), 7, 86, 90, 139
Savage Streets (1983), 112
Saved by the Bell television show, 30
Save the Last Dance (2001), xiii, 94, 213, *262*
Saxon, John, 4
Say Anything... (1989), 33, 209, 218–220, *219,* 284n.10, 288n.2
Scarred (1984), 113
Scary Movie (2000), 141, 178, 246
Scent of a Woman (1992), 50
Schachter, Felice, 192
Schatz, Thomas, 13–14
Scheiner, Georganne, 284
school: as an educational site, 3–4, 80, 92–93, 107, 113, 135; as a setting in films, 2, 7, 9, 26–27, 41–42, 44–48, 54, 57–59, 61, 63, 78, 289n.20; as a youth film subgenre, 8–9, 16, 18, 26–79, 81, 259–260, 263. *See also* athletes; delinquents, in school; nerds; popularity; rebels; teachers' relationship to youth
School Ties (1992), 53
Schrader, Paul, 13
Schreiber, Liev, 165
Schwartzman, Jason, 54
Schwarzbaum, Lisa, 39, 298n.11
science as a youth film subgenre, 8, 180–208, 260, 263. *See also* computers and youth; technology and youth; video games
Scott, Larry B., 188
Scream (1996), 10, 122, 141–142, 148, 154, 161, 164–168, 178, 295n.36
Scream 2 (1997), 166
Scream 3 (2000), 166–167
Screwballs (1984), 7, 211
Secret Admirer (1985), 217
secret societies, 9, 44, 54, 70, 117, 205
Set It Off (1996), 118
Seven (1995), 298n.13
Seven Minutes in Heaven (1986), 211
7th Heaven television show, 10
Sevigny, Chloe, 234
sex comedies. *See* comedies, sexual
sex education, x
Sexton, Brendan, Jr., 39
sexuality of youth, 3, 5, 7–9, 21, 29, 86, 90–91, 93, 99, 111, 128, 138–139, 142, 145, 151, 153, 155–158, 161, 163, 170, 176, 187, 192, 202, 207, 209–212, 226–254, 260, 298n.14; connected to death, 7–8, 137, 139, 142, 146, 148–155, 161–163, 166–168, 170, 172, 232; as a youth film subgenre, 7–9, 261, 263. *See also* homosexuality; masturbation; orgasm; pregnancy; rape; romance and youth; virginity
sexually transmitted disease, 209, 213, 214, 227, 229, 231, 233, 259, 261. *See also* AIDS

S.F.W. (1995), 182–183
Shabba-Doo, 92
Shag (1989), 91, 290n.24
Shakespeare, William, 8
Shaking the Tree (1992), 297n.16
Shary, Timothy, x
Shawn, Dick, 113
Sheedy, Ally, 29, *31,* 52, 202–*203*
Sheen, Charlie, 36, 104–*105*
Sheen, Martin, 189
Shelly, Adrienne, 220–221
Shepherd, John, 152
She's All That (1999), 10, 29–30, 33, 37, 39–40, 69, 110, 212, 225
She's Out of Control (1989), 33, 218, 220
Shields, Brooke, 216
shopping malls, 6. *See also* multiplex movie theaters
Shrunken Heads (1994), 173
Sidekicks (1993), 70, 76
Silverstone, Alicia, 65, *66,* 223
Sing (1989), 91
Singer, Lori, 88
Singles (1992), 21
Singleton, John, 125, 128, 293n.33, 294n.45
Sister Act 2: Back in the Habit (1993), 42, 47
Sixteen Candles (1984), 211, 213
Sixth Sense, The (1999), 178
Six Ways to Sunday (1999), 85
Skye, Ione, 218–*219,* 250
Slacker (1991), 21
slasher/stalker films, 8, 81, 137, 139–141, 146, 147–168, 169, 256. See also *Friday the 13th* series; *Halloween* series; *A Nightmare on Elm Street* series; *Slumber Party Massacre* trilogy
Slater, Christian, 56–*58,* 114, 189
Slater, Helen, 114–*115*
Slaughter High (1986), 164
Sleepaway Camp trilogy, 141, 148
Sloane, Lance, 232
Sloniowski, Jeannette, 48
Slumber Party Massacre trilogy, 141, 148, 161–163; *Slumber Party Massacre* (1982), 7, 137, 161–162, 164; *Slumber Party Massacre II* (1987), 162–163; *Slumber Party Massacre III* (1990), 162
Smith, Shawnee, 172
Smokers, The (2000), 122
Smooth Talk (1985), 213
Snowballing (1985), 84
Snow Day (2000), 9
social representation in film, 11–12, 255–258. *See also* media (at large), representation of youth
Society (1992), 141, 147
Solarbabies (1986), 181, 193, 195
Soldier's Daughter Never Cries, A (1998), 122
Soles, P. J., 51
Solondz, Todd, 1
Some Kind of Wonderful (1987), 211
Sorority House Massacre (1986), 164
Sorority House Massacre 2: Nighty Nightmare (1992), 164
Soul Food (1997), 124
South Central (1992), 293n.38
Space Camp (1986), 187–189
Spacek, Sissy, 30
space shuttle Challenger, 184, 187–189
Spader, James, 43
Spanking the Monkey (1994), 212
Spielberg, Steven, ix, 137
Spitfire (1994), 119
Splendor in the Grass (1961), 5, 30, 216
sports. *See* athletes
Square Dance (1987), 211, 216
Squeeze (1997), 292n.31
Staiger, Janet, 15–17
Stand and Deliver (1988), 28, 30, 42, 46, 48, 93, 289n.21
Stand By Me (1986), 100
Stark, Susan, 190
Star Kid (1997), 296n.8
Star Wars (1977), 108, 139, 296n.9
Sterile Cuckoo, The (1969), 52

Sterritt, David, 189
Stevens, Fisher, 206
Stiles, Julia, *262*
Stille, Robin, 161
Stockwell, John, 170
Straight Out of Brooklyn (1991), 81, 126–127, 129, 134
Strangeland (1998), 147
Strawberry Statement, The (1970), 6
Street Fighter (1994), 296n.9
Strick, Philip, 222
Strike (1998). See *All I Wanna Do*
Student Bodies (1981), 140, 164, 178, 294n.6
Student Confidential (1987), 289n.17
subgenres of youth films, 8–9, 14–16, 23, 27, 79, 81, 83, 85, 183, 256–258, 263, 300n.38. *See also* delinquency; horror; romance and youth; school; science as a youth film subgenre; sexuality of youth
Subkoff, Tara, 245
Substitute, The (1996), 41, 48, 297n.16
Substitute: Failure Is Not an Option, The (2000), 290n.23
Substitute 2: School's Out, The (1998), 290n.23
Substitute 3, The (1999), 290n.23
Suburbia (1984), 84
Sugar and Spice (2001), 62, 300n.45
suicide, 35, 51, 53, 56–58, 64, 120, 175, 200–201, 222, 225, 239, 242
summer camp movies, 7, 140, 151, 227
Summer School (1987), 42
Sunset Park (1996), 76, 290n.32
Superman (1978), 139
Superman 3 (1983), 204
Super Mario Brothers (1993), 296n.9
supernatural movies, 8, 75, 141, 147, 168–177
Supreme Court, x, 4
Sure Thing, The (1985), 231
Swank, Hillary, 70
Swanson, Kristy, 195
Swayze, Patrick, 90, 104–*105*
Swing Kids (1993), 93–94
Sylvester (1985), 95

Taffel, Ron, ix
Tales from the Darkside television show, 159
Tales from the Hood (1995), 141, 147
Taming of the Shrew (William Shakespeare), 67
Taps (1981), 53–54
Tate, Larenz, 130
Taxi Driver (1976), 114, 216
Taylor, Christine, 68
Taylor, Elizabeth, 4
Taylor, Lili, 120
Taylor, Robert, 87
Tea and Sympathy (1956), 238
Teachers (1984), 28, 41, 45, 48, 51, 247–248
teachers' relationship to youth, 43, 45, 57–58, 66, 68, 76, 188, 248, 289n.20; "inspiring" or "reforming" roles, 28, 41–42, 45–49, 53, 61, 92–93, 131, 190, 289n.21
Teaching Mrs. Tingle (1999), 47, 49
technology and youth, 8, 58, 109, 181–183, 185, 187, 191–196, 200–208, 221, 259–260, 263
Teenage Bad Girl (1959), 112
Teenage Crime Wave (1955), 5, 235
Teenage Devil Dolls (1952), 5
Teenage Doll (1957), 112
Teenage Exorcist (1993), 173
Teenage Strangler (1964), 5, 138
teen angst. *See* angst
Teen Research Unlimited, 10
teens. *See* youth
Teen Witch (1989), 173
Teen Wolf (1985), 75
television and youth, 1, 4, 10, 30, 124, 135, 165, 183, 196, 200, 206, 263, 284n.11. *See also* media (at large)
Temple, Shirley, 3

10 Things I Hate About You (1999), 29, 33, 67, 122, 212, 223, 235
Terminal Bliss (1992), 85
Terror Squad (1987), 109
Terror Train (1980), 140
Testament (1983), 106
Texas Chainsaw Massacre (1974), 139, 143
That Darn Cat (1997), 122
That Thing You Do! (1996), 212
Thelma and Louise (1991), 135
There's Nothing Out There (1990), 178
Thinkin' Big (1986), 211
This Boy's Life (1993), x, 299n.29
This Rebel Breed (1960), 5
Thomas, Dylan, 48
Thomas, Eddie Kaye, 237
Thomas, Heather, 192
Thomas, Kevin, 119, 242–243
Thomas, Sean Patrick, *262*
Thompson, Lea, 188
3 Ninjas franchise, 76, 290n.33
Three O'Clock High (1987), 35, 41–42
Ticks (1993), 147
Tiger Heart (1996), 76, 85
Tin Man (1983), 204
Titanic (1997), 10, 212, 213, 220, 226, 235
To Die For (1995), 212, 213
Toilers and the Wayfarers, The (1997), 243
Tomb Raider (2001), 122, 296n.9
Tommy (1975), 297n.11
Top Gun (1986), 108
Torch Song Trilogy (1988), 239
Totally Fucked Up (1994), 241–242
tough girls, 53, 71, 82, 85, 102, 109, 110–122, 135, 157, 172–173, 200–201, 256
Toy Soldiers (1991), 110
Traffic (2000), 85
Travolta, John, 7
Trick or Treat (1986), 147
Trojan War (1997), 235
Troma studio, 224
Tromeo and Juliet (1995), 224
Tron (1982), 197, 296n.9
Truck Stop Women (1974), 289n.18
True, Rachel, 176
True Crime (1995), 119
Trust (1991), 218, 220–222, 250
Tudor, Andrew, 13–14, 16
Tuff Turf (1985), 41–44, 216, 289n.15
Tunney, Robin, 175
Turner, Tyrin, 130
Turturro, John, 133
Twentieth-Century Fox, 187
twenty-first century films, xiii, 9, 122, 300n.1
20-somethings, 19, 21, 94, 150, 154, 221, 243, 287n.42, 294n.45. *See also* Generation X
Twisted (1985), 185

Ulrich, Skeet, 165, 175
Unbelievable Truth, The (1990), 33, 220
Uncommon Valor (1983), 104, 108
Unguarded Moment, The (1956), 4
Up Against the Wall (1991), 125
Up the Academy (1980), 41

Valley Girl (1983), 213
vampires, 147, 231. *See also* horror
Van Der Beek, James, 77
Van Patten, Timothy, 45
Van Peebles, Mario, 125
Van Sant, Gus, 240
Vargas, Jacob, 118
Varsity Blues (1999), 9–10, 29–30, 69, 77
venereal disease. *See* sexually transmitted disease
video (movies on), 18–19, 141–142, 198, 238, 288n.2
video games, 8, 108, 181, 196–202, 207, 296n.9, 297n.11
Vietnam War, 6, 20, 55, 104, 109, 290n.24
Virgin High (1990), 227, 233
virginity, 7, 9, 30, 33–34, 67, 73, 74, 139, 141, 143, 146, 149–151, 162–163, 165–166, 171, 176, 206, 209, 211, 213–214, 223, 225, 226–238, 245, 298n.16. *See also* deflowering

Virgin Queen of St. Francis High, The (1988), 298n.16
Virgin Suicides, The (2000), 212, 226, 235
Vision Quest (1985), 73–74, 239, 290n.32

Wacko (1981), 178
Wahlberg, Mark, 223
Waiting to Exhale (1996), 124
Walker, Justin, *66*
Walker, Kim, *64*
war and youth, 100, 105, 199, 201–205, 207. *See also* Cold War; military; nuclear war; patriotic purpose; Persian Gulf War; Vietnam War; World War II
Ward, Megan, 200
WarGames (1983), 8, 104, 180, 182, 197, 201, 202–204, *203*, 205, 207
War Party (1989), 84
Warriors, The (1979), 293n.34
Washington, Isaiah, 132
Wayne's World (1992), 182–183
Weeks, Janet, 22
Weinraub, Bernard, 122
Weird Science (1985), 182, 193–194, 195
Welcome to Normal (1989), 299n.28
Welcome to the Dollhouse (1996), x, 1, 33, 37–38, 218, 225, 235, 289n.11
Wes Craven's New Nightmare (1994), 154, 157, 160–161, 295n.33
West Side Story (1961), 4, 91
Wet Hot American Summer (2001), xiii
Whale of a Tale (1976), 96
Whatever (1998), 122
What's Eating Gilbert Grape (1993), 220, 223
Where the Day Takes You (1992), 85
Where the Heart Is (2000), 253
White, Armond, 24, 258
White Fang (1991), 95
White Fang 2: Myth of the White Wolf (1994), 95
White House Office of National Drug Control Policy, x
White Squall (1996), 100
White Water Summer (1987), 100
White Wolves. See *Cry in the Wild/White Wolves* franchise
Whiz Kids television show, 197
whizzes. *See* nerds
Wilcox, Lisa, 158–159
Wild America (1997), 96
Wild Angels (1966), 5
Wildcats (1986), 75–76, 290n.32
wilderness survival films, 99–103
Wild Hearts Can't Be Broken (1991), 95
Wild in the Streets (1968), 6
Wild Life, The (1984), 7, 29, 84
Wild One, The (1953), 4, 82
Wild Pony (1983), 95
Wild Style (1983), 87
Wild Things (1997), 122, 212, 235
Wilkes, Donna, 113
Willemen, Paul, 12
Williams, Olivia, 55
Williams, Treat, 290n.23
William Shakespeare's Romeo + Juliet (1996), 10, 220, 223, 224–226
Williamson, Judith, 155
Williamson, Kevin, 10, 49, 141
Wilmington, Michael, 44
Windrunner (1994), 75
Wing Commander (1999), 296n.9
Winnicott, D. W., 20, 286n.34
Winter, Alex, 55
Wise, Robert, 91
witches. *See* occult topics
Witherspoon, Reese, 67, 223, 236
Wizard, The (1989), 200, 297n.11
Wizard of Oz, The (1939), 113
Wonder Years television show, 30
Wood, John, 203
Wood, Natalie, 4, 30
Wood, Robin, 13, 145, 171
Woods, James, 249
World War II, 3
Wraith, The (1986), 169
wrestling, 69, 72–74. *See also* athletes

Young Love: Lemon Popsicle 7 (1987), 298n.14
youth: culture of, 3–4, 7, 10–11, 20–21, 24, 27, 86, 207, 235, 258, 261, 264; definitions of, 3, 17–18, 20–23, 257; power of, 8, 41, 44, 65, 68, 83, 111, 113, 116–117, 120, 122, 144, 177, 183, 185, 196, 198, 203–208, 214, 254, 260–262; studies of, 19–25, 258, 263–264, 286nn.34,37, 287n.40. *See also* fear of youth
youth film as a genre, 2–3, 6–8, 10–12, 15, 17, 23–25, 124, 255–264, 265–282, 284nn.10,11, 287n.55
You've Got Mail (1998), 208

Zapped (1982), 182, 191–192
Zapped Again (1989), 196
Zebrahead (1992), 293n.38
Zeffirelli, Franco, 297n.4
Zero Boys (1986), 100
zombies, 141, 147, 256. *See also* horror
Zornow, Edith, 25